# Software Engineering Essentials

# Software Engineering Essentials

Edited by **Cheryl Jollymore**

New York

Published by NY Research Press,
23 West, 55th Street, Suite 816,
New York, NY 10019, USA
www.nyresearchpress.com

**Software Engineering Essentials**
Edited by Cheryl Jollymore

International Standard Book Number: 978-1-63238-421-8 (Hardback)

Printed in the United States of America.

# Contents

# Preface

There are innumerable new professions that are being created on a regular basis, needing to cater to the wants and needs of a changing and evolving world. Software Engineering comes under such a category, though the term itself is under contention. Simply speaking, it is the study and application of any kind of engineering to software and its design, development and eventual maintenance. One of the most sought after and a fastest growing job profile, software engineering came into its own after the technology boom in the last century and is the youngest field in engineering, with the appearance of the first digital computers in the early 1940s. There are numerous sub disciplines of software engineering itself, ranging from software design to software quality and maintenance. The scope of software engineering is growing exponentially, keeping pace with the fast changing technologies in this modern age. There has been a huge impact of globalization on this field as outsourcing has affected the percentage of software engineers in the global market. Another core issue in this field is the criticism that its approach is not really empirical and often derided for being feasible only in a 'theoretical' environment.

I would like to thank the people whose hard work went behind this research. I would also like to thank my family and friends for their unwavering support.

**Editor**

# Statistical and Machine Learning Methods for Software Fault Prediction Using CK Metric Suite: A Comparative Analysis

**Yeresime Suresh, Lov Kumar, and Santanu Ku. Rath**

*Department of Computer Science and Engineering, National Institute of Technology, Rourkela, Odisha 769008, India*

Correspondence should be addressed to Yeresime Suresh; suresh.vec04@gmail.com

Academic Editors: K. Framling, Z. Shen, and S. K. Shukla

Experimental validation of software metrics in fault prediction for object-oriented methods using statistical and machine learning methods is necessary. By the process of validation the quality of software product in a software organization is ensured. Object-oriented metrics play a crucial role in predicting faults. This paper examines the application of linear regression, logistic regression, and artificial neural network methods for software fault prediction using Chidamber and Kemerer (CK) metrics. Here, fault is considered as dependent variable and CK metric suite as independent variables. Statistical methods such as linear regression, logistic regression, and machine learning methods such as neural network (and its different forms) are being applied for detecting faults associated with the classes. The comparison approach was applied for a case study, that is, Apache integration framework (AIF) version 1.6. The analysis highlights the significance of weighted method per class (WMC) metric for fault classification, and also the analysis shows that the hybrid approach of radial basis function network obtained better fault prediction rate when compared with other three neural network models.

## 1. Introduction

Present day software development is mostly based on object-oriented paradigm. The quality of object-oriented software can be best assessed by the use of software metrics. A number of metrics have been proposed by researchers and practitioners to evaluate the quality of software. These metrics help to verify the quality attributes of a software such as effort and fault proneness.

The usefulness of these metrics lies in their ability to predict the reliability of the developed software. In practice, software quality mainly refers to reliability, maintainability, and understandability. Reliability is generally measured by the number of faults found in the developed software. Software fault prediction is a challenging task for researchers before the software is released. Hence, accurate fault prediction is one of the major goals so as to release a software having the least possible faults.

This paper aims to assess the influence of CK metrics, keeping in view of predicting faults for an open-source software product. Statistical methods such as linear regression and logistic regression are used for classification of faulty classes. Machine learning algorithms such as artificial neural network (ANN), functional link artificial neural network (FLANN), and radial basis function network (RBFN) are applied for prediction of faults, and probabilistic neural network (PNN) is used for classification of faults. It is observed in literature that metric suites have been validated for small data sets. In this approach, the results achieved for an input data set of 965 classes were validated by comparing with the results obtained by Basili et al. [1] for statistical analysis.

The rest of the paper is organized as follows. Section 2 summarizes software metrics and their usage in fault prediction. Section 3 highlights research background. Section 4 describes the proposed work for fault prediction by applying various statistical and machine learning methods. Section 5 highlights the parameters used for evaluating the performance of each of the applied techniques. Section 6 presents the results and analysis of fault prediction. Section 7 concludes the paper with scope for future work.

## 2. Related Work

This section presents a review of the literature on the use of software metrics and their application in fault prediction. The most commonly used metric suites, indicating the quality of any software, are McCabe [2], Halstead [3], Li and Henry [4], CK metric [5], Abreu MOOD metric suite [6], Lorenz and Kidd [7], Martin's metric suite [8], Tegarden et al. [9], Melo and Abreu [10], Briand et al. [11], Etzkorn et al. [12], and so forth. Out of these metrics, CK metric suite is observed to be used very often by the following authors as mentioned in Table 1 for predicting faults at class level.

Basili et al. [1] experimentally analyzed the impact of CK metric suite on fault prediction. Briand et al. [13] found out the relationship between fault and the metrics using univariate and multivariate logistic regression models. Tang et al. [14] investigated the dependency between CK metric suite and the object-oriented system faults. Emam et al. [15] conducted empirical validation on Java application and found that export coupling has great influence on faults. Khoshgoftaar et al. [16, 17] conducted experimental analysis on telecommunication model and found that ANN model is more accurate than any discriminant model. In their approach, nine software metrics were used for modules developed in procedural paradigm. Since then, ANN approach has taken a rise in their usage for prediction modeling.

## 3. Research Background

The following subsections highlight the data set being used for fault prediction. Data are normalized to obtain better accuracy, and then dependent and independent variables are chosen for fault prediction.

*3.1. Empirical Data Collection.* Metric suites are used and defined for different goals such as fault prediction, effort estimation, reusability, and maintenance. In this paper, the most commonly used metric, that is, CK metric suite, [5] is used for fault prediction.

The CK metric suite consists of six metrics, namely, weighted method per class (WMC), depth of inheritance tree (DIT), number of children (NOC), coupling between objects (CBO), response for class (RFC), and lack of cohesion (LCOM) [5]. Table 2 gives a short note on the six CK metrics and the threshold for each of the six metrics.

The metric values of the suite are extracted using Chidamber and Kemerer Java Metrics (CKJM) tool. CKJM tools extract object-oriented metrics by processing the byte code of compiled Java classes. This tool is being used to extract metric values for three versions of Apache integration framework (AIF, an open-source framework) available in the Promise data repository [18]. The versions of the AIF used from the repository are developed in Java language. The CK metric values of the AIF are used for fault prediction.

*3.2. Data Normalization.* ANN models accept normalized data which lie in the range of 0 to 1. In the literature it is

TABLE 1: Fault prediction using CK metrics.

| Author | Prediction technique |
| --- | --- |
| Basili et al. [1] | Multivariate logistic regression |
| Briand et al. [13] | Multivariate logistic regression |
| Kanmani and Rymend [29] | Regression, neural network |
| Nagappan and Laurie [30] | Multiple linear regression |
| Olague et al. [31] | Multivariate logistic regression |
| Aggarwal et al. [32] | Statistical regression analysis |
| Wu [33] | Decision tree analysis |
| Kapila and Singh [34] | Bayesian inference |

observed that techniques such as Min-Max normalization, $Z$-Score normalization, and Decimal scaling are being used for normalizing the data. In this paper, Min-Max normalization [19] technique is used to normalize the data.

Min-Max normalization performs a linear transformation on the original data. Each of the actual data $d$ of attribute $p$ is mapped to a normalized value $d'$ which lies in the range of 0 to 1. The Min-Max normalization is calculated by using the equation:

$$\text{Normalized} (d) = d' = \frac{d - \min (P)}{\max (p) - \min (p)}, \quad (1)$$

where $\min(p)$ and $\max(p)$ represent the minimum and maximum values of the attribute, respectively.

*3.3. Dependent and Independent Variables.* The goal of this study is to explore the relationship between object-oriented metrics and fault proneness at the class level. In this paper, a fault in a class is considered as a dependent variable and each of the CK metrics is an independent variable. It is intended to develop a function between fault of a class and CK metrics (WMC, DIT, NOC, CBO, RFC, and LCOM). Fault is a function of WMC, DIT, NOC, CBO, RFC, and LCOM and can be represented as shown in the following equation:

$$\text{Faults} = f (\text{WMC}, \text{DIT}, \text{NOC}, \text{CBO}, \text{RFC}, \text{LCOM}). \quad (2)$$

## 4. Proposed Work for Fault Prediction

The following subsections highlight the various statistical and machine learning methods used for fault classification.

*4.1. Statistical Methods.* This section describes the application of statistical methods for fault prediction. Regression analysis methods such as linear regression and logistic regression analysis are applied. In regression analysis, the value of unknown variable is predicted based on the value of one or more known variables.

*4.1.1. Linear Regression Analysis.* Linear regression is a statistical technique and establishes a linear (i.e., straight-line) relationship between variables. This technique is used when faults are distributed over a wide range of classes.

TABLE 2: CK metric suite.

| CK metric | Description | Value |
| --- | --- | --- |
| WMC | Sum of the complexities of all class methods | Low |
| DIT | Maximum length from the node to the root of the tree | <six |
| NOC | Number of immediate subclasses subordinate to a class in the class hierarchy | Low |
| CBO | Count of the number of other classes to which it is coupled | Low |
| RFC | A set of methods that can potentially be executed in response to a message received by an object of that class | Low |
| LCOM | Measures the dissimilarity of methods in a class via instanced variables | Low |

Linear regression analysis is of two types:

(a) univariate linear regression, and

(b) multivariate linear regression.

Univariate linear regression is based on

$$Y = \beta_0 + \beta_1 X, \tag{3}$$

where $Y$ represents dependent variables (accuracy rate for this case) and $X$ represents independent variables (CK metrics for this case).

In case of multivariate linear regression, the linear regression is based on

$$Y = \beta_0 + \beta_1 X_1 + \beta_2 X_2 + \beta_3 X_3 + \cdots + \beta_p X_p, \tag{4}$$

where $X_i$ is the independent variable, $\beta_0$ is a constant, and $y$ is the dependent variable. Table 8 shows the result of linear regression analysis for three versions of AIF.

### 4.1.2. Logistic Regression Analysis.

Logistic regression analysis is used for predicting the outcome of dependent variables based on one or more independent variable(s). A dependent variable can take only two values. So the dependent variable of a class containing bugs is divided into two groups, one group containing zero bugs and the other group having at least one bug.

Logistic regression analysis is of two types:

(a) univariate logistic regression, and

(b) multivariate logistic regression.

*(a) Univariate Logistic Regression Analysis.* Univariate logistic regression is carried out to find the impact of an individual metric on predicting the faults of a class. The univariate logistic regression is based on

$$\pi(x) = \frac{e^{\beta_0 + \beta_1 X_1}}{1 + e^{\beta_0 + \beta_1 X_1}}, \tag{5}$$

where $x$ is an independent variable and $\beta_0$ and $\beta_1$ represent the constant and coefficient values, respectively. Logit function can be developed as follows:

$$\text{logit}\,[\pi(x)] = \beta_0 + \beta_1 X, \tag{6}$$

where $\pi$ represents the probability of a fault found in the class during validation phase.

The results of univariate logistic regression for AIF are tabulated in Table 9. The values of obtained coefficient are the estimated regression coefficients. The probability of faults being detected for a class is dependent on the coefficient value (positive or negative). Higher coefficient value means greater probability of a fault being detected. The significance of coefficient value is determined by the $P$ value. The $P$ value was assessed based on the significance level ($\alpha$). $R$ coefficient is the proportion of the total variation in the dependent variable explained in the regression model. High value of $R$ indicates greater correlation between faults and the CK metrics.

*(b) Multivariate Logistic Regression Analysis.* Multivariate logistic regression is used to construct a prediction model for the fault proneness of classes. In this method, metrics are used in combination. The multivariate logistic regression model is based on the following equation:

$$\pi(x) = \frac{e^{\beta_0 + \beta_1 X_1 + \beta_2 X_2 + \beta_3 X_3 + \cdots + \beta_p X_p}}{1 + e^{\beta_0 + \beta_1 X_1 + \beta_2 X_2 + \beta_3 X_3 + \cdots + \beta_p X_p}}, \tag{7}$$

where $x_i$ is the independent variable, $\pi$ represents the probability of a fault found in the class during validation phase, and $p$ represents the number of independent variables. The Logit function can be formed as follows:

$$\text{logit}\,[\pi(x)] = \beta_0 + \beta_1 X_1 + \beta_2 X_2 + \beta_3 X_3 + \cdots + \beta_p X_p. \tag{8}$$

Equation (8) shows that logistic regression is really just a standard linear regression model, where the dichotomous outcome of the result is transformed by the logit transform. The value of $\pi(x)$ lies in the range $0 > \pi(x) < 1$. After the logit transforms the value of $\pi(x)$ lies in the range $-\infty > \pi(x) < +\infty$.

### 4.2. Machine Learning Methods.

Besides the statistical approach, this paper also implements four other machine learning techniques. Machine learning techniques have been used in this paper to predict the accuracy rate in fault prediction using CK metric suite.

This section gives a brief description of the basic structure and working of machine learning methods applied for fault prediction.

### 4.2.1. Artificial Neural Network.

Figure 1 shows the architecture of ANN, which contains three layers, namely, input layer, hidden layer, and output layer. Computational features involved in ANN architecture can be very well applied for fault prediction.

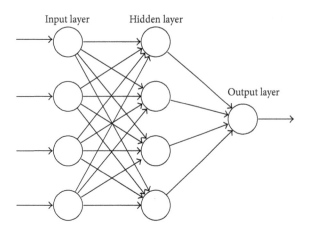

FIGURE 1: A typical FFNN.

In this paper for input layer, linear activation function has been used; that is, the output of the input layer "$O_i$" is input of the input layer "$I_i$," which is represented as follows:

$$O_i = I_i. \tag{9}$$

For hidden layer and output layer, sigmoidal (squashed-S) function is used. The output of hidden layer $O_h$ for input of hidden layer $I_h$ is represented as follows:

$$O_h = \frac{1}{1 + e^{-I_h}}. \tag{10}$$

Output of the output layer "$O_o$" for the input of the output layer "$O_i$" is represented as follows:

$$O_o = \frac{1}{1 + e^{-O_i}}. \tag{11}$$

A neural network can be represented as follows:

$$Y' = f(W, X), \tag{12}$$

where $X$ is the input vector, $Y'$ is the output vector, and $W$ is weight vector. The weight vector $W$ is updated in every iteration so as to reduce the mean square error (MSE) value. MSE is formulated as follows:

$$\text{MSE} = \frac{1}{n} \sum_{i=1}^{n} (y_i' - y_i)^2, \tag{13}$$

where $y$ is the actual output and $y'$ is the expected output. In the literature, different methods are available to update weight vector ("$W$") such as Gradient descent method, Newton's method, Quasi-Newton method, Gauss Newton Conjugate-gradient method, and Levenberg Marquardt method. In this paper, Gradient descent and Levenberg Marquardt methods are used for updating the weight vector $W$.

*(a) Gradient Descent Method.* Gradient descent is one of the methods for updating the weight during learning phase [20]. Gradient descent method uses first-order derivative of total error to find the *minima* in error space. Normally gradient

vector $G$ is defined as the first-order derivative of error function. Error function is represented as follows:

$$E_k = \frac{1}{2}(T_k - O_k)^2 \tag{14}$$

and $G$ is given as:

$$G = \frac{\partial d}{\partial dW}(E_k) = \frac{\partial d}{\partial dW}\left(\frac{1}{2}(T_k - O_k)^2\right). \tag{15}$$

After computing the value of gradient vector $G$ in each iteration, weighted vector $W$ is updated as follows:

$$W_{k+1} = W_k - \alpha G_k, \tag{16}$$

where $W_{k+1}$ is the updated weight, $W_k$ is the current weight, $G_k$ is a gradient vector, and $\alpha$ is the learning parameter.

*(b) Levenberg Marquardt (LM) Method.* LM method locates the minimum of multivariate function in an iterative manner. It is expressed as the sum of squares of nonlinear real-valued functions [21, 22]. This method is used for updating the weights during learning phase. LM method is fast and stable in terms of its execution when compared with gradient descent method (LM method is a combination of steepest descent and Gauss-Newton methods). In LM method, weight vector $W$ is updated as follows:

$$W_{k+1} = W_k - \left(J_k^T J_k + \mu I\right)^{-1} J_k e_k, \tag{17}$$

where $W_{k+1}$ is the updated weight, $W_k$ is the current weight, $J$ is Jacobian matrix, and $\mu$ is combination coefficient; that is, when $\mu$ is very small then it acts as Gauss-Newton method and if $\mu$ is very large then it acts as Gradient descent method.

Jacobian matrix is calculated as follows:

$$J = \begin{bmatrix} \frac{\partial d}{\partial dW_1}(E_{1,1}) & \frac{\partial d}{\partial dW_2}(E_{1,1}) & \cdots & \frac{\partial d}{dW_N}(E_{1,1}) \\ \frac{\partial d}{\partial dW_1}(E_{1,2}) & \frac{\partial d}{\partial dW_2}(E_{1,2}) & \cdots & \frac{\partial d}{\partial dW_N}(E_{1,2}) \\ \vdots & \vdots & \vdots & \vdots \\ \frac{\partial d}{\partial dW_1}(E_{P,M}) & \frac{\partial d}{\partial dW_2}(E_{P,M}) & \cdots & \frac{\partial d}{\partial dW_N}(E_{P,M}) \end{bmatrix}, \tag{18}$$

where $N$ is number of weights, $P$ is the number of input patterns, and $M$ is the number of output patterns.

*4.2.2. Functional Link Artificial Neural Network (FLANN).* FLANN, initially proposed by Pao [23], is a flat network having a single layer; that is, the hidden layers are omitted. Input variables generated by linear links of neural network are linearly weighed. Functional links act on elements of input variables by generating a set of linearly independent functions. These links are evaluated as functions with the variables as the arguments. Figure 2 shows the single layered

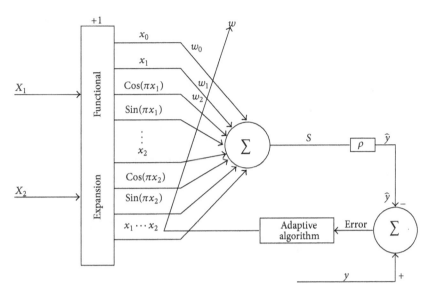

FIGURE 2: Flat net structure of FLANN.

architecture of FLANN. FLANN architecture offers less computational overhead and higher convergence speed when compared with other ANN techniques.

Using FLANN, output is calculated as follows:

$$\widehat{y} = \sum_{i=1}^{n} W_i X_i, \tag{19}$$

where $\widehat{y}$ is the predicted value, $W$ is the weight vector, and $X$ is the functional block, and is defined as follows:

$$X$$
$$= \left[1, x_1, \sin\left(\pi x_1\right), \cos\left(\pi x_1\right), x_2, \sin\left(\pi x_2\right), \cos\left(\pi x_2\right), \ldots\right] \tag{20}$$

and weight is updated as follows:

$$W_i\left(k+1\right) = W_i\left(k\right) + \alpha e_i\left(k\right) x_i\left(k\right) \tag{21}$$

having $\alpha$ as the learning rate and $e_i$ as the error value. "$e_i$" is formulated as follows:

$$e_i = y_i - \widehat{y}_i, \tag{22}$$

here $y$ and $\widehat{y}$ represent actual and the obtained (predicted) values, respectively.

*4.2.3. Radial Basis Function Network (RBFN).* RBFN is a feed-forward neural network (FFNN), trained using supervised training algorithm. RBFN is generally configured by a single hidden layer, where the activation function is chosen from a class of functions called basis functions.

RBFN is one of the ANN techniques which contains three layers, namely, input, hidden, and output layer. Figure 3 shows the structure of a typical RBFN in its basic form involving three entirely different layers. RBFN contains $h$ number of hidden centers represented as $C_1, C_2, C_3, \ldots, C_h$.

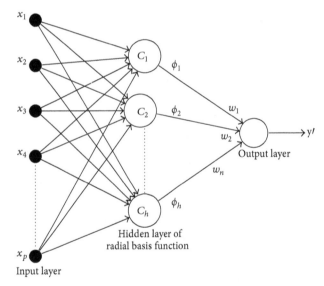

FIGURE 3: RBFN network.

The target output is computed as follows:

$$y' = \sum_{i=1}^{n} \phi_i W_i, \tag{23}$$

where $W_i$ is the weight of the $i$th center, $\phi$ is the radial function, and $y'$ is the target output. Table 3 shows the various radial functions available in the literature.

In this paper, Gaussian function is used as a radial function, and $z$ the distance vector is calculated as follows:

$$z = \left\| x_j - c_j \right\|, \tag{24}$$

where $x_j$ is input vector that lies in the receptive field for center $c_j$. In this paper, gradient descent learning and hybrid learning techniques are used for updating weight and center, respectively.

TABLE 3: Radial function.

| Radial function | Mathematical expression |
|---|---|
| Gaussian radial function | $\phi(z) = e^{-(z^2/2\sigma^2)}$ |
| Thin plate spline | $\phi(z) = z^2 \log z$ |
| Quadratic | $\phi(z) = (z^2 + r^2)^{1/2}$ |
| Inverse quadratic | $\phi(z) = \dfrac{1}{(z^2 + r^2)^{1/2}}$ |

The advantage of using RBFN lies in its training rate which is faster when compared with propagation networks and is less susceptible to problem with nonstationary inputs.

*(a) Gradient Descent Learning Technique.* Gradient descent learning is a technique used for updating the weight $W$ and center $C$. The center $C$ in gradient learning is updated as:

$$C_{ij}(k+1) = C_{ij}(k) - \eta_1 \frac{\partial d}{\partial C_{ij}}(E_k) \tag{25}$$

and weight $W$ is updated as:

$$W_i(k+1) = W_i(k) - \eta_2 \frac{\partial d}{\partial W_i}(E_k), \tag{26}$$

where $\eta_1$ and $\eta_2$ are the learning coefficients for updating center and weight, respectively.

*(b) Hybrid Learning Technique.* In hybrid learning technique, radial function relocates their center in self-organized manner while the weights are updated using learning algorithm. In this paper, least mean square (LMS) algorithm is used for updating the weights while the center is updated only when it satisfies the following conditions:

(a) Euclidean distance between the input pattern and the nearest center is greater than the threshold value, and

(b) MSE is greater than the desired accuracy.

After satisfying the above conditions, the Euclidean distance is used to find the centers close to $x$ and then the centers are updated as follows:

$$C_i(k+1) = C_i(k) + \alpha(x - C_i(k)). \tag{27}$$

After every updation, the center moves closer to $x$.

*4.2.4. Probabilistic Neural Network (PNN).* PNN was introduced by Specht [24]. It is a feed-forward neural network, which has been basically derived from Bayesian network and statistical algorithm.

In PNN, the network is organized as multilayered feed-forward network with four layers such as input, hidden, summation, and output layer. Figure 4 shows the basic architecture of PNN.

The input layer first computes the distance from input vector to the training input vectors. The second layer consists of a Gaussian function which is formed using the given set of data points as centers. The summation layers sum up the contribution of each class of input and produce a net output which is vector of probabilities. The fourth layer determines the fault prediction rate.

PNN technique is faster when compared to multilayer perceptron networks and also is more accurate. The major concern lies in finding an accurate smoothing parameter "$\sigma$" to obtain better classification. The following function is used in hidden layer:

$$\phi(z) = e^{-(z^2/\sigma^2)}, \tag{28}$$

where $z = \|x - c\|$,

$x$ is the input,

$c$ is the center, and

$z$ is the Euclidean distance between the center and the input vector.

## 5. Performance Evaluation Parameters

The following subsections give the basic definitions of the performance parameters used in statistical and machine learning methods for fault prediction.

*5.1. Statistical Analysis.* The performance parameters for statistical analysis can be determined based on the confusion matrix [25] as shown in Table 4.

*5.1.1. Precision.* It is defined as the degree to which the repeated measurements under unchanged conditions show the same results:

$$\text{Precision} = \frac{\text{TP}}{\text{FP} + \text{TP}}. \tag{29}$$

*5.1.2. Correctness.* Correctness as defined by Briand et al. [13] is the ratio of the number of modules correctly classified as fault prone to the total number of modules classified as fault prone:

$$\text{Correctness} = \frac{\text{TP}}{\text{FP} + \text{TP}}. \tag{30}$$

*5.1.3. Completeness.* According to Briand et al. [13], completeness is the ratio of number of faults in classes classified as fault prone to the total number of faults in the system:

$$\text{Completeness} = \frac{\text{TP}}{\text{FN} + \text{TP}}. \tag{31}$$

TABLE 4: Confusion matrix to classify a class as faulty and not-faulty.

| | No (prediction) | Yes (prediction) |
|---|---|---|
| No (actual) | True negative (TN) | False positive (FP) |
| Yes (actual) | False negative (FN) | True positive (TP) |

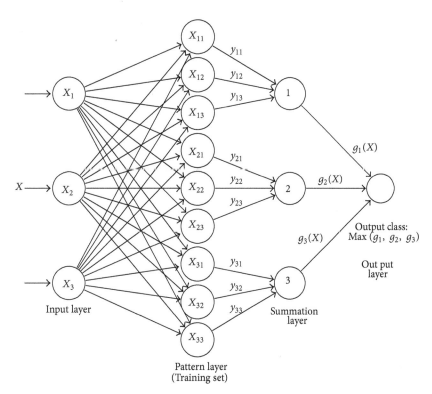

FIGURE 4: Basic structure of PNN.

*5.1.4. Accuracy.* Accuracy as defined by Yaun et al. [26] is the proportion of predicted fault prone modules that are inspected out of all modules:

$$\text{Accuracy} = \frac{\text{TN} + \text{TP}}{\text{TN} + \text{FP} + \text{FN} + \text{TP}}. \qquad (32)$$

*5.1.5. $R^2$ Statistic.* $R^2$, also known as coefficient of multiple determination, is a measure of power of correlation between predicted and actual number of faults [25]. The higher the value of this statistic the more is the accuracy of the predicted model

$$R^2 = 1 - \frac{\sum_{i=1}^{n} (y_i - \hat{y}_i)^2}{\sum_{i=1}^{n} (y_i - \overline{y})^2}, \qquad (33)$$

where $y_i$ is the actual number of faults, $\hat{y}_i$ is the predicted number of faults, and $\overline{y}$ is the average number of faults.

*5.2. Machine Learning.* Fault prediction accuracy for four of the applied ANN is determined by using performance evaluation parameters such as mean absolute error (MAE), mean absolute relative error (MARE), root mean square error (RMSE), and standard error of the mean (SEM).

*5.2.1. Mean Absolute Error (MAE).* This performance parameter determines how close the values of predicted and actual fault (accuracy) rate differ:

$$\text{MAE} = \frac{1}{n} \sum_{i=1}^{n} \left| y_i - y_i' \right|. \qquad (34)$$

*5.2.2. Mean Absolute Relative Error (MARE).* Consider

$$\text{MARE} = \frac{1}{n} \sum_{i=1}^{n} \frac{\left| y_i - y_i' \right|}{y_i}. \qquad (35)$$

In (35), a numerical value of 0.05 is added in the denominator in order to avoid numerical overflow (division by zero). The modified MARE is formulated as:

$$\text{MARE} = \frac{1}{n} \sum_{i=1}^{n} \frac{\left| y_i - y_i' \right|}{y_i + 0.05}. \qquad (36)$$

*5.2.3. Root Mean Square Error (RMSE).* This performance parameter determines the differences in the values of predicted and actual fault (accuracy) rate:

$$\text{RMSE} = \sqrt{\frac{1}{n} \sum_{i=1}^{n} (y_i - y_i')^2}. \qquad (37)$$

In (35), (36), and (37), $y_i$ is actual value and $y_i'$ is expected value.

*5.2.4. Standard Error of the Mean (SEM).* It is the deviation of predicted value from the actual fault (accuracy) rate:

$$\text{SEM} = \frac{\text{SD}}{\sqrt{n}}, \qquad (38)$$

where SD is sample standard deviation and "$n$" is the number of samples.

TABLE 5: Distribution of bugs for AIF version 1.6.

| Number of classes | Percentage of bugs | Number of associated bugs |
|---|---|---|
| 777 | 80.5181 | 0 |
| 101 | 10.4663 | 1 |
| 32 | 3.3161 | 2 |
| 16 | 1.6580 | 3 |
| 14 | 1.4508 | 4 |
| 6 | 0.6218 | 5 |
| 2 | 0.2073 | 6 |
| 3 | 0.3109 | 7 |
| 5 | 0.5181 | 8 |
| 1 | 0.1036 | 9 |
| 1 | 0.1036 | 10 |
| 3 | 0.3109 | 11 |
| 1 | 0.1036 | 13 |
| 1 | 0.1036 | 17 |
| 1 | 0.1036 | 18 |
| 1 | 0.1036 | 28 |
| 965 | 100.00 | 142 |

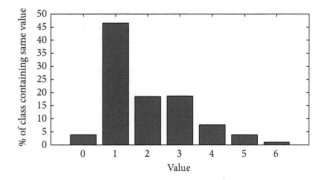

FIGURE 6: DIT of AIF version 1.6.

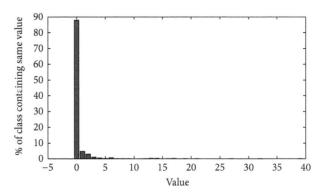

FIGURE 7: NOC of AIF version 1.6.

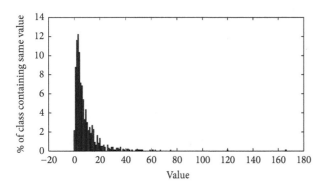

FIGURE 5: WMC of AIF version 1.6.

# 6. Results and Analysis

In this section, the relationship between value of metrics and the fault found in a class is determined. In this approach, the comparative study involves using six CK metrics as input nodes and the output is the achieved fault prediction rate. Fault prediction is performed for AIF version 1.6.

*6.1. Fault Data.* To perform statistical analysis, bugs were collected from Promise data repository [18]. Table 5 shows the distribution of bugs based on the number of occurrences (in terms of percentage of class containing number of bugs) for AIF version 1.6.

AIF version 1.6 contains 965 numbers of classes in which 777 classes contain zero bugs (80.5181%), 10.4663% of classes contain at least one bug, 3.3161% of classes contain a minimum of two bugs, 1.6580% of classes contain three bugs, 1.4508% of classes contain four bugs, 0.6218% of classes contain five bugs, 0.2073% of the classes contain six bugs,

0.3109% of classes contain seven and eleven bugs, 0.5181% of classes contain eight bugs, and 0.1036% of the class contain nine, thirteen, seventeen, eighteen, and twenty-eight bugs.

*6.2. Metrics Data.* CK metric values for WMC, DIT, NOC, CBO, RFC, and LCOM, respectively, for AIF version 1.6 are graphically represented in Figures 5, 6, 7, 8, 9, and 10.

*6.3. Descriptive Statistics and Correlation Analysis.* This subsection gives the comparative analysis of the fault data, descriptive statistics of classes, and the correlation among the six metrics with that of Basili et al. [1]. Basili et al. studied object-oriented systems written in C++ language. They carried out an experiment in which they set up eight project groups each consisting of three students. Each group had the same task of developing small/medium-sized software system. Since all the necessary documentation (for instance, reports about faults and their fixes) were available, they could search for relationships between fault density and metrics. They used the same CK metric suite. Logistic regression was employed to analyze the relationship between metrics and the fault proneness of classes.

The obtained CK metric values of AIF version 1.6 are compared with the results of Basili et al. [1]. In comparison with Basili, the total number of classes considered is much greater; that is, 965 classes were considered (Vs. 180). Table 6 shows the comparative statistical analysis results obtained for

TABLE 6: Descriptive statistics of classes.

|  | WMC | DIT | NOC | CBO | RFC | LCOM |
|---|---|---|---|---|---|---|
| Basili et al. [1] | | | | | | |
| Max. | 99.00 | 9.00 | 105.00 | 13.00 | 30.00 | 426.00 |
| Min. | 1.00 | 0.00 | 0.00 | 0.00 | 0.00 | 0.00 |
| Median | 9.50 | 0.00 | 19.50 | 0.00 | 5.00 | 0.00 |
| Mean | 13.40 | 1.32 | 33.91 | 0.23 | 6.80 | 9.70 |
| Std Dev. | 14.90 | 1.99 | 33.37 | 1.54 | 7.56 | 63.77 |
| AIF version 1.6 | | | | | | |
| Max. | 166.00 | 6.00 | 39.00 | 448.00 | 322.00 | 13617 |
| Min. | 0.00 | 0.00 | 0.00 | 0.00 | 0.00 | 0.00 |
| Median | 5.00 | 1.00 | 0.00 | 7.00 | 14.00 | 4.00 |
| Mean | 8.57 | 1.95 | 0.052 | 11.10 | 21.42 | 79.33 |
| Std Dev. | 11.20 | 1.27 | 2.63 | 22.52 | 25.00 | 523.75 |

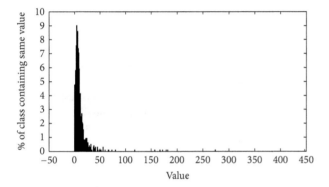

FIGURE 8: CBO of AIF version 1.6.

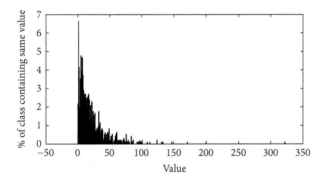

FIGURE 9: RFC of AIF version 1.6.

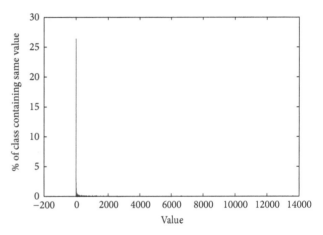

FIGURE 10: LCOM of AIF version 1.6.

From Table 7, w.r.t AIF version 1.6, it is observed that correlation between WMC and RFC is 0.77 which is highly correlated; that is, these two metrics are very much linearly dependent on each other. Similarly, correlation between WMC and DIT is 0, which indicates that they are loosely correlated; that is, there is no dependency between these two metrics.

### 6.4. Fault Prediction Using Statistical Methods

*6.4.1. Linear Regression Analysis.* Table 8 shows results obtained for linear regression analysis, in which the fault is considered as the dependent variable and the CK metrics are the independent variables.

"$R$" represents the coefficient of correlation; "$P$" refers to the significance of the metric value. If $P < 0.001$, then the metrics are of very great significance in fault prediction.

*6.4.2. Logistic Regression Analysis.* The logistic regression method helps to indicate whether a class is faulty or not but does not convey anything about the possible number of faults in the class. Univariate and multivariate logistic regression techniques are applied to predict whether the

Basili et al. and AIF version 1.6 for CK metrics indicating Max, Min, Median, and Standard deviation.

The dependency between CK metrics is computed using Pearson's correlations ($R^2$: coefficient of determination) and compared with Basili et al. [1] for AIF version 1.6. The coefficient of determination, $R^2$, is useful because it gives the proportion of the variance (fluctuation) of one variable that is predictable from the other variable. It is a measure that allows a researcher to determine how certain one can be in making predictions from a certain model/graph. Table 7 shows the Pearson's correlations for the data set used by Basili et al. [1] and the correlation metrics of AIF version 1.6.

TABLE 7: Correlations between metrics.

|  | WMC | DIT | NOC | CBO | RFC | LCOM |
|---|---|---|---|---|---|---|
| Basili et al. [1] |  |  |  |  |  |  |
| WMC | 1.00 | 0.02 | 0.24 | 0.00 | 0.13 | 0.38 |
| DIT |  | 1.00 | 0.00 | 0.00 | 0.00 | 0.01 |
| NOC |  |  | 1.00 | 0.00 | 0.00 | 0.00 |
| CBO |  |  |  | 1.00 | 0.31 | 0.01 |
| RFC |  |  |  |  | 1.00 | 0.09 |
| LCOM |  |  |  |  |  | 1.00 |
| AIF version 1.6 |  |  |  |  |  |  |
| WMC | 1.00 | 0.00 | 0.03 | 0.10 | 0.77 | 0.60 |
| DIT |  | 1.00 | 0.00 | 0.00 | 0.00 | 0.01 |
| NOC |  |  | 1.00 | 0.024 | 0.025 | 0.027 |
| CBO |  |  |  | 1.00 | 0.08 | 0.05 |
| RFC |  |  |  |  | 1.00 | 0.42 |
| LCOM |  |  |  |  |  | 1.00 |

TABLE 8: Linear regression analysis.

| Version | $R$ | $P$ value | Std. error |
|---|---|---|---|
| 1.2 | 0.5360 | 0.000 | 0.1114 |
| 1.4 | 0.5024 | 0.000 | 0.1450 |
| 1.6 | 0.5154 | 0.000 | 0.0834 |

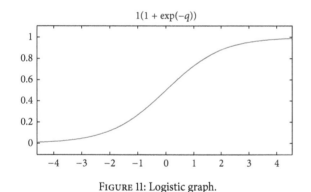

$1(1 + \exp(-q))$

FIGURE 11: Logistic graph.

class is faulty or not. Univariate regression analysis is used to examine the effect of each metric on fault of the class while multivariate regression analysis is used to examine the common effectiveness of metrics on fault of the class. The results of three versions of AIF are compared considering these two statistical techniques. Figure 11 shows the typical "$S$" curve obtained (similar to Sigmoid function) for the AIF version 1.6 using multivariate logistic regression. Tables 9 and 10 contain the tabulated values for the results obtained by applying univariate and multivariate regression analysis, respectively.

From Table 9, it can be observed that all metrics of CK suite are highly significant except for DIT. The $P$ value for the three versions (w.r.t DIT) is 0.335, 0.108, and 0.3527, respectively. Higher values of "$P$" are an indication of less significance.

Univariate and multivariate logistic regression statistical methods were used for classifying a class as faulty or not faulty. Logistic regression was applied with a threshold value 0.5; that is, $\pi > 0.5$ indicates that a class is classified as "faulty," otherwise it is categorized as "not faulty" class.

Tables 11 and 12 represent the confusion matrix for number of classes with faults before and after applying regression analysis, respectively, for AIF version 1.6. From Table 11 it is clear that before applying the logistic regression, a total number of 777 classes contained zero bugs and 188 classes contained at least one bug. After applying logistic regression (Table 12), a total of 767 + 16 classes are classified correctly with accuracy of 81.13%.

The performance parameters of all three versions of the AIF are shown in Table 13, obtained by applying univariate and multivariate logistic regression analysis. Here precision, correctness, completeness, and accuracy [1, 13, 27, 28] are taken as a performance parameters. By using multivariate logistic regression, accuracy of AIF version 1.2 is found to be 64.44%, accuracy of AIF version 1.4 is 83.37%, and that of AIF version 1.6 is 81.13%.

From the results obtained by applying linear and logistic regression analysis, it is found that out of the six metrics WMC appears to have more impact in predicting faults.

### 6.5. Fault Prediction Using Neural Network

*6.5.1. Artificial Neural Network.* ANN is an interconnected group of nodes. In this paper, three layers of ANN are considered, in which six nodes act as input nodes, nine nodes represent the hidden nodes, and one node acts as output node.

ANN is a three-phase network; the phases are used for learning, validation and testing purposes. So in this article, 70% of total input pattern is considered for learning phase, 15% for validation, and the rest 15% for testing. The regression analysis carried out classifies whether a class is faulty or not faulty. The prediction models of ANN and its forms such as

TABLE 9: Analysis of univariate regression.

| | Coefficient | | | Constant | | | P value | | | R value | | |
| | ver 1.2 | ver 1.4 | ver 1.6 | ver 1.2 | ver 1.4 | ver 1.6 | ver 1.2 | ver 1.4 | ver 1.6 | ver 1.2 | ver 1.4 | ver 1.6 |
|---|---|---|---|---|---|---|---|---|---|---|---|---|
| WMC | 0.028 | 0.05 | 0.03 | −0.83 | −2.11 | −1.77 | 0.0013 | 0.0007 | 0.00 | 0.130 | 0.240 | 0.18 |
| DIT | −0.067 | 0.10 | 0.05 | −0.46 | −1.83 | −1.53 | 0.335 | 0.108 | 0.3257 | −0.039 | 0.054 | 0.02 |
| NOC | 0.137 | 0.09 | 0.13 | −0.66 | −1.67 | −1.50 | 0.0007 | 0.00 | 0.00 | 0.136 | 0.13 | 0.16 |
| CBO | 0.011 | 0.01 | 0.02 | −0.71 | −1.80 | −1.66 | 0.017 | 0.00 | 0.00 | 0.096 | 0.15 | 0.17 |
| RFC | 0.012 | 0.02 | 0.01 | −0.86 | −2.15 | −1.79 | 0.0014 | 0.00 | 0.00 | 0.130 | 0.23 | 0.17 |
| LCOM | 0.007 | 0.007 | 0.007 | −0.64 | −1.67 | −1.48 | 0.0349 | 0.0004 | 0.0007 | 0.085 | 0.11 | 0.11 |

TABLE 10: Multivariate logistic regression analysis.

| | Coefficient | | |
| | AIF version 1.2 | AIF version 1.4 | AIF version 1.6 |
|---|---|---|---|
| WMC | 0.0195 | 0.0574 | 0.0320 |
| DIT | −0.041 | 0.000 | 0.000 |
| NOC | 0.1231 | 0.000 | 0.000 |
| CBO | 0.005 | 0.008 | 0.001 |
| RFC | 0.0071 | 0.0081 | 0.0109 |
| LCOM | 0 | −0.001 | 0 |
| Constant | −0.917 | −2.785 | −2.157 |

TABLE 11: Before applying regression.

| | Not-faulty | Faulty |
|---|---|---|
| Not-Faulty | 777 | 0 |
| Faulty | 188 | 0 |

TABLE 12: After applying regression.

| | Not-faulty | Faulty |
|---|---|---|
| Not-Faulty | 767 | 10 |
| Faulty | 172 | 16 |

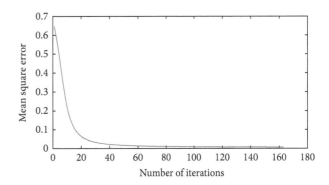

FIGURE 12: MSE versus number of epoch w.r.t Gradient descent NN.

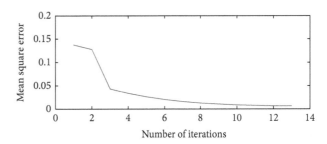

FIGURE 13: MSE versus number of epoch w.r.t Levenberg-marquardt NN.

PNN, RBFN, and FLANN, not only classify the class as faulty or not faulty but also highlight the number of bugs found in the class and these bugs are fixed in the testing phase of software development life cycle.

In this paper six CK metrics are taken as input, and output is the fault prediction accuracy rate required for developing the software. The network is trained using Gradient descent method and Levenberg Marquardt method.

*(a) Gradient Descent Method.* Gradient descent method is used for updating the weights using (15) and (16). Table 14 shows the performance metrics of AIF version 1.6. Figure 12 shows the graph plot for variation of mean square error values w.r.t no of epoch (or iteration) for AIF version 1.6.

*(b) Levenberg Marquardt Method.* Levenberg Marquardt method [21, 22] is a technique for updating weights. In case of Gradient descent method, learning rate $\alpha$ is constant but in Levenberg Marquardt method, learning rate $\alpha$ varies in every iteration. So this method consumes less number of iterations

to train the network. Table 15 shows the performance metrics for AIF version 1.6 using Levenberg Marquardt method.

Figure 13 shows the graph plot for variation of mean square error values w.r.t number of epoch for AIF version 1.6.

TABLE 13: Precision, correctness, completeness, and accuracy for three versions of AIF.

|        | Precision (%) | | | Correctness (%) | | | Completeness (%) | | | Accuracy (%) | | |
|--------|---------|---------|---------|---------|---------|---------|---------|---------|---------|---------|---------|---------|
|        | ver 1.2 | ver 1.4 | ver 1.6 | ver 1.2 | ver 1.4 | ver 1.6 | ver 1.2 | ver 1.4 | ver 1.6 | ver 1.2 | ver 1.4 | ver 1.6 |
| WMC    | 61.11   | 41.17   | 57.14   | 61.11   | 41.17   | 57.14   | 5.09    | 4.82    | 4.25    | 66.13   | 84.02   | **81.71** |
| DIT    | —       | —       | —       | —       | —       | —       | 0       | 0       | 0       | 64.47   | 83.37   | 80.51   |
| NOC    | 75      | 75      | 66.66   | 75      | 75      | 66.66   | 5.55    | 2.06    | 5.31    | 65.78   | 83.6    | 81.03   |
| CBO    | 60      | 57.14   | 77.77   | 60      | 57.14   | 77.77   | 2.77    | 2.75    | 3.72    | 64.8    | 83.48   | 81.03   |
| RFC    | 66.66   | 36.36   | 50      | 66.66   | 36.36   | 50      | 4.62    | 2.75    | 2.12    | 65.29   | 83.02   | 80.51   |
| LCOM   | 66.66   | 50      | 60      | 0.66    | 0.5     | 0.6     | 2.77    | 6.8     | 1.59    | 64.96   | 83.37   | 80.62   |
| MULTI  | 68.75   | 50      | 61.53   | 68.75   | 50      | 61.53   | 10.18   | 7.58    | 8.51    | 66.44   | 83.37   | 81.13   |

TABLE 14: Accuracy prediction using gradient descent NN.

| MAE    | MARE  | RMSE   | R        | P value | Std. error | Accuracy (%) |
|--------|-------|--------|----------|---------|------------|--------------|
| 0.0594 | 1.093 | 0.0617 | −0.2038  | 0.0044  | 0.0048     | 94.0437      |

TABLE 15: Accuracy prediction using Levenberg Marquardt.

| MAE    | MARE   | RMSE   | R        | P value | Std. error | Accuracy (%) |
|--------|--------|--------|----------|---------|------------|--------------|
| 0.0023 | 1.1203 | 0.0308 | −0.2189  | 0.0022  | 0.0041     | 90.4977      |

TABLE 16: Accuracy prediction using FLANN.

| MAE    | MARE   | RMSE   | R      | P value       | Std. error | Accuracy (%) |
|--------|--------|--------|--------|---------------|------------|--------------|
| 0.0304 | 0.7097 | 0.0390 | 0.3308 | $2.4601e-06$  | 0.0050     | 96.3769      |

TABLE 17: Accuracy prediction using basic RBFN.

| MAE    | MARE   | RMSE   | R      | P value | Std. error | Accuracy (%) |
|--------|--------|--------|--------|---------|------------|--------------|
| 0.0279 | 0.3875 | 0.0573 | 0.1969 | 0.059   | 0.006      | 97.2792      |

*6.5.2. Functional Link Artificial Neural Network (FLANN).* FLANN architecture for software fault prediction is a single layer feed-forward neural network consisting of an input and output layer. FLANN does not incorporate any hidden layer and hence has less computational cost. In this paper, adaptive algorithm has been used for updating the weights as shown in (21). Figure 14 shows the variation of mean square values against number of epochs for AIF version 1.6. Table 16 shows the performance metrics of FLANN.

*6.5.3. Radial Basis Function Network.* In this paper, Gaussian radial function is used as a radial function. Gradient descent learning and hybrid learning methods are used for updating the centers and weights, respectively.

Three layered RBFN has been considered, in which six CK metrics are taken as input nodes, nine hidden centers are taken as hidden nodes, and output is the fault prediction rate. Table 17 shows the performance metrics for AIF version 1.6.

*(a) Gradient Descent Learning Method.* Equations (25) and (26) are used for updating center and weight during training phase. After simplifying (25), the equation is represented as:

$$C_{ij}(k+1) = C_{ij}(k) - \eta_1 (y' - y) Wi \frac{\phi_i}{\sigma^2} (x_j - C_{ij}(k)) \quad (39)$$

and the modified Equation (26) is formulated as:

$$W_i(k+1) = W_i(k) + \eta_2 (y' - y) \phi_i, \quad (40)$$

where $\sigma$ is the width of the center and $k$ is the current iteration number. Table 18 shows the performance metrics for AIF version 1.6. Figure 15 indicates the variation of MSE w.r.t number of epochs.

*(b) Hybrid Learning Method.* In Hybrid learning method, centers are updated using (27) while weights are updated using supervised learning methods. In this paper, least mean square error (LMSE) algorithm is used for updating the weights. Table 19 shows the performance matrix for AIF version 1.6. Figure 16 shows the graph for variation of MSE versus number of epochs.

*6.5.4. Probabilistic Neural Network (PNN).* As mentioned in Section 4.2.4, PNN is a multilayered feed-forward network with four layers such as input, hidden, summation, and output layer.

In PNN, 50% of faulty and nonfaulty classes are taken as input for hidden layers. Gaussian elimination (28) is used as a hidden node function. The summation layers sum

TABLE 18: Accuracy prediction using RBFN gradient.

| MAE | MARE | RMSE | R | P value | Std. Error | Accuracy (%) |
|---|---|---|---|---|---|---|
| 0.0207 | 0.2316 | 0.0323 | 0.3041 | $1.6302e - 05$ | 0.0041 | 97.2475 |

TABLE 19: Accuracy prediction using hybrid RBFN.

| MAE | MARE | RMSE | R | P value | Std. Error | Accuracy (%) |
|---|---|---|---|---|---|---|
| 0.0614 | 0.1032 | 0.0316 | 0.9184 | $3.1834e - 79$ | 0.0013 | 98.4783 |

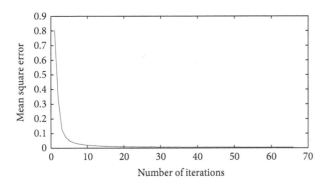

FIGURE 14: Graph plot for MSE versus number of iterations (epoch) w.r.t FLANN.

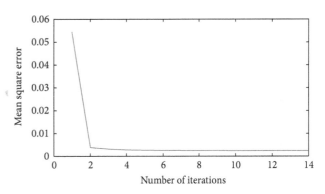

FIGURE 16: MSE versus number of epochs w.r.t hybrid RBFN.

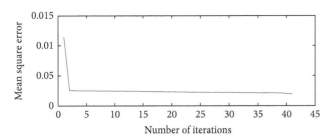

FIGURE 15: MSE versus number of epochs w.r.t gradient RBFN.

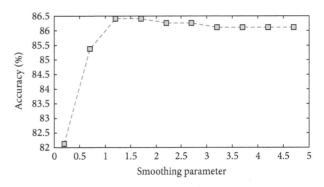

FIGURE 17: Accuracy rate versus smoothing parameter.

contribution of each class of input patterns and produce a net output which is a vector of probabilities. The output pattern having maximum summation value is classified into respective class. Figure 17 shows the variation of accuracy for different values of smoothing parameter.

*6.6. Comparison.* Table 20 shows the tabulated results for the obtained performance parameter values, number of epochs, and accuracy rate by applying three neural network techniques. This performance table is an indication of better fault prediction model. In this comparative analysis, the performance parameter mean square error (MSE) was taken as a criterion to compute the performance parameters (such as MARE, MSE, number of epochs, and accuracy rate) when four neural network techniques were applied. During this process the MSE value of 0.002 was set a threshold for evaluation. Based on the number of iterations and the accuracy rate obtained by the respective NN technique, best prediction model was determined.

From Table 20 it is evident that gradient NN method obtained an accuracy rate of 94.04% in 162 epochs (iterations). LM technique, which is an improvised model of ANN, obtained 90.4% accuracy rate. This accuracy rate is less than gradient NN but this approach (LM method) took only 13 epochs. PNN method achieved a classification rate of 86.41%.

The three types of RBFN, namely, basic RBFN, gradient, and hybrid methods obtained a prediction rate of 97.27%, 97.24%, and 98.47%, respectively. Considering the number of epochs, RBFN hybrid method obtained better prediction rate of 98.47% in only 14 epochs when compared with gradient method (41 epochs) and basic RBFN approaches.

FLANN architecture obtained 96.37% accuracy rate with less computational cost involved. FLANN obtained accuracy rate in 66 epochs as it has no hidden layer involved in its architecture.

TABLE 20: Performance metrics.

| AI technique | Epoch | Performance parameters | | | | |
| --- | --- | --- | --- | --- | --- | --- |
| | | MAE | MARE | RMSE | Std. Error | Accuracy |
| Gradient descent | 162 | 0.0594 | 1.0930 | 0.0617 | 0.0048 | 94.04 |
| LM | 13 | 0.0023 | 1.1203 | 0.0308 | 0.0041 | 90.49 |
| RBFN basic | — | 0.0279 | 0.3875 | 0.0573 | 0.06 | 97.27 |
| RBFN gradient | 41 | 0.0207 | 0.2316 | 0.0323 | 0.0041 | 97.24 |
| RBFN hybrid | **14** | 0.0614 | 0.1032 | 0.0316 | 0.0013 | **98.47** |
| FLANN | 66 | 0.0304 | 0.7097 | 0.0390 | 0.0050 | 96.37 |

The performance of PNN is shown in Figure 17. Highest accuracy in prediction was obtained for smoothing parameter value of 1.7. PNN obtained a classification rate of 86.41%.

RBFN using hybrid learning model gives the least values for MAE, MARE, RMSE, and high accuracy rate. Hence, from the obtained results by using ANN techniques it can be concluded that RBFN hybrid approach obtained the best fault prediction rate in less number of epochs when compared with other three ANN techniques.

## 7. Conclusion

System analyst use of prediction models to classify fault prone classes as faulty or not faulty is the need of the day for researchers as well as practitioners. So, more reliable approaches for prediction need to be modeled. In this paper, two approaches, namely, statistical methods and machine learning techniques were applied for fault prediction. The application of statistical and machine learning methods in fault prediction requires enormous amount of data and analyzing this huge amount of data is necessary with the help of a better prediction model.

This paper proposes a comparative study of different prediction models for fault prediction for an open-source project. Fault prediction using statistical and machine learning methods were carried out for AIF by coding in MATLAB environment. Statistical methods such as linear regression and logistic regression were applied. Also machine learning techniques such as artificial neural network (gradient descent and Levenberg Marquardt methods), Functional link artificial neural network, radial basis function network (RBFN basic, RBFN gradient, and RBFN hybrid), and probabilistic neural network techniques were applied for fault prediction analysis.

It can be concluded from the statistical regression analysis that out of six CK metrics, WMC appears to be more useful in predicting faults. Table 20 shows that hybrid approach of RBFN obtained better fault prediction in less number of epochs (14 iterations) when compared with the other three neural network techniques.

In future, work should be replicated to other open-source projects like Mozilla using different AI techniques to analyze which model performs better in achieving higher accuracy for fault prediction. Also, fault prediction accuracy should be measured by combining multiple computational intelligence techniques.

## Conflict of Interests

The authors declare that there is no conflict of interests regarding the publication of this paper.

## References

[1] V. R. Basili, L. C. Briand, and W. L. Melo, "A validation of object-oriented design metrics as quality indicators," *IEEE Transactions on Software Engineering*, vol. 22, no. 10, pp. 751–761, 1996.

[2] T. J. McCabe, "A Complexity Measure," *IEEE Transactions on Software Engineering*, vol. 2, no. 4, pp. 308–320, 1976.

[3] M. H. Halstead, *Elements of Software Science*, Elsevier Science, New York, NY, USA, 1977.

[4] W. Li and S. Henry, "Maintenance metrics for the Object-Oriented paradigm," in *Proceedings of the 1st International Software Metrics Symposium*, pp. 52–60, 1993.

[5] S. R. Chidamber and C. F. Kemerer, "Metrics suite for object oriented design," *IEEE Transactions on Software Engineering*, vol. 20, no. 6, pp. 476–493, 1994.

[6] F. B. E. Abreu and R. Carapuca, "Object-Oriented software engineering: measuring and controlling the development process," in *Proceedings of the 4th International Conference on Software Quality*, pp. 1–8, McLean, Va, USA, October 1994.

[7] M. Lorenz and J. Kidd, *Object-Oriented Software Metrics*, Prentice Hall, Englewood, NJ, USA, 1994.

[8] R. Martin, "OO design quality metrics—an analysis of dependencies," in *Proceedings of the Workshop Pragmatic and Theoretical Directions in Object-Oriented Software Metrics (OOPSLA '94)*, 1994.

[9] D. P. Tegarden, S. D. Sheetz, and D. E. Monarchi, "A software complexity model of object-oriented systems," *Decision Support Systems*, vol. 13, no. 3-4, pp. 241–262, 1995.

[10] W. Melo and F. B. E. Abreu, "Evaluating the impact of object-oriented design on software quality," in *Proceedings of the 3rd International Software Metrics Symposium*, pp. 90–99, Berlin, Germany, March 1996.

[11] L. Briand, P. Devanbu, and W. Melo, "Investigation into coupling measures for C++," in *Proceedings of the IEEE 19th International Conference on Software Engineering Association for Computing Machinery*, pp. 412–421, May 1997.

[12] L. Etzkorn, J. Bansiya, and C. Davis, "Design and code complexity metrics for OO classes," *Journal of Object-Oriented Programming*, vol. 12, no. 1, pp. 35–40, 1999.

[13] L. C. Briand, J. Wüst, J. W. Daly, and D. Victor Porter, "Exploring the relationships between design measures and software quality in object-oriented systems," *The Journal of Systems and Software*, vol. 51, no. 3, pp. 245–273, 2000.

[14] M.-H. Tang, M.-H. Kao, and M.-H. Chen, "Empirical study on object-oriented metrics," in *Proceedings of the 6th International Software Metrics Symposium*, pp. 242–249, November 1999.

[15] K. El Emam, W. Melo, and J. C. Machado, "The prediction of faulty classes using object-oriented design metrics," *Journal of Systems and Software*, vol. 56, no. 1, pp. 63–75, 2001.

[16] T. M. Khoshgoftaar, E. B. Allen, J. P. Hudepohl, and S. J. Aud, "Application of neural networks to software quality modeling of a very large telecommunications system," *IEEE Transactions on Neural Networks*, vol. 8, no. 4, pp. 902–909, 1997.

[17] R. Hochman, T. M. Khoshgoftaar, E. B. Allen, and J. P. Hudepohl, "Evolutionary neural networks: a robust approach to software reliability problems," in *Proceedings of the 8th International Symposium on Software Reliability Engineering (ISSRE '97)*, pp. 13–26, November 1997.

[18] T. Menzies, B. Caglayan, E. Kocaguneli, J. Krall, F. Peters, and B. Turhan, "The PROMISE Repository of empirical software engineering data," West Virginia University, Department of Computer Science, 2012, http://promisedata.googlecode.com.

[19] Y. Kumar Jain and S. K. Bhandare, "Min max normalization based data perturbation method for privacy protection," *International Journal of Computer and Communication Technology*, vol. 2, no. 8, pp. 45–50, 2011.

[20] R. Battiti, "First and Second-Order Methods for Learning between steepest descent and newton's method," *Neural Computation*, vol. 4, no. 2, pp. 141–166, 1992.

[21] K. Levenberg, "A method for the solution of certain non-linear problems in least squares," *Quarterly of Applied Mathematics*, vol. 2, no. 2, pp. 164–168, 1944.

[22] D. W. Marquardt, "An algorithm for the lest-squares estimation of non-linear parameters," *SIAM Journal of Applied Mathematics*, vol. 11, no. 2, pp. 431–441, 1963.

[23] Y. H. Pao, *Adaptive Pattern Recognition and Neural Networks*, Addison-Wesley, Reading, UK, 1989.

[24] D. F. Specht, "Probabilistic neural networks," *Neural Networks*, vol. 3, no. 1, pp. 109–118, 1990.

[25] C. Catal, "Performance evaluation metrics for software fault prediction studies," *Acta Polytechnica Hungarica*, vol. 9, no. 4, pp. 193–206, 2012.

[26] X. Yaun, T. M. Khoshgoftaar, E. B. Allen, and K. Ganesan, "Application of fuzzy clustering to software quality prediction," in *Proceedings of the 3rd IEEE Symposium on Application-Specific Systems and Software Engineering Technology (ASSEST '00)*, pp. 85–91, March 2000.

[27] T. Gyimóthy, R. Ferenc, and I. Siket, "Empirical validation of object-oriented metrics on open source software for fault prediction," *IEEE Transactions on Software Engineering*, vol. 31, no. 10, pp. 897–910, 2005.

[28] G. Denaro, M. Pezzè, and S. Morasca, "Towards industrially relevant fault-proneness models," *International Journal of Software Engineering and Knowledge Engineering*, vol. 13, no. 4, pp. 395–417, 2003.

[29] S. Kanmani and U. V. Rymend, "Object-Oriented software quality prediction using general regression neural networks," *SIGSOFT Software Engineering Notes*, vol. 29, no. 5, pp. 1–6, 2004.

[30] N. Nagappan and W. Laurie, "Early estimation of software quality using in-process testing metrics: a controlled case study," in *Proceedings of the 3rd Workshop on Software Quality*, pp. 1–7, St. Louis, Mo, USA, 2005.

[31] H. M. Olague, L. H. Etzkorn, S. Gholston, and S. Quattlebaum, "Empirical validation of three software metrics suites to predict fault-proneness of object-oriented classes developed using highly Iterative or agile software development processes," *IEEE Transactions on Software Engineering*, vol. 33, no. 6, pp. 402–419, 2007.

[32] K. K. Aggarwal, Y. Singh, A. Kaur, and R. Malhotra, "Empirical analysis for investigating the effect of object-oriented metrics on fault proneness: a replicated case study," *Software Process Improvement and Practice*, vol. 14, no. 1, pp. 39–62, 2009.

[33] F. Wu, "Empirical validation of object-oriented metrics on NASA for fault prediction," in *Proceedings of theInternational Conference on Advances in Information Technology and Education*, pp. 168–175, 2011.

[34] H. Kapila and S. Singh, "Analysis of CK metrics to predict software fault-proneness using bayesian inference," *International Journal of Computer Applications*, vol. 74, no. 2, pp. 1–4, 2013.

# 2

# Understanding Contributor to Developer Turnover Patterns in OSS Projects: A Case Study of Apache Projects

**Aftab Iqbal**

*INSIGHT, NUI, Galway, Ireland*

Correspondence should be addressed to Aftab Iqbal; aftab.iqbal@deri.org

Academic Editors: Y. Dittrich and Y. K. Malaiya

OSS projects are dynamic in nature. Developers contribute to a project for a certain period of time and later leave the project or join other projects of high interest. Hence, the OSS community always welcomes members who can attain the role of a developer in a project. In this paper, we investigate contributions made by members who have attained the role of a developer. In particular, we study the contributions made by the members in terms of bugs reported, comments on bugs, source-code patch submissions, and their social relation with other members of an OSS community. Further, we study the significance of nondevelopers contribution and investigate if and to what extent they play a role in the long-term survival of an OSS project. Moreover, we investigate the ratio of contributions made by a member before and after attaining the role of a developer. We have outlined 4 research questions in this regard and further discuss our findings based on the research questions by taking into account data from software repositories of 4 different *Apache* projects.

## 1. Introduction and Motivation

Open source software (OSS) is a good example of global software development. It has gained a lot of attraction from the public and the software engineering community over the past decade. The success of an OSS project is highly dependent on the infrastructure provided by the community to the developers and users in order to collaborate with each other [1]. It is important to understand how the OSS project and the community surrounding it evolve over time. During the project and community evolution, the roles of the members change significantly, depending on how much the member wants to get involved into the community. Unlike a project member in a software company whose role is determined by a project manager and remains unchanged for a long period of time until the member is promoted or leaves, the role in an OSS project is not preassigned and is assumed by a member as he/she interacts with other members. An active and determined member usually becomes a "core member" through the following path: a newcomer starts as a "reader", reading messages on the mailing lists, going through the wiki pages and other documentation, and so forth, in

order to understand how the system works. Later, he starts to discover and report bugs, which does not require any technical knowledge, and becomes a "bug reporter". After gaining good understanding of the system and community, he may start fixing small and easy bugs which he identifies himself or are reported by other members of the system, hence playing the role of either a "bug fixer," "peripheral developer," or an "active developer." To this stage, his bug fixes are usually accepted through patches submitted on the mailing lists or bug tracking system. Finally, after some important contributions are accepted by the core developers, the member may obtain the right of committing source code directly to the source control repository, hence becoming the "core member" of the project. This process is also called "joining script" [2], also referred to as "immigration process" [3]. The general layered structure of OSS communities as discussed above is further depicted in Figure 1, in which the role closer to the center has a larger radius of influence on the system.

The figure depicts an ideal model of role change in the OSS community. However, not all members want to be or become the "core member." Some remain "passive user" and some stop somewhere in the middle. The key point is that OSS makes it possible for an aspiring and determined developer to be part of the "core members" group of developers through continuous contributions. On the other hand, the sustainability of an OSS project is related to the growth of the developer community. The community surrounding an OSS must regenerate itself through the contributions of their members and continuous emergence of new "core members" otherwise the project is going to stop or fail. An example is the GIMP project (http://www.gimp.org/) [5], which started as an academic project. When the creators left the university and decided to work on something else, the project stopped for more than a year until someone else decided to take over the control and resume working on the project. Therefore, attracting or integrating new members is an important aspect to keep the system and the community evolve over time.

Given these precedents, the research goal of the study presented in this paper is to understand the pattern of contributions made by members who eventually attained the role of a developer in an OSS project, that is, joining the "core members" group of developers. We are interested to investigate the key factors which led members towards attaining the role of a developer. We studied the immigration process in OSS projects as done in the past by others but using a quantitative approach based on extensive data mining. The contribution of this paper is manifolds: we study the contributions made by the members in terms of bugs reported, comments on different bugs, attachments or source-code patch submissions to fix certain bugs, and social relation with other members on the mailing list in a particular OSS community/project. Further, we analyze the contributions made by members before and after attaining the role of a developer. Moreover, we compute the ratio of average contributions made by a developer (before attaining the role of a developer) and compare it with the average contributions made by other members of the project.

The rest of the paper is structured as follows: the related work comparable to our approach will be discussed in Section 2. Research questions are outlined in Section 3. In Section 4, the methodology we used to extract information from different software repositories is described. Section 5 presents the results based on the research questions, and finally, in Section 6, we conclude our work.

## 2. Related Work

The process of joining an OSS project has been studied by many researchers in the past. In this line, the best known model which describes the organizational structure of an OSS project is the "onion model" [10] (cf. Figure 1), a visual analogy which depicts how the members of an OSS project are positioned within a community. The onion-like structure represents only a static picture of the project, lacking the time dimension which is required to study the role transformation (i.e., promotion) from being a passive user to the core member of the project. Ye et al. complemented this shortcoming with a more theoretical identification and description of roles [5]. According to this model, a core

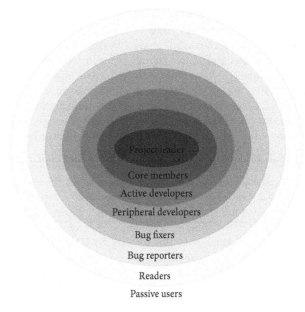

FIGURE 1: General structure of an OSS community based on the onion model described in [4].

member is supposed to go through all the roles, starting as a passive user, until he/she attains the role of a core member. In this regard, Jensen and Scacchi also studied and modeled the process of role migration in OSS projects [11], focusing on end users who eventually become core members. They identified different paths for the joining process and concluded that the organizational structure of studied OSS projects is highly dynamic in nature.

Von Krogh et al. studied the joining and specialization process of FreeNet project [2]. Based on the data gathered from publicly available documents, mailing list archives, and the source control repository, they discovered that offering bug fixes is much common among newcomers who eventually become core members of the project. They also found that a certain period of time, ranging from couple of weeks to several months, was required before a newcomer could contribute to a technical discussion. There also exist few research studies which have reported and quantified the onion-like structure of a community for many OSS projects. For example, Mockus et al. [12] studied the *Apache httpd server* and *Mozilla web browser* projects and Dinh-Trong and Bieman [13] studied the *FreeBSD* project. According to their findings, the "core members" group is composed of small number of members. Surrounding the "core members" group is a large group of contributors (i.e., active developers, peripheral developers, etc.) who submit bug reports, offer bug fixes and participate heavily in discussions on the mailing lists.

In an ethnographic study, Ducheneaut studied the *Python* project in order to investigate the contribution of the members during their role transition from being a newcomer towards attaining the role of a core member by taking into account data from mailing lists and source control repository [14]. He found that prior technical commitment and good social standing in the community were strong factors in joining the core members group of developers having write-access to the source control repository. Bird et al. [3] used the mailing lists and source control repository to investigate the time required for members to be invited into the "core members" group of an OSS project. They applied hazard rate analysis or survival analysis [15] to model the time-dependent phenomena such as employment duration. They used survival analysis to understand which factors influence the duration and occurrence of such events and to what degree. They modeled the duration between activities by considering the first appearance of a member on the mailing list to the first commit on the source control repository. One of their findings was that prior patch submission had a strong effect on becoming part of the "core members" group of a project. Herraiz et al. [16] studied the GNOME project and found two different patterns of joining the project: (1) volunteers/contributors who follow the "onion model", and (2) firm/organization sponsored developers who do not. They found that hired developers gain knowledge quickly enough to start writing code than the volunteers.

Although these research studies were carried out in detail on different OSS projects, they considered data only from mailing lists and source control repositories. However, we also take into account bug repositories and quantify the contributions made by members in terms of the following bugs reported, comments on bugs, social relation with other members based on comments, social relation with other members based on email exchanges on the mailing list, and patch submissions on bug repositories. In addition to that, there is no published work known to us which studies the contributions made by a member *before* and *after* attaining the role of a developer in an OSS project. Therefore, we have quantified and analyzed the average rate of contributions made by a member *before* and *after* attaining the role of a developer which makes this work unique in contrast to other related pieces of work which have been done so far in this area.

## 3. Research Questions

As mentioned earlier, the success of an OSS project is in its long-term survival which is potentially due to the existence of a community surrounding the project. We are particularly interested to identify the role of a community in the long-term survival of an OSS project as well as the key factors which promote a nondeveloper (In this paper, we will use the term "nondeveloper" to refer to all those members who do not have write-access to the source control repository.) to the role of a developer (In this paper, we will use the term "developer" to refer to all those members who have write-access to the source control repository.). Further, we are interested to know if the potential developers (In this paper, we will use the term "potential developer" to refer to all those members who started as a passive user and later attained the role of a developer.) follow the onion model or if there is a sudden integration of developers into the "core members" group of an OSS project. In order to address these key points, we have outlined few research questions in the following

which will be addressed using data from publicly available software repositories of few selected *Apache* projects:

(1) RQ-1: *What is the ratio of contributions made by the developers and nondevelopers to the project over the period of time?*

Previous studies [12, 17] on various OSS projects have shown that most part of the source-code development is carried out by the developers of those projects. We will investigate what are the contributions of nondevelopers if the source-code development is mostly done by the developers of those projects? In particular, we will investigate the contributions of nondevelopers in terms of reporting bugs, commenting on bugs, and exchanging emails. Further, we are interested to investigate the role of nondevelopers in the long-term success and maturity of an OSS project.

(2) RQ-2: *What is the ratio of contributions made by a potential developer before and after attaining the role of a developer?*

Attaining a higher role comes with more responsibilities and commitments to the project. We will investigate if a potential developer after attaining the role of a developer contributes (except source-code modification or bug fixing) more in contrast to contributing as a nondeveloper. Does the contribution pattern change with the change in role of a potential developer? To be more precise, does his/her contribution to the project in terms of bugs reporting and interaction with the community increase or decrease? We hypothesize that after attaining the role of a developer, he/she will participate actively in technical discussions on the bug tracking systems or on the mailing lists and report bugs effectively.

(3) RQ-3: *What is the average rate of contributions made by a potential developer comparing to other members of the project before attaining the role of a developer?*

We will investigate if the average contributions made by a potential developer are more than the average contributions made by nondevelopers who were also active during his/her time period. It has been addressed in previous studies [3] that demonstration of technical commitment and social status with other members will positively influence in attaining the role of a developer. We will investigate if a potential developer was more active (i.e., technically skilled and higher social status) than nondevelopers before attaining the role of a developer.

(4) RQ-4: *Does a potential developer follow onion model in order to attain the role of a developer?*

We will investigate if a potential developer follows the onion model in order to attain the role of a developer, that is, joining the "core members" group of the project. Not every member who is contributing to an OSS project eventually becomes a developer. It depends on the level of involvement of a member in an OSS project and also on the needs to promote

TABLE 1: Apache projects data range.

| Apache projects | Date range |
|---|---|
| Apache Ant [6] | 2000–2010 |
| Apache Lucene [7] | 2001–2010 |
| Apache Maven [8] | 2003–2010 |
| Apache Solr [9] | 2006–2010 |

TABLE 2: Dataset overview.

| | Attachments | Bugs | Commits | Emails |
|---|---|---|---|---|
| Apache Ant | 1,345 | 5,480 | 6,025 | 84,737 |
| Apache Lucene | 2,865 | 3,116 | 5,790 | 59,616 |
| Apache Maven | 1,169 | 3,902 | 8,815 | 87,611 |
| Apache Solr | 2,146 | 2,528 | 4,288 | 25,173 |

a nondeveloper to the role of a developer. There is no static or standard timeline for a member to join the "core members" group of a project. The time period required to attain the role of a developer varies from project to project and also from member to member. Members often start contributing to a project by participating in the mailing list conversations to get themselves familiar with the project before contributing source-code patches to the project. We will study the appearance of a potential developer on different software repositories by comparing the time-stamp value of their first activity on these software repositories in order to validate if he/she actually followed the onion model.

## 4. Data Extraction Process

In this section, we describe our data extraction methodology and the *Apache* projects selected for evaluation. We extracted data from 4 different *Apache* projects as shown in Table 1. The range of data selected for each project is different because of the difference in the starting date of each project. The reason of choosing these *Apache* projects is that the repositories of these projects are on the Web and available to be downloaded (i.e., mailing list archives, bugs, subversion logs, etc.).

Most *Apache* projects have at least 3 different mailing lists: user, dev, and commits, but some have more than 3 mailing lists (e.g., announcements, notifications, etc.). For our study, we downloaded only the dev mailing list archives of each *Apache* project under consideration. The reason is that software developers communicate often with each other on the dev mailing list rather than on any other mailing lists. We developed our own scripts which were used to extract information from mailing list archives in a similar manner to previous research [12, 18]. For example, each email was processed to extract information like *sender name, email address, subject, date, message-id*, and *reference*. The *reference* field contains *message-id(s)*, if the email is a reply to previous thread(s). We used the *reference* field information to build a social network correspondence and computed social network measures [19] of all the members of a project.

We retrieved all the bugs (related to the *Apache* projects we considered for our study) which are publicly available through the Bugzilla and JIRA Web interface (https://issues .apache.org/) and extracted the required information using our custom written scripts. For further details on the information extracted from each email and bug, we refer the readers to [20]. We computed the social relation correspondence among members on the bug tracking system based on the bug

comments exchanged among themselves. Bird et al. [21] findings indicated the detection and acceptance of source-code patches through the mailing list, but we discovered that source-code patches were always attached to the respective bugs on the bug tracking system rather than sending it on the mailing list. Prior research has indicated the importance of offering bug fixing and its acceptance as an influential factor in gaining the developer status [14]; therefore, we have also analyzed how many source-code patches were submitted by the members on bug repositories.

In order to get information from source control repository, we wrote our script (see [22] for details) and extracted necessary information (i.e., *log number, date of commit, author id, and files committed*). We only considered those subversion logs where a particular source-code file (i.e., "*.java*" because *Apache* projects under consideration are Java-based) was committed. These subversion log files were further analyzed by our script in order to identify if it fixes any bug by looking for patterns, such as, "PR:xxx," "MNG-xxx," "SOLR-xxx," "LUCENE-xxx," and patch acceptance acknowledgements such as "patch provided by xxx", "patch submitted by xxx." On the identification of such patterns, the bugs were queried to retrieve source-code patches associated with those bugs. This would help to identify source-code patches that are accepted by the "core members" group of the project. Further, it allows to identify members who possess strong technical skills required for attaining the role of a developer in the project. Table 2 gives an overview on the raw data sources we extracted from different software repositories of the selected *Apache* projects based on the methodology described.

The values for *Apache Ant* show that there were 1,345 source-code patches found for a total of 5,480 bugs reported on the bug tracking system. Further, 6,025 subversion logs were extracted from the source control repository where source-code files (i.e., *.java) were committed and 84,737 emails were extracted from the *Apache Ant* mailing list archives between 2000 and 2010.

## 5. Empirical Analysis

Before we address each of the research questions in detail, we present a high level overview on the development activity of each *Apache* project under consideration over the period of time in Figure 2. This would give an insight into how much contributions were made each year to a project and the peak development years of a project. For each *Apache* project under consideration, we computed the number of contributions with respect to the number of people who made those contributions. For example, we computed the number

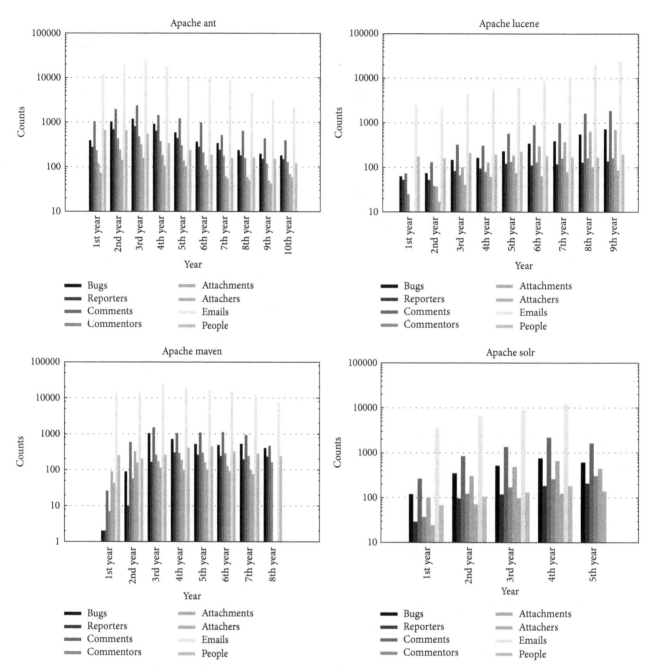

FIGURE 2: Development activity of Apache projects over the period of time.

of distinct bugs reported each year along with the number of distinct reporters who submitted those bug reports (cf. Figure 2). This would make it easier to answer simple questions like: how many bugs were reported and how many members were involved in the bug reporting process during the 2nd year of a project?

*Preliminaries*: let $\mathbf{C}$ be the total number of members (i.e., developers, nondevelopers, etc.) who worked on the project:

$$\mathbf{C} = \{c_1, c_2, \ldots, c_n\}. \qquad (1)$$

Let $\mathbf{Y}$ be the total number of years of a project under consideration:

$$\mathbf{Y} = \{y_1, y_2, \ldots, y_n\}, \qquad (2)$$

where $y_1$ is considered to be the first year of the project, $y_2$ is considered to be the second year of the project, and so on. Let $\grave{\mathbf{C}}$ be the set of members (i.e., developers, nondevelopers, etc.) who were active in a time period $y$:

$$\grave{\mathbf{C}} = \{c_1, c_2, \ldots, c_n\}, \quad \grave{\mathbf{C}} \subseteq \mathbf{C}, \qquad (3)$$

and let `Immig` be the immigrants (i.e., potential developers) who started as contributors and later become the developers of the project. We classified only those members as immigrants/potential developers who had an activity in the project (i.e., number of bugs reported, number of bugs commented, number of patches submitted, or number of emails sent) at least 4 months prior to their first commit on the source control repository

$$\mathbf{Immig} = \{\mathrm{Immig}_1, \mathrm{Immig}_2, \ldots, \mathrm{Immig}_n\},$$
$$\mathbf{Immig} \subseteq D_y \subseteq \mathbf{C}. \tag{4}$$

Let $D_y$ be the set of developers who have made commits before and during time period $y$ such that $D_y \subseteq \mathbf{C}$. Let the total number of bugs reported and commented and emails sent by a set of members in a time period y be represented as follows:

$$\mathrm{Contribution}_{\mathrm{bugs}}(C, y),$$
$$\mathrm{Contribution}_{\mathrm{comments}}(C, y), \tag{5}$$
$$\mathrm{Contribution}_{\mathrm{emails}}(C, y),$$

whereas the number of bugs reported and commented and emails sent by the developers in a given period of time $y$ is represented as

$$\mathrm{Contribution}_{\mathrm{bugs}}(D_y, y),$$
$$\mathrm{Contribution}_{\mathrm{comments}}(D_y, y), \tag{6}$$
$$\mathrm{Contribution}_{\mathrm{emails}}(D_y, y),$$

respectively. Let $d$ be a single developer and let commitDate($d$) return the first commit date of a developer. The yearly average contribution of a member before and after attaining the role of a developer is represented as

$$\mathrm{Contribution}_{\mathrm{before}}(d, \mathrm{commitDate}(d)),$$
$$\mathrm{Contribution}_{\mathrm{after}}(d, \mathrm{commitDate}(d)), \tag{7}$$

and the total number of bugs reported and commented and emails sent by an immigrant before becoming a developer is represented as

$$\mathrm{Contribution}_{\mathrm{bugs}}(\mathrm{Immig}, \mathrm{commitDate}(\mathrm{Immig})),$$
$$\mathrm{Contribution}_{\mathrm{comments}}(\mathrm{Immig}, \mathrm{commitDate}(\mathrm{Immig})), \tag{8}$$
$$\mathrm{Contribution}_{\mathrm{emails}}(\mathrm{Immig}, \mathrm{commitDate}(\mathrm{Immig})).$$

*RQ-1: What is the ratio of contributions made by the developers and nondevelopers to the project over the period of time?*

In order to compute the contributions, we need to distinguish between the developers and nondevelopers of the project. As each subversion log has a time stamp associated to it, we queried all subversion logs from the *start date* of the project till the last *commit date* of the year under consideration. Based on this, we get a list of all developers IDs who have contributed to the source control repository

TABLE 3: Average rate of contributions made by developers and non developers.

| Variable | Contributions | | Participants | |
|---|---|---|---|---|
| | Dev. | Non dev. | Dev. | Non dev. |
| Apache Ant | | | | |
| bugs reported | 29.70 | 509.30 | 6.30 | 377.40 |
| bug comments | 681.50 | 416.01 | 11.30 | 248.90 |
| emails | 4,773.91 | 5,628.00 | 14.54 | 284.91 |
| Apache Lucene | | | | |
| bugs reported | 141.11 | 156.77 | 8.66 | 91.33 |
| bug comments | 507.11 | 241.33 | 10.77 | 95.33 |
| emails | 3,547.00 | 5,745.66 | 13.66 | 173.22 |
| Apache Maven | | | | |
| bugs reported | 204.87 | 268.25 | 11.00 | 165.00 |
| bug comments | 569.28 | 334.28 | 13.85 | 195.14 |
| emails | 4,328.37 | 9,505.75 | 13.37 | 260.87 |
| Apache Solr | | | | |
| bugs reported | 201.10 | 265.60 | 10.20 | 116.00 |
| bug comments | 819.03 | 432.80 | 11.00 | 166.60 |
| emails | 1,808.25 | 6,047.75 | 9.00 | 112.50 |

till that particular year. For each developer ID, we computed the contributions (i.e., bugs reported, comments on bugs, emails, etc.) made to the project on yearly basis and add up the contributions made by all the developers for each year. Similarly, we computed the contributions made by nondevelopers on yearly basis and add up all their contributions for each year. Later, we plotted the contributions made by the developers and nondevelopers for each year in the form of a chart which is shown in Figure 3. Figure 3 shows the comparison of contributions made by the developers and nondevelopers of each *Apache* project under consideration. Further, we computed the average rate of contributions made by the developers and nondevelopers as well as the average number of developers and nondevelopers who made those contributions per year, which is shown in Table 3. For example, the number of bugs reported by the nondevelopers in a given period of time y is computed as follows:

$$\mathrm{Contribution}_{\mathrm{bugs}}\left(\frac{C}{D_y}, y\right), \tag{9}$$

and the average number of bugs reported by the developers and nondevelopers is computed as follows:

$$\sum_{y \in Y} \frac{\mathrm{Contribution}_{\mathrm{bugs}}(D_y, y)}{|y|},$$
$$\sum_{y \in Y} \frac{\mathrm{Contribution}_{\mathrm{bugs}}(C/D_y, y)}{|y|}. \tag{10}$$

Let us assume that the nondevelopers who were active in a certain period of time is calculated by nonDev($\dot{C}/D_y, y$),

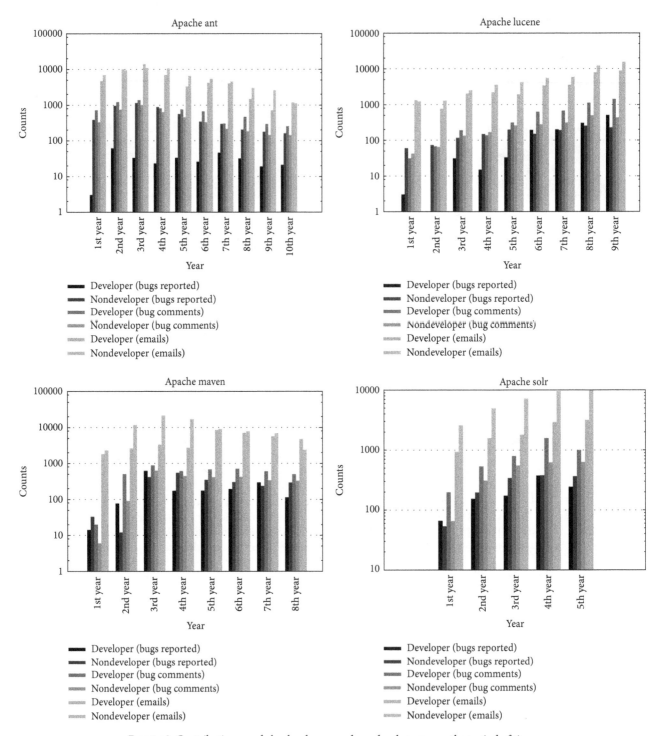

FIGURE 3: Contributions made by developers and nondevelopers over the period of time.

the average participation ratio of developers and nondevelopers is computed as follows:

$$\sum_{y \in \mathbf{Y}} \frac{D_y}{|y|}, \qquad \sum_{y \in \mathbf{Y}} \frac{\text{nonDev}\left(\dot{\mathbf{C}}/D_y, y\right)}{|y|}. \qquad (11)$$

The results in Table 3 show that nondevelopers are highly involved (i.e., contributing more than the developers)

in reporting bugs and participating in discussions on the mailing list. One potential reason for this is the existence of a huge community surrounding these *Apache* projects. Given that discussing/commenting on a bug report requires technical knowledge about the project which is why developers appear to be more active in commenting on the bug reports than nondevelopers, it is quite obvious from Table 3 (also see Figure 3) that nondevelopers play a significant role in the projects under consideration, and hence it is one of the major factors in the long-term survival, success and maturity of these projects over the period of time.

The high ratio of nondevelopers involvement in the project (cf. Figure 3 and Table 3) allows the core members to select or vote for the potential developers to be invited to the "core members" group of the project.

*RQ-2: What is the ratio of contributions made by a potential developer before and after attaining the role of a developer?*

We are only interested in those developers who did not start contributing directly to the project but instead follows the onion model (cf. Figure 1). In order to select those developers, we retrieved all developers from subversion logs. Later for each developer, we compared his first commit date on the project to his first appearance on any of the project repositories (i.e., first bug reporting date, bug comment date, attachment, or email date) in order to compute the number of days or months before he started to contribute as a developer. Although there is no fixed or standard timeline for attaining the role of a developer in the project, we considered only those developers who had an activity (bug report, bug comment, attachment or email) on the project at least 4 months prior to their first commit on the source control repository of the project.

For each of those selected developers, we queried the contributions made to the project *before* and *after* the first *commit date* of each developer. As the time period of attaining the role of a developer is different for each developer, we computed the average yearly rate of contributions made by a developer *before* and *after* attaining the role of a developer. We do not show each individual's contribution to the project due to the privacy issues, and hence we have summarized the aggregated results of each project as shown in Table 4. All the variables (except *n*) used in our study represent the contribution of potential developers on yearly basis. For each *Apache* project, *n* represents the number of potential developers who have attained the role of a developer. The average yearly rate of contributions by a potential developer *before* and *after* attaining the role of a developer is calculated as follows:

$$\sum_{d \in \mathbf{Immig}} \frac{\text{Contribution}_{\text{before}}\left(d, \text{commitDate}\left(d\right)\right)}{|d|},$$

$$\sum_{d \in \mathbf{Immig}} \frac{\text{Contribution}_{\text{after}}\left(d, \text{commitDate}\left(d\right)\right)}{|d|}. \quad (12)$$

Based on Table 4, we find that the bugs reporting pattern does not change much *before* and *after* attaining the role of a developer in *Apache Maven* and *Apache Solr* projects. However, in *Apache Ant*, it decreased tremendously after attaining the role of a developer. As shown in Figure 3, there are only few bugs reported by the developers in contrast to nondevelopers in the *Apache Ant* project which is also reflected by the value of `bugs reported` variable for the *Apache Ant* project. Members after joining the "core members" group participate more often in technical discussions on the bug tracking system which is reflected by

TABLE 4: Yearly average contribution ratio of a potential developer before and after attaining the role of a developer.

| Variable | Mean | | St. Dev | |
|---|---|---|---|---|
| | Before | After | Before | After |
| Apache Ant (*n* = 13) | | | | |
| bugs reported | 17.23 | 2.35 | 17.98 | 3.65 |
| bug comments | 41.44 | 39.02 | 37.66 | 34.83 |
| bug social relation | 44.65 | 31.57 | 51.41 | 23.34 |
| emails | 230.49 | 280.34 | 259 | 224.52 |
| email social relation | 30.5 | 20.31 | 30.35 | 13.55 |
| Apache Lucene (*n* = 22) | | | | |
| bugs reported | 14.12 | 23.73 | 9.12 | 32.74 |
| bug comments | 24.84 | 73.21 | 18.18 | 91.85 |
| bug social relation | 33.57 | 34.67 | 23.75 | 30.02 |
| emails | 130 | 398.71 | 124.87 | 508.02 |
| email social relation | 19.59 | 21.69 | 16.53 | 15.32 |
| Apache Maven (*n* = 21) | | | | |
| bugs reported | 28.40 | 27.82 | 53.27 | 79.49 |
| bug comments | 16.42 | 27.86 | 12.07 | 58.68 |
| bug social relation | 27.16 | 24.08 | 21.43 | 30.85 |
| emails | 158.41 | 185.55 | 218.27 | 174.89 |
| email social relation | 18.33 | 23.34 | 18.31 | 15.73 |
| Apache Solr (*n* = 13) | | | | |
| bugs reported | 24.77 | 23.75 | 30.38 | 17.50 |
| bug comments | 44.72 | 84.77 | 41.35 | 86.25 |
| bug social relation | 68.04 | 80.46 | 52.18 | 52.39 |
| emails | 156.01 | 313.82 | 227.57 | 333.19 |
| email social relation | 14.72 | 38.47 | 7.85 | 33.04 |

the value of `bug comment` variable. However, an increase in the participation in technical discussions did not increase the social relation of the developers on the bug tracking system (i.e., `bug social relation`) in the case of *Apache Ant* and *Apache Maven* project. One reason could be that, after attaining the role of a developer, they focused only on certain modules of a project and hence involved in discussions on bugs relevant to those modules with other developers of the project. There is also a tremendous increase in the number of emails sent by the members after attaining the role of a developer which eventually increases the value of `email social relation` variable.

Based on the *Apache* projects under consideration, we found that members after attaining the role of a developer tend to participate actively in technical discussions either on the mailing list or bug tracking system which also increases their social relation networks except the case of *Apache Ant* project. The bugs reporting behavior of these members varies in our studied *Apache* projects, and hence it is difficult to say if they report more bugs after attaining the role of a developer.

*RQ-3: What is the average rate of contributions made by a potential developer comparing to other members of the project before attaining the role of a developer?*

For each potential developer, we took the first time-stamp value where he first appears on the project and the second time-stamp value when he actually made the first commit

TABLE 5: Average contribution rate of a potential developer comparing to other members of the project before attaining the role of a developer.

| Variable | Mean | St. dev |
|---|---|---|
| Apache Ant ($n = 13$) | | |
| bugs reported | 11.15 | 13.25 |
| bug comments | 10.43 | 8.35 |
| bug social relation | 8.42 | 6.65 |
| emails | 19.89 | 16.25 |
| email social relation | 10.97 | 8.42 |
| Apache Lucene ($n = 22$) | | |
| bugs reported | 4.53 | 3.09 |
| bug comments | 4.08 | 2.89 |
| bug social relation | 3.18 | 1.73 |
| emails | 3.91 | 3.27 |
| email social relation | 6.23 | 4.42 |
| Apache Maven ($n = 21$) | | |
| bugs reported | 4.05 | 3.68 |
| bug comments | 2.36 | 2.01 |
| bug social relation | 2.44 | 1.98 |
| emails | 4.05 | 5.76 |
| email social relation | 4.31 | 3.34 |
| Apache Solr ($n = 13$) | | |
| bugs reported | 4.56 | 5.77 |
| bug comments | 4.4 | 4.72 |
| bug social relation | 2.52 | 2.15 |
| emails | 1.05 | 1.07 |
| email social relation | 2.71 | 1.95 |

TABLE 6: Appearance of a potential developer on different software repositories prior to attaining the role of a developer.

| Apache projects | Patch submission (no. of days) | Bugs reported (no. of days) | Emails (no. of days) |
|---|---|---|---|
| Apache Ant | 544.15 | 553.84 | 706.53 |
| Apache Lucene | 457.41 | 526.32 | 706.22 |
| Apache Maven | 385.00 | 396.31 | 709.71 |
| Apache Solr | 269.30 | 237.92 | 452.46 |

to the source control repository of the project. We extracted the contributions (i.e., bugs reported, comments, emails, etc.) made by a potential developer between those time-stamp values. Using the same time-stamp values, we computed the contributions made by other members who were also active during that specific time period. Later, we divided the contributions of a potential developer by the average contributions of all other members in order to determine the average rate of contributions made by a potential developer comparing to other members of the project. We do not show each individual's contribution rate due to the privacy issues, and hence we have summarized the aggregated results of each project which is shown in Table 5. For example, the average rate of bugs reported by an immigrant comparing to other members who were active during the same time-stamp is calculated as follows:

$$\sum_{\text{Immig} \in \textbf{Immig}} \frac{\text{Contribution}_{\text{bugs}}\left(\text{Immig}, \text{commitDate}\left(\text{Immig}\right)\right)}{\sum_{c \in C} \text{Contribution}_{\text{bugs}}\left(c, \text{commitDate}\left(\text{Immig}\right)\right) / |c|}. \tag{13}$$

The results in Table 5 can be understand as follows: the average rate of reporting bugs by a potential developer of *Apache Lucene* project is 4.53 times the average rate of reporting bugs by all other members who were active during that time period. Although the average rate of contributions

made by potential developers varies in all the projects under consideration, it is quite obvious from each variable value that the contributions made by potential developers are more than the average contributions of all other members. Hence, we can say that they were the most active contributors (i.e., technically skilled and higher social status) before attaining the developer status in the project.

*RQ-4: Does a potential developer follow onion model in order to attain the role of a developer?*

For each potential developer, we computed the time-stamp value between his/her first commit date to his/her first activity on the different software repositories in terms of days. Table 6 presents the appearance of a potential developer in terms of average number of days on different software repositories prior to attaining the role of a developer. The result shows that all the potential developers started from the mailing list (cf. Table 6) because the email activity is the oldest for all *Apache* projects under consideration followed by the bugs reporting/commenting, and the latest activity before attaining the role of a developer was the source-code patch submissions (i.e., bugs fixing). The results shown in Table 6 closely match to the onion model (see Figure 1) where a member starts as a reader followed by reporting bugs and later fixing bugs before attaining the role of a developer.

Let `ActivityDate(Immig,mL)` return the number of days between the first commit date of an immigrant (i.e., potential developer) on the source control repository to his first activity date on the mailing list of a project. The average number of days for an immigrant to appear on a mailing list prior to his/her first commit date is calculated as follows:

$$\sum_{\text{Immig} \in \textbf{Immig}} \frac{\text{ActivityDate}\left(\text{Immig}, ml\right)}{|\textbf{Immig}|}. \tag{14}$$

The results (Table 6) also show that it took almost 2 years for a potential developer of *Apache Ant, Apache Lucene,* and *Apache Maven* projects to attain the role of a developer. However, we cannot say that it is the standard time as the time varies dramatically from project to project as it can be seen in the results of *Apache Solr* project comparing to other *Apache* projects under consideration.

## 6. Conclusion

In this paper, we have investigated in detail the patterns of contributions made by those members who have attained the role of a developer in the project. First, we investigated the significant role played by nondevelopers in the long-term survival of an OSS project and observed that nondevelopers who do not have write-access to the source control repository participate actively in reporting bugs and email discussions, thus contributing to the maturity of an OSS project. Our investigation based on the contribution of potential developers before and after attaining the role of a developer showed that after attaining a higher position in the community, developers tend to contribute more efficiently than nondevelopers of the project by actively participating in technical discussions along with fixing bugs. Moreover, we observed that the members who attained the role of a developer had more contributions in contrast to the average number of contributions made by other members of the project who were active during his/her time period. This makes it obvious that one of the important factors in order to attain the role of a developer is the demonstration of technical skills and commitment to the project in an efficient manner.

## Conflict of Interests

The authors declare that there is no conflict of interests regarding the publication of this paper.

## References

[1] B. Shibuya and T. Tamai, "Understanding the process of participating in open source communities," in *Proceedings of the ICSE Workshop on Emerging Trends in Free/Libre/Open Source Software Research and Development (FLOSS '09)*, pp. 1–6, IEEE Computer Society, Washington, DC, USA, May 2009.

[2] G. Von Krogh, S. Spaeth, and K. R. Lakhani, "Community, joining, and specialization in open source software innovation: a case study," *Research Policy*, vol. 32, no. 7, pp. 1217–1241, 2003.

[3] C. Bird, A. Gourley, P. Devanbu, A. Swaminathan, and G. Hsu, "Open borders? Immigration in open source projects," in *Proceedings of the 4th International Workshop on Mining Software Repositories (MSR '07)*, Washington, DC, USA, May 2007.

[4] M. Antikainen, T. Aaltonen, and J. Väisänen, "The role of trust in OSS communities—case Linux Kernel community," *IFIP International Federation for Information Processing*, vol. 234, pp. 223–228, 2007.

[5] Y. Ye, K. Nakakoji, Y. Yamamoto, and K. Kishida, "The co-evolution of systems and communities in Free and Open Source Software Development," in *Free/Open Source Software Development*, pp. 59–82, Idea Group, Hershey, Pa, USA, 2004.

[6] http://ant.apache.org/.

[7] http://lucene.apache.org/.

[8] http://maven.apache.org/.

[9] http://lucene.apache.org/solr/.

[10] K. Crowston and J. Howison, "The social structure of free and open source software development," in *Proceedings of the International Conference on Information Systems*, Seattle, Wash, USA, 2003.

[11] C. Jensen and W. Scacchi, "Modelling recruitment and role migration process in oosd projects," in *Proceedings of the 6th International Workshop on Software Process Simulation and Modeling*, St. Louis, Mo, USA, 2005.

[12] A. Mockus, R. T. Fielding, and J. D. Herbsleb, "Two case studies of open source software development: apache and mozilla," *ACM Transactions on Software Engineering and Methodology*, vol. 11, no. 3, pp. 309–346, 2002.

[13] T. Dinh-Trong and J. M. Bieman, "Open source software development: a case study of freeBSD," in *Proceedings of the 10th International Symposium on Software Metrics (METRICS '04)*, pp. 96–105, Washington, DC, USA, September 2004.

[14] N. Ducheneaut, "Socialization in an open source software community: a socio-technical analysis," *Computer Supported Cooperative Work*, vol. 14, no. 4, pp. 323–368, 2005.

[15] D. Cox and D. Oakes, *Analysis of Survival Data: Monographs on Statistics and Applied Probability*, Chapman and Hall, 1984.

[16] I. Herraiz, G. Robles, J. J. Amor, T. Romera, and J. M. G. Barahona, "The processes of joining in global distributed software projects," in *Proceedings of the International Workshop on Global Software Development for the Practitioner (GSD '06)*, pp. 27–33, 2006.

[17] W. Scacchi, J. Feller, B. Fitzgerald, S. Hissam, and K. Lakhani, "Understanding free/open source software development processes," *Software Process Improvement and Practice*, vol. 11, no. 2, pp. 95–105, 2006.

[18] M. Fischer, M. Pinzger, and H. Gall, "Populating a release history database from version control and bug tracking systems," in *Proceedings of the International Conference on Software Maintenance (ICSM '03)*, pp. 23–32, IEEE Computer Society, Washington, DC, USA, September 2003.

[19] S. Wasserman and K. Faust, *Social Network Analysis: Methods and Applications*, Cambridge University Press, 1994.

[20] A. Iqbal and M. Hausenblas, "Interlinking developer identities within and across open source projects: the linked data approach," *ISRN Software Engineering*, vol. 2013, Article ID 584731, 12 pages, 2013.

[21] C. Bird, A. Gourley, and P. Devanbu, "Detecting patch submission and acceptance in OSS projects," in *Proceedings of the 4th International Workshop on Mining Software Repositories (MSR '07)*, Washington, DC, USA, May 2007.

[22] A. Iqbal, O. Ureche, M. Hausenblas, and G. Tummarello, "LD2SD: linked data driven software development," in *Proceedings of the 21st International Conference on Software Engineering and Knowledge Engineering (SEKE '09)*, pp. 240–245, Boston, Mass, USA, July 2009.

# 3

# Towards the Consolidation of a Diagramming Suite for Agent-Oriented Modelling Languages

**Brian Henderson-Sellers**

*University of Technology, Sydney, Broadway, NSW 2007, Australia*

Correspondence should be addressed to Brian Henderson-Sellers; brian.henderson-sellers@uts.edu.au

Academic Editors: X. He, S. Sutton, and M. Viroli

Whilst several agent-oriented modelling languages have been developed by independent research groups, it is now appropriate to consider a consolidation of these various approaches. There are arguably three things that need consolidation and future standardization: individual symbols, the underpinning metamodel, and the diagram types. Here we address only the third issue by extending an earlier analysis that resulted in recommendations for various diagram types for the modelling of a multiagent system (MAS). Here, we take each of these previously recommended diagram types and see how each is realized in a wide variety (over 20) of current agent-oriented software engineering (AOSE) methodologies. We also take the opportunity to express, as exemplars, some of these diagram types using the recently published FAML notation.

## 1. Introduction

Any software development benefits from the use of a methodology. Part of such a methodological approach is a means to depict interim work products, typically documented using a graphical notation (a.k.a. concrete syntax). Symbols are used to represent single concepts, defined in an appropriate modelling language (ML), itself typically represented, at least in part, by a metamodel (e.g., [1]). These symbols can then be grouped in heterogeneous yet semantically related ways. A coherent model, thus depicted, is often said to be of a specific *diagram type*. In other words, a diagram type refers to a collection of classes in the metamodel, that is, it defines which metaclasses can be appropriately instantiated for this particular scope and focus.

For agent-oriented software engineering (AOSE), such modelling languages (and their notations and recommended diagram types) are in their infancy. A large number of AOSE methodological approaches exist, all with their own notational elements. As part of a community goal of standardizing agent-oriented modelling languages, collaborative notations have been proposed (e.g., [2]), as well as mergers at the conceptual level (e.g., [3, 4]), the latter of these being complemented more recently by a concrete syntax [5].

Notations need to have a high degree of usability, which can often be accomplished based on semiotic principles (e.g., [6–8]). Information is needed not only about individual agents and interagent communications, but also on the context of the environment in which they are situated. Current practice in many methodological approaches is to utilize standard object-oriented diagramming techniques, typically using UML [9–11] as a notation, whenever possible, although there are many concepts in AOSE not so representable. For example, Garcia et al. [12] comment on the need to include specific agenthood properties, including interaction/communication, autonomy, and adaptation with possible additional properties of learning, mobility, collaboration, and roles. A similar list, yet with a BDI (BDI = beliefs, desires, and intentions (e.g., [13, 14])) slant, is given by Sturm and Shehory [15, 16] as agent, belief, desire, intention, message, norm, organization, protocol, role, society, and task. Taveter and Wagner [17] identify the most important concepts as including agents, events, actions, communication, and message, underpinning these in terms of ontological theory (e.g., endurants and perdurants). Bertolini et al. [18] focus primarily on the Goal Diagram and the Actor Diagram in their presentation of TAOM4E—an Eclipse-based tool to support the Tropos methodology and based solidly on a metamodel.

Beydoun et al. [4] present a generic metamodel which itself contains four connected perspectives. In this case, the discrimination is between organization as compared to agent level and between design time and run time. However, they do not explicitly link these to diagram types, although there is in fact a weak relationship.

Diagram types are often divided into two loosely defined groups: static or structural diagrams and dynamic (a.k.a. behavioural) diagrams (e.g., [69, 70])—a grouping that will also be utilized here. The former depict aspects that might be termed architectural, typified by variants of an OO class diagram; the latter depict some forms of functionality and time-dependent actions.

Torres da Silva et al. [71] have presented MAS-ML as a metamodel-based modelling language for agent-oriented software engineering. As well as introducing new agent-focussed concepts, as discussed below, they also recommend a suite of diagram types—three static and two dynamic:

(i) Extended UML Class Diagram,

(ii) Organization Diagram,

(iii) Role Diagram,

(iv) Extended UML Sequence Diagram,

(v) Extended UML Activity Diagram.

In contrast to the approach taken in the ML proposed by Beydoun et al. [4] that focusses first on a viewpoint and later on the detailed concepts, Torres da Silva et al. [71] propose not viewpoints but specific diagram types, although they neglect to give a clear problem statement for which these diagram types are the proposed solution. In other words, whilst useful, they are at the diagram level rather than the viewpoint level as advocated in Henderson-Sellers [19]. We will therefore comment on each of these diagrams in the appropriate place in Sections 5 and 6.

In summary, we aim here to make a contribution towards future standardization of agent-oriented modelling languages—focussing here on diagram suites. Section 2 outlines the approach taken in determining an appropriate framework, which we then use to analyze over 20 contemporary agent-oriented methodologies in terms of the kinds of diagrams that they support and recommend. Section 3 discusses notational aspects, introducing the FAML notation [5] that we use in later examples in comparison with the notations used by these individual AOSE methodologies. Following an overview of diagram types in Section 4, in the next two sections, we describe in detail static diagram types (Section 5) and then dynamic diagram types (Section 6). In each of these two sections, we categorize diagrams using the several views derived in Section 2. Section 7 provides a final discussion and indicates some other related work not otherwise cited followed by a brief conclusion section (Section 8) including some ideas for future research. From this detailed comparison, we aim to draw out commonalities and variations in the suite of diagram types utilized across all extant agent-modelling languages as a precursor to future international standardization.

TABLE 1: Set of diagram types recommended in Henderson-Sellers [19] in the light of his analysis of AOSE methodologies. These diagram types should then be supplemented by textual based templates and descriptors as shown in Table 2.

| Static diagram types | Dynamic diagram types |
| --- | --- |
| Environment description | Agent goal-based use case |
| Environmental connectivity | Use case map |
| External organization structure chart | Conversation a.k.a. interaction |
| Architecture | Protocol (a kind of conversation) |
| Agent society | Workflow |
| Agent role | Agent state |
| Role dependency | Task specification |
| Agent internals | Task state |
| Agent overview | |
| Goal decomposition | |
| Ontology | |
| Plan | |
| Capability | |
| Service | |
| Task decomposition | |
| Deployment | |
| UI design | |

TABLE 2: Textual work products (static and dynamic).

| Static textual diagram types | Dynamic textual diagram types |
| --- | --- |
| System requirements | Goal-based use case template |
| Role definition template | Contractual template |
| Agent descriptors | Event descriptors |
| CRC cards | Data descriptors |
| Plan descriptor | Plan descriptors |
| Capability descriptors | Task template |
| Service diagram | Protocol descriptors |
| Task template | Message descriptors |
| Percept descriptor | Action descriptor |
| | Process descriptor |

## 2. Research Approach

As detailed in Henderson-Sellers [19], in order to analyze the various options for a suite of AOSE relevant diagrams, the first step was to identify static versus dynamic diagram types (Tables 1 and 2) and then to group these in terms of their relevance to a number of views or viewpoints as previously discussed in the AOSE literature (e.g., [20, 48]). Seven such views were identified (Table 3), and, for each, both static and dynamic diagram types were identified (Table 4). (Details of the several iterations needed to derive Table 4 are to be found by Henderson-Sellers [19] and are not replicated here.) Finally, the atomic elements identified for each of these diagram types are listed in Table 5. However, this list is not absolute in that different methodologies offer different interpretations and consequently use different atomic elements on

TABLE 3: Seven views recommended in the analysis of Henderson-Sellers [19]. Note that the original analysis was based on the AOSE literature which essentially eschews aspects of user interface. To these seven, an eighth one, UI, needs to be added (reprinted from [19], copyright 2010, with permission from IOS Press).

| View name | Focus of view |
| --- | --- |
| Environment | External context, including system requirements |
| Architecture | High level structure of system independent of agent technology |
| Agent societies | Structure of agents into groups together with interactions and information exchange, typically within the group |
| Agent workflow | Workflows |
| Agent knowledge | Roles of individual agents, their responsibilities, and purpose |
| Agent services | Services offered, tasks to be undertaken, goals to be attained, and detailed capabilities. Applied to a small number of interacting agents |
| Deployment | Interface with run-time platform |

TABLE 4: Two dimensional matrix for views versus static/dynamic aspects for various AOSE diagram types (modified and reprinted from [19], copyright 2010, with permission from IOS Press).

| View | Static diagram types | Dynamic diagram types |
| --- | --- | --- |
| Environment | Environment description; environmental connectivity; system requirements; use case | N/A |
| Architecture | Agent societies/organization | N/A |
| Agent societies | Agent society details; agent role | Conversation (including interaction and protocol); task |
| Agent workflow | N/A | Workflow |
| Agent knowledge | Goal; agent type; agent role; plan; ontology | Goal; agent state; capability |
| Agent services | Agent society details; agent type; goal; ontology | Goal; task; capability |
| Deployment | Allocation to run-time platform | N/A |
| UI | User interface design | States and transitions related to interface |

any one named diagram—for example, Padgham et al. [2] note that in the Prometheus methodology an Agent Society model shows actions and percepts but would not use an Ontology diagram, whereas users of the PASSI methodology would use a separate Ontology diagram.

As the knowledge of AOSE increases, the diagram suite suggested in Table 4 and the details of Table 5 will almost certainly require further changes—this paper offers further comments based on further investigation of the extant literature.

An initial assessment [19] resulted in some suggested recommendations for each diagram type in Table 4. Here, we commence with those recommendations and evaluate how each particular diagram type is utilized in methodologies not previously discussed. With the recent advent of a proposed notational standard for FAML [5], we take the opportunity of including an evaluation of how the symbols in this modelling language (summarized in Figure 2) can be useful. In cases where problems are identifiable, this could lead to improvements to be proposed to the FAML notation itself.

## 3. Notations

Notations (a.k.a. concrete syntax) currently utilized for agent-oriented methodologies are typically individualistic. However, there are efforts under way to systematize these. Two

proposed notations, AML [72, 73] and AUML [74, 75], are essentially extensions of an object-oriented modelling language—whether this is appropriate is discussed in, for example, Torres da Silva and de Lucena [76], Choren and Lucena [77], and Beydoun et al. [4].

In AML, UML class diagrams are used with subtypes of Ontology Diagrams, Society Diagrams, Behavior Decomposition Diagrams, and Mental Diagrams (with a further subtype of Goal-Based Requirements Diagram). Composite Structure Diagrams (from UML) can be either Entity or Service Diagrams in AML; UML sequence diagrams are used as Protocol Sequence Diagrams with a subtype of Service Protocol Sequence Diagram. Finally, UML communication diagrams are realized as Protocol Communication Diagrams, a subtype of which is the Service Protocol Communication Diagram.

These UML-based notations are not readily related to the seven views identified by Henderson-Sellers [19] (see Table 3), although they do discuss static versus dynamic aspects of each diagram (Table 1).

Secondly, a number of methodologies use as their main notation that of $i^*$ [78] (later mapped in the agent-oriented context to UML by Mylopoulos et al. [79]). Designed for requirements engineering, $i^*$'s usage in AOSE has been primarily in the requirements and architectural design stages of Tropos (in later stages Tropos uses AUML/UML diagrams)

TABLE 5: Atomic elements and diagram types.

| Diagram type | Atomic elements to be displayed |
| --- | --- |
| (1) *Static diagram types* | |
| Environment description | Entities represented by classes; relationships between the modelled entities |
| Environmental connectivity | Agents/MASs, internal and external resources, relationships across the MAS/environment interface |
| External organization structure chart | Organizational units in the real-life business |
| Architecture | Technology-independent large-scale structure |
| Agent society | Agents inside the MAS, how they associate with each other |
| Agent role | Links between the agents and the roles they play |
| Role dependency | Hierarchical structure of many roles |
| Agent internals | Constituent elements in an individual agent or role |
| Agent overview | High level view of an agent |
| Goal decomposition | Goals, subgoals |
| Ontology | The underpinning semantic structure |
| Plan | The (process) steps needed to effect a task and accomplish a goal |
| Capability | The ability or responsibility of an agent |
| Service | Functionality offered by the agent |
| Task decomposition | Tasks, subtasks |
| Deployment | Allocation of MAS elements to nodes of the run-time platform |
| UI design | TBD (the topic of proposed future research). (See brief discussion in Sections 5.7 and 6.5 on the relevant, non-AOSE UI literature) |
| (2) *Dynamic diagram types* | |
| Agent goal-based use case | Functionality offered by the MAS |
| Use case map | Threads across many agents to realize a use case |
| Conversation | Dynamic interaction details |
| Protocol | Rules associated with interactions |
| Workflow | Large-scale processes relating to problem solving (in the real world) |
| Agent state | Attribute values determining the current state of an agent |
| Task specification | Definitions of tasks needed to accomplish a specific goal |
| Task state | The current state of a task, in terms of how far through the task enactment |

because that agent-oriented methodology uses requirements engineering concepts throughout the development process. However, more recently this notation has been more widely evaluated. For example, Lapouchnian and Lespérance [80] map between $i^*$ and CASL (Cognitive Agents Specification Language [81]) representing agents' goals and knowledge as mental states; Franch [82] assesses the predictability of $i^*$ models; Estrada et al. [83] undertake an empirical evaluation of $i^*$ using industrial case studies and conclude that extensions and modifications are needed for $i^*$ to address its lack of modularization.

Although most methodologists devise their own notation, there has been over the last few years a groundswell of opinion that notations (and metamodels) should be applicable to more than just a single methodological approach. In that spirit, Padgham et al. [2] suggest a notation based on a merger between the notations that are part of O-MaSE, Tropos, Prometheus, and PASSI. (Sources/citations for the various AOSE methodologies are found in Table 7). Although a huge step forward in the future creation of a widely acceptable standard AOML, Henderson-Sellers et al. [5]

offered some areas for improvement, based on semiotic considerations. Using that experience (of Padgham et al. [2]), they then offered a notation that has a stronger semiotic basis whilst retaining ideas from Padgham et al. [2] when appropriate. This notation has elements that are conformant to the FAML metamodel of Beydoun et al. [4].

In their definition of a modelling language, which contains more detail than we seek at present, Beydoun et al. [4] split their metamodel diagrams into four parts, which correspond interestingly with the viewpoints discussed in Henderson-Sellers [19] and outlined above. Beydoun et al. [4] discriminate between internal versus external (to an agent) and design versus runtime perspectives. Their System-level diagram corresponds to the Organization view of Table 3 together with some aspects of the Knowledge view (specifically in terms of role modelling) and their Environment level diagram to the Environment view. Their agent-definition metamodel fragment depicts specifications for agent types, messages, and plans, *inter alia*, and would therefore seem to have a reasonable correlation with the Services view in Table 3, whereas the agent-level (runtime) portion of the

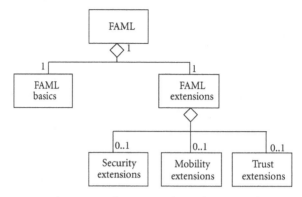

FIGURE 1: Organizational structure of FAML into basic elements and extensional elements.

TABLE 6: Initially proposed families and their members.

| Family | Members | Shape | Colour (optional) | Source and/or influence for notation |
|---|---|---|---|---|
| Agents and roles[1] | Agent, role, group, position, organization | Circle atop mask or rectangle | Yellow | INGENIAS [20] |
| Tasks and plans | Action specification, FAML task, plan specification | Curvilinear | Green | ISO/IEC [21] |
| Events and resources | Event, resource | Triangular | Blue/green | |
| Goals | Hard goal, soft goal, belief | Complex curvilinear | Brown | |
| Ontology | Ontology, service, capability | Polygonal | Dark blue | |
| Use cases | Scenario, actor | Double oval, stick figure | None | Padgham et al. [2] |
| Messages | Conversation, message in, message out | Arrow heads | B/W | Padgham et al. [2] |

[1] Strictly agent types and role types (design time concepts) rather than their run-time equivalents of individual agents and individual roles.

metamodel goes somewhat beyond the views of Table 3, since it describes metamodelling support for the runtime "Actions" of individual agents, moving on from plan descriptors, for example, to plan enactment. Run-time concepts can thus be linked to some of the dynamic diagram types discussed by other authors (and one of the two discriminators used in this survey). An important distinction is made between agent types (the equivalent to OO classes in a class diagram) and (runtime) agents, which are individuals (equivalent to objects in an OO environment) (see also [59, page 93]). This distinction was made after surveying the literature wherein agent types are often (mis)labelled agents.

The initial studies for the derivation of FAML's metamodel and notation were confined to what might be called "basics" (Figure 1), in that they did not take into account security, mobility, or trust. These are to be regarded as FAML Extensions, the detailed derivation of which is yet to be undertaken.

The set of symbols proposed for the FAML Basics (Figure 1) by Henderson-Sellers et al. [5] have since been slightly modified as a result of questions and discussions at the conference presentation. Figure 2 shows this final set, which we evaluate further in this paper. The principles behind the choice of symbol include ease of drawing, that "families" of symbols should have the same shape and colour (Table 6) and that colour should be an enhancer and not a

determinant; that is, the shapes should be understandable in black and white as well as colour. These, and other principles, accord well with the semiotic discussion and principles of Constantine and Henderson-Sellers [6, 84] and Moody [7].

Symbols for agents and roles utilize the role "mask" and its variations. Process-style symbols are similar to those in ISO/IEC [21], topologically similar and green in colour. Events and resources, whilst being a little difficult to defend as a "family", have, nevertheless, similar shapes and colours. Goals, on the other hand, are linked to beliefs as part of the mental state of agents. They use a familiar representation using Yu's [78] $i^*$ notation, as used in agent methodologies like Tropos and Secure Tropos [85]. When used, the fill colour is brown. Ontology, service, and capability are grouped together because both Service and Ontology are linked to Role in FAML. Finally, both scenarios and actors can be linked by their common usage in use case style diagrams. For these, we simply adopt the symbols proposed by Padgham et al. [2].

Agent interactions utilize various variants of an arrowhead (Figure 3). Two alternatives (for MessageIn and MessageOut) were also proposed, but discussants at the EMM-SAD conference in June 2012 at which these ideas were first presented were undecided whether the symbols in Figure 3 or in Figure 4 were preferable. Here, we use those of Figure 3.

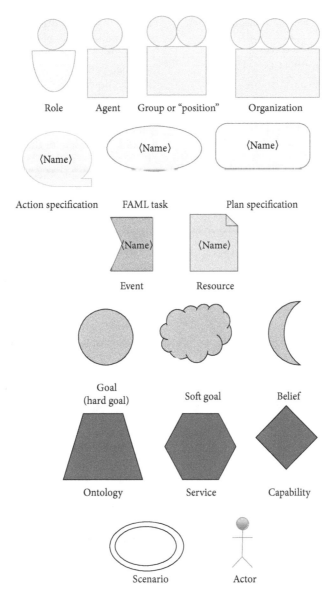

FIGURE 2: Symbols selected for FAML's notation.

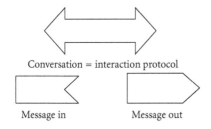

FIGURE 3: Communication symbols in FAML (after [5]).

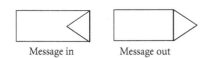

FIGURE 4: Some suggested alternative representations of agent communication.

## 4. Diagram Types Used in Current AOSE Methodologies

Henderson-Sellers [19] proposed a number of static and dynamic diagram types for the seven identified views, see Table 4. He then discussed a small selection of methodologies that supported each diagram type, the methodologies being selected from over 20 contemporary AOSE methodologies (Table 7)—excluding those dealing with mobility, for example, Hachicha et al. [86], security (Low et al. [87] discuss security diagrams, offering them as *extensions* to existing diagrams—as shown here in Figure 4), for example, Mouratidis [85], and Bresciani et al. [66], or with noncooperative and adaptive agents. (We, however, do include aspects of ADELFE relevant to cooperative agents), for example, Georgé et al. [88] and Steegmans et al. [89], which introduce additional specifically-focussed concepts, symbols, and diagram

TABLE 7: Prime references for the AOSE methodologies quoted here.

| Methodology name | Main references |
| --- | --- |
| ADELFE | Picard and Gleizes [22] |
| Agent factory | Collier et al. [23, 24] |
| CAMLE | Shan and Zhu [25] |
| Cassiopeia | Collinot et al. [26] Collinot and Dragoul [27] |
| Elammari and Lalonde | Elammari and Lalonde [28] |
| Gaia | Wooldridge et al. [29] Zambonelli et al. [30, 31] |
| ROADMAP extensions to Gaia | Juan et al. [32] Sterling et al. [33] |
| INGENIAS | Pavón and Gómez-Sanz [34] Pavón et al. [20] |
| ISLANDER | Sierra et al. [35, 36] |
| MAS-CommonKADS | Iglesias and Garijo [37] Iglesias et al. [38, 39] |
| MaSE | Wood and DeLoach [40] DeLoach [41–43] DeLoach and Kumar [44] |
| O-MaSE | Garcia-Ojeda et al. [45] DeLoach and Garcia-Ojeda [46] |
| MESSAGE | Caire et al. [47, 48] Garijo et al. [49] |
| MOBMAS | Tran et al. [50] Tran and Low [51] |
| OperA | Dignum [52] Mensonides et al. [53] |
| PASSI | Burrafato and Cossentino [54] Cossentino [55, 56] Cossentino and Potts [57, 58] |
| Prometheus | Padgham and Winikoff [59, 60] Winikoff and Padgham [61] Khallouf and Winikoff [62] |
| RAP/AOR | Taveter and Wagner [17] |
| SODA | Omicini [63] |
| SONIA | Alonso et al. [64] |
| Tropos | Bresciani et al. [65, 66] Giorgini et al. [67] |

types. Furthermore, Tran and Low [51] note that all are deficient in at least one of the three areas of agent internal design, agent interaction design, and MAS organization modelling. The numbers for each diagram type proposed in each of the methodologies of Table 7 are given in Table 8, although it should be noted that some diagram types could be classified under different headings.

In determining to which view (of Table 3) any specific methodological diagram type should be allotted, terminology definitions were sometimes found to be absent, ambiguous, or apparently contradictory. There are several sets of such

terms including (i) organization and domain, (ii) interaction diagram and protocol diagram, (iii) goal and task, and (iv) "capability," "service," "responsibility," and "functionality".

Since some authors are using their own definitions, for example, in categorizing views/perspectives, the scoping we have established in Table 3 is sometimes not matched by particular methodological approaches. In particular, our anticipation that the Architecture view should be independent of technology chosen for the solution, as described, for instance, in Giorgini et al. [67], is not met (see further discussion in Section 5.2). In other methodologies, the different use of terms such as "model," "diagram," "view," and "viewpoint" is often unclear (e.g., [20, 29, 31, 39, 49, 90]). As another example, PASSI confounds work product terms with process terms by using model/diagram names to describe tasks.

Another challenge in developing a standard diagramming suite, useful for all AOSE methodologies, is that, while some published methodologies recommend a set of diagrams that occurs in every publication (e.g., [17, 44, 45]), other methodologies continue to evolve so that examination of any one methodology-specific paper often results in difficulty in our determining of what diagrams are recommended for that particular methodology at the present time, although some authors do make it clear what changes have been made (e.g., [62]). In other words, some methodologies contain a stable set of work products, whilst in others the recommended diagramming suite has not yet stabilized.

While Henderson-Sellers [19] attempted to be comprehensive, here we will emphasize those diagram types and diagram usages recommended therein, extending the discussion and incorporating new ideas on AOML notations [5]. When standard UML (OO) diagrams are recommended, we will not include a pictorial representation of what (we assume) will be a diagram well known to readers, being part of the International Standard 19501 [93].

We do not undertake a side-by-side methodology comparison, as is done, for example, in Tran and Low [94] or, more recently, in Dam and Winikoff [95]. Rather, we try to exemplify some of the differences in representational style for diagrams pertinent to each of the several views identified in Henderson-Sellers [19] and summarized below.

In the following two sections, we analyze diagram types currently used in a number of AOSE methodologies using the framework of Table 4. Section 5 discusses the various static diagram types and Section 6 the dynamic counterparts. For both sections, we adopt the seven views deduced in Henderson-Sellers [19] plus the added UI view (Table 3) and try to make additional suggestions, where appropriate, regarding appropriate notations for these identified diagram types.

The *Environment View* is used either to describe the interface between the MAS and the external entities in the problem domain and/or the externalities to the MAS (Figure 5). Indeed, domain modelling is seen by Müller [96], Parunak and Odell [97], and Dignum and Dignum [98] as being crucial.

Relevant diagram types may be solely focussed on the environment (a.k.a. domain), but there are many methodologies in which an organizational diagram type, as discussed

TABLE 8: Summary of the number of distinct usages of each diagram type per methodology.

| | View | | | | | | | | | | |
| | Environment | | Architecture | Agent societies | | Agent knowledge | | Agent services | | Deployment | User interface |
| | Static | Dynamic | Static | Static | Dynamic | Static | Dynamic | Static | Dynamic | Static | |
|---|---|---|---|---|---|---|---|---|---|---|---|
| ADELFE | | 1 | | 1 | 1 | | | | | | |
| Agent factory | | 1 | | 1 | 3 | | | | | | |
| CAMLE | | | | 1 | 1 | 2 | | | | | |
| Cassiopeia | | | | 1 | | | | | | | |
| Elammari and Lalonde | | 1 | 1 | 1 + 2 textual | | 1 textual | | | | | |
| Gaia | 1 | | 1 | 2 + 1 textual | | 2 textual | | | | | |
| ROADMAP extensions to Gaia | | 1 | | 1 textual | | 1 | | | | | |
| INGENIAS | 1 | | 2 | | 2 | 1 | | 1 | | | |
| ISLANDER | | | | 2 | | 1 + 1 textual | 1 | 1 | 1 | | |
| MAS-CommonKADS | | 1 | 1 | 1 | 2 | 4 + 1 textual | | | 1 | 2 | |
| MaSE | | 1 | 1 | 2 | 2 | 1 | 2 | | 1 | 1 | |
| O-MaSE (extras) | | | | 2 | 1 | 3 | | | | | |
| MESSAGE | 4 | | | 5 | 1 | 2 | 1 | 2 | | | |
| MOBMAS | 4 | | 1 | 2 | 2 | 7 + 1 textual | 1 | | | 1 | |
| OperA | | | | 4 + 5 textual | 1 | 1 + 1 textual | | | | | |
| PASSI | 1 | 1 | | 2 | 3 | 2 | 1 | | 1 | 1 + 1 textual | |
| Prometheus | | 2 | | 2 | 2 | 5 + 2 textual | | | 1 | | |
| RAP/AOR | | 2 | | 5 | 2 | | | | | 1 | |
| SODA | 1 | | | 2 | | 2 textual | | | | | |
| SONIA | | | | | | 3 | | 1 | | | |
| Tropos | | | | | 1 | 5 | | | | 1 | |

in Section 5.3, serves a second purpose: that of including not only the agent organization but also its interface with the environment, whilst retaining the (perhaps confusing) name of "organizational diagram." This is especially seen in methodological approaches such as MAS-CommonKADS and MESSAGE. For the organizational model of the former, it is clear that the organization model is intended to serve also beyond the agent organization and to interface with the environment, since the recommended notation for the organizational model (Figure 6) includes sensors and actuators (a.k.a. effectors) in the agent symbol (actually an agent type—see earlier discussion).

In other words, some of the diagram types discussed in Section 5.1 could well be equally allocated to Section 5.3 (and vice versa). (For a more detailed and more philosophical discussion of environment abstractions, see Viroli et al. [99]). Environment was also recently a major topic of conversation

within the OMG as part of their emerging interests in agents [100].

For the *Architecture View*, we note that the term "architecture" can have many interpretations in the context of an MAS. Here, we use it to describe large-scale features that are independent of the technology used to undertake the implementation of the MAS. In different AOSE methodologies, the level of detail can vary—some diagrams include agents and their roles whilst others do not.

Both the Environment View and the Architecture View diagrams are restricted to static diagram types.

In the *Agent Societies View*, diagrams depict agent societies or organizations. (As noted earlier, the term organization can be used both as a synonym for society and to represent the environment); for example, Ferber and Gutknecht [102] provide more detail than that of an architecture diagram. They typically focus on agent interaction

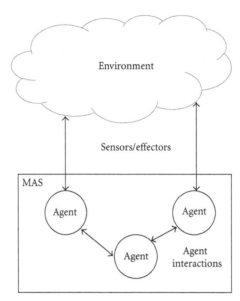

FIGURE 5: Agents in an MAS interact with their environment using sensors and effectors.

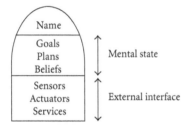

FIGURE 6: Organizational model notation for MAS-CommonKADS (based on [37], reprinted by permission of the publisher © IGI Global).

rather than system structure (e.g., [63, 103]). Indeed, the architectural diagrams identified in Section 5.2 for various AOSE methodologies can also be extended to depict agent society details.

Furthermore, "organizational patterns" (i.e., patterns applied to agent societies) are discussed in Zambonelli et al. [30] and Gonzalez-Palacios and Luck [104]. Typical examples include pipeline, single hierarchy, and multiple hierarchies.

Here, we seek to depict how agents interact in terms of such an interacting society of agents and/or roles, again dividing the discussion into static and dynamic aspects.

The *Agent Workflow View* relates solely to dynamic diagram types since a workflow reflects agent behaviour. This can involves concepts such as process, actions, and interagent messaging.

For the *Agent Knowledge View* we need to represent the internal structure and behaviour of individual agents. Concepts such as goals, beliefs, commitments, plans, capabilities, perceptions, protocols, events, sensors, actuators, and services are all considered by one or more authors. In Section 5.4 we focus particularly on goals, ontologies, and plans.

The *Agent Services View* can involve a number of different diagramming techniques (see Table 4) including goals, tasks, capabilities, and a domain ontology. Services can be described as encapsulated blocks of offered functionality [30, 32, 105]. In AOSE, a service may be described in terms of capabilities, where a capability is defined as "the ability of an actor of defining, choosing and executing a plan for the fulfillment of a goal, given certain world conditions and in presence of a specific event" [65], a definition similar to that used in Prometheus.

For the *Deployment View*, the allocation of software components to hardware nodes has traditionally been the focus; for AOSE a greater emphasis is placed on agent conversations.

Finally, the *UI View* is ill represented in current AOSE methodologies. Our discussion therefore makes suggestions from outside the agent-oriented methodology community.

In the following two sections, citations to specific methodologies will be by methodology name rather than author name(s)—these are found in Table 7—unless a specific paper needs a direct citation. We introduce methodology-specific examples of diagram types not discussed in Henderson-Sellers [19] and assess their match to the previous recommendations. We also describe a selection of these diagrams with the new FAML notation [5], merely as an illustration of the visualization resulting from the combination of a specific diagram type and this notation. We introduce an oversimplified running example in the Travel Agent domain. None of these diagrams are intended to be a complete depiction but rather should be regarded as merely illustrations of the diagramming style to which they refer.

## 5. Static Diagram Types

*5.1. Environment View.* For an MAS, the environment is relevant to two separate phases of the development lifecycle.

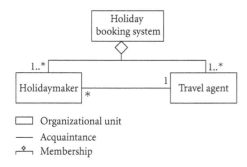

FIGURE 7: Organization context chart in MOBMAS.

TABLE 9: Example of a goal-based use case, here for the business process type "Process the request for a quote" (after [17], reprinted by permission of the publisher © IGI Global).

| Use case 1 | | Process the request for a quote |
|---|---|---|
| Goal of the primary actor | | To receive from the seller the quote |
| Goal of the focus actor | | To provide the buyer with the quote |
| Scope and level | | Seller, primary task |
| Success end condition | | The buyer has received from the seller the quote |
| Primary actor | | Buyer |
| Secondary actors | | |
| Triggering event | | A request for a quote by the buyer |
| Description | Step | Action |
| | 1 | Check and register the availability of the product items included in the request for a quote |
| | 2 | Send the quote to the buyer. |

Initially, requirements will relate to real-life problems, and the MAS will itself interact with this environment. This interaction will be evident in both the analysis and design phases. Secondly, environment issues are relevant in the deployment phase, when allocation of software code to a specific run-time platform node is necessitated. This second interface occasion is described in Section 5.6.

The recommended diagram type [19] for the environment description diagram, which models the external environment, is a UML-style class diagram with entities representing domain entities. For the environmental connectivity diagram, which shows the interfacial linkages between the environment and the top level agents in the MAS, particularly in terms of how agents are likely to access external resources such as databases, actors, and other MASs, a UML-style class diagram can also be useful. A third diagram type (more optional) is an *External organization structure chart*: a UML-style class diagram with entities = organizational unit, decomposition using the membership relation and acquaintance relationships between collaborating organizational units (see, e.g., Figure 7, which shows the use of this style of diagram in MOBMAS).

Environment description diagrams are also used in SODA and PASSI. INGENIAS offers an Environment Viewpoint diagram (Figure 8) depicting the external entities with which the MAS-to-be-constructed will interact.

A second style of diagram is often used to describe the functionality aspects relevant to the interaction between external stakeholders and the software system. This often relates to an early stage in the lifecycle, when requirements need to be identified and documented. Here, it is fairly common practice to use some sort of use case diagram, identical or very similar to that proposed in UML [10]. Henderson-Sellers [19] recommends that, to appropriately support the agent aspects more accurately, a goal-based use diagram that extends the "User-Environment-Responsibility (UER) case" diagram of Iglesias and Garijo [106] is useful for showing agent actors as well as human actors. An example of this is shown in Figure 9. To accompany this, a set of completed use case templates is necessary, such as that provided in Prometheus or by Taveter and Wagner [17], as originally proposed by Cockburn [107] (see example in Table 9). Here, the internal and external actors correspond directly to internal and external agents in AOR modelling.

As is the case with the use of use cases in object-oriented software development, the use case diagram only offers a high level viewpoint on requirements. Of more value [107] is the textual description of each use case. In the Prometheus approach, Padgham and Winikoff [59] note that, since agents have abilities beyond those of objects, it is necessary to provide a textual template significantly beyond those found in OO requirements engineering. Specifically, their textual template (called a "functionality descriptor") describes the system functionality in terms of name, description, percepts, actions, data used/produced, and a brief discussion of interactions with other functionality. While these functionality descriptors are said to be intermediate work products, a final work product that is cross-checked (Figure 10) with them is the use case scenarios (or "scenarios" for short). These are again textual—a typical scenario descriptor in Prometheus is given in Table 10. Each step described in the scenario is a small piece of functionality.

Other methodologies use UML use cases "as-is," for example, MaSE, ROADMAP, ADELFE, MAS-Common-KADS and PASSI where it is called a "domain descriptor diagram."

*5.2. Architecture View.* Henderson-Sellers [19] recommends a UML-style package diagram as the Organization-based architecture diagram (Figure 11) similar to that used in MESSAGE [49] (Figure 12), although this diagram often has a different name, using different basic shapes, for example, organization structure model in Gaia [29] (Figure 13), or as a jurisdictional diagram (as in Figure 14).

In INGENIAS, the generic elements of Figure 15 are used to depict an exemplar organizational viewpoint model in Figure 16 (notational key is given in Figure 17).

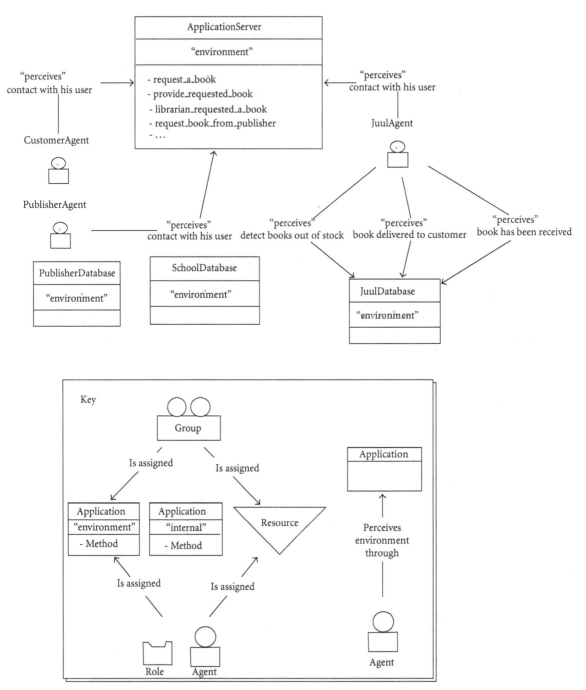

FIGURE 8: Example of an INGENIAS environment viewpoint diagram (after [20]), with key showing typical elements (after [20], reprinted by permission of the publisher © IGI Global).

*5.3. Agent Societies View.* A large number of AOSE methodologies have a strong focus on agent societies, especially SODA, ISLANDER, and OperA. Social structures were added to the earlier version of Gaia by Zambonelli et al. [30].

The style of an agent society diagram recommended in Henderson-Sellers [19] is that of a UML-style class diagram showing all agents and all interrelationships. Other information that may be chosen for display includes percepts, actions, capabilities, plans, data, and messages represented by entities rather than relationships. An example is seen in Figure 18, which uses Prometheus notation and depicts individual messages in the style of Padgham and Winikoff [60], for example, their Figure 5 (p. 123). An alternative depiction is given in Figure 19, which gathers messages into interaction protocols, following the style of Padgham and Winikoff [60], for example, their figure in page 93; part of which is also represented with FAML's notation in Figure 20.

Other diagram styles can be seen in, for instance, MAS-CommonKADS (Figure 21), which shows the mental state and internal attributes of an agent (e.g., goals, beliefs, and

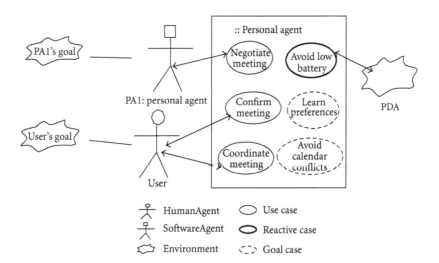

FIGURE 9: Recommended diagram for an agent goal-based use case diagram, (reprinted from [19], copyright 2010, with permission from IOS Press).

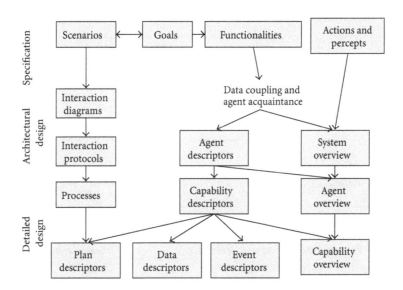

FIGURE 10: Phases and work products defined in Prometheus (after [60], reprinted by permission of the publisher © IGI Global).

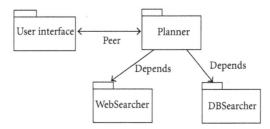

FIGURE 11: Recommended diagram style for an Architecture Diagram.

plans) (upper box) together with the external attributes of the agent (e.g., services, sensors, and effectors) (lower box) (Figure 6); MASE (Figure 22), in which the connections between classes denote conversations that are held between agent classes, and the second label in each agent class represents the role the agent plays in a conversation; MOB-MAS (Figure 23), which shows acquaintances between agent classes and connections between these and any wrapped resources, a diagram that may also be enhanced to show protocols and associated ontologies; AOR (Figure 24), which

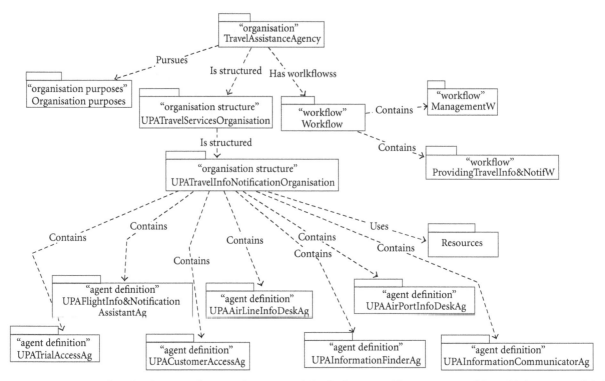

FIGURE 12: Organization-based architecture diagram of MESSAGE (after [49], reprinted by permission of the publisher © IGI Global).

TABLE 10: Example of a Prometheus scenario descriptor (after [60], reprinted by permission of the publisher © IGI Global).

Name: new meeting scheduled

Description: the user adds a new meeting

Trigger: new meeting requested by user

Steps:

| No. | Type | Name | Functionality | Data |
|---|---|---|---|---|
| 1 | Percept | Request meeting | User interaction | |
| 2 | Goal | Propose time meeting user preferences | Meeting scheduler | MeetDB(R), Prefs(R) |
| 3 | Goal | Negotiate with other users | Negotiator | MeetDB(R), Prefs(R) |
| 4 | Goal | Update user's diary | Meeting manager | MeetDB(W) |
| 5 | Goal | Inform others of meeting | Contact notify | |
| 6 | Other | Wait for day of meeting | | |
| 7 | Goal | Remind user of meeting | User notify | MeetDB(R), Prefs(R) |
| 8 | Goal | Remind others of meeting | Contact notify | ContactInfo(R) |

Variations:

(i) Steps 2-3 may be repeated in order to obtain agreement.

(ii) If agreement on a meeting time is not reached then steps 4–8 are replaced with notifying the user that the meeting could not be scheduled.

(iii) The meeting can be rescheduled or cancelled during step 6 (waiting).

Key:

(i) MeetDB(R): meetings database read.

(ii) Prefs(R): user preferences read.

(iii) MeetDB(W): meetings database written.

(iv) ContactInfo(R): contact information read.

depicts agent types, their internal agents, and the relationships between them; PASSI (Figure 25); and ADELFE (Figure 26), which depicts the connectivity between cooperative agents, for which ADELFE was specifically designed (Figure 26).

Another approach to agent societies is to utilize a version of the UML collaboration diagram, although the omission of any sequencing of communications makes this use somewhat dubious. Typically, they depict static aspects of the agent society rather than being dynamic interaction diagrams (as

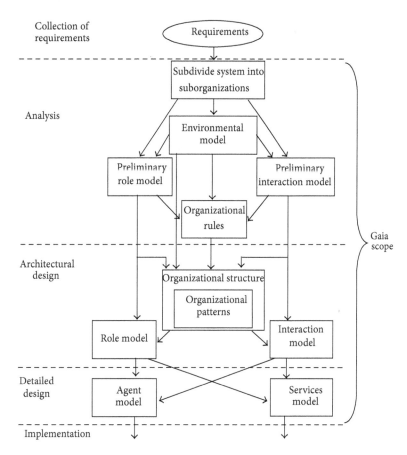

FIGURE 13: Phases and work products ("models") defined in Gaia (after [31], reprinted by permission of the publisher © IGI Global).

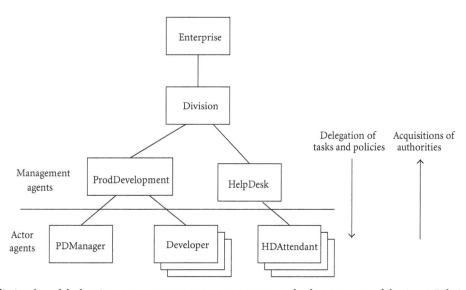

FIGURE 14: A jurisdictional model, showing management agents, actor agents, and subagents, part of the Agent Relationship Model (after [28]).

any true variant on a UML collaboration would be classified). Hence, they are summarized in this subsection.

The event flow diagram of MAS-CommonKADS [39], for example, represents events (the exchange of messages) (Figure 27) but does not depict any message sequencing.

A somewhat similar diagram is to be found in OperA (Figure 28).

Visually different are the interaction-frame diagrams of RAP/AOR. This is used at both the class level (Figure 29) and the agent-instance level (Figure 30). In these diagrams, the

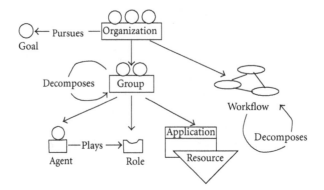

FIGURE 15: Typical elements in an INGENIAS organization viewpoint (structural description of an MAS organization) (after [20], reprinted by permission of the publisher © IGI Global).

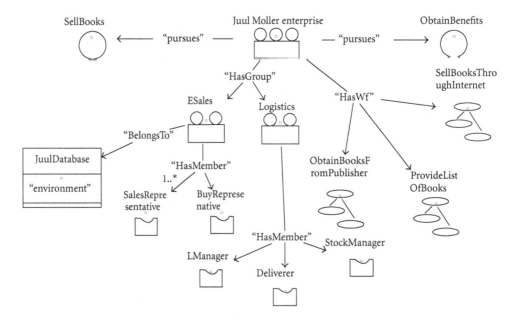

FIGURE 16: Example of an INGENIAS organization viewpoint (structural) description (after [20], reprinted by permission of the publisher © IGI Global).

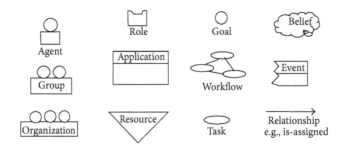

FIGURE 17: Notational key for INGENIAS diagrams.

solid arrows indicate a noncommunicative action event type, and the chain dashed arrows are message types.

Whilst not a methodology, MAS-ML [71] suggests, in this context, the use of two diagrams that have a UML style class diagram to them: (i) the organization diagram and (ii) an extended UML Class Diagram that shows the "structural aspects of classes, agents, organizations, environments, and the relationships between these entities," by introducing additional concepts (i.e., additional to those of UML Class Diagrams), including Environment Class,

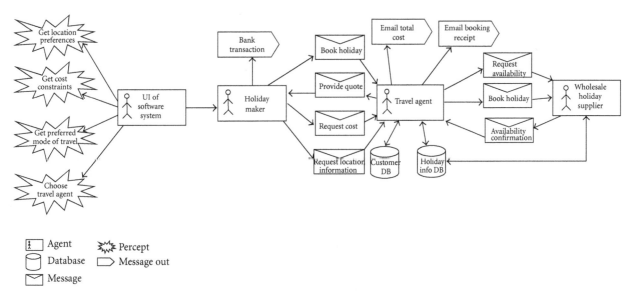

FIGURE 18: Prometheus style "system overview diagram" depicting messages.

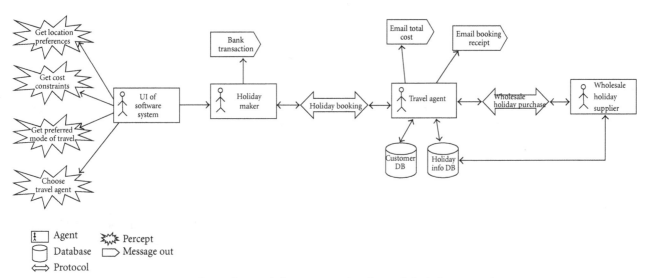

FIGURE 19: Prometheus style "system overview diagram" depicting protocols.

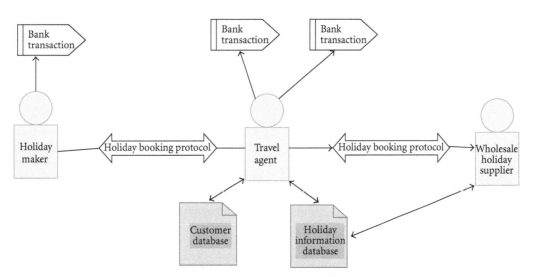

FIGURE 20: A portion of Figure 19 "translated" into FAML notation.

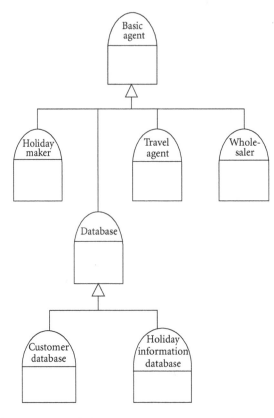

FIGURE 21: Example organizational model as recommended in MAS-CommonKADS. In the lower part of each symbol are shown the mental state and external interface as shown in Figure 6.

FIGURE 22: MaSE agent class diagram.

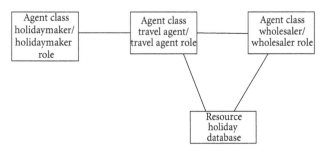

FIGURE 23: MOBMAS agent relationship diagram.

Organization Class, and Agent Class. The notation used (both for these two diagrams and their role diagram—see later discussion) is shown in Figure 31.

*5.3.1. Roles.* Although supported to some degree in object-oriented modelling languages, the much greater importance of roles in AOSE modelling [109–113] requires separate

consideration, despite the common adoption of a UML-style class diagram to depict roles (Figure 32), for example, as used in Agent Factory, MOBMAS, PASSI, and O-MaSE. It should be noted that, in Figure 32, each role class is characterized by its associated so-called protocol identifiers, while each agent class is characterized by a list of protocol identifiers (any not specified in the associated role) and activities. Consequently, it is argued that a two-compartment symbol is needed for roles, and a three-compartment symbol for agents. In ROADMAP also, roles are explicitly linked to agents, as shown in Figure 33 [114]. Such role-focussed diagrams should be supplemented by a Role definition template (see, e.g., Table 11). The original ROADMAP template [115] was later simplified by Sterling et al. [33] as shown in Table 12.

A second role-focussed diagram is the role dependency diagram: a simple role decomposition diagram, using just names and unadorned lines. Figure 34 is one such example. This may be supplemented by a textual description of all the roles and their dependencies (Table 13).

Whilst not a methodology, MAS-ML [71] uses a UML-like Role Diagram using the notation given in Figure 31 to show "structural aspects of agents roles and object roles defined in the organisations" and their interrelationships. Concepts additional to those of UML Class Diagrams include Object Role Class to represent resources utilized by an Agent Role Class.

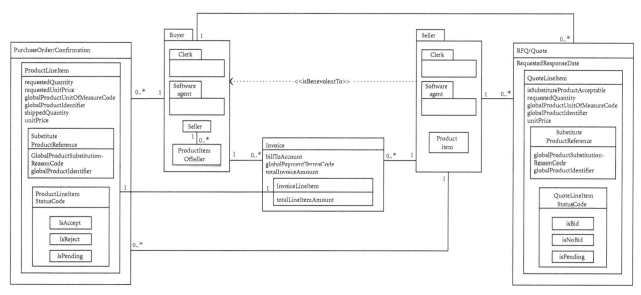

FIGURE 24: AOR agent diagram for the domain of B2B e-commerce (after [17], reprinted by permission of the publisher © IGI Global).

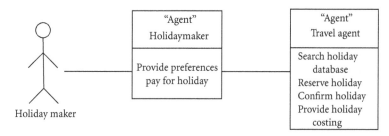

FIGURE 25: PASSI's Multiagent Structure Definition Diagram.

TABLE 11: Role definition as used in OperA (after [52]).

---

**Role: PC member**

*Objectives:*

Paper_reviewed(Paper, Report)

*Subobjectives:*

{read(P), report_written(P, Rep), review_received(org, P, Rep)}

*Rights:*

access-confman-programme(*me*)

*Norms:*

OBLIGED understand(English)

IF DONE assigned(P, *me*, Deadline)

  THEN OBLIGED paper_reviewed(P, Rep) BEFORE Deadline

IF DONE paper_assigned(P, *me*, _) AND is_a_direct_colleague(author(P))

  THEN OBLIGED review_refused(P) BEFORE TOMORROW

*Type:*

External

---

Figures 35 and 36 show how the role dependency diagram of Figure 34 and the Agent-role dependency diagram of Figure 33 can be depicted using the FAML notation of Figure 4.

5.4. *Agent Knowledge View.* The static knowledge of individual agents is encapsulated in symbols for each agent type, typically by extending a basic icon, such as the UML rectangle or the MOSES tablet (as used, for instance, in Figure 21). Suggestions here include goals, beliefs, commitments, and plans added to the basic class symbol (Figure 37); however, several authors (e.g., [76]) argue that it is not yet clear whether the attributes and operations are valid features of an agent type. Since these are derived (via the metamodel) from the UML Classifier, their rejection would negate the generalization relationship between Agent and Classifier (as shown in Figure 36). (This is another illustration of the confounding in the literature between agent and agent type. Often what is referred to as an agent is an agent type, that is, the word is used to describe an entity that conforms to some subtype of Classifier in the metamodel. Although in our following analysis we will continue to use "agent" when quoting from the AOSE literature, it should be remembered that usually this should be replaced by "agent type").

Thus this suggests the need for an agent modelling language *not* based on UML (see revisions, proposed here, in Figure 38). Other proposals are to explicitly depict

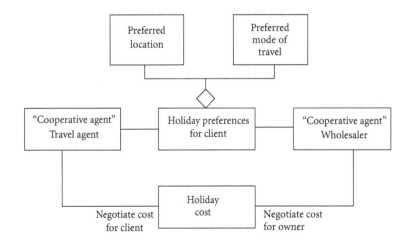

FIGURE 26: Typical ADELFE class diagram showing two cooperative agents and their interrelationships with other classes.

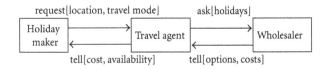

FIGURE 27: Event flow diagram using MAS-CommonKADS notation.

TABLE 12: Simplified version of the role template as used in more recent versions of ROADMAP—here for an Intruder Handler agent (reprinted from [33], copyright 2006, with permission from IOS Press).

---

*Role name*

Intruder handler

*Description*

Identifies and responds to the intruder detected

*Responsibilities*

Detect the presence of a person in the environment

Check the house schedule for strangers scheduled to be there

Take an image of the person

Compare the image against the database of known people

Contact the police and send the image to them

Check the house schedule for planned visitors

Send a message to stay away to each visitor expected that day

Inform the owner that the police are on their way and the visitors have been warned not to enter the house

*Constraints*

The owner and each person pointed out by him/her needs to provide in advance personal information (face) to be recognised

A subject to be detected needs to be seen within the camera's image area

The user must maintain the schedule

Visitors must be within the coverage area of mobile communication with their mobile access terminals switched on

TABLE 13: Social structure definition in OperA (after [52]).

---

Social structure definition

---

*Roles:*

A list of role definitions

*Role dependencies:*

A list of triples of two role names and the name of the relationship between them

*Groups:*

A list of sets of roles

---

capabilities, perceptions, protocols, and organizations (Figure 39); belief conceptualization and events (Figure 40); or sensors, actuators, and services (Figure 6); these often being supplemented by agent descriptors (see, e.g., Boxes 1 and 2). Textual templates for agent roles are recommended in Gaia [29]. Such a schema (one per role) gives information about the protocols, permissions, and responsibilities (liveness and safety) as well as an overall description for each agent role. It is also used by Suganthy and Chithralekha [118] and in SODA.

Knowledge is often expressed in terms of the "mental state" (Figure 41) of an agent, as described, for instance, in the Agent viewpoint of INGENIAS [20]—see example in Figure 42. This idea of "mental state" is also found in AOR (Figure 43) and in Silva et al. [119] who link the set of beliefs, goals, plans, and actions to the mental state of the agent.

Agent internals are represented in Prometheus in terms of an Agent Overview diagram (one for each agent). For the Travel Agent agent in Figure 19, Figure 44 shows its capabilities, percepts, and messages utilized. It is similar in style to the System Overview diagram of Figure 19 but at a finer granularity (Figure 45). Then each capability in the Agent Overview diagram can be expanded in a Capability Overview diagram (Figures 46 and 47).

In SONIA, the knowledge model is represented differently, by blocks of knowledge that group concepts and

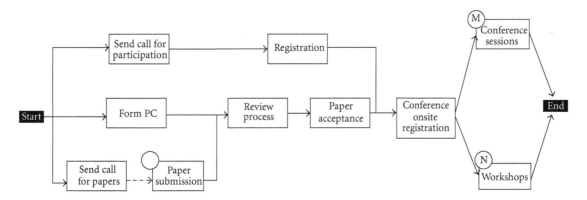

FIGURE 28: Interaction diagram from OperA for the "Conference" society (after [52]).

Name: Travel agent
Description: Arranges holiday for holidaymaker client
Cardinality: One per holidaymaker client
Lifetime: Duration of interaction with Holidaymaker
Initialization: Reads Customer database, receives messages from Holidaymaker
Demise: Closes open database connections
Functionalities included: Obtaining wholesale product, supplying packaged holiday to holidaymaker
Uses data: Customer database, Holiday information database
Produces data: Recommendation to holidaymaker client
Goals: Respond to queries; obtain best deal for wholesaler; package wholesale products for client
Percepts responded to: Logon by holidaymaker
Actions: Advice of cost; Send receipt
Protocols and interactions: Holiday booking protocol, Wholesale holiday purchase

Box 1: Example agent descriptor in Prometheus format.

Agent: Travel agent
Role: Arranger of holidays for holidaymaker clients
Location: Inside holiday booking agent society
Description: This agent manages client requests and interfaces with wholesaler of holidays
Objective: Get best deal for holidaymaker client subject to client preferences
Exceptions: Missing preferences or fully booked holidays
Input parameter: Client preferences
Output parameter: Recommendations to client including costing
Services: Recommendation to holidaymaker client; holiday booking with wholesaler
Expertise: Respond to queries; obtain best deal for wholesaler; package wholesale products for client
Communication: Holidaymaker agent; Wholesaler agent
Coordination: Wholesaler agent

Box 2: Example of an agent definition template as proposed in MAS-CommonKADS—a format suggested by Peyravi and Taghyareh [68].

associations from the structural model. These knowledge blocks may be used internally or shared between agents.

*5.4.1. Goals.* Another aspect of agent knowledge is that of goals: agent goals as well as system goals. A goals is said to represent a state that is to be achieved, for example, Braubach et al. [120]—although other kinds of goals are possible, and goals may conflict with each other, for example, Van Riemsdijk et al. [121]. Goals are achieved by means of actions (a.k.a. tasks) (Figures 48 and 49), the combination of

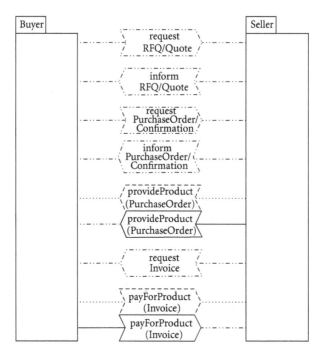

FIGURE 29: AOR interaction frame between agents of the types Buyer and Seller (after [17], reprinted by permission of the publisher © IGI Global).

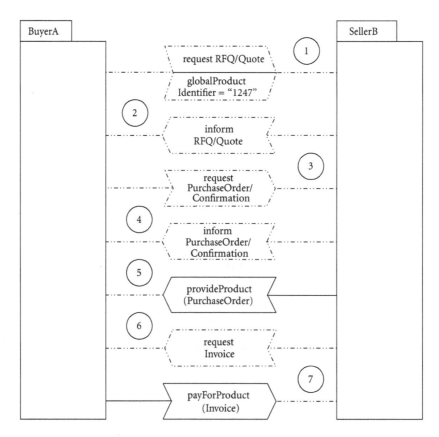

FIGURE 30: AOR interaction sequence between agent instances BuyerA and SellerB (after [17], reprinted by permission of the publisher © IGI Global).

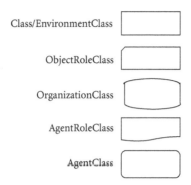

FIGURE 31: Notation used in MAS-ML.

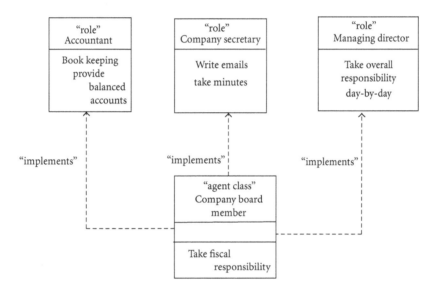

FIGURE 32: Example of Agent Factory's agent model.

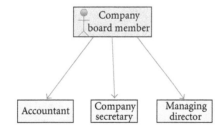

FIGURE 33: Agent-role coupling diagram of ROADMAP.

actions and goals forming the plan body. Tasks are discussed later in Section 6.4.

Goal-focussed diagrams are found in Prometheus (Figure 50), in MaSE, and in MESSAGE's "Level 0 Goal/Task Implication Diagram" (Figure 51). Prometheus also suggests a textual goal descriptor—with three lines only: name, description, and subgoals. (We note that in Figure 50,

following Prometheus' guidelines, the names of the goals are almost task-like (i.e., verbs). Here, from Figure 48, we argue for state-like names for goals, as shown in Figure 52).

Relationships between goals are captured in MOBMAS's agent-goal diagram (Figure 53) and in the two goal-focussed diagrams of Tropos (Figures 54 and 55). The actor diagram (Figure 54) links actors to goals, whereas the goal

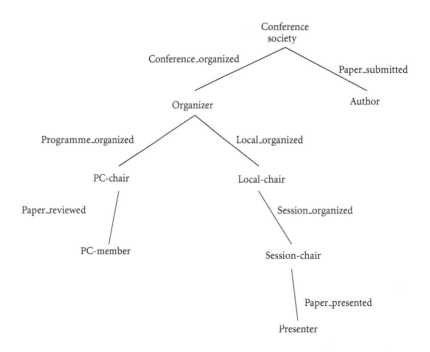

FIGURE 34: Role dependency diagram as used in OperA for the "Conference Society" (after [52]).

diagram (Figure 55) expands the internal details of the goal itself—here using the $i^*$ notation of Yu [78] which permits discrimination between hard goals and soft goals. (It can be determined whether or not a hard goal has been satisfied; in contrast soft goals do not have well-defined achievement criteria and can only be "satisficed" (e.g., [65, page 207]). Hard goals are associated with capturing functional requirements and soft goals with nonfunctional requirements, e.g., Braubach et al. [120]). The goals, labelled Gx in Figure 53, are also captured in the third partition of the Agent class diagram (Figure 40).

A diagram type that appears to have some ambiguity in terms of its scoping (system versus agent) is found in MaSE, called the "goal hierarchy diagram" (Figure 56) (called Goal Model in OMaSE), and in MESSAGE, where it is called an agent goal decomposition diagram linking goals, tasks, actions, and facts. In both methodologies, it is a relatively simple tree structure where goals are represented as boxes and goal-subgoal relationships as directed arrows from parent to children (MASE) or children to parent (MESSAGE). (Clearly, such directional contradictions form an ideal target for standardization). It is interesting to observe that this would appear to be topologically isomorphic with Graham's [122] task decomposition diagram (using hierarchical task analysis). Indeed, based on our earlier discussion, Figure 56 is, more realistically, either a task (not a goal) diagram or else is a goal diagram with poorly named goals.

Goal hierarchy diagrams are also used in Hermes [123] but associated with agent interactions (Figure 57), and a goal-oriented interaction modelling technique is also introduced

into Prometheus by Cheong and Winikoff [124] to replace the previous interaction protocol modelling techniques used in Prometheus.

A more elaborated version of this approach, based on the well-established AND/OR approach to goal modelling, is shown in Figure 58, as presented in OMaSE. The numbers indicate a precedence ordering of the goals, again suggesting tasks rather than goals, although goals are, of course, closely linked to tasks (see Section 6.4), as shown in the metamodel of Figure 48.

Notwithstanding, this pair of concepts ("task" and "goal") are frequently confused. In an etymological analysis of these terms, Henderson-Sellers et al. [101] recommend goals as future-desired states that, when committed to, require the enactment of a task (sometimes called "action") in order to achieve such a desired state (Figure 48). Thus the enactment of a task requires a duration. At the point of time at which this ends, the goal has been achieved (Figure 59). This means that goal names should be state names; that is, nouns, whereas task names should be more verb-like. Splitting up the achievement of a final goal into a set of intermediate or subgoals, as shown here, permits a differentiation (goal/subgoal) that could be seen as commensurate with the action/task differentiation of Figure 60; that is, a goal is achieved by an action, which can be broken down into more granular sections each of which depicts a subgoal being achieved by a task. However, in some methodologies these two terms (goal and task) are equated; that is, used as synonyms. This can often lead to names that are cognitive misdirectional, for example, in such methodologies, the names of goals are typically imperative

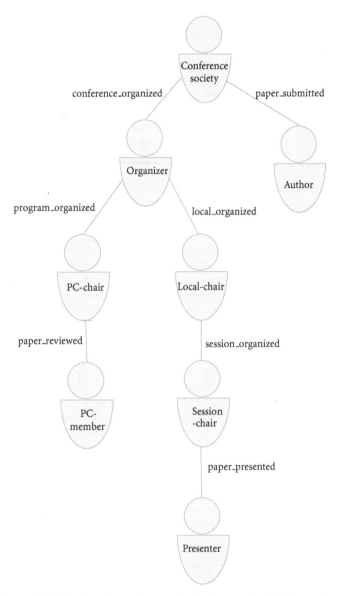

FIGURE 35: Role dependency diagram depicted using the FAML notation.

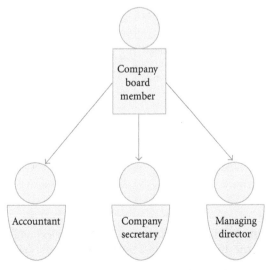

FIGURE 36: Agent-role coupling diagram depicted using the FAML notation.

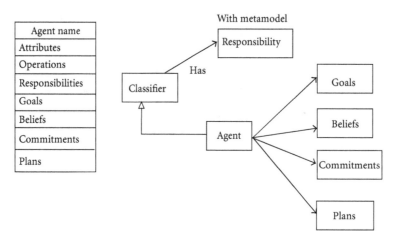

FIGURE 37: One proposal for extended UML notation for an individual agent type plus the underpinning metamodel fragment (after [91]).

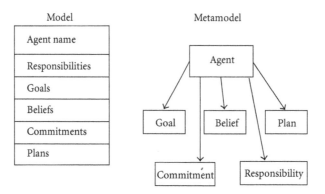

FIGURE 38: Revised proposal for an agent representation (model-scope symbol plus supporting metamodel fragment).

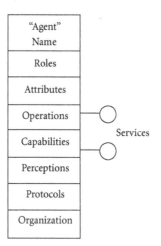

FIGURE 39: Agent symbol illustrating the kind of information proposed by Huget [92] to show agent attributes.

verb-like which, at first glance, suggests tasks rather than goals. This, therefore, needs to be borne in mind when reading or writing such diagrams.

*5.4.2. Ontologies and Plans.* Also in this group of recommendations (for static diagram types relevant to agent knowledge) are the ontology diagram and the plan diagram.

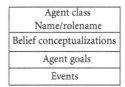

FIGURE 40: Agent class definition diagram of MOBMAS.

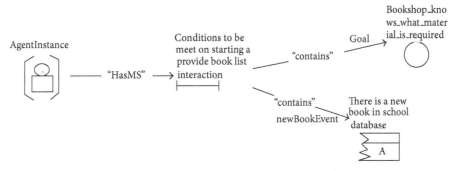

FIGURE 41: Example of an agent's mental state (which links mental state to facts, beliefs, and events and involves goals, tasks, and roles) as depicted by INGENIAS (after [20], reprinted by permission of the publisher © IGI Global).

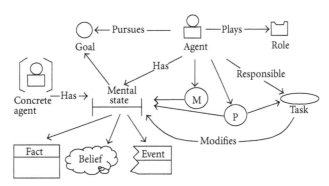

FIGURE 42: Typical elements in the agent viewpoint and the agent's mental state as depicted by INGENIAS (after [20], reprinted by permission of the publisher © IGI Global).

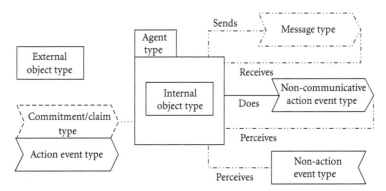

FIGURE 43: Core mental state structure modelling elements of external AOR diagrams (after [17], reprinted by permission of the publisher © IGI Global).

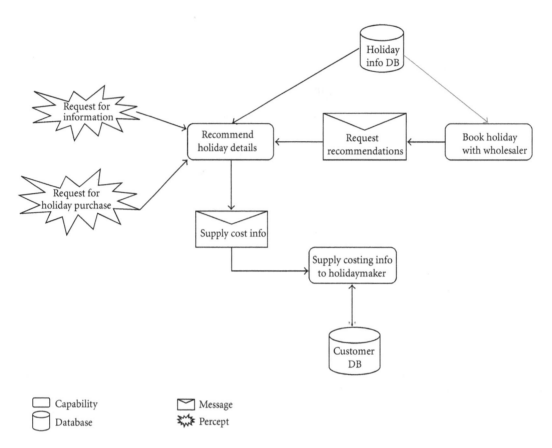

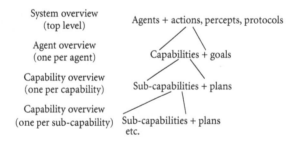

FIGURE 44: Example of Prometheus Agent Overview diagram showing some of the details of the Travel Agent agent and including percepts.

FIGURE 45: Increasing detail from system overview diagram to agent overview diagram to capability overview diagrams (as envisaged in the Prometheus methodology).

Ontologies are explicit in only a handful of methodological approaches: PASSI and MAS-CommonKADS, MOBMAS and AML [105], and, to a lesser extent, in OperA and ISLANDER. Ontologies, particularly domain ontologies as need here, represent knowledge that is effectively static. It is thus reasonable to depict that knowledge as a fairly standard UML class diagram (Figure 61).

Plans depict the internal details of how a task is to be performed and a goal attained. Plans are typically internal to a single agent and are linked to the tasks (or actions) needed to attain goals (Figure 48) or to the capabilities (Figures 44 and 46). Since the execution of plans may or may not be successful, alternative paths must be included (Figure 62). These alternatives may utilize AND/OR gates, which can be used either in context of an activity diagram or a state transition diagram—depending upon whether the developer wishes to have as his/her prime focus the process or the product aspect. In Tropos, the internal structure of a plan can be summarized as a single node on a Capability diagram (e.g., Figure 46). Plan diagrams may be based on the UML activity diagram as in Tropos or UML STD diagram as in O-MaSE. Mylopoulos et al. [79] show how the Tropos plan diagram can also be depicted using UML notations. Plan diagrams are also used in MOBMAS.

Plan name: Identify location and dates
Description: Ascertain possible holiday places and date
Trigger: Request from client
Context: Holiday not already booked
Data used and produced: Holiday brochures/database
Goal: Recommend time and place(s)
Failure: All likely holidays booked
Failure recovery: Change dates and/or place
Procedure: (1) Search data for location commensurate with client's desire
          (2) Check dates holiday is possible
          (3) Create list of possible place/date combinations

Box 3: Prometheus-style plan descriptor for the plan to identify holiday location and dates of Figure 46.

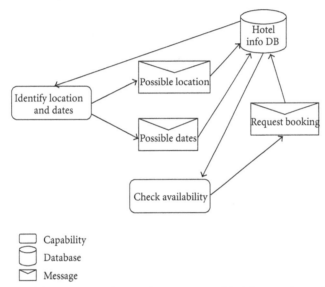

FIGURE 46: Example of Prometheus Capability Overview diagram for Recommend Holiday Details capability of Figure 44. This also shows a subcapability of identify location and dates, which, in turn, could be depicted graphically by another Capability Overview diagram.

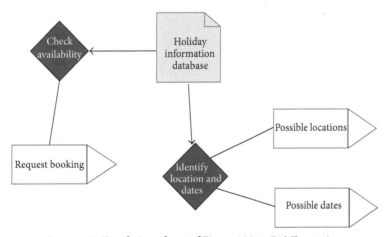

FIGURE 47: Translation of part of Figure 46 into FAML notation.

Plan diagrams, whether of the activity diagram style or the STD style, can be augmented by text in the form of a plan descriptor (Box 3), as used, for example, in MOBMAS, which defines the plan in terms of initial state, goals, strategies, actions, and events, and Prometheus, which defines a plan in terms of triggering events, messages, actions, and plan steps (a completed example of which is shown in Box 3).

Thangarajah et al. [125] note that there may be several acceptable plans for achieving a single goal such that there is an overlap. This led these authors to formulate mathematical

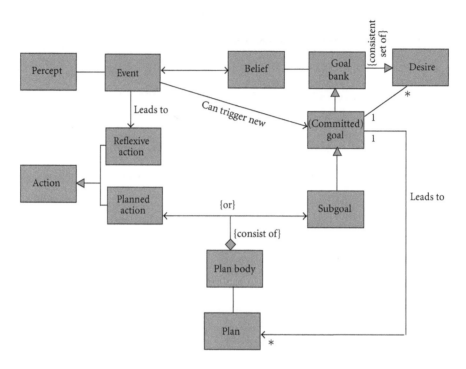

FIGURE 48: Metamodel fragment relevant to goals, tasks, and plans (after [101]).

FIGURE 49: Generic model of plans, tasks, and goals conformant to a fragment of the metamodel of Figure 48.

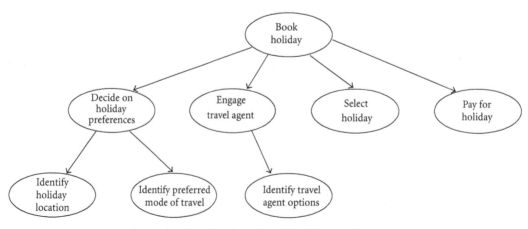

FIGURE 50: Example Prometheus Goal Overview Diagram.

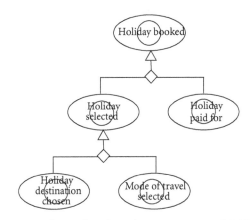

FIGURE 51: Level 0 Goal/Task Implication Diagram of MESSAGE.

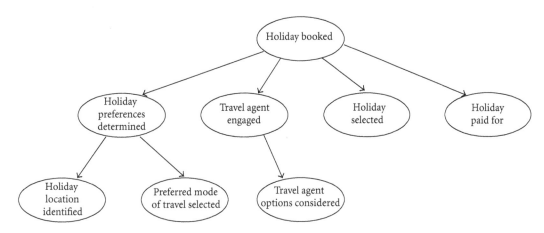

FIGURE 52: Example of Prometheus Goal Overview Diagram with state-like goal names.

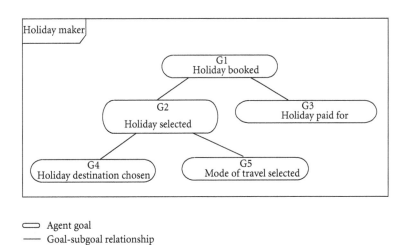

FIGURE 53: MOBMAS's agent-goal diagram.

expressions for this overlap and also the coverage. Overlap is readily represented using a Venn diagram; a typical goal-plan hierarchy is shown in Figure 63.

5.5. *Agent Services View.* UML-style class diagram is supplemented by UML-style activity diagrams to show details for each capability to expand a portion of the Capability

(a)                                                                                (b)

FIGURE 54: (a) Example actor diagram showing goals attached to actors. (b) Example of actor diagram showing an explicit depender (Holidaymaker), dependee (Travel Agent), and dependum (Select good travel agent).

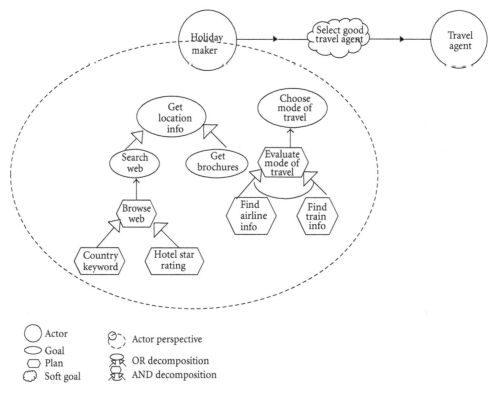

FIGURE 55: Example of a Tropos goal diagram.

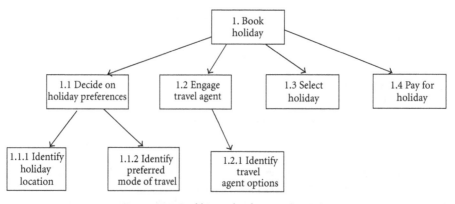

FIGURE 56: Goal hierarchy diagram (MaSE).

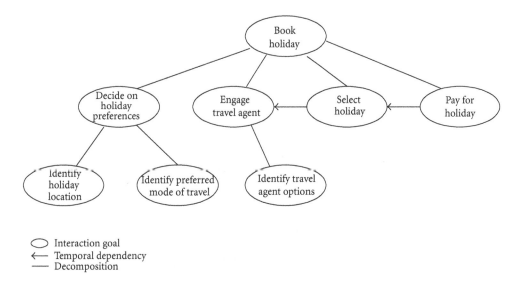

FIGURE 57: Interaction goal hierarchy of Hermes/Prometheus.

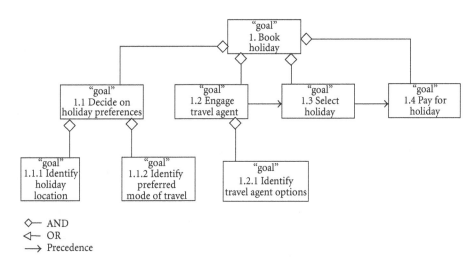

FIGURE 58: Refined GMoDS goal model using AND/OR decomposition technique (O-MaSE).

Overview diagram of Figure 46 into a more detailed Capability diagram—one diagram for each subcapability. An example, compatible with the Check availability capability of Figure 64, is given in Figure 65 (Prometheus notation). A textual template to accompany the diagram might also be useful to present in textual format details of goals, processes protocols, messages, percepts, actions, capabilities, plans, and data utilized in different ways. Figure 66 shows the alternative use of an Activity Diagram in this context, Capability Diagrams being used in Tropos (Figure 66 for a specific agent) wherein each node may be expanded into a Plan Diagram (see Section 5.4.2).

Services can alternatively be represented directly in either graphical or tabular form, the latter following, for example, the Gaia Service Model, which lists Services and their Inputs, Outputs, Preconditions and Postconditions, the former as depicted in the Level 1 analysis phase of MESSAGE [48, page 186], wherein a service is realized by a partially ordered set of tasks (see later discussion of Figure 81). Direct representation of service protocols is found also in AML (see later discussion of Figures 76 and 77) and in the Service Model of ISLANDER [35].

*5.6. Deployment View.* Henderson-Sellers [19] recommends using a fairly standard UML (or AUML) deployment diagram. MaSE uses a similar diagram (Figure 67) but notes that it differs from the standard use of the UML Deployment Diagram since

(i) the three-dimensional boxes represent agents in MASE, whereas they represent (hardware) nodes in UML,

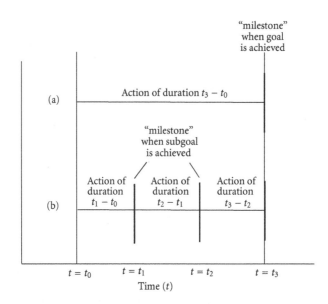

FIGURE 59: Milestones, subgoals, and goals: (a) a single action attains the goal or (b) several actions are needed, each achieving a subgoal (after [101]).

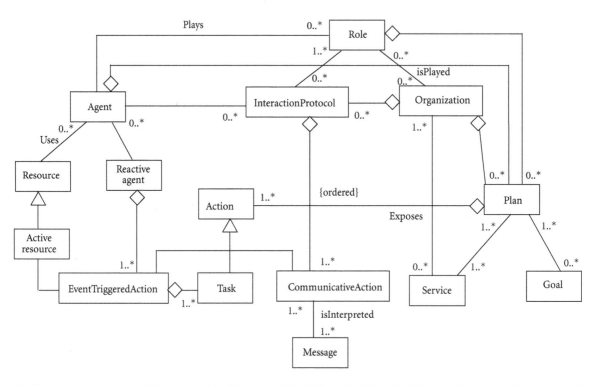

FIGURE 60: The action perspective of the metamodel of Azaiez et al. [108], (reprinted from [108], copyright 2007, with permission from IOS Press).

(ii) the connecting lines represent conversations between agents in MASE whereas in UML they represent physical connections between nodes,

(iii) MASE uses dashed-line box around agents to indicate that these agents are housed on the same physical platform.

Other methodologies adopting this UML style of deployment diagram include PASSI and RAP/AOR. Most other approaches neglect it. Whilst not employing such a diagram, Tropos does discuss implementation issues as related to its use of class diagrams (Figure 68). SODA only hints at implementation in terms of their environment model, preferring to

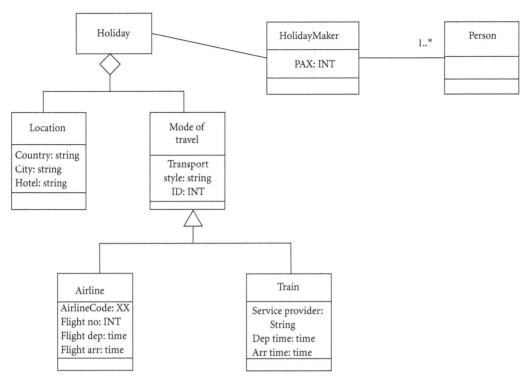

FIGURE 61: Ontology diagram as used in MOBMAS.

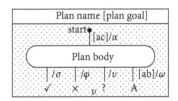

FIGURE 62: Plan diagram in which ac is the activation condition and $\alpha$ is the activation action. Stop states are labeled as success states "$\checkmark$" (success action "$\sigma$"), fail states "$\times$" (fail action "$\varphi$"), unknown states "?" (unknown action "$\upsilon$"), or abort states "A" (abort condition "ab"; abort action "$\omega$") (after [116], reprinted by permission of the publisher © IGI Global).

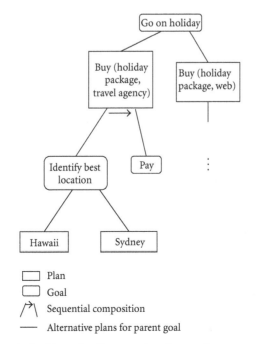

FIGURE 63: An example goal-plan hierarchy diagram using the notation proposed by Shapiro et al. [117].

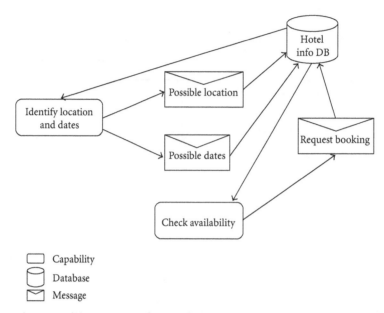

FIGURE 64: Duplicate of Prometheus Capability Overview diagram for Recommend Holiday Details capability of Figure 44 in comparison with Figure 65.

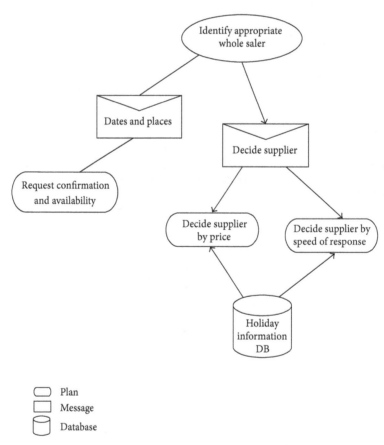

FIGURE 65: Example of Prometheus Capability diagram showing the plans for the Check availability capability of the Travel Agent agent shown in Figure 64.

defer such details to specific implementation methodologies. PASSI and O-MaSE seem to be the only methodologies that discuss implementation issues directly (i.e., at the code level).

5.7. UI View. Henderson-Sellers [19] noted the lack, in published AOSE methodologies, of any diagrams relating to the user interface. He therefore recommended adding (at least) a

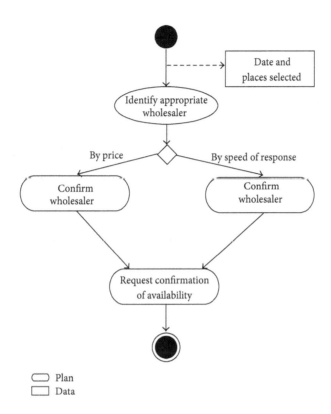

FIGURE 66: Example of a Tropos-style capability diagram for the capability of Check availability of Figure 64.

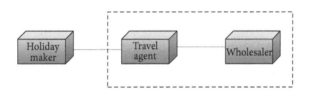

FIGURE 67: Example deployment diagram using MaSE notation.

UI design diagram, which could likely be represented using a semantic net (Figure 69). Henderson-Sellers [19] offers this as a placeholder; that is, a generic "UI design" diagram type pending future empirical work and utilization of the visual design theories of, for example, Ware [127] and the insights of Graham [122] and Constantine and Lockwood [128] (see also http://www.foruse.com/). This latter book also recommends user role maps and structure role models (where "role" refers to human roles in the software development process). These authors also provide heuristics on menu design, the use of iconic interfaces, and other more innovative interface design approaches. The topic was also explored in a non-AOSE context by Gonzalez-Perez [129].

Other suggestions in the literature, although sparse, include a placeholder for a UI prototype in ADELFE's (http://www.irit.fr/ADELFE/) Activities 8 and 9 (see also Jorquera et al. [130] who discuss UI prototyping as a work unit but do not offer a notation for the resultant work product).

## 6. Dynamic Diagram Types

*6.1. Agent Societies View.* Agent behaviour is usually depicted in terms of agent-agent interactions, including message passing. A typical agent-oriented interaction diagram also shows the order of these messages needed to effect a single service. Consequently, a standard AUML [75] or AML [73] interaction diagram can be used as the basic interaction diagram (a.k.a. conversation diagram) (Figure 70). Further addition of more formal protocol information to the basic conversation diagram, again using, say, AUML or AML as the notation, would result in a protocol diagram. Prometheus optionally enhances these interaction diagrams with percepts and actions; that is, messages to and from an invisible timeline/agent. In addition to percepts, input from the environment and other events, including those self-generated, for example, by a clock, can be shown [131]. Events typically generate an action within the agent. The result is really

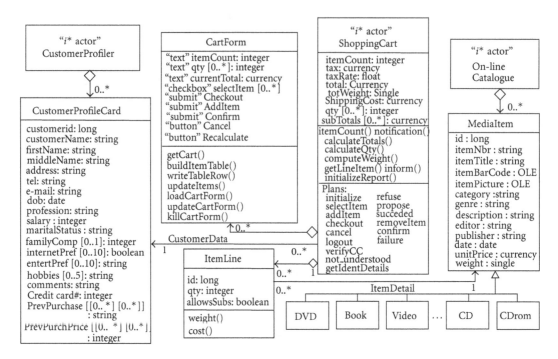

FIGURE 68: Partial class diagram for a Tropos implementation in their Store Front case study (after [67], reprinted by permission of the publisher © IGI Global).

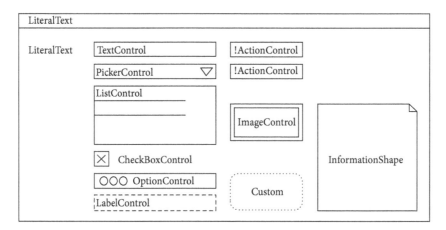

Parameter: type

FIGURE 69: An OPEN/Metis user interface sketch (after [126]).

highly notation dependent but with AUML might look like Figure 71 and with AML it would look like Figure 72. This can then be supplemented by protocol descriptors and message descriptors. In Prometheus, Padgham and Winikoff [59] recommend fields for the protocol descriptor as Description, Scenarios, Agent names, a list of Messages in the protocol, and a final field to contain other miscellaneous information. For the Message descriptor, they recommend a natural language descriptor, the source and target of the message together with

a statement on its purpose, and the information carried by the message.

Behavioural diagrams used in AOSE often adopt (or adapt) one of the two basic kinds of UML interaction diagram: sequence charts and collaboration diagrams (said to be semantically equivalent), the latter renamed as Communication diagram in UML Version 2.

Sequence-style diagrams are used in MaSE (e.g., [44]), PASSI, ADELFE, and MOBMAS as well as in OperA and

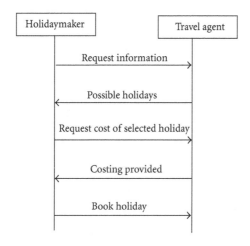

FIGURE 70: Interaction diagram between Holidaymaker agent and Travel_Agent agent.

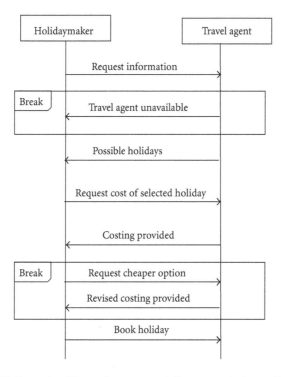

FIGURE 71: Example of Prometheus protocol diagram equivalent to Figure 70.

Agent Factory (Figure 73), where it is called a "protocol" and a "protocol model," respectively, and in MESSAGE (Figure 74) and Tropos (Figure 75). MOBMAS uses a slightly different version of an AUML sequence diagram in which ACL messages are replaced by tuples.

A specialized form of the AML Interaction Protocol Diagram (Figure 72) is the Service Protocol Diagram (Figure 76), used only within the context of the service specification.

Whilst not a methodology, MAS-ML [71] uses an extended UML Sequence Diagram to show interactions and their sequencing. These authors use this approach to depict the

modelling of plans and actions, of protocols, and of role commitment.

Collaboration-style diagrams are used in Agent Factory, CAMLE, and AML (Figure 77) but seldom elsewhere wherein the sequence-style diagram is the preferred option.

6.2. *Workflow View.* Workflows reflect agent behaviour so that a standard workflow diagram would seem appropriate. UML-style activity diagrams are used in Prometheus to illustrate processes within an agent, including allusions to

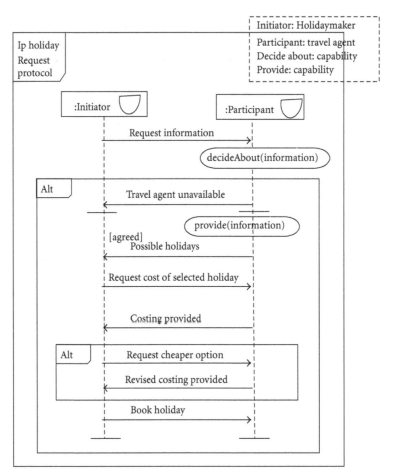

FIGURE 72: Example of AML Interaction Protocol as a sequence diagram.

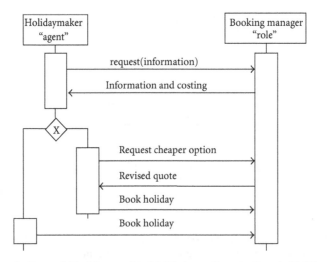

FIGURE 73: Example Protocol Model as used in MaSE, Agent Factory, OperA, PASSI, and ADELFE.

interactions with other agents. Figure 78 shows an example of a Prometheus Process Diagram. In this diagram, details of a process are shown together with interactions with other agents; these are depicted minimalistically by a single (envelope-shaped) icon. A Process Diagram can then be supplemented by a process descriptor listing activities, triggers, messages, and protocols. Whilst these diagrams show the higher level view, details can be presented textually

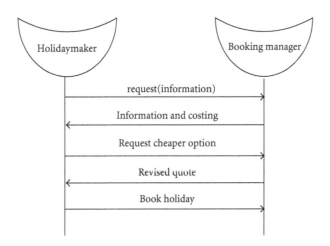

FIGURE 74: Example of an MESSAGE interaction protocol diagram.

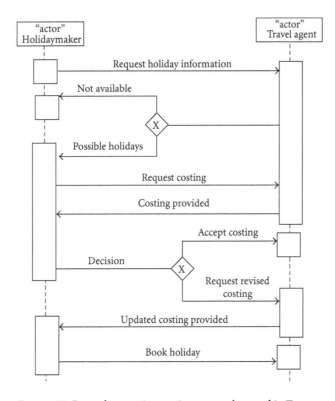

FIGURE 75: Example agent interaction protocol as used in Tropos.

[132]: for percepts, actions, and events. The percept descriptor lists the information gleaned by the agent in its interaction with the environment, whereas the action descriptor depicts the effect of the agent on the environment. An event descriptor defines an event in terms of its purpose, together with the data that the event carries. (For details of these templates, see [59, Chapter 7]).

UML-style activity diagrams are also used in Agent Factory, called there an "activity model." These illuminate all the "activity scenarios," wherein each swimlane represents the processing of a role involved in the scenario. In PASSI, a similar use is made of swimlanes to specify the methods of each agent or of each agent's task.

Workflows are also represented explicitly in INGENIAS (Figure 79) using the notation shown in Figure 80. In this approach, a workflow is created from the tasks identified in the interaction specification diagram together with the goal/task view (see later discussion of Figure 84). Similarly,

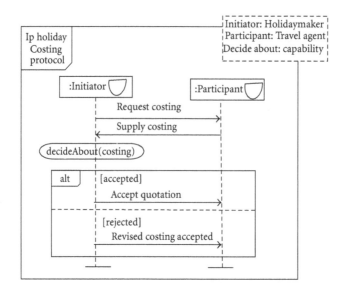

FIGURE 76: Example of AML Service Protocol as a sequence diagram.

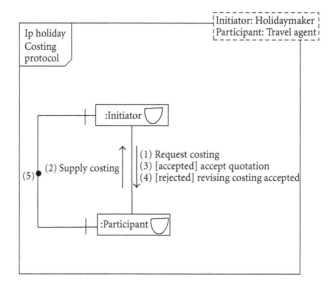

FIGURE 77: Example of AML Service Protocol as a communication diagram showing the same information as Figure 76.

MESSAGE depicts a workflow in terms of a partially ordered set of tasks that realize a service (Figure 81). AOR also uses workflow as the basis for its activity diagram (Figure 82).

MAS-ML [71] includes extensions proposed to the UML Activity Diagram in order to depict "a flow of execution through the sequencing of subordinate units called action." In this way, the authors can model plans and actions; goals; and messages, roles, organizations, and environment (for full details, see [133]).

*6.3. Agent Knowledge View.* The dynamic aspects of agent behaviour are addressed in several methodologies, both in terms of interagent behaviour and single agent behaviour. This is exemplified in MaSE's "communication class diagram" a.k.a. conversation diagram [43], based on the notation of a UML State Transition Diagram. It should be noted that

this diagram type focusses on the states of an agent *during a particular conversation.* This means that for a conversation between two agents (initiator and responder) two state diagrams are required. Actions specified within a state represent processing required by the agent.

STD-style diagrams are recommended by PASSI, MESSAGE (Figure 83), and MOBMAS. Also with a slightly different visualization is the state machine-focussed Interaction Structure of ISLANDER, which shows dialogues called scenes. These then define protocols.

*6.4. Agent Services View: Task Diagrams.* Tasks represent the dynamic counterbalance to goals. Indeed, they are closely linked, as shown in the metamodel of Figure 48 and in INGENIAS (Figure 84). Indeed, in the SONIA methodology, a task model is one of the first to be developed, although

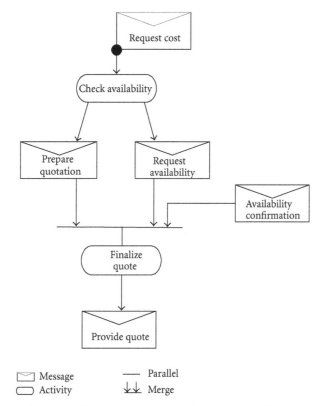

FIGURE 78: Example process diagram for the Request cost functionality.

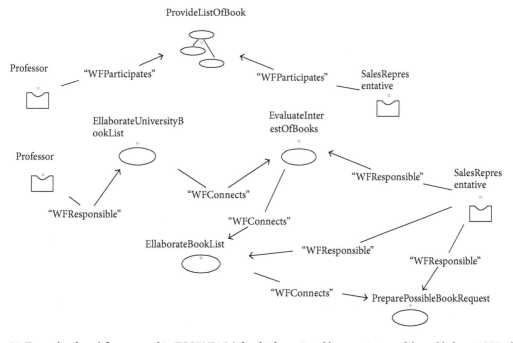

FIGURE 79: Example of workflow as used in INGENIAS (after [20], reprinted by permission of the publisher © IGI Global).

goals are not considered until later, in a Goal Model. Tasks are accomplished by the enactment of a Plan (see Section 5.4.2).

Several AOSE methodologies address task descriptions and task decomposition, for example, using a UML activity diagram with two swimlanes (Figure 85) or incorporating AND/OR task decomposition (Figure 86) to create a task hierarchy. Both diagram styles can be supplemented by Task templates. For the current state(s) of any task, a standard UML-style Statechart diagram can be used.

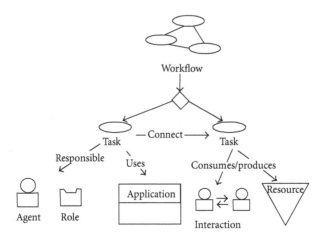

FIGURE 80: Typical elements in an INGENIAS's workflow (after [20], reprinted by permission of the publisher © IGI Global).

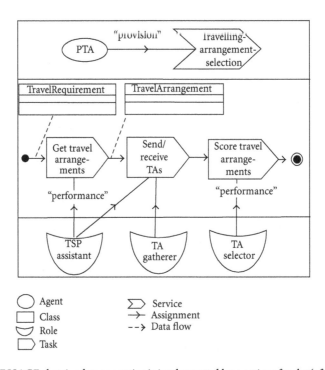

FIGURE 81: Task workflow from MESSAGE showing how a service is implemented by a series of tasks (after [49], reprinted by permission of the publisher © IGI Global).

A task model is also included in the diagram suite of MAS-CommonKADS. It consists of two elements for each task: a "task hierarchy diagram" and a "task textual template." Peyravi and Taghyareh [68] suggest the addition to MAS-CommonKADS of a standard activity diagram to represent the activity flow of a task together with a textual template for each individual task within the activity flow, together with a tabular rendering of task knowledge. Task models are also found in MaSE and in ISLANDER.

Interestingly, Fuentes-Fernández et al. [134] investigate the ideas of Activity Theory [135] as applied to AOSE.

They propose mapping these activities to tasks and possibly to workflows or interactions. This is clearly a topic for further discussion beyond the standard methodological use of diagram types as outlined here.

*6.5. UI View.* In Section 5.7, we noted the possibility of introducing, as a static diagram type, a UI design diagram. There is also a need for a dynamic view on the UI. Gonzalez-Perez [126] suggests a service state diagram (Figure 87) to represent the various states of the UI and linking this directly to UI design diagram of Figure 69. Constantine

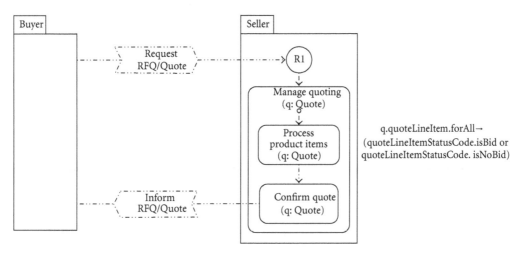

FIGURE 82: Incomplete AOR activity diagram for the quoting business process type from the perspective of the Seller agent (after [17], reprinted by permission of the publisher © IGI Global).

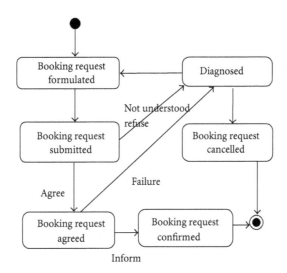

FIGURE 83: State chart in MESSAGE for a Booking Manager role (after [49], reprinted by permission of the publisher © IGI Global).

and Lockwood [128] also recommend the utilization of task modelling, essential use cases, and context navigation maps to describe the dynamic aspects of user interface design.

## 7. Discussion and Related Work

Recommendations for a standardized agent-oriented modelling language are still indeterminate with several approaches being investigated. These include use of many UML diagrams with little or no change (e.g., [20, 37, 49, 59, 136]) or bundled as a UML profile (e.g., [17, page 286]). Formal proposals to create an agent-oriented extension to UML include AUML [74, 137, 138] and AML [73]. They provide all the fine detail of the UML, also making some recommendations for diagram types in passing. Here, we have taken the results of the deliberations of Henderson-Sellers [19] regarding appropriate diagram types that could be recommended as part of a future standardized agent-oriented modelling language and have investigated a wider range of examples from the literature.

In addition, we have introduced the FAML notation in order to see whether (i) the recommended diagram types can be visualized using this notation and (ii) there are any deficiencies in the FAML notation.

Our discussion here has focussed solely on the suite of diagram types, whilst recognizing that there are two other major elements of any modelling language: notation of individual atomic elements (e.g., [2, 100]) and the defining metamodel (e.g., [1]). In the latter case, there have been attempts to combine existing metamodels synergistically for (a) work products (e.g., [4, 71, 139]) and (b) method elements (e.g., [3, 140–142]).

In the A&A (agents and artifacts) approach [143], the three basic categories identified of agent, society, and environment align well with three of the views presented here (Tables 3 and 4). The aim of these authors is to be able to manipulate agent societies and the MAS environment as first-class entities. Their utilization of a multidisciplinary approach including speech act analysis [144] and activity theory [135]

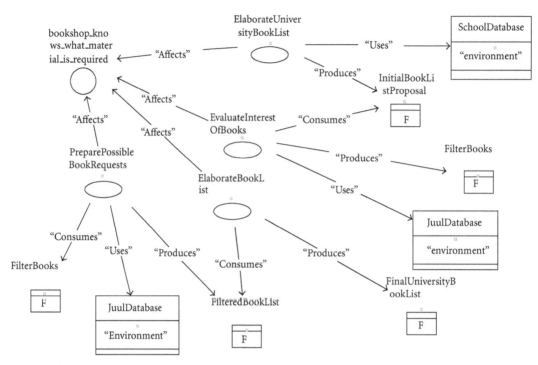

FIGURE 84: Goal-task relationships in INGENIAS (after [20]). For notation see Figure 17, it is reprinted by permission of the publisher © IGI Global.

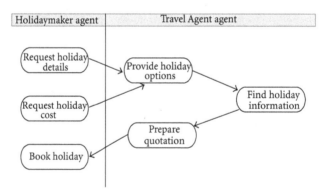

FIGURE 85: Example of PASSI task specification diagram.

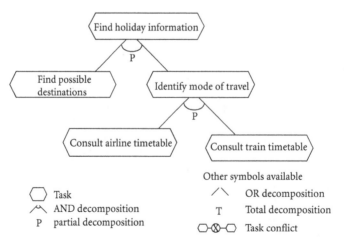

FIGURE 86: MOBMAS's use of a task decomposition diagram.

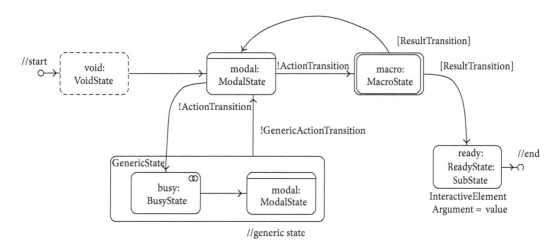

FIGURE 87: An OPEN/Metis service state diagram in which some of the annotations on arcs and nodes refer back to elements in the user interface sketch of Figure 69 (after [126]).

is a promising approach to gain a well-grounded conceptual foundation for agent-oriented modelling.

It should also be noted that all work products go through their own "lifecycle" in the sense that they are first created, and then modified towards maturity of a final state. This means that there will likely be several versions of each work product (e.g., [145, Appendix G]); that is, the notion of a "state" can be associated with each work product (e.g., [45, 146]).

As well as agent-oriented metamodelling treatises, some authors have sought to set their work in the context of model-driven engineering (MDE) or model-driven development (MDD), for example, Amor et al. [147]; Fischer et al. [148]; Taveter and Sterling [149] and the proposal by Benguria et al. [150] of Platform Independent Model (PIM) for Service-Oriented Architecture (SOA) named PIM4SOA. Others (e.g., Liu et al. [151]) have examined the possible utilization of agents for developing web services and in SOA (Service-Oriented Architecture). Internet development is also discussed by Zambonelli et al. [152].

There is also an emerging trend to adopt a method engineering mindset for agent-oriented software construction (e.g., [153]). In a recent paper on O-MaSE [46], the authors tabulate their recommended diagram types in the form of method fragments (Table 14).

In addition to these related works on notation and metamodelling, we were only able to find a small number of additional papers in the main topic area that are not already cited above. In particularly, although differently named in part, the six diagram types proffered by Juan et al. [154] in their "skeleton methodology" are commensurate with those discussed here. They are given as Use-case model, Environmental Interface Model, Agent Model, Service Model, Acquaintance Model, and Interaction Model. In addition, they proffer (i) from Prometheus: System Overview Diagram, Agent Overview Diagram, Capability Diagram, and Event, Data, Plan, and Capability Descriptors; and (ii) from ROADMAP: Environment Model, Knowledge Model, and Role Model.

Our use of FAML notation has only been indicative rather than the provision of any conclusive results. We have anticipated following the comprehensive evaluation method of the notation for ISO/IEC 24744 International Standard [21] as undertaken by Sousa et al. [8]. However, it turns out that there are significant differences between the mode of utilization of symbols in creating a process model (for which ISO/IEC 24744 was designed) and the way symbols are used in an AOML. In the former, not only are the symbols evaluated but also, perhaps more critically, the superposition of various combinations in terms of their usability vis-a-vis their shape and colour turns out to be the more important aspect. On the contrary, for an AOML, there is little (or zero) need to superpose symbols rather than to have a collection of them related to each other in any specific diagram type. This means that a symbol set for a AOSE diagramming suite need have little concern for juxtapositioning and superpositioning issues but simply be evaluated in terms of its semiotic value in terms of the degree to which each symbol successfully represents each AOSE concept. That means that our illustration of only a few diagram types, chosen to illustrate elements of the different "families" of Figure 2, indicates that further one-to-one translation of symbols between, say, Prometheus and FAML or between INGENIAS and FAML should be as successful. In terms of the goals of this current paper, the profferings of FAML diagram types are adequate, whilst leaving to future work (Section 8) comprehensive user and usability studies.

Thus, creating a standard, for which this paper is intended to be a potential precursor, needs careful mappings between the various methodology-linked diagram types by consideration of their associated semantics (i.e., not just names and notations). Once these similarities and any overlaps have been identified, it is likely that the number of diagram types needed for AOSE can be significantly reduced from the sum

TABLE 14: Diagram types recommended in O-MaSE depicted as method fragments (after [46]) and reprinted by permission of the publisher © Inderscience.

| Activities | Tasks | Work products created or modified | Responsible method roles |
|---|---|---|---|
| Requirements gathering | Requirements specification | Requirements specification | Requirements engineer |
| Problem analysis | Model goals | Goal model | Goal modeller |
| | Refine goals | | |
| | Model domain | Domain model | Domain modeller |
| Solution analysis | Model organization interfaces | Organization model | Organization modeller |
| | Model roles | Role model | Role modeller |
| | Define roles | Role description document | |
| | Define role goals | Role goal model | |
| Architecture design | Model agent classes | Agent class model | Agent class modeller |
| | Model protocols | Protocol model | Protocol modeller |
| | Model policies | Policy model | Policy modeller |
| Low level design | Model plans | Agent plan model | Plan modeller |
| | Model capabilities | Capabilities model | Capabilities modeller |
| | Model actions | Action model | Action modeller |
| Code generation | Generate code | Source code | Programmer |

of all the diagram types across all AOSE methodologies—the aim of this current project.

## 8. Conclusions and Future Work

Using the list of over two dozen proposed diagram types in the AOSE literature, we have here extended the analysis of Henderson-Sellers [19] commencing with his recommendations and assessing to what extent these recommendations are seen in this wide range of AOSE methodologies. We have also taken the opportunity, as indicated in the Future Work Section of Henderson-Sellers [19], to express several of these recommended diagram types using the new FAML notation [5], itself conformant to the metamodel of Beydoun et al. [4], and derived in part from the suggestions of Padgham et al. [2] and DeLoach et al. [155], and taking into account the semiotic advice of Moody [7].

In summary, we have added further evaluations of the recommendations of Henderson-Sellers [19] by consideration of a wider range of diagram types in the AOSE methodologies listed in Table 7, the motivation being a small additional contribution to standards efforts current in organizations like FIPA, OMG, and ISO.

As noted in Henderson-Sellers et al. [5], further empirical research is required to evaluate the usability of these various diagram types using FAML's notation. We plan to undertake an experiment in which creative design students are asked to supply appropriate symbols for the FAML concepts as well as evaluating our current proposals (Figure 2). We also intend to conduct a comprehensive evaluation using a large group (20 plus) of experts followed by a usability study in a real world case study.

## Acknowledgments

The author wishes to thanks Cesar Gonzalez-Perez for helpful comments on an earlier draft of this paper. This is contribution 12/06 of the Centre for Object Technology Applications and Research at the University of Technology, Sydney.

## References

[1] A. Susi, A. Perini, J. Mylopoulos, and P. Giorgini, "The Tropos metamodel and its use," *Informatica*, vol. 29, no. 4, pp. 401–408, 2005.

[2] L. Padgham, M. Winikoff, S. Deloach, and M. Cossentino, "A unified graphical notation for AOSE?" in *Agent-Oriented Software Engineering IX: 9th International Workshop (AOSE '08) Estoril, Portugal, May 12-13, 2008 Revised Selected Papers*, M. Luck and J. J. Gomez-Sanz, Eds., vol. 5386 of *Lecture Notes in Computer Science*, pp. 116–130, Springer, Berlin, Germany, 2009.

[3] C. Bernon, M. Cossentino, M.-P. Gleizes, P. Turci, and F. Zambonelli, "A study of some multiagent meta-models," in *Proceedings of the 5th International Workshop on Agent-Oriented Software Engineering V (AOSE '04)*, J. Odell, P. Giorgini, and J. P. Müller, Eds., vol. 3382 of *Lecture Notes in Computer Science*, pp. 62–77, Springer, Berlin, Germany, 2004.

[4] G. Beydoun, G. Low, B. Henderson-Sellers et al., "FAML: a generic metamodel for MAS development," *IEEE Transactions on Software Engineering*, vol. 35, no. 6, pp. 841–863, 2009.

[5] B. Henderson-Sellers, G. C. Low, and C. Gonzalez-Perez, "Semiotic considerations for the design of an agent-oriented modelling language, enterprise, business-process and information systems modeling," in *Proceedings of the 13th International Conference and 17th International Conference (Emmsad '12)*, I. Bider, T. Halpin, J. Krogstie et al., Eds., vol. 113 of *Lecture*

*Notes in Business Information Processing*, pp. 422–434, Springer, Heidelberg, Germany, 2012.

[6] L. L. Constantine and B. Henderson-Sellers, "Notation matters: part 1—framing the issues," *Report on Object Analysis and Design*, vol. 2, no. 3, pp. 25–29, 1995.

[7] D. Moody, "The physics of notations: toward a scientific basis for constructing visual notations in software engineering," *IEEE Transactions on Software Engineering*, vol. 35, no. 6, pp. 756–779, 2009.

[8] K. Sousa, J. Vanderdonckt, B. Henderson-Sellers, and C. Gonzalez Perez, "Evaluating a graphical notation for modelling software development methodologies," *Journal of Visual Languages and Computing*, vol. 23, no. 4, pp. 195–212, 2012.

[9] OMG, "Unified Modelling Language Specification," formal/01-09-68 through 80 (13 documents). Object Management Group, 2001.

[10] OMG, Unified Modeling Language: superstructure, Version 2.0, formal/05-07-04, 709pp, 2005.

[11] OMG, OMG Unified Modeling Language (OMG UML), Superstructure, V2.1.2, formal/2007-11-02, 738pp, 2007.

[12] A. F. Garcia, C. J. P. De Lucena, and D. D. Cowan, "Agents in object-oriented software engineering," *Software*, vol. 34, no. 5, pp. 489–521, 2004.

[13] A. S. Rao and M. P. Georgeff, "BDI agents: from theory to practice," Technical Note 56, Australian Artificial Intelligence Institute, 1995.

[14] D. Kinny, M. Georgeff, and A. Rao, "A methodology and modelling technique for systems of BDI agents," in *Proceedings of the 17th European Workshop on Modelling Autonomous Agents in a Multi-Agent World (MAAMAW '96)*, pp. 56–71, Eindhoven, The Netherlands, 1996.

[15] A. Sturm and O. Shehory, "A framework for evaluating agent-oriented methodologies," in *Proceedings of the 5th International Bi-Conference on Agent-Oriented Information Systems*, P. Giorgini and M. Winikoff, Eds., pp. 60–67, 2003.

[16] A. Sturm and O. Shehory, "A comparative evaluation of agent-oriented methodologies," in *Methodologies and Software Engineering for Agent Systems. The Agent-Oriented Software Engineering Handbook*, F. Bergenti, M. P. Gleizes, and F. Zambonelli, Eds., chapter 7, pp. 127–149, Kluwer Academic Publishers, Boston, Mass, USA, 2004.

[17] K. Taveter and G. Wagner, "Towards radical agent-oriented software engineering processes based on AOR modelling," in *Agent-Oriented Methodologies*, B. Henderson-Sellers and P. Giorgini, Eds., chapter 10, pp. 277–316, Idea Group, 2005.

[18] D. Bertolini, A. Novikau, A. Susi, and A. Perini, "TAOM4E: an Eclipse ready tool for agent-oriented modeling," Issue on the Development Process, IRST Report, Trento, Italy, 2006.

[19] B. Henderson-Sellers, "Consolidating diagram types from several agent-oriented methodologies," *Frontiers in Artificial Intelligence and Applications*, vol. 217, pp. 293–345, 2010.

[20] J. Pavón, J. J. Gómez-Sanz, and R. Fuentes, "The INGENIAS methodology and tools," in *Agent-Oriented Methodologies*, B. Henderson-Sellers and P. Giorgini, Eds., chapter 9, pp. 236–276, Idea Group, 2005.

[21] ISO/IEC, "Software Engineering. Metamodel for Development Methodologies," ISO/IEC International Standard 24744, Annex A—Notation, ISO, Geneva, Switzerland, 2010.

[22] G. Picard and M. P. Gleizes, "The ADELFE methodology," in *Methodologies and Software Engineering for Agent Systems. the Agent-Oriented Software Engineering Handbook*, F. Bergenti,

M. P. Gleizes, and F. Zambonelli, Eds., chapter 8, pp. 157–175, Kluwer Academic Publishers, Boston, Mass, USA, 2004.

[23] R. Collier, G. O'Hare, T. Lowen, and C. Rooney, "Beyond prototyping in the factory of agents," in *Multi-Agent Systems and Applications III*, V. Marik, J. Muller, and M. Pechoucek, Eds., vol. 2691 of *Lecture Notes in Computer Science*, pp. 383–393, Springer, New York, NY, USA, 2003.

[24] R. Collier, G. O'Hare, and C. Rooney, "A UML-based software engineering methodology for agent factory," in *Proceedings of the 16th International Conference on Software Engineering & Knowledge Engineering (SEKE '04)*, F. Maurer and G. Ruhe, Eds., pp. 25–30, Banff, Canada, June 2004.

[25] L. Shan and H. Zhu, "CAMLE: a caste-centeric agent-oriented modeling language and environment," in *Software Engineering for Multi-Agent Systems III*, R. Choren, A. Garcia, C. Lucena, and A. Romanovsky, Eds., vol. 3390 of *Lecture Notes in Computer Science*, pp. 144–161, Springer, Berlin, Germany, 2005.

[26] A. Collinot, A. Drogoul, and P. Benhamou, "Agent oriented design of a soccer robot team," in *Proceedings of the 2nd International Conference on Multi-Agent Systems (ICMAS '96)*, M. Tokoro, Ed., pp. 41–47, AAAI Press, Menlo Park, Calif, USA, 1996.

[27] A. Collinot and A. Drogoul, "Using the Cassiopeia method to design a robot soccer team," *Applied Artificial Intelligence*, vol. 12, no. 2-3, pp. 127–147, 1998.

[28] M. Elammari and W. Lalonde, "An agent-oriented methodology: high-level and intermediate models," in *Proceedings of the 1st International Workshop on Agent-Oriented Information Systems (AOIS '99)*, Heidelberg, Germany, June 1999.

[29] M. Wooldridge, N. R. Jennings, and D. Kinny, "The Gaia methodology for agent-oriented analysis and design," *Autonomous Agents and Multi-Agent Systems*, vol. 3, no. 3, pp. 285–312, 2000.

[30] F. Zambonelli, N. R. Jennings, and M. Wooldridge, "Developing multiagent systems: the Gaia methodology," *ACM Transactions on Software Engineering and Methodology*, vol. 12, no. 3, pp. 317–370, 2003.

[31] F. Zambonelli, N. Jennings, and M. Wooldridge, "Multi-agent systems as computational organizations: the Gaia methodology," in *Agent-Oriented Methodologies*, B. Henderson-Sellers and P. Giorgini, Eds., chapter 6, pp. 136–171, Idea Group, 2005.

[32] T. Juan, A. Pearce, and L. Sterling, "ROADMAP: extending the Gaia methodology for complex open systems," in *Proceedings of the 1st International Joint Conference on Autonomous Agents adn Multiagent Systems*, pp. 3–10, Bologna, Italy, July 2002.

[33] L. Sterling, K. Taveter, and The Daedalus Team, "Building agent-based appliances with complementary methodologies," in *Knowledge-Based Software Engineering*, E. Tyugu and T. Yamaguchi, Eds., pp. 223–232, IOS Press, 2006.

[34] J. Pavón and J. J. Gómez-Sanz, "Agent-oriented software engineering with INGENIAS," in *Proceedings of the 3rd International/Central and Eastern European Conference on Multi-Agent Systems (CEEMAS '03)*, V. Marik, J. Muller, and M. Pechoucek, Eds., vol. 2691 of *Lecture Notes in Artificial Intelligence*, pp. 394–403, Springer, Berlin, Germany, 2003.

[35] C. Sierra, J. Thangarajah, L. Padgham, and M. Winikoff, "Designing institutional multi-agent systems," in *Agent-Oriented Software Engineering VII*, L. Padgham and F. Zambonelli, Eds., vol. 4405 of *Lecture Notes in Computer Science*, pp. 84–103, Springer, Berlin, Germany, 2007.

[36] C. Sierra, J. A. Rodríguez-Aguilar, and J. L. Arcos, "Helios: harmonious electronic institution operational scheme," Tech. Rep. IIIA-TR-2009-10, IIIA, CSIC, Barcelona, Spain, 2009.

[37] C. A. Iglesias and M. Garijo, "The agent-oriented methodology MAS-CommonKADS," in *Agent-Oriented Methodologies*, B. Henderson-Sellers and P. Giorgini, Eds., chapter 3, pp. 46–78, Idea Group, Hershey, Pa, USA, 2005.

[38] C. A. Iglesias, M. Garijo, J. C. Gonzalez, and J. R. Velasco, "A methodological proposal for multiagent systems development extending CommonKADS," in *Proceedings of the 10th Knowledge Acquisition Workshop (KAW '96)*, SRDG Publications, Department of Computer Science, University of Calgary, Banff, Canada, 1996.

[39] C. A. Iglesias, M. Garijo, J. C. Gonzalez, and J. R. Velasco, "Analysis and design of multi-agent systems using MAS-CommonKADS," in *Intelligent Agents IV*, M. P. Singh, A. Rao, and M. J. Wooldridge, Eds., vol. 1365 of *Lecture Notes in Artificial Intelligence*, pp. 313–328, Springer, Berlin, Germany, 1998.

[40] M. F. Wood and S. A. DeLoach, "An overview of the multiagent systems engineering methodology," in *Proceedings of the 1st International Workshop on Agent-Oriented Software Engineering (AOSE '00)*, P. Ciancarini and M. J. Wooldridge, Eds., vol. 1957 of *Lecture Notes in Computer Science*, pp. 207–221, Springer, Berlin, Germany, 2000.

[41] S. A. DeLoach, "Multiagent systems engineering: a methodology and language for designing agent systems," in *Proceedings of the Agent-Oriented Information Systems (AOIS '99)*, Seattle, Wash, USA, May 1999.

[42] S. A. DeLoach, "Modeling organizational rules in the multi-agent systems engineering methodology," in *Proceedings of the Advances in Artificial Intelligence (AI '02)*, R. Cohen and B. Spencer, Eds., vol. 2338 of *Lecture Notes in Artificial Intelligence*, pp. 1–15, Springer, Berlin, Germany, 2002.

[43] S. A. DeLoach, "The MaSE methodology," in *Methodologies and Software Engineering for Agent Systems the Agent-Oriented Software Engineering Handbook*, F. Bergenti, M. P. Gleizes, and F. Zambonelli, Eds., chapter 6, pp. 107–125, Kluwer Academic Publishers, Boston, Mass, USA, 2004.

[44] S. A. DeLoach and M. Kumar, "Multiagent systems engineering: an overview and case study," in *Agent-Oriented Methodologies*, B. Henderson-Sellers and P. Giorgini, Eds., chapter 11, pp. 317–340, Idea Group, Hershey, Pa, USA, 2005.

[45] J. C. Garcia-Ojeda, S. A. DeLoach, Robby, W. H. Oyenan, and J. Valenzuela, "O-MaSE: a customizable approach to developing multiagent development processes," in *Proceedings of the 8th International Workshop on Agent Oriented Software Engineering VIII (AOSE '07)*, M. Luck, Ed., vol. 4951 of *Lecture Notes in Computer Science*, pp. 1–15, Springer, Berlin, Germany, 2007.

[46] S. A. DeLoach and J. C. Garcia-Ojeda, "O-MaSE: a customisable approach to designing and building complex, adaptive multi-agent systems," *International Journal of Agent-Oriented Software Engineering*, vol. 4, no. 3, pp. 244–280, 2010.

[47] G. Caire, W. Coulier, F. Garijo et al., "Agent oriented analysis using MESSAGE/UML," in *Proceedings of the 2nd International Workshop on Agent-Oriented Software Engineering II (AOSE '01)*, M. J. Wooldridge, G. Weiß, and P. Ciancarini, Eds., vol. 2222 of *Lecture Notes in Computer Science*, pp. 119–135, Springer, Berlin, Germany, 2001.

[48] G. Caire, W. Coulier, F. Garijo et al., "The MESSAGE methodology," in *Methodologies and Software Engineering for Agent Systems. The Agent-Oriented Software Engineering Handbook*, F. Bergenti, M.-P. Gleizes, and F. Zambonelli, Eds., chapter 9, pp. 177–194, Kluwer Academic Publishers, 2004.

[49] F. J. Garijo, J. J. Gómez-Sanz, and Ph. Massonet, "The MESSAGE methodology for agent-oriented analysis and design," in *Agent-Oriented Methodologies*, B. Henderson-Sellers and P. Giorgini, Eds., chapter 8, pp. 203–235, Idea Group, 2005.

[50] Q. N. N. Tran, G. Low, and G. Beydoun, "A methodological framework for ontology centric oriented software engineering," *Computer Systems Science and Engineering*, vol. 21, no. 2, pp. 117–132, 2006.

[51] Q. N. N. Tran and G. Low, "MOBMAS: a methodology for ontology-based multi-agent systems development," *Information and Software Technology*, vol. 50, no. 7-8, pp. 697–722, 2008.

[52] V. Dignum, *A model for organizational interaction based on agents, founded in logic [Ph.D. thesis]*, SIKS, Amsterdam, The Netherlands, 2004, SIKS Dissertation Series No. 2004-1.

[53] M. Mensonides, B. Huisman, and V. Dignum, "Towards agent-based scenario development for strategic decision support," in *Proceedings of the 8th International Bi-Conference Workshop on Agent-Oriented Information Systems IV (AOIS '06)*, P. Bresciani, A. Garcia, A. Ghose, B. Henderson-Sellers, M. Kolp, and H. Mouratidis, Eds., vol. 4898 of *Lecture Notes in Artificial Intelligence*, pp. 53–72, Springer, Berlin, Germany, 2006.

[54] P. Burrafato and M. Cossentino, "Designing a multi-agent solution for a bookstore with the PASSI methodology," in *Proceedings of the 4th International Bi-Conference Workshop on Agent-Oriented Information Systems (AOIS '02)*, P. Giorgini, Y. Lespérance, G. Wagner, and E. S. K. Yu, Eds., Toronto, Canada, May 2002, CEUR Workshop Proceedings 57, CEUR-WS.org.

[55] M. Cossentino, "Different perspectives in designing multi-agent systems," in *Proceedings of the Agent Technology and Software Engineering Workshop at (NODe '02)*, Erfurt, Germany, October 2002.

[56] M. Cossentino, "From requirements to code with the PASSI methodology," in *Agent-Oriented Methodologies*, B. Henderson-Sellers and P. Giorgini, Eds., pp. 79–106, Idea Group, 2005.

[57] M. Cossentino and C. Potts, "PASSI: a process for specifying and implementing multi-agent systems using UML," 2002, http://citeseerx.ist.psu.edu/viewdoc/summary?doi=10.1.1.4.3182.

[58] M. Cossentino and C. Potts, "A CASE tool supported methodology for the design of multi-agent systems," in *Proceedings of the International Conference on Software Engineering Research and Practice (SERP '02)*, Las Vegas, Nev, USA, June 2002.

[59] L. Padgham and M. Winikoff, *Developing Intelligent Agent Systems: A Practical Guide*, J. Wiley and Sons, Chichester, UK, 2004.

[60] L. Padgham and M. Winikoff, "Prometheus: a practical agent-oriented methodology," in *Agent-Oriented Methodologies*, B. Henderson-Sellers and P. Giorgini, Eds., chapter 5, pp. 107–135, Idea Group, 2005.

[61] M. Winikoff and L. Padgham, "The Prometheus methodology," in *Methodologies and Software Engineering for Agent Systems. The Agent-Oriented Software Engineering Handbook*, F. Bergenti, M. P. Gleizes, and F. Zambonelli, Eds., chapter 11, pp. 217–234, Kluwer Academic Publishers, Boston, Mass, USA, 2004.

[62] J. Khallouf and M. Winikoff, "The goal-oriented design of agent systems: a refinement of Prometheus and its evaluation," *International Journal of Agent-Oriented Software Engineering*, vol. 3, no. 1, pp. 88–112, 2009.

[63] A. Omicini, "SODA: societies and infrastructures in the analysis and design of agent-based systems," in *Proceedings of the Agent-Oriented Software Engineering (AOSE '00)*, P. Ciancarini and

M. J. Wooldridge, Eds., vol. 1957 of *Lecture Notes in Computer Science*, pp. 185–193, Springer, Berlin, Germany, 2000.

[64] F. Alonso, S. Frutos, L. Martínez, and F. J. Soriano, "The synthesis stage in the software agent development process," in *Proceedings of the 4th International Central and Eastern European Conference on Multi-Agent Systems and Applications (CEEMAS '05)*, M. Pěchouček, P. Petta, and L. Z. Varga, Eds., vol. 3690 of *Lecture Notes in Artificial Intelligence*, pp. 193–202, Springer, Berlin, Germany, 2005.

[65] P. Bresciani, A. Perini, P. Giorgini, F. Giunchiglia, and J. Mylopoulos, "Tropos: an agent-oriented software development methodology," *Autonomous Agents and Multi-Agent Systems*, vol. 8, no. 3, pp. 203–236, 2004.

[66] P. Bresciani, P. Giorgini, H. Mouratidis, and G. Manson, "Multi-agent systems and security requirements analysis," in *Advances in Software Engineering for Multi-Agent Systems*, C. Lucena, A. Garcia, A. Romanovsky, J. Castro, and P. Alencar, Eds., vol. 2940 of *Lecture Notes in Computer Science*, pp. 35–48, Springer, Berlin, Germany, 2004.

[67] P. Giorgini, M. Kolp, J. Mylopoulos, and J. Castro, "Tropos: a requirements-driven methodology for agent-oriented software," in *Agent-Oriented Methodologies*, B. Henderson-Sellers and P. Giorgini, Eds., chapter 2, pp. 20–45, Idea Group, Hershey, Pa, USA, 2005.

[68] F. Peyravi and F. Taghyareh, "Applying mas-commonkads methodology in knowledge management problem in call centers," in *Proceedings of the IASTED International Conference on Software Engineering (SE '07)*, pp. 99–104, February 2007.

[69] G. Booch, J. Rumbaugh, and I. Jacobson, *The Unified Modeling Language User Guide*, Addison-Wesley, Reading, Mass, USA, 1999.

[70] L. Shan and H. Zhu, "Unifying the semantics of models and meta-models in the multi-layered UML meta-modelling hierarchy," *International Journal of Software and Informatics*, vol. 6, no. 2, pp. 163–200, 2012.

[71] V. Torres da Silva, R. Choren, and C. J. P. de Lucena, "MAS-ML: a multiagent system modelling language," *International Journal of Agent-Oriented Software Engineering*, vol. 2, no. 4, pp. 382–421, 2008.

[72] I. Trencansky and R. Cervenka, "Agent Modeling Language (AML): a comprehensive approach to modeling MAS," *Informatica*, vol. 29, no. 4, pp. 391–400, 2005.

[73] R. Cervenka and I. Trencansky, *AML. The Agent Modeling Language*, Birkhäuser, Basel, Switzerland, 2007.

[74] B. Bauer, J. P. Müller, and J. Odell, "Agent UML: a formalism for specifying multiagent software systems," *International Journal of Software Engineering and Knowledge Engineering*, vol. 11, no. 3, pp. 207–230, 2001.

[75] M. P. Huget and J. Odell, "Representing agent interaction protocols with agent UML," in *Proceedings of the 5th International Workshop on Agent-Oriented Software Engineering V (AOSE '04)*, J. Odell, P. Giorgini, and J. P. Müller, Eds., vol. 3382 of *Lecture Notes in Computer Science*, pp. 16–30, Springer, Berlin, Germany, 2004.

[76] V. Torres da silva and C. J. P. de Lucena, "Form a conceptual framework for agents and objects to a multi-agent system modeling language," *Autonomous Agents and Multi-Agent Systems*, vol. 9, no. 1-2, pp. 145–189, 2004.

[77] R. Choren and C. Lucena, "The ANote modelling language for agent-oriented specification," in *Proceedings of the Software Engineering for Multi-Agent Systems III (SELMAS '04)*, R. Choren, A. Garcia, C. Lucena, and A. Romanovsky, Eds., vol. 3390 of *Lecture Notes in Computer Science*, pp. 198–212, Springer, Berlin, Germany, 2004.

[78] E. S. K. Yu, *Modelling strategic relationships for process reengineering [Ph.D. thesis]*, University of Toronto, 1995.

[79] J. Mylopoulos, M. Kolp, and J. Castro, "UML for agent-oriented software development: the Tropos proposal," in *Proceedings of the 4th International Conference on the Unified Modeling Language (UML '01)*, M. Gogolla and C. Kobryn, Eds., vol. 2185 of *Lecture Notes in Computer Science*, pp. 422–441, Springer, Berlin, Germany, 2001.

[80] A. Lapouchnian and Y. Lespérance, "Modeling mental states in agent-oriented requirements engineering," in *Proceedings of the 18th International Conference on Advanced Information Systems Engineering (CAiSE '06)*, E. Dubois and K. Pohl, Eds., vol. 4001 of *Lecture Notes in Computer Science*, pp. 480–494, Springer, Berlin, Germany, 2006.

[81] S. Shapiro and Y. Lespérance, "Modeling multiagent systems with the Cognitive Agents Specification Language—a feature interaction resolution application," in *Proceedings of the 7th International Workshop (ATAL '00)*, vol. 1986 of *Lecture Notes in Artificial Intelligence*, pp. 244–259, Springer, Berlin, 2000.

[82] X. Franch, "On the quantitative analysis of agent-oriented models," in *Proceedings of the Advanced Information Systems Engineering (CAiSE '06)*, E. Dubois and K. Pohl, Eds., vol. 4001 of *Lecture Notes in Computer Science*, pp. 495–509, Springer, Berlin, Germany, 2006.

[83] H. Estrada, A. Martínez Rebollar, O. Pastor, and J. Mylopoulos, "An empirical evaluation of the i* framework in a model-based software generation environment," in *Proceedings of the Advanced Information Systems Engineering (CAiSE '06)*, E. Dubois and K. Pohl, Eds., vol. 4001 of *Lecture Notes in Computer Science*, pp. 513–527, Springer, Berlin, Germany, 2006.

[84] L. L. Constantine and B. Henderson-Sellers, "Notation matters: part 2—applying the principles," *Report on Object Analysis and Design*, vol. 2, no. 4, pp. 20–23, 1995.

[85] H. Mouratidis, *A security oriented approach in the development of multiagent systems: applied to the management of health and social care needs of older people in England [Ph.D. thesis]*, Department of Computer Science, University of Sheffield, 2004.

[86] H. Hachicha, A. Loukil, and K. Ghédira, "MA-UML: a conceptual approach for mobile agents' modelling," *International Journal of Agent-Oriented Software Engineering*, vol. 3, no. 2-3, pp. 277–305, 2009.

[87] G. Low, H. Mouratidis, and B. Henderson-Sellers, "Using a situational method engineering approach to identify reusable method fragments from the secure TROPOS methodology," *Journal of Object Technology*, vol. 9, no. 4, pp. 93–125, 2010.

[88] J. P. George, B. Edmonds, and P. Glize, "Making self-organising adaptive multiagent systems work," in *Methodologies and Software Engineering for Agent Systems. The Agent-Oriented Software Engineering Handbook*, F. Bergenti, M. P. Gleizes, and F. Zambonelli, Eds., chapter 16, pp. 321–340, Kluwer Academic Publishers, Boston, Mass, USA, 2004.

[89] E. Steegmans, D. Weyns, T. Holvoet, and Y. Berbers, "A design process for adaptive behaviour of situated agents," in *Proceedings of the 5th International Conference on Agent-Oriented Software Engineering (AOSE '04)*, J. Odell, P. Giorgini, and J. P. Müller, Eds., vol. 3382 of *Lecture Notes in Computer Science*, pp. 109–125, Springer, Berlin, Germany, 2004.

[90] Y. Demazeau, *La Méthode VOYELLES, Dans Systèmes Multi-Agents. Des Théories Organisationnelles Aux Applications Industrielles*, Hermès, Oslo, Norway, 2001.

[91] B. Henderson-Sellers, Q.-N. Tran, and J. N. Debenham, "Incorporating elements from the Prometheus agent-oriented methodology in the OPEN Process Framework," in *Proceedings of the Agent-Oriented Information Systems II*, P. Bresciani, P. Giorgini, B. Henderson-Sellers, G. Low, and M. Winikoff, Eds., vol. 3508 of *Lecture Notes in Artificial Intelligence*, pp. 140–156, Springer, Berlin, Germany, 2005.

[92] M. P. Huget, "Agent UML class diagrams revisited," in *Proceedings of the Agent Technology Workshops*, R. Kowalczyk, J. Müller, H. Tianfield, and R. Unland, Eds., vol. 2592 of *Lecture Notes in Artificial Intelligence*, pp. 49–60, Springer, Berlin, Germany, 2003.

[93] ISO/IEC, "Unified Modeling Language (UML) Version 1. 4. 2," ISO/IEC 19501, International Organization for Standardization/International Electrotechnical Commission, Geneva, Switzerland, 2005.

[94] Q. N. N. Tran and G. Low, "Comparison of ten agent-oriented methodologies," in *Agent-Oriented Methodologies*, B. Henderson-Sellers and P. Giorgini, Eds., chapter 12, pp. 341–367, Idea Group, 2005.

[95] H. K. Dam and M. Winikoff, "Towards a next-generation AOSE methodology," *Science of Computer Programming*. In press.

[96] J. P. Müller, *The Design of Intelligent Agents*, Springer, Berlin, Germany, 1996.

[97] H. V. D. Parunak and J. J. Odell, "Representing social structures in UML," in *Proceedings of the Agent-Oriented Software Engineering (AOSE '01)*, M. Wooldridge, P. Ciancarini, and G. Weiss, Eds., vol. 2222 of *Lecture Notes in Computer Science*, pp. 1–16, Springer, Berlin, Germany, 2001.

[98] V. Dignum and F. Dignum, "Designing agent systems: state of the practice," *International Journal of Agent-Oriented Software Engineering*, vol. 4, no. 3, pp. 224–243, 2010.

[99] M. Viroli, T. Holvoet, A. Ricci, K. Schelfthout, and F. Zambonelli, "Infrastructures for the environment of multiagent systems," *Autonomous Agents and Multi-Agent Systems*, vol. 14, no. 1, pp. 49–60, 2007.

[100] OMG, Agent Metamodel and Profile (AMP). Request For Proposal, OMG Document: ad/2008-08-10, 2008.

[101] B. Henderson-Sellers, Q. N. N. Tran, and J. Debenham, "An etymological and metamodel-based evaluation of the terms "goals and tasks" in agent-oriented methodologies," *Journal of Object Technology*, vol. 4, no. 2, pp. 131–150, 2005.

[102] J. Ferber and O. Gutknecht, "A meta-model for the analysis and design of organizations in multi-agent systems," in *Proceedings of the 3rd International Conference on Multi Agent Systems (ICMAS '98)*, pp. 128–135, IEEE Computer Society, Los Alamitos, CA, USA, 1998.

[103] V. Dignum and H. Weigand, "Toward an organization-oriented design methodology for agent societies," in *Intelligent Agent Software Engineering*, V. Plekhanova, Ed., chapter 9, pp. 191–212, Idea Group Publishing, 2003.

[104] J. Gonzalez-Palacios and M. Luck, "A framework for patterns in Gaia: a case-study with organisations," in *Proceedings of the 5th International Workshop on Agent-Oriented Software Engineering (AOSE '04)*, J. Odell, P. Giorgini, and J. P. Müller, Eds., vol. 3382 of *Lecture Notes in Computer Science*, pp. 174–188, Springer, Berlin, Germany, 2004.

[105] R. Cervenka, I. Trencansky, M. Calisti, and D. Greenwood, "AML: agent modeling language toward industry-grade agent-based modelling," in *Proceedings of the 5th International Conference on Agent-Oriented Software Engineering (AOSE '04)*, J. Odell, P. Giorgini, and J. P. Müller, Eds., vol. 3382 of *Lecture Notes in Computer Science*, pp. 31–46, Springer, Berlin, Germany, 2004.

[106] C. A. Iglesias and M. Garijo, "UER technique: conceptualization for agent-oriented development," in *Proceedings of the 3rd World Multi Conference on Systemics, Cybernetics and Informatics (SCI '99) and 5th International Conference on Information Systems Analysis and Synthesis (ISAS '99)*, vol. 5, pp. 535–540, International Institute of Informatics and Systemics, 1999.

[107] A. Cockburn, *Writing Effective Use Cases*, Addison-Wesley, Boston, Mass, USA, 2001.

[108] S. Azaiez, M. P. Huget, and F. Oquendo, "An approach for multiagent metamodelling," *Multiagent and Grid Systems*, vol. 2, no. 4, pp. 435–454, 2007.

[109] E. A. Kendall, "Role modeling for agent system analysis, design, and implementation," *IEEE Concurrency*, vol. 8, no. 2, pp. 34–41, 2000.

[110] E. A. Kendall, "Agent software engineering with role modelling," in *Proceedings of the 1st International Workshop on Agent-Oriented Software Engineering*, vol. 1957 of *Lecture Notes in Computer Science*, pp. 163–170, Springer, Berlin, Germany, 2001.

[111] J. J. Odell, H. V. D. Parunak, and M. Fleischer, "The role of roles in designing effective agent organizations," in *Proceedings of the Software Engineering for Large-Scale Multi-Agent Systems (SELMAS '02)*, . Garcia, C. Lucena, F. Zambonelli, A. Omicini, and J. Castro, Eds., vol. 2603 of *Lecture Notes in Computer Science*, pp. 27–38, Springer, Berlin, Germany, 2002.

[112] J. J. Odell, H. V. D. Parunak, and M. Fleischer, "Modeling agent organizations using roles," *Software and Systems Modeling*, vol. 2, no. 2, pp. 76–81, 2003.

[113] C. B. Ward and B. Henderson-Sellers, "Utilizing dynamic roles for agents," *Journal of Object Technology*, vol. 8, no. 5, pp. 177–198, 2009.

[114] L. Sterling, "Agent-oriented modelling: declarative or procedural?" in *Proceedings of the Declarative Agent Languages and Technologies V (DALT '07)*, M. Baldoni, T. C. Son, M. B. van Riemsdijk, and M. Winikoff, Eds., vol. 4897 of *Lecture Notes in Artificial Intelligence*, pp. 1–17, Springer, Berlin, Germany, 2007.

[115] L. Cernuzzi, T. Juan, L. Sterling, and F. Zambonelli, "The Gaia methodology: basic concepts and extensions," in *Methodologies and Software Engineering for Agent Systems. The Agent-Oriented Software Engineering Handbook*, F. Bergenti, M.-P. Gleizes, and F. Zambonelli, Eds., chapter 4, pp. 69–88, Kluwer Academic Publishers, Boston, Mass, USA, 2004.

[116] J. Debenham and B. Henderson-Sellers, "Designing agent-based process systems—extending the OPEN Process Framework," in *Intelligent Agent Software Engineering*, V. Plekhanova, Ed., chapter 8, pp. 160–190, Idea Group Publishing, 2003.

[117] S. Shapiro, S. Sardina, J. Thangarajah, L. Cavedon, and L. Padgham, "Revising conflicting intention sets in BDI agents," in *Proceedings of the 11th International Conference on Autonomous Agents and Multiagent Systems (AAMAS '12)*, V. Conitzer, M. Winikoff, W. van der Hoek, and L. Padgham, Eds., pp. 1081–1088, International Foundation for Autonomous Agents and Multiagent Systems, Valencia, Spain, June 2012.

[118] A. Suganthy and T. Chithralekha, "Domain-specific architecture for software agents," *Journal of Object Technology*, vol. 7, no. 6, pp. 77–100, 2008.

[119] V. Silva, A. Garcia, A. Brandão, C. Chavez, C. Lucena, and P. Alencar, "Taming agents and objects in software engineering," in *Proceedings of the Software Engineering for Large-Scale Multi-Agent Systems: Research Issues and Practical Applications (SEL-MAS '02)*, A. Garcia, C. Lucena, F. Zambonelli, A. Omicini, and J. Castro, Eds., vol. 2603 of *Lecture Notes in Computer Science*, pp. 1–26, Springer, Berlin, Germany, 2002.

[120] L. Braubach, A. Pokahr, D. Moldt, and W. Lamersdorf, "Goal representation for BDI agent systems," in *Proceedings of the 2nd International Conference on Programming Multi-Agent Systems (ProMAS '04)*, R. H. Bordini, M. Dastani, J. Dix, and A. E. F. Seghrouchni, Eds., vol. 3346 of *Lecture Notes in Artificial Intelligence*, pp. 44–65, Springer, Berlin, Germany, 2004.

[121] M. B. Van Riemsdijk, M. Dastani, and J. J. C. Meyer, "Goals in conflict: semantic foundations of goals in agent programming," *Autonomous Agents and Multi-Agent Systems*, vol. 18, no. 3, pp. 471–500, 2009.

[122] I. Graham, *Migrating to Object Technology*, Addison-Wesley, Wokingham, UK, 1995.

[123] C. Cheong and M. Winikoff, "Hermes: designing goal-oriented agent interactions," in *Proceedings of the 6th International Workshop on Agent-Oriented Software Engineering (AOSE '05)*, J. P. Müller and F. Zambonelli, Eds., vol. 3950 of *Lecture Notes in Computer Science*, pp. 16–27, Springer, Berlin, Germany, 2005.

[124] C. Cheong and M. Winikoff, "Improving flexibility and robustness in agent interactions: extending Prometheus with Hermes," in *Proceedings of the Software Engioneering for Large-Scale Multi-agent Systems (SELMAS '05)*, A. Garcia, R. Choren, C. Lucena, P. Giorgini, T. Holvoet, and A. Romanovsky, Eds., vol. 3914 of *Lecture Notes in Computer Science*, pp. 189–206, Springer, Berlin, Germany, 2005.

[125] J. Thangarajah, S. Sardina, and L. Padgham, "Measuring plan coverage and overlap for agent reasoning," in *Proceedings of the 11th International Conference on Autonomous Agents and Multiagent Systems (AAMAS '12)*, V. Conitzer, M. Winikoff, W. van der Hoek, and L. Padgham, Eds., pp. 1049–1056, International Foundation for Autonomous Agents and Multiagent Systems, Valencia, Spain, June 2012.

[126] C. Gonzalez-Perez, "OPEN/Metis. The Integral Object-Oriented Software Development Framework," 2004, http://www.openmetis.com

[127] C. Ware, *Visual Thinking for Design*, Elsevier, Amsterdam, The Netherlands, 2008.

[128] L. L. Constantine and L. A. D. Lockwood, *Software for Use*, Addison-Wesley, Reading, Mass, USA, 1999.

[129] C. Gonzalez-Perez, "Filling the voids: from requirements to deployment with OPEN/Metis," in *Proceedings of the 5th International Conference on Software and Data Technologies (ICSOFT '10)*, Athens, Greece, July 2010.

[130] T. Jorquera, C. Maurel, F. Migeon, M. P. Gleizes, C. Bernon, and N. Bonjean, "ADELFE fragmentation," Rapport IRIT/RR-2009-26-FR, Université Paul Sabatier, Toulouse, France, 2009.

[131] M. Winikoff, L. Padgham, and J. Harland, "Simplifying the development of intelligent agents," in *Proceedings of the 14th Australian Joint Conference on Artificial Intelligence (AI '01)*, Adelaide, December 2001.

[132] L. Padgham and M. Winikoff, "Prometheus: a pragmatic methodology for engineering intelligent agents," in *Proceedings of the Workshop on Agent-Oriented Methodologies (OOPSLA '02)*, J. Debenham, B. Henderson-Sellers, N. Jennings, and J. J. Odell, Eds., Centre for Object Technology Applications and Research, Sydney, Australia, 2002.

[133] V. Torres da Silva, R. Choren, and C. J. P. de Lucena, "Modeling MAS properties with MAS-ML dynamic diagrams," in *Proceedings of the 8th International Bi-Conference Workshopon Agent-Oriented Information Systems IV (AOIS '06)*, M. Kolp, B. Henderson-Sellers, H. Mouratidis, A. Garcia, A. Ghose, and P. Bresciani, Eds., vol. 4898 of *Lecture Notes in Artificial Intelligence*, pp. 1–8, Springer, Berlin, Germany, 2006.

[134] R. Fuentes-Fernández, J. J. Gomez-Sanz, and J. Pavón, "Model integration in agent-oriented development," *International Journal of Agent-Oriented Software Engineering*, vol. 1, no. 1, pp. 2–27, 2007.

[135] L. S. Vygotsky, *Mind and Society*, Harvard University Press, Cambridge, Mass, USA, 1978.

[136] M. P. Gervais, "ODAC: an agent-oriented methodology based on ODP," *Autonomous Agents and Multi-Agent Systems*, vol. 7, no. 3, pp. 199–228, 2003.

[137] J. Odell, H. V. D. Parunak, and B. Bauer, "Extending UML for agents," in *Proceedings of the Agent-Oriented Information Systems Workshop at the 17th National Conference on Artificial Intelligence*, G. Wagner, Y. Lesperance, and E. Yu, Eds., pp. 3–17, Austin, Tex, USA, 2000.

[138] B. Bauer, "UML class diagrams revisited in the context of agent-based systems," in *Proceedings of the Agent-Oriented Software Engineering (AOSE '01)*, M. Wooldridge, P. Ciancarini, and G. Weiss, Eds., vol. 2222 of *Lecture Notes in Computer Science*, pp. 101–118, Springer, Berlin, Germany, 2001.

[139] G. Beydoun, C. Gonzalez-Perez, G. Low, and B. Henderson-Sellers, "Synthesis of a generic MAS metamodel," in *Proceedings of the 4th International Workshop on Software Engineering for Large-Scale Multi-Agent Systems (SELMAS '05)*, A. Garcia, R. Choren, C. Lucena, A. Romanovsky, T. Holvoet, and P. Giorgini, Eds., pp. 27–31, IEEE Computer Society Press, Los Alamitos, CA, USA, 2005.

[140] B. Henderson-Sellers and C. Gonzalez-Perez, "A comparison of four process metamodels and the creation of a new generic standard," *Information and Software Technology*, vol. 47, no. 1, pp. 49–65, 2005.

[141] ISO/IEC, "Software engineering. Metamodel for development methodologies," ISO/IEC International Standard 24744, ISO, Geneva, Switzerland, 2007.

[142] C. Gonzalez-Perez and B. Henderson-Sellers, *Metamodelling for Software Engineering*, J. Wiley & Sons, Chichester, UK, 2008.

[143] A. Omicini, A. Ricci, and M. Viroli, "Artifacts in the A&A metamodel for multi-agent systems," *Autonomous Agents and Multi-Agent Systems*, vol. 17, no. 3, pp. 432–456, 2008.

[144] J. Searle, *Speech Acts: An Essay in the Philosophy of Language*, Cambridge University Press, 1969.

[145] D. G. Firesmith and B. Henderson-Sellers, *The OPEN Process Framework. An Introduction*, Addison-Wesley, 2002.

[146] D. G. Firesmith and B. Henderson-Sellers, "Improvements to the OPEN process metamodel," *Journal of Object-Oriented Programming*, vol. 12, no. 7, pp. 30–35, 1999.

[147] M. Amor, L. Fuentes, and A. Vallecillo, "Bridging the gap between agent-oriented design and implementation using MDA," in *Proceedings of the 5th International Workshop on Agent-Oriented Software Engineering V (AOSE '04)*, J. Odell, P. Giorgini, and J. P. Müller, Eds., vol. 3382 of *Lecture Notes in Computer Science*, pp. 93–108, Springer, Berlin, Germany, 2004.

[148] K. Fischer, C. Hahn, and C. Madrigal-Mora, "Agent-oriented software engineering: a model-driven approach," *International Journal of Agent-Oriented Software Engineering*, vol. 1, no. 3-4, pp. 334–369, 2007.

[149] K. Taveter and L. Sterling, "An expressway from agent-oriented models to prototypes," in *Proceedings of the Agent-Oriented Software Engineering VIII (AOSE '07)*, M. Luck and L. Padgham, Eds., vol. 4951 of *Lecture Notes in Computer Science*, pp. 147–163, Springer, Berlin, Germany, 2007.

[150] G. Benguria, X. Larrucea, B. Elvesæter, T. Neple, A. Beardsmore, and M. Friess, "A platform independent model for service oriented architectures," in *Enterprise Interoperability New Challenges and Approaches*, G. Doumeingts, J. Müller, G. Morel, and B. Vallespir, Eds., pp. 23–32, Springer, London, UK, 2006.

[151] L. Liu, Q. Liu, and C. H. Chi, "Towards a service requirements modelling ontology based on agent knowledge and intentions," *International Journal of Agent-Oriented Software Engineering*, vol. 2, no. 3, pp. 324–349, 2008.

[152] F. Zambonelli, N. Jennings, A. Omicini, and M. Wooldridge, "Agent-oriented software engineering for internet applications," in *Coordination of Internet Agents: Models, Technologies, and Applications*, A. Omicini, F. Zambonelli, M. Klusch, and R. Tolkdorf, Eds., pp. 326–346, Springer, Heidelberg, Germany, 2001.

[153] B. Henderson-Sellers, "Creating a comprehensive agent-oriented methodology—using method engineering and the OPEN metamodel," in *Agent-Oriented Methodologies*, B. Henderson-Sellers and P. Giorgini, Eds., chapter 13, pp. 368–397, Idea Group, 2005.

[154] T. Juan, L. Sterling, and M. Winikoff, "Assembling agent oriented software engineering methodologies from features," in *Agent-Oriented Software Engineering III*, F. Giunchiglia, J. Odell, and G. Weiss, Eds., vol. 2585 of *Lecture Notes in Computer Science*, pp. 198–209, Springer, Berlin, Germany, 2003.

[155] S. A. DeLoach, L. Padgham, A. Perini, A. Susi, and J. Thangarajah, "Using three AOSE toolkits to develop a sample design," *International Journal of Agent-Oriented Software Engineering*, vol. 3, no. 4, pp. 416–476, 2009.

# 4

# Business Process Management: A Comprehensive Survey

## Wil M. P. van der Aalst

*Department of Mathematics and Computer Science, Technische Universiteit Eindhoven, 5612 AZ Eindhoven, The Netherlands*

Correspondence should be addressed to Wil M. P. van der Aalst; w.m.p.v.d.aalst@tue.nl

Academic Editors: F. Barros, X. He, J. A. Holgado-Terriza, and C. Rolland

Business Process Management (BPM) research resulted in a plethora of methods, techniques, and tools to support the design, enactment, management, and analysis of operational business processes. This survey aims to structure these results and provide an overview of the state-of-the-art in BPM. In BPM the concept of a *process model* is fundamental. Process models may be used to configure information systems, but may also be used to analyze, understand, and improve the processes they describe. Hence, the introduction of BPM technology has both managerial and technical ramifications and may enable significant productivity improvements, cost savings, and flow-time reductions. The practical relevance of BPM and rapid developments over the last decade justify a comprehensive survey.

## 1. Introduction

*Business Process Management* (BPM) is the discipline that *combines knowledge from information technology and knowledge from management sciences and applies this to operational business processes* [1, 2]. It has received considerable attention in recent years due to its potential for significantly increasing productivity and saving costs. Moreover, today there is an abundance of *BPM systems*. These systems are *generic software systems that are driven by explicit process designs to enact and manage operational business processes* [3].

BPM can be seen as an extension of *Workflow Management* (WFM). WFM primarily focuses on the automation of business processes [4–6], whereas BPM has a broader scope: from process automation and process analysis to operations management and the organization of work. On the one hand, BPM aims to improve operational business processes, possibly without the use of new technologies. For example, by modeling a business process and analyzing it using simulation, management may get ideas on how to reduce costs while improving service levels. On the other hand, BPM is often associated with software to manage, control, and support operational processes. This was the initial focus of WFM. However, traditional WFM technology aimed at the automation of business processes in a rather mechanistic manner without much attention for human factors and management support.

*Process-Aware Information Systems* (PAISs) include traditional WFM systems and modern BPM systems, but also include systems that provide more flexibility or support specific processes [7]. For example, larger ERP (Enterprise Resource Planning) systems (e.g., SAP and Oracle), CRM (Customer Relationship Management) systems, case-handling systems, rule-based systems, call center software, and high-end middleware (e.g., WebSphere) can be seen as process-aware, although they do not necessarily control processes through some generic workflow engine. Instead, these systems have in common that there is an explicit process notion and that the information system is aware of the processes it supports. Also a database system or e-mail program may be used to execute steps in some business process. However, such software tools are not "aware" of the processes they are used in. Therefore, they are not actively involved in the management and orchestration of the processes they are used for. BPM techniques are not limited to WFM/BPM systems, but extend to any PAIS. In fact, BPM techniques such as *process mining* [8] can be used to discover and analyze emerging processes that are supported by systems that are not even "aware" of the processes they are used in.

The notion of a *process model* is foundational for BPM. A process model aims to capture the different ways in which a *case* (i.e., process instance) can be handled. A plethora of notations exists to model operational business processes (e.g., Petri nets, BPMN, UML, and EPCs). These notations have in common that processes are described in terms of activities (and possibly subprocesses). The ordering of these activities is modeled by describing causal dependencies. Moreover, the process model may also describe temporal properties, specify the creation and use of data, for example, to model decisions, and stipulate the way that resources interact with the process (e.g., roles, allocation rules, and priorities).

Figure 1 shows a process model expressed in terms of a Petri net. The model allows for the scenario $\langle a, c, e, f, g, i, j, k, l \rangle$. This is the scenario where a car is booked (activity $a$), extra insurance is added (activity $c$), the booking is confirmed (activity $e$), the check-in process is initiated (activity $f$), more insurance is added (activity $g$), a car is selected (activity $i$), the license is checked (activity $j$), the credit card is charged (activity $k$), and the car is supplied (activity $l$). Another example scenario is $\langle a, c, d, d, e, f, h, k, j, i, l \rangle$ where the booking was changed two times (activity $d$) and no extra insurance was taken at check-in (activity $h$).

Figure 1 focuses on control flow and does *not* model data, decisions, resources, and so forth. The *control-flow perspective* (modeling the ordering of activities) is often the backbone of a process model. However, other perspectives such as the *resource perspective* (modeling roles, organizational units, authorizations, etc.), the *data perspective* (modeling decisions, data creation, forms, etc.), the *time perspective* (modeling durations, deadlines, etc.), and the *function perspective* (describing activities and related applications) are also essential for comprehensive process models.

The Petri net notation is used to model the control flow in Figure 1. However, various alternative notations (e.g., BPMN, UML, and EPCs) could have been used. Discussions on different notations tend to distract BPM professionals from the key issues. The workflow patterns [9] describe the key functionalities in a language-independent manner. Obviously, there are differences in expressiveness and suitability among languages; however, these are only relevant for the more advanced patterns. Moreover, the study in [10] revealed that business process modelers typically only use a fraction of an elaborate language like BPMN. This illustrates the disconnect between BPM standardization efforts and the real needs of BPM professionals.

The model shown in Figure 1 could have been made by hand or discovered using process mining [8]. As a matter of fact, models can have very different origins. Moreover, models may also serve very different purposes. The model in Figure 1 can be used to configure a BPM system. After configuration, new cases are handled according to the rules specified in the model. However, the model can also be used for analysis (without aiming at system support); for example, after adding timing information and frequencies it can be used for "what-if" analysis using simulation. Sometimes, process models are merely used for discussion or training.

Figure 2 provides a high-level view on four-key BPM-related activities: *model*, *enact*, *analyze*, and *manage*. Process models obtained through modeling can be used for enactment (e.g., execution using a BPM or WFM system) and analysis (e.g., what-if analysis using simulation). BPM is a continuous effort; that is, processes need to be managed and BPM does not stop after completing the process design or system implementation. Changing circumstances may trigger process adaptations and generate new analysis questions. Therefore, it is important to continuously monitor processes (e.g., using process mining).

This paper aims to survey the maturing BPM discipline. Section 2 provides a historic overview of BPM. Section 3 further structures the BPM discipline. For example, processes are classified using BPM-relevant properties. Section 4 lists various *BPM use cases*. These use cases refer to the creation of process models and their usage to improve, enact, and manage processes. Section 5 discusses six *key BPM concerns* in more detail: process modeling languages, process enactment infrastructures, process model analysis, process mining, process flexibility, and process reuse. Section 6 concludes the paper with an outlook on the future of BPM.

## 2. History of BPM

Business Process Management (BPM) has various roots in both computer science and management science. Therefore, it is difficult to pinpoint the starting point of BPM. Since the industrial revolution, productivity has been increasing because of technical innovations, improvements in the organization of work, and the use of information technology. Adam Smith (1723–1790) showed the advantages of the division of labor. Frederick Taylor (1856–1915) introduced the initial principles of scientific management. Henry Ford (1863–1947) introduced the production line for the mass production of "black T-Fords." It is easy to see that these ideas are used in today's BPM systems.

Around 1950, computers and digital communication infrastructures started to influence business processes. This resulted in dramatic changes in the organization of work and enabled new ways of doing business. Today, innovations in computing and communication are still the main drivers behind change in almost all business processes. Business processes have become more complex, heavily rely on information systems, and may span multiple organizations. *Therefore, process modeling has become of the utmost importance.* Process models assist in managing complexity by providing insight and by documenting procedures. Information systems need to be configured and driven by precise instructions. Cross-organizational processes can only function properly if there is common agreement on the required interactions. As a result, process models are widely used in today's organizations.

In the last century many process modeling techniques have been proposed. In fact, the well-known Turing machine described by Alan Turing (1912–1954) can be viewed as a process model. It was instrumental in showing that many questions in computer science are undecidable. Moreover, it added a data component (the tape) to earlier transition

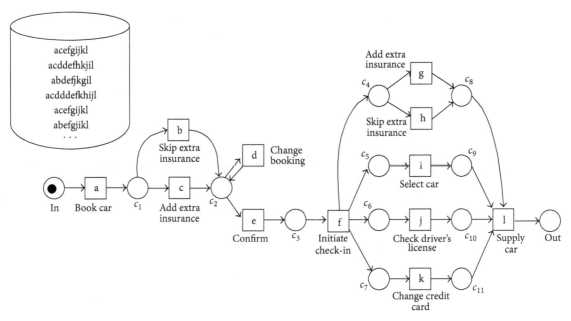

FIGURE 1: A process model expressed in terms of a Petri net and an event log with some example traces.

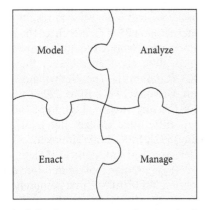

FIGURE 2: A high-level view on BPM showing the four key activities: *model* (creating a process model to be used for analysis or enactment), *enact* (using a process model to control and support concrete cases), *analyze* (analyzing a process using a process model and/or event logs), and *manage* (all other activities, e.g., adjusting the process, reallocating resources, or managing large collections of related process models).

systems. Petri nets play an even more prominent role in BPM as they are graphical and able to model concurrency. In fact, most of the contemporary BPM notations and systems use token-based semantics adopted from Petri nets. Petri nets were proposed by Carl Adam Petri (1926–2010) in 1962. This was the first formalism treating concurrency as a first-class citizen. Concurrency is very important as in business processes many things may happen in parallel. Many cases may be handled at the same time and even within a case there may be various enabled or concurrently running activities. Therefore, a BPM system should support concurrency natively.

Since the seventies there has been consensus on the modeling of data (cf. the Relational Model by Codd [11] and the Entity-Relationship Model by Chen [12]). Although there are different languages and different types of Database Management (DBM) systems, there has been consensus on the fundamental concepts for the information-centric view of information systems for decades. The process-centric view on information systems on the other hand can be characterized by the term "divergence." There is little consensus on its fundamental concepts. Despite the availability of established formal languages (e.g., Petri nets and process calculi), industry has been pushing ad hoc/domain-specific languages. As a result there is a plethora of systems and languages available today (BPMN, BPEL, UML, EPCs, etc.), some of which will be discussed in Section 5.1.

Figure 3 sketches the emergence of BPM systems and their role in the overall information system architecture. Initially, information systems were developed from scratch; that is, everything had to be programmed, even storing and retrieving data. Soon people realized that many information systems had similar requirements with respect to data management. Therefore, this generic functionality was subcontracted to a DBM system. Later, generic functionality related to user interaction (forms, buttons, graphs, etc.) was subcontracted to tools that can automatically generate user interfaces. The trend to subcontract recurring functionality to generic tools continued in different areas. BPM systems can be seen in this context: a BPM system takes care of process-related aspects. Therefore, the application can focus on supporting individual/specific tasks. In the mid 1990s, many WFM systems became available. These systems focused on automating workflows with little support for process analysis, process flexibility, and process management. BPM systems provide much broader support, for example, by supporting simulation, business process intelligence, case management,

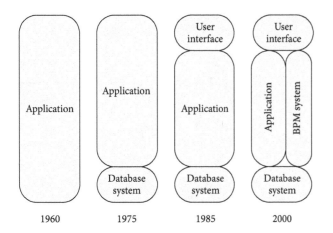

FIGURE 3: Historic view on information systems' development illustrating that BPM systems can be used to push "process logic" out of the application (adapted from [13]).

and so forth. However, compared to the database market, the BPM market is much more diverse and there is no consensus on notations and core capabilities. This is not a surprise as process management is much more challenging than data management.

A good starting point for exploring the scientific origins of BPM is the early work on *office information systems*. In the seventies, people like Skip Ellis, Anatol Holt, and Michael Zisman already worked on the so-called office information systems, which were driven by explicit process models [1, 14–22]. Ellis et al. [14–16, 23] developed office automation prototypes such as Officetalk-Zero and Officetalk-D at Xerox PARC in the late 1970s. These systems used Information Control Nets (ICN), a variant of Petri nets, to model processes. Office metaphors such as inbox, outbox, and forms were used to interact with users. The prototype office automation system SCOOP (System for Computerizing of Office Processes) developed by Michael Zisman also used Petri nets to represent business processes [20–22]. It is interesting to see that pioneers in office information systems already used Petri-net-based languages to model office procedures. During the seventies and eighties, there was great optimism about the applicability of office information systems. Unfortunately, few applications succeeded. As a result of these experiences, both the application of this technology and research almost stopped for a decade. Consequently, hardly any advances were made in the eighties. In the nineties, there was a clear revival of the ideas already present in the early office automation prototypes [4]. This is illustrated by the many commercial WFM systems developed in this period.

In the mid-nineties, there was the expectation that WFM systems would get a role comparable to Database Management (DBM) systems. Most information systems subcontract their data management to DBM systems and comparatively there are just a few products. However, these products are widely used. Despite the availability of WFM/BPM systems, process management is not subcontracted to such systems at a scale comparable to DBM systems. The application of "pure" WFM/BPM systems is still limited to specific industries such as banking and insurance. However, WFM/BPM technology is often hidden inside other systems. For example, ERP systems like SAP and Oracle provide workflow engines. Many other platforms include workflow-like functionality. For example, integration and application infrastructure software such as IBM's WebSphere and Cordys Business Operations Platform (BOP) provides extensive process support. In hindsight, it is easy to see why process management cannot be subcontracted to a standard WFM/BPM system at a scale comparable to DBM systems. As illustrated by the varying support for the workflow patterns [9, 24, 25], process management is much more "thorny" than data management. *BPM is multifaceted, complex, and difficult to demarcate.* Given the variety in requirements and close connection to business concerns, it is often impossible to use generic BPM/WFM solutions. Therefore, BPM functionality is often embedded in other systems. Moreover, BPM techniques are frequently used in a context with conventional information systems.

BPM has become a mature discipline. Its relevance is acknowledged by practitioners (users, managers, analysts, consultants, and software developers) and academics. This is illustrated by the availability of many BPM systems and a range of BPM-related conferences.

In this survey we will often refer to results presented at the Annual International BPM Conference. The International BPM Conference just celebrated its 10th anniversary and its proceedings provide a good overview of the state-of-the-art: BPM 2003 (Eindhoven, The Netherlands) [26], BPM 2004 (Potsdam, Germany) [27], BPM 2005 (Nancy, France) [28], BPM 2006 (Vienna, Austria) [29], BPM 2007 (Brisbane, Australia) [30], BPM 2008 (Milan, Italy) [31], BPM 2009 (Ulm, Germany) [32], BPM 2010 (Hoboken, NJ, USA) [33], BPM 2011 (Clermont-Ferrand, France) [34], and BPM 2012 (Tallinn, Estonia) [35]. Other sources of information are the following books on WFM/BPM: (first comprehensive WFM book focusing on the different workflow perspectives and the MOBILE language [5]), [36] (edited book that served as the basis for the BPM conference series), [4] (most cited WFM book; a Petri-net-based approach is used to model, analyze, and enact workflow processes), [19] (book relating WFM systems to operational performance), [7] (edited book on process-aware information systems), [6] (book on production WFM systems closely related to IBM's workflow products), [37] (visionary book linking management perspectives to the pi calculus), [2] (book presenting the foundations of BPM, including different languages and architectures), [38] (book based on YAWL and the workflow patterns), [8] (book focusing on process mining and BPM), and [39] (book on supporting flexibility in process-aware information systems). Most of these books also provide a historical perspective on the BPM discipline.

## 3. Structuring the BPM Discipline

Before discussing typical BPM use cases and some of the key concerns of BPM, we first structure the domain by describing the BPM life-cycle and various classifications of processes.

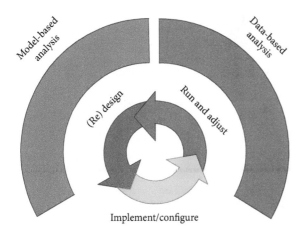

FIGURE 4: The BPM life cycle consisting of three phases: (1) *(re)design*, (2) *implement/configure*, and (3) *run* and *adjust*.

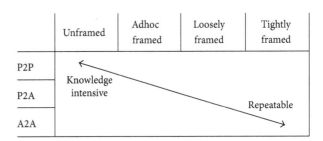

FIGURE 5: Classification of processes: most processes can be found around the diagonal.

Figure 4 shows the *BPM life-cycle*. In the *(re)design phase*, a process model is designed. This model is transformed into a running system in the *implementation/configuration phase*. If the model is already in executable form and a WFM or BPM system is already running, this phase may be very short. However, if the model is informal and needs to be hardcoded in conventional software, this phase may take substantial time. After the system supports the designed processes, the *run* and *adjust phase* starts. In this phase, the processes are enacted and adjusted when needed. In the run and adjust phase, the process is not redesigned and no new software is created; only predefined controls are used to adapt or reconfigure the process. Figure 4 shows two types of analysis: *model-based analysis* and *data-based analysis*. While the system is running, event data are collected. These data can be used to analyze running processes, for example, discover bottlenecks, waste, and deviations. This is input for the redesign phase. During this phase process models can be used for analysis. For example, simulation is used for what-if analysis or the correctness of a new design is verified using model checking.

The scope of BPM extends far beyond the implementation of business processes. Therefore, the role of model-based and data-based analyses is emphasized in Figure 4.

Business processes can be classified into human-centric and system-centric [40] or more precisely into *Person-to-Person* (P2P), *Person-to-Application* (P2A), and *Application-to-Application* (A2A) processes [7].

In P2P processes, the participants involved are primarily people; that is, the processes predominantly involve activities that require human intervention. Job tracking, project management, and groupware tools are designed to support P2P processes. Indeed, the processes supported by these tools are not composed of fully automated activities only. In fact, the software tools used in these processes (e.g., project tracking servers, e-mail clients, video-conferencing tools, etc.) are primarily oriented towards supporting computer-mediated interactions. Recently, the importance of social networks increased significantly (facebook, twitter, linkedin, etc.) and

BPM systems need to be able to incorporate such computer-mediated human interactions [41]. The term "Social BPM" refers to exploiting such networks for process improvement.

On the other end of the spectrum, A2A processes are those that only involve activities performed by software systems. Financial systems may exchange messages and money without any human involvement; logistic information systems may automatically order products when inventory falls below a predefined threshold, Transaction processing systems, EAI platforms, and Web-based integration servers are examples of technologies to support A2A processes.

P2A processes involve both human activities and interactions between people, and activities and interactions involving applications which act without human intervention. Most BPM/WFM systems fall in the P2A category. In fact, most information systems aim at making people and applications work in an integrated manner.

Note that the boundaries between P2P, P2A, and A2A are not crisp. Instead, there is a continuum of processes, techniques, and tools covering the spectrum from P2P (i.e., manual, human-driven) to A2A (automated, application-driven).

Orthogonal to the classification of processes into P2P, P2A, and A2A, we distinguish between *unframed*, *ad hoc framed*, *loosely framed*, and *tightly framed* processes [7] (cf. Figure 5).

A process is said to be *unframed* if there is no explicit process model associated with it. This is the case for collaborative processes supported by groupware systems that do *not* offer the possibility of defining process models.

A process is said to be *ad hoc framed* if a process model is defined a priori but only executed once or a small number of times before being discarded or changed. This is the case in project management environments where a process model (i.e., a project chart) is often only executed once. The same holds for scientific computing environments, where a scientist may define a process model corresponding to a computation executed on a grid and involving multiple datasets and computing resources [42]. Such a process is often executed only once (although parts may be reused for other experiments).

A *loosely framed* process is one for which there is a priori defined process model and a set of constraints, such that the predefined model describes the "normal way of doing things" while allowing the actual executions of the process to deviate from this model (within certain limits). Case-handling systems aim to support such processes; that is, they support the ideal process and implicitly defined deviations (e.g., skipping activities or rolling back to an earlier point in the process).

Finally, a *tightly framed* process is one which consistently follows an a priori defined process model. Tightly framed processes are best supported by traditional WFM systems.

As Figure 5 shows, the degree of framing of the underlying processes (unframed, ad hoc, loosely, or tightly framed) and the nature of the process participants (P2P, P2A, and A2A) are correlated. Most processes are found around the diagonal. Knowledge-intensive processes tend to be less framed and more people-centric. Highly repeatable processes tend to be tightly framed and automated.

As with P2P, P2A, and A2A processes, the boundaries between unframed, ad hoc framed, loosely framed, and tightly framed processes are not crisp. In particular, there is a continuum between loosely and tightly framed processes. For instance, during its operational life a process considered to be tightly framed can start deviating from its model so often and so unpredictably, that at some point in time it may be considered to have become loosely framed. Conversely, when many instances of a loosely framed process have been executed, a common structure may become apparent, which may then be used to frame the process in a tighter manner.

Figures 4 and 5 illustrate the breadth of the BPM spectrum. A wide variety of processes—ranging from unframed and people-centric to tightly framed and fully automated—may be supported using BPM technology. Different types of support are needed in three main phases of the BPM lifecycle (cf. Figure 4). Moreover, various types of analysis can be used in these phases: some are based on models only whereas others also exploit event data. In the remainder we present a set of twenty *BPM use cases* followed by a more detailed discussion of six *key concerns*. The use cases and key concerns are used to provide a survey of the state-of-the-art in BPM research. Moreover, the proceedings of past BPM conferences are analyzed to see trends in the maturing BPM discipline.

## 4. BPM Use Cases

To further structure the BPM discipline and to show "how, where, and when" BPM techniques can be used, we provide a set of twenty BPM use cases. Figures 6, 7, 8, 9, 10, 11, 12, and 13 show graphical representations of these use cases. Models are depicted as pentagons marked with the letter "*M*." A model may be descriptive (*D*), normative (*N*), and/or executable (*E*). A "*D|N|E*" tag inside a pentagon means that the corresponding model is descriptive, normative, or executable. Tag "*E*" means that the model is executable. Configurable models are depicted as pentagons marked with "CM." Event data (e.g., an event log) are denoted by a disk symbol (cylinder shape) marked with the letter "*E*." Information systems used to support processes at runtime are depicted as squares with rounded corners and marked with the letter "*S*." Diagnostic information is denoted by a star shape marked with the letter "*D*." We distinguish

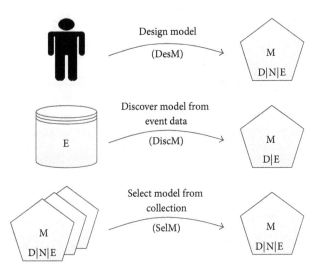

FIGURE 6: Use cases to obtain a descriptive, normative, or executable process model.

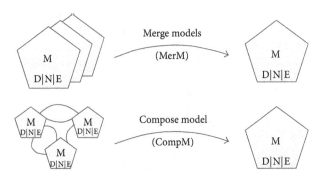

FIGURE 7: Use cases to obtain a process model from other models.

between conformance-related diagnostics (star shape marked with "CD") and performance-related diagnostics (star shape marked with "PD").

The twenty atomic use cases can be chained together in so-called *composite* use cases. These composite cases correspond to realistic BPM scenarios.

*4.1. Use Cases to Obtain Models.* The first category of use cases we describe have in common that a process model is produced (cf. Figures 6 and 7).

*4.1.1. Design Model (DesM).* Use case *design model* (DesM) refers to the creation of a process model from scratch by a human. Figure 6 shows the creation of a model represented by a pentagon marked with the letter "*M*." This is still the most common way to create models. The handmade model may be descriptive, normative, or executable. Descriptive models are made to describe the as-is or to-be situation. A descriptive model may describe undesirable behavior. If the model only describes the desired behavior, is called normative. A normative model may describe a rule like "activities $x$ and $y$ should never be executed by the same person for a given case" even though in reality the rule is often violated and not enforced. An executable model can

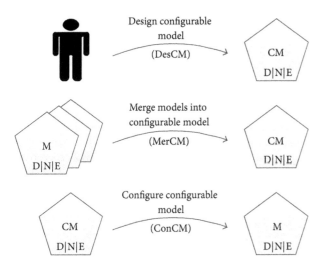

FIGURE 8: Use cases to obtain and use configurable process models.

be interpreted unambiguously by software, for example, to enact or verify a process. Given a state or sequence of past activities, the model can determine the set of possible next activities. A model may be executable and descriptive or normative; that is, the three classes are not mutually exclusive and combinations are possible.

### 4.1.2. Discover Model from Event Data (DiscM).
The term "Big Data" is often used to refer to the incredible growth of event data in recent years [43]. More and more organizations realize that the analysis of event data is crucial for process improvement and achieving competitive advantage over competitors. Use case *discover model from event data* (DiscM) refers to the automated generation of a process model using process mining techniques [8].

The goal of process mining is to extract knowledge about a particular (operational) process from event logs; that is, process mining describes a family of *a posteriori* analysis techniques exploiting the information recorded in audit trails, transaction logs, databases, and so forth (cf. Section 5.4). Typically, these approaches assume that it is possible to *sequentially record events* such that each event refers to an *activity* (i.e., a well-defined step in the process) and is related to a particular *case* (i.e., a process instance). Furthermore, some mining techniques use additional information such as the performer or *originator* of the event (i.e., the person/resource executing or initiating the activity), the *timestamp* of the event, or *data elements* recorded with the event (e.g., the size of an order).

A discovery technique takes an event log and produces a model without using any a priori information. An example is the $\alpha$-algorithm [44]. This algorithm takes an event log and produces a Petri net explaining the behavior recorded in the log. For example, given sufficient example executions of the process shown in Figure 1, the $\alpha$-algorithm is able to automatically construct the corresponding Petri net without using any additional knowledge. If the event log contains

information about resources, one can also discover resource-related models, for example, a social network showing how people work together in an organization.

### 4.1.3. Select Model from Collection (SelM).
Large organizations may have repositories containing hundreds of process models. There may be variations of the same model for different departments or products. Moreover, processes may change over time resulting in different versions. Because of these complexities, (fragments of) process models may be reinvented without reusing existing models. As a result, even more process models need to coexist, thus further complicating model management. Therefore, reuse is one of the key concerns in BPM (cf. Section 5.6).

Use case *select model from collection* (SelM) refers to the retrieval of existing process models, for example, based on keywords or process structures. An example of a query is "return all models where activity *send invoice* can be followed by activity *reimburse*." Another example is the query "return all models containing activities that need to be executed by someone with the role *manager*."

### 4.1.4. Merge Models (MerM).
Use case SelM selects a complete model from some repository. However, often new models are created from existing models. Use case *merge models* (MerM) refers to the scenario where different parts of different models are merged into one model. For example, the initial part of one model is composed with the final part of another process, a process model is extended with parts taken from another model, or different process models are unified resulting in a new model. Unlike classical composition the original parts may be indistinguishable.

### 4.1.5. Compose Model (CompM).
Use case *compose model* (CompM) refers to the situation where different models are combined into a larger model. Unlike use case MerM the different parts can be related to the original models used in the composition.

The five use cases shown in Figures 6 and 7 all produce a model. The resulting model may be used for analysis or enactment as will be shown in later use cases.

### 4.2. Use Cases Involving Configurable Models.
A configurable process model represents a *family of process models*, that is, a model that through configuration can be customized for a particular setting. For example, configuration may be achieved by *hiding* (i.e., bypassing) or *blocking* (i.e., inhibiting) certain fragments of the configurable process model [45]. In this way, the desired behavior is selected. From the viewpoint of generic BPM software, configurable process models can be seen as a mechanism to add "content" to these systems. By developing comprehensive collections of configurable models, particular domains can be supported. From the viewpoint of ERP software, configurable process models can be seen as a means to make these systems more process-centric, although in the latter case quite some refactoring is needed as processes are often hidden in table structures and application code. Various configurable languages have been

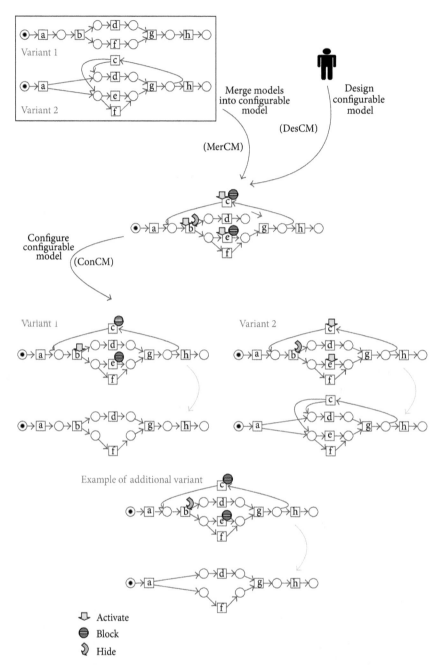

FIGURE 9: Abstract example illustrating the use cases related to configurable process models. A configurable model may be created from scratch (use case DesCM) or from existing process models (use case MerCM). The resulting configurable model can be used to generate concrete models by hiding and blocking parts (use case ConCM).

proposed as extensions of existing languages (e.g., C-EPCs [46], and C-SAP, C-BPEL) but few are actually supported by enactment software (e.g., C-YAWL [47]). Traditional reference models [48–50] can be seen as configurable process models. However, configuration is often implicit or ad hoc and often such reference models are not executable.

Figure 8 shows three use cases related to configurable process models.

### 4.2.1. Design Configurable Model (DesCM).
Configurable process models can be created from scratch as shown by use case *design configurable model* (DesCM). Creating

a configurable model is more involved than creating an ordinary nonconfigurable model. For example, because of hiding and/or blocking selected fragments, the instances of a configured model may suffer from behavioral anomalies such as deadlocks and livelocks. This problem is exacerbated by the many possible configurations a model may have, and by the complex domain dependencies which may exist between various configuration options [51].

### 4.2.2. Merge Models into Configurable Model (MerCM).
A configurable process model represents a family of process models. A common approach to obtain a configurable model

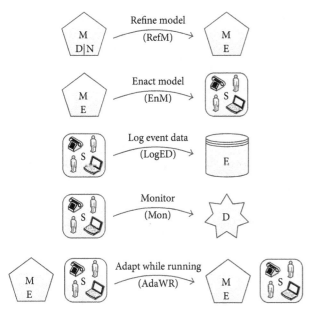

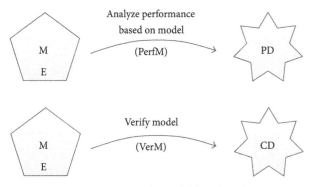

FIGURE 10: Use cases to enact models, to log event data, and to monitor running processes.

FIGURE 11: Use cases for model-based analysis.

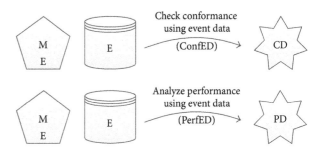

FIGURE 12: Use cases where diagnostics are obtained using both model and log.

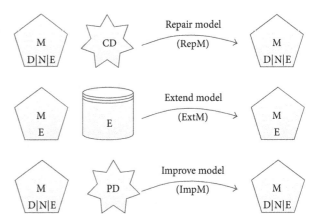

FIGURE 13: Use cases to repair, extend, or improve process models.

is to merge example members of such family into a model that is able to generate a least of the example variants. The merging of model variants into a configurable model is analogous to the discovery of process models from example traces.

Figure 9 illustrates the use case *merge models into configurable model* (MerCM). Two variants of the same process are shown in the top-left corner. Variant 1 models a process where activity *a* is followed by activity *b*. After completing *b*, activities *d* and *f* can be executed in any order, followed by activity *g*. Finally, *h* is executed. Variant 2 also starts with activity *a*. However, now *a* is followed by activities *d* and *f* or *d* and *e*. Moreover, after completing *g* the process can loop back to a state where again there is a choice between *d* and *f* or *d* and *e*.

The two variants can be merged into the configurable model shown in the center of Figure 9. Activities *c* and *e* can be blocked and activity *b* can be hidden. If we block *c* and *e* and do not hide *b* (i.e., *b* is activated), we obtain the first variant. If we do not block *c* and *e* and hide *b*, we obtain the second variant.

*4.2.3. Configure Configurable Model (ConCM).* Figure 9 also illustrates use case *configure configurable model* (ConCM). This use case creates a concrete model from some configurable process model by selecting a concrete variant; that is, from a family of process variants one member is selected. The bottom part of Figure 9 shows a variant created by blocking activities *c* and *e* and hiding activity *b*.

Figure 9 is a bit misleading as it only shows the control flow. Data-related aspects and domain modeling play an important role in process configuration. For example, when configuring ERP systems like SAP R/3 the data-perspective is most prominent.

*4.3. Use Cases Related to Process Execution.* BPM systems are used to enact processes based on executable process models. In fact, the initial focus of WFM systems was on process automation and implementation and not on the management, analysis, and improvement of business processes (cf. Figure 10).

*4.3.1. Refine Model (RefM).* Only executable models can be enacted. Therefore, use case *refine model* (RefM) describes the scenario of converting a model tagged with "*D*|*N*" into a model tagged with "*E*;" that is, a descriptive or normative model is refined into a model that is also executable. To make a model executable one needs to remove all ambiguities; that is, the supporting software should understand its meaning. Moreover, it may be necessary to detail aspects not considered relevant before. For example, it may be necessary to design a form where the user can enter data.

### 4.3.2. Enact Model (EnM).

Executable models can be interpreted by BPM systems and used to support the execution of concrete cases. Use case *enact model* (EnM) takes as input a model and as output a running system. The running system should be reliable, usable, and have a good performance. Therefore, issues like exception handling, scalability, and ergonomics play an important role. These factors are typically not modeled when discussing or analyzing processes. Yet they are vital for the actual success of the system. Therefore, Section 5.2 discusses the process enactment infrastructure as one of the key concerns of BPM.

### 4.3.3. Log Event Data (LogED).

When process instances (i.e., cases) are handled by the information system, they leave traces in audit trails, transaction logs, databases, and so forth. Even when no BPM/WFM systems is used, relevant events are often recorded by the supporting information system. Use case *log event data* (LogED) refers to the recording of event data, often referred to as *event logs*. Such event logs are used as input for various process mining techniques. Section 5.4 discusses the use of event data as one of the key concerns of BPM.

### 4.3.4. Monitor (Mon).

Whereas process mining techniques center around event data and models (e.g., models are discovered or enriched based on event logs), monitoring techniques simply measure without building or using a process model. For example, it is possible to measure response times without using or deriving a model. Modern BPM systems show dashboards containing information about Key Performance Indicators (KPIs) related to costs, responsiveness, and quality. Use case *monitor* (Mon) refers to all measurements done at runtime without actively creating or using a model.

### 4.3.5. Adapt While Running (AdaWR).

BPM is all about making choices. When designing a process model choices are made with respect to the ordering of activities. At runtime, choices may be resolved by human decision making. Also process configuration is about selecting the desired behavior from a family of process variants. As will be explained in Section 5.5, flexibility can be viewed as the ability to make choices at different points in time (design time, configuration time, or runtime). Some types of flexibility require changes of the model at runtime. Use case *adapt while running* (AdaWR) refers to the situation where the model is adapted at runtime. The adapted model may be used by selected cases (ad hoc change) or by all new cases (evolutionary change). Adapting the system or process model at runtime may introduce all kinds of complications. For example, by making a concurrent process more sequential, deadlocks may be introduced for already running cases.

### 4.4. Use Cases Involving Model-Based Analysis.

Process models are predominantly used for discussion, configuration, and implementation. Interestingly, process models can also be used for analysis. This is in fact one of the key features of BPM. Instead of directly hard-coding behavior in software, models can be analyzed before being put into production.

### 4.4.1. Analyze Performance Based on Model (PerfM).

Executable process models can be used to analyze the expected performance in terms of response times, waiting times, flow times, utilization, costs, and so forth. Use case *analyze performance based on model* (PerfM) refers to such analyses. Simulation is the most widely applied analysis technique in BPM because of its flexibility. Most BPM tools provide a simulation facility. Analytical techniques using, for example, queueing networks or Markov chains can also be used to compute the expected performance. However, these are rarely used in practice due to the additional assumptions needed.

### 4.4.2. Verify Model (VerM).

Before a process model is put into production, one would like to get assurance that the model is correct. Consider, for example, the notion of soundness [13, 52]. A process model is sound if cases cannot get stuck before reaching the end (termination is always possible) and all parts of the process can be activated (no dead segments). Use case *verify model* (VerM) refers to the analysis of such properties using techniques such as model checking.

Section 5.3 elaborates on model-based analysis as one of the key concerns of BPM.

### 4.5. Use Cases Extracting Diagnostics from Event Data.

A process model may serve as a pair of glasses that can be used to look at reality. As Figure 12 shows, we identify two use cases where diagnostic information is derived from both model and event data.

### 4.5.1. Check Conformance Using Event Data (ConfED).

Event data and models can be compared to see where modeled and observed behavior deviates. For example, one may replay history on a process model and see where observed events do not "fit" the model. Use case *check conformance using event data* (ConfED) refers to all kinds of analysis aiming at uncovering discrepancies between modeled and observed behaviors. Conformance checking may be done for auditing purposes, for example, to uncover fraud or malpractices.

### 4.5.2. Analyze Performance Using Event Data (PerfED).

Event data often contain timing information; that is, events have timestamps that can be used for performance analysis. Use case *analyze performance using event data* (PerfED) refers to the combined use of models and timed event data. By replaying an event log with timestamps on a model, one can measure delays, for example, the time in-between two subsequent activities. The result can be used to highlight bottlenecks and gather information for simulation or prediction techniques.

### 4.6. Use Cases Producing New Models Based on Diagnostics or Event Data.

Diagnostic information and event data can be used to repair, extend, or improve models (cf. Figure 13).

*4.6.1. Repair Model (RepM).* Use case ConfED can be used to see where reality and model deviate. The corresponding diagnostics can be used as input for use case *repair model* (RepM;) that is, the model is adapted to match reality better [53]. On the one hand, the resulting model should correspond to the observed behavior. On the other hand, the repaired model should be as close to the original model as possible. The challenge is to balance both concerns.

*4.6.2. Extend Model (ExtM).* Event logs refer to activities being executed and events may be annotated with additional information such as the person/resource executing or initiating the activity, the timestamp of the event, or data elements recorded with the event. Use case *extend model* (ExtM) refers to the use of such additional information to enrich the process model. For example, timestamps of events may be used to add delay distributions to the model. Data elements may be used to infer decision rules that can be added to the model. Resource information can be used to attach roles to activities in the model. This way it is possible to extend a control-flow-oriented model with additional perspectives.

*4.6.3. Improve Model (ImpM).* Performance-related diagnostics obtained through use case PerfED can be used to generate alternative process designs aiming at process improvements, for example, to reduce costs or response times. Use case *improve model* (ImpM) refers to BPM functionality helping organizations to improve processes by suggesting alternative process models. These models can be used to do "what-if" analysis. Note that unlike RepM the focus of ImpM is on improving the process itself.

*4.7. Composite Use Cases.* The twenty atomic use cases should not be considered in isolation; that is, for practical BPM scenarios these atomic use cases are chained together into composite use cases. Figure 14 shows three examples.

The first example (Figure 14(a)) is the classical scenario where a model is constructed manually and subsequently used for performance analysis. Note that the use cases *design model* (DesM) and *analyze performance based on model* (PerfM) are chained together. A conventional simulation not involving event data would fit this composite use case.

The second composite use case in Figure 14 combines three atomic use cases: the observed behavior extracted from some information system (LogED) is compared with a manually designed model (DesM) in order to find discrepancies (ConfED).

Figure 14(c) shows a composite use case composed of five atomic use cases. The initially designed model (DesM) is refined to make it executable (RefM). The model is used for enactment (EnM) and the resulting behavior is logged (LogED). The modeled behavior and event data are used to reveal bottlenecks (PerfED); that is, performance-related information is extracted from the event log and projected onto the model.

The composite use cases in Figure 14 are merely examples; that is, a wide range of BPM scenarios can be supported by composing the twenty atomic use cases.

*4.8. Analysis of BPM Conference Proceedings Based on Use Cases.* After describing the twenty BPM uses cases, we evaluate their relative importance in BPM literature [54]. As a reference set of papers we used all papers in the proceedings of past BPM conferences, that is, BPM 2003–BPM 2011 [26–34] and the edited book *Business Process Management: Models, Techniques, and Empirical Studies* [36]. The edited book [36] appeared in 2000 and can be viewed as a predecessor of the first BPM conference.

In total, 289 papers were analyzed by tagging each paper with the use cases considered [54]. As will be discussed in Section 5.7, we also tagged each paper with the key concerns addressed. Since the BPM conference is the premier conference in the field, these 289 papers provide a representative view on BPM research over the last decade.

Most papers were tagged with one dominant use case, but sometimes more tags were used. In total, 367 tags were assigned (on average 1.18 use cases per paper). For example, the paper "Instantaneous soundness checking of industrial business process models" [55] presented at BPM 2009 is a typical example of a paper tagged with use case *verify model* (VerM). In [55], 735 industrial business process models are checked for soundness (absence of deadlock and lack of synchronization) using three different approaches. The paper "Graph matching algorithms for business process model similarity search" [56] presented at the same conference was tagged with the use case *select model from collection* (SelM) since the paper presents an approach to rank process models in a repository based on some input model. These examples illustrate the tagging process.

By simply counting the number of tags per use case and year, the relative frequency of each use case per year can be established. For example, for BPM 2009 four papers were tagged with use case *discover model from event data* (DiscM). The total number of tags assigned to the 23 BPM 2009 papers is 30. Hence, the relative frequency of DiscM is 4/30 = 0.133. Table 1 shows all relative frequencies including the one just mentioned. The table also shows the average relative frequency of each use case over all ten years. These averages are shown graphically in Figure 15.

Figure 15 shows that use cases *design model* (DesM) and *enact model* (EnM) are most frequent. This is not very surprising as these use cases are less specific than most other use cases. The third most frequent use case—*verify model* (VerM)—is more surprising (relative frequency of 0.144). An example paper having such a tag is [55] which was mentioned before. Over the last decade there has been considerable progress in this area and this is reflected by various verification papers presented at BPM. In this context it is remarkable that the use cases *monitor* (Mon) and *analyze performance using event data* (PerfED) have a much lower relative frequency (resp., 0.009 and 0.015). Given the practical needs of BPM one would expect more papers presenting techniques to diagnose and improve the performance of business processes.

Figure 16 shows changes of relative frequencies over time. The graph shows a slight increase in process-mining-related topics. However, no clear trends are visible due to the many use cases and small number of years and papers per year.

(a) A conventional simulation study not involving any event data can be viewed as a composite use case obtained by chaining two atomic use cases (DesM and PerfM)

(b) A composite use case obtained by chaining three atomic use cases (LogED, DesM, and ConfED)

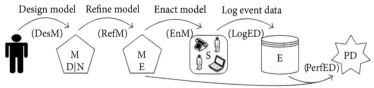

(c) A composite use case obtained by chaining five use cases: DesM, RefM, EnM, LogED, and PerfED

FIGURE 14: Three composite use cases obtained by chaining atomic use cases.

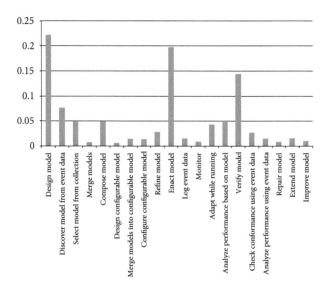

FIGURE 15: Average relative importance of use cases (taken from Table 1).

Therefore, the 289 BPM papers were also analyzed based on the six key concerns presented next (cf. Section 5.7).

## 5. BPM Key Concerns

The use cases refer to the practical/intended use of BPM techniques and tools. However, BPM research is not equally distributed over all of these use cases. Some use cases provide important engineering or managerial challenges, but these are not BPM specific or do not require additional BPM research. Other use cases require foundational research and are not yet encountered frequently in practice. Therefore, we now zoom in on six key concerns addressed by many BPM papers: process modeling languages, process enactment

infrastructures, process model analysis, process mining, process flexibility, and process reuse.

*5.1. Process Modeling Languages.* The modeling and analysis of processes plays a central role in business process management. Therefore, the choice of language to represent an organization's processes is essential. Three classes of languages can be identified.

(i) *Formal languages*: processes have been studied using theoretical models. Mathematicians have been using Markov chains, queueing networks, and so forth to model processes. Computer scientists have been using Turing machines, transition systems, Petri nets, temporal logic, and process algebras to model processes. All of these languages have in common that they have *unambiguous semantics* and allow for *analysis*.

(ii) *Conceptual languages*: users in practice often have problems using formal languages due to the rigorous semantics (making it impossible to leave things intentionally vague) and low-level nature. They typically prefer to use higher-level languages. Examples are BPMN (Business Process Modeling Notation, [57, 58]), EPCs (Event-Driven Process Chains, [59–61]), UML activity diagrams, and so forth (see Figure 17 for some examples). These languages are typically *informal*; that is, they do not have a well-defined semantics and do not allow for analysis. Moreover, the lack of semantics makes it impossible to directly execute them.

(iii) *Execution languages*: formal languages typically abstract from "implementation details" (e.g., data structures, forms, and interoperability problems) and conceptual languages only provide an approximate description of the desired behavior. Therefore, more technical languages are needed for enactment.

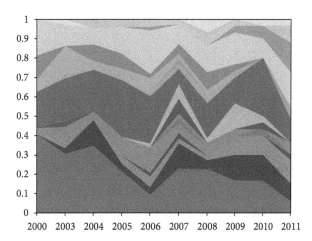

- ▨ Improve model (ImpM)
- ▨ Extend model (ExtM)
- ▨ Repair model (RepM)
- ▨ Analyze performance using event data (PerfED)
- ▨ Check conformance using event data (ConfED)
- ▨ Verify model (VerM)
- ▨ Analyze performance based on model (PerfM)
- ▨ Adapt while running (adaWR)
- ▨ Monitor (Mon)
- ▨ Log event data (LogED)
- ▪ Enact model (EnM)
- ▨ Refine model (RefM)
- ▪ Configure configurable model (ConCM)
- ▨ Merge models into configurable model (MerCM)
- ▨ Design configurable model (DesCM)
- ▨ Compose model (CompM)
- ▪ Merge models (MerM)
- ▨ Select model from collection (SelM)
- ▪ Discover model from event data (DiscM)
- ▪ Design model (DesM)

FIGURE 16: Development of the relative importance of each use case plotted over time (derived from Table 1).

An example is the BPEL (Business Process Execution Language, [62]) language. Most vendors provide a proprietary execution language. In the latter case, the source code of the implemented tool determines the exact semantics.

Note that fragments of languages like BPMN, UML, BPEL, and EPCs have been formalized by various authors [63, 64]. However, these formalizations typically cover only selected parts of the language (e.g., abstract from data or OR-joins). Moreover, people tend to use only a small fragment of languages like BPMN [10]. To illustrate problems related to the standardization of industry-driven languages, consider the OR-join semantics described in the most recent BPMN standard [57]. Many alternative semantics have been proposed and are used by different tools and formalizations [65–68]. There is a tradeoff between accuracy and performance and due to the "vicious circle" [66, 69] it is impossible to provide "clean semantics" for all cases. In fact, the OR-join semantics of [57] is not supported by any of the many tools claiming to support BPMN.

Figure 18 illustrates the "vicious circle" paradox [66, 69]. The intuitive semantics of an OR-join is to wait for all tokens to arrive. In the state shown in Figure 18, each OR-join has a token on one of its input arcs (denoted by the two black dots). The top OR-join should occur if it cannot receive a token via its second input arc. By symmetry, the same holds for the second OR-join. Suppose that one OR-join needs to wait for a second token to arrive, then also the other OR-join needs to wait due to symmetry. However, in this case the process deadlocks and no second token will be received by any of the OR-joins; that is, none of the OR-joins should have blocked. Suppose that one OR-join does not wait for a second token to arrive, then, by symmetry, also the other OR-join can move forward. However, in this case each OR-join receives a second token and in hindsight both should have blocked. The example shown has no obvious interpretation; however, the paradox revealed by the "vicious circle" also appears in larger, more meaningful, examples where one OR-join depends on another OR-join.

Thus far, we only considered procedural languages like Petri nets, BPMN, UML activity diagrams, and BPEL.

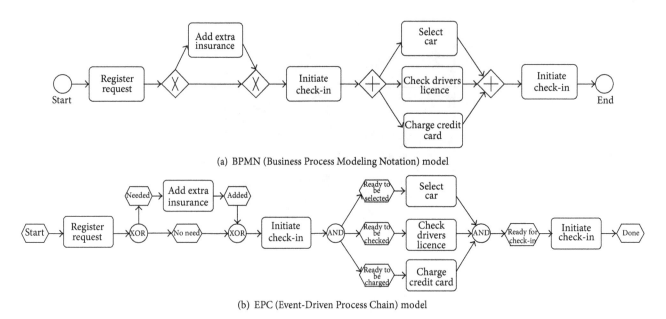

(a) BPMN (Business Process Modeling Notation) model

(b) EPC (Event-Driven Process Chain) model

FIGURE 17: Two examples of conceptual procedural languages: (a) BPMN (Business Process Modeling Notation, [57]) and (b) EPC (Event-Driven Process Chain, [59]).

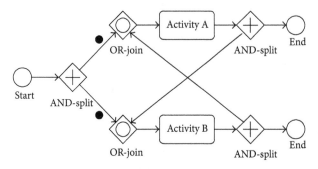

FIGURE 18: An example of a so-called "vicious circle" in a BPMN model with two OR-joins.

Although lion's share of BPM research is focusing on such languages, there is also BPM research related to more *declarative* forms of process modeling. Procedural process models take an "inside-to-outside" approach; that is, all execution alternatives need to be specified explicitly and new alternatives must be explicitly added to the model. Declarative models use an "outside-to-inside" approach: anything is possible unless explicitly forbidden. To illustrate the "outside-to-inside" approach of modeling we use the example shown in Figure 19. The example is expressed in terms of the *Declare* language [70, 71] and is intended to be witty; it does not model a realistic business process but illustrates the modeling constructs. The Declare model consists of four activities ($a$ = eat food, $b$ = feel bad, $c$ = drink beer, and $d$ = drink wine) and four constraints ($c1$, $c2$, $c3$, and $c4$). Without any constraints any sequence of activities is allowed as only constraints can limit the allowed behavior.

Declare is grounded in *Linear Temporal Logic* (LTL) with finite-trace semantics; that is, each constraint is mapped onto an LTL formula using temporal operators such as always ($\square$),

eventually ($\lozenge$), until ($\sqcup$), weak until ($W$), and next time ($\circ$) [72, 73]. The construct connecting activities $c$ and $d$ is the so-called *noncoexistence constraint*. In terms of LTL constraint $c1$ means "$\neg((\lozenge c) \wedge (\lozenge d))$;" that is, $\lozenge c$ and $\lozenge d$ cannot both be true. Hence, it is not allowed that both $c$ and $d$ happen for the same case (beer and wine do not mix well). However, in principle, one of them can occur an arbitrary number of times. There are two *precedence constraints* ($c2$ and $c3$). The semantics of precedence constraint $c2$ which connects $a$ to $c$ can also be expressed in terms of LTL: "$(\neg c)Wa$;" that is, $c$ should not happen before $a$ has happened. Since the weak until ($W$) is used in "$(\neg c)Wa$", traces without any $a$ and $c$ events also satisfy the constraint. Similarly, $d$ should not happen before $a$ has happened: "$(\neg d)Wa$." There is one branched *response constraint*: $c4$. The LTL formalization of the constraint connecting $b$ to $c$ and $d$ is "$\square(b \Rightarrow (\lozenge c \vee \lozenge d))$;" that is, every occurrence of $b$ should eventually be followed by $c$ or $d$. However, there does not need to be a one-to-one correspondence; for example, four occurrences of activity $b$ may be followed by just one occurrence of activity $c$. For example, trace $\langle a, c, c, a, b, b, b, c \rangle$ is allowed. Whereas in a procedural model, everything is forbidden unless explicitly enabled, a declarative model allows for anything unless explicitly forbidden. Trace $\langle a, a, c, d \rangle$ is not allowed as it violates $c1$ (cannot drink both wine and beer). Trace $\langle b, c, c \rangle$ is not allowed as it violates $c2$ (cannot drink beer before eating food). Trace $\langle a, c, b \rangle$ is not allowed as it violates $c4$ (after feeling bad one should eventually drink beer or wine). For processes with a lot of flexibility, declarative models are often more appropriate [70, 71].

Recently, more and more authors realized that conventional process modeling languages such as BPMN, UML ADs, Statecharts, BPEL, YAWL, WF-nets, and EPCs provide only a *monolithic view* on the real process of interest. The process is "flattened" to allow for a diagram that describes

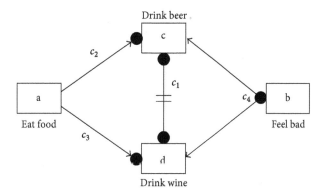

FIGURE 19: Example illustrating the declarative style of process modeling where anything is possible unless explicitly forbidden by constraints.

the life-cycle of one case in isolation. *Proclets* [74] are one of the few business process modeling languages not forcing the modeler to *straightjacket* processes into one monolithic model. Instead, processes can be decomposed into a collection of interacting proclets that may have one-to-many or many-to-many relationships (following the cardinalities in the corresponding data model). For example, one order may result in multiple deliveries and one delivery may involve order lines of different orders. This cannot be handled by the classical refinement of activities. However, order, order line, and delivery proclets may coexist independent of one another and are only loosely coupled. For example, an orderline exists because it was created in the context of order. However, the actual delivery of the corresponding item depends on inventory levels, transportation planning, and competing orders.

Object-oriented and artifact-centric approaches use ideas related to proclets [75–80]. These approaches aim to provide a better balance between process-centric and data-centric modeling.

There is an increasing interest in understanding and evaluating the comprehensibility of process models [81–83]. The connection between complexity and process model understanding has been shown empirically in recent publications (e.g., [84–87]) and mechanisms have been proposed to alleviate specific aspects of complexity (e.g., [88–90]). In [82, 83], various change patterns have been proposed. The goal of these patterns is to modify the process model to make it more understandable. The collection of patterns for concrete syntax modifications described in [82] includes mechanisms for arranging the layout, for highlighting parts of the model using enclosure, graphics, or annotations, for representing specific concepts explicitly or in an alternative way, and for providing naming guidance. A collection of patterns for abstract syntax modifications has been presented in [83]. These patterns affect the formal structure of process model elements and their interrelationships (and not just the concrete syntax). For example, a process model may be converted into a behavioral equivalent process model, that is block structured and thus easier to understand.

The existence and parallel use of a plethora of languages causes many problems. The lack of consensus makes it difficult to exchange models. The gap between conceptual languages and execution languages leads to rework and a disconnect between users and implementers. Moreover, conceptual languages and execution languages often do not allow for analysis.

The Workflow Patterns Initiative [91] was established in the late nineties with the aim of delineating the fundamental requirements that arise during business process modeling on a recurring basis and describe them in an imperative way. Based on an analysis of contemporary workflow products and modeling problems encountered in various workflow projects, a set of twenty patterns covering the control-flow perspective of BPM was created [9]. Later this initial set was extended and now also includes workflow resource patterns [24], workflow data patterns [25], exception handling patterns [92], service-interaction patterns [93], and change patterns [94].

These collections of workflow patterns can be used to compare BPM/WFM languages and systems. Moreover, they help focusing on the core issues rather than adding new notations to the "Tower of Babel for Process Languages." The lack of consensus on the modeling language to be used resulted in a plethora of similar but subtly different languages inhibiting effective and unified process support and analysis. This "Tower of Babel" and the corresponding discussions obfuscated more foundational questions.

*5.2. Process Enactment Infrastructures.* The Workflow Management Coalition (WfMC) was founded in August 1993 as an international nonprofit organization. In the early 1990s, the WfMC developed their so-called *reference model* [95, 96]. Although the detailed text describing the reference model refers to outdated standards and technologies, it is remarkable to see that after almost twenty years the reference model of the WfMC still adequately structures the desired functionality of a WFM/BPM system. Figure 20 shows an overview of the reference model. It describes the major components and interfaces within a workflow architecture. In our description of the reference model we use the original terminology. Therefore, "business processes" are often referred to as "workflows" when explaining the reference model.

The core of any WFM/BPM system is the so-called *workflow enactment service*. The workflow enactment service

TABLE 1: Relative importance of use cases in [26–34, 36]. Each of the 289 papers was tagged with, on average, 1.18 use cases (typically 1 or 2 use cases per paper). The table shows the relative frequency of each use case per year. The last row shows the average over 10 years. All rows add up to 1.

| Year | Design model | Discover model from event data | Select model from collection | Merge models | Compose model | Design configurable model | Merge models into configurable model | Configure configurable model | Refine model | Enact model | Log event data | Monitor | Adapt while running | Analyze performance based on model | Verify model | Check conformance using event data | Analyze performance using event data | Repair model | Extend model | Improve model |
|---|---|---|---|---|---|---|---|---|---|---|---|---|---|---|---|---|---|---|---|---|
| | DesM | DiscM | SelM | MerM | CompM | DesCM | MerCM | ConCM | RefM | EnM | LogED | Mon | AdawR | PerfM | VerM | ConfED | PerfED | RepM | ExtM | ImpM |
| 2000 | 0.406 | 0.000 | 0.000 | 0.000 | 0.031 | 0.000 | 0.000 | 0.000 | 0.000 | 0.188 | 0.000 | 0.000 | 0.063 | 0.125 | 0.188 | 0.000 | 0.000 | 0.000 | 0.000 | 0.000 |
| 2003 | 0.306 | 0.028 | 0.056 | 0.000 | 0.056 | 0.000 | 0.000 | 0.028 | 0.000 | 0.222 | 0.028 | 0.000 | 0.139 | 0.000 | 0.111 | 0.000 | 0.000 | 0.000 | 0.028 | 0.000 |
| 2004 | 0.348 | 0.130 | 0.000 | 0.000 | 0.043 | 0.000 | 0.000 | 0.000 | 0.000 | 0.217 | 0.000 | 0.000 | 0.043 | 0.087 | 0.087 | 0.000 | 0.000 | 0.000 | 0.000 | 0.043 |
| 2005 | 0.216 | 0.039 | 0.039 | 0.000 | 0.098 | 0.000 | 0.000 | 0.000 | 0.000 | 0.294 | 0.000 | 0.000 | 0.059 | 0.078 | 0.137 | 0.000 | 0.000 | 0.000 | 0.000 | 0.039 |
| 2006 | 0.094 | 0.038 | 0.057 | 0.019 | 0.132 | 0.000 | 0.000 | 0.000 | 0.019 | 0.245 | 0.019 | 0.000 | 0.075 | 0.019 | 0.226 | 0.019 | 0.019 | 0.000 | 0.000 | 0.019 |
| 2007 | 0.231 | 0.128 | 0.026 | 0.026 | 0.051 | 0.026 | 0.026 | 0.077 | 0.077 | 0.077 | 0.026 | 0.026 | 0.026 | 0.051 | 0.103 | 0.000 | 0.026 | 0.023 | 0.000 | 0.000 |
| 2008 | 0.227 | 0.045 | 0.023 | 0.000 | 0.045 | 0.000 | 0.023 | 0.000 | 0.023 | 0.182 | 0.045 | 0.000 | 0.023 | 0.091 | 0.136 | 0.000 | 0.045 | 0.023 | 0.068 | 0.000 |
| 2009 | 0.167 | 0.133 | 0.023 | 0.000 | 0.033 | 0.000 | 0.033 | 0.000 | 0.133 | 0.133 | 0.033 | 0.000 | 0.000 | 0.033 | 0.167 | 0.033 | 0.033 | 0.000 | 0.000 | 0.000 |
| 2010 | 0.167 | 0.133 | 0.067 | 0.000 | 0.000 | 0.033 | 0.000 | 0.033 | 0.033 | 0.300 | 0.033 | 0.000 | 0.000 | 0.000 | 0.100 | 0.067 | 0.000 | 0.000 | 0.033 | 0.000 |
| 2011 | 0.061 | 0.091 | 0.121 | 0.030 | 0.000 | 0.000 | 0.061 | 0.000 | 0.000 | 0.121 | 0.000 | 0.061 | 0.000 | 0.000 | 0.182 | 0.152 | 0.030 | 0.061 | 0.030 | 0.000 |
| Average | 0.222 | 0.077 | 0.049 | 0.007 | 0.049 | 0.006 | 0.014 | 0.014 | 0.029 | 0.198 | 0.015 | 0.009 | 0.043 | 0.048 | 0.144 | 0.027 | 0.015 | 0.008 | 0.016 | 0.010 |

provides the run-time environment which takes care of the control and execution of workflows. For technical or managerial reasons the workflow enactment service may use multiple *workflow engines*. A workflow engine handles selected parts of the workflow and manages selected parts of the resources. The *process definition tools* are used to specify and analyze workflow process definitions and/or resource classifications. These tools are used at design time. In most cases, the process definition tools can also be used for business process modeling and analysis. Most WFM/BPM systems provide three process definition tools: (1) a tool with a graphical interface to define workflow processes, (2) a tool to specify resource classes (organizational model describing roles, groups, etc.), and (3) an analysis tool to analyze a specified workflow (e.g., using simulation or verification). The end user communicates with the workflow system via the *workflow client applications*. An example of a workflow client application is the well-known *in-basket* also referred to as *work-list*. Via such an in-basket work items are offered to the end user. By selecting a work item, the user can execute a task for a specific case. If necessary, the workflow engine invokes applications via Interface 3. The *administration and monitoring tools* are used to monitor and control the workflows. These tools are used to register the progress of cases and to detect bottlenecks. Moreover, they are also used to set parameters, allocate people, and handle abnormalities. Via Interface 4 the workflow system can be connected to other workflow systems.

To standardize the five interfaces shown in Figure 20, the WfMC aimed at a common *Workflow Application Programming Interface* (WAPI). The WAPI was envisaged as a common set of API calls and related interchange formats which may be grouped together to support each of the five interfaces (cf. [96]). The WfMC also started to work on a common language to exchange process models soon after it was founded. This resulted in the Workflow Process Definition Language (WPDL) [97] presented in 1999. Although many vendors claimed to be WfMC compliant, few made a serious effort to support this language. At the same time, XML emerged as a standard for data interchange. Since WPDL was not XML based, the WfMC started working on a new language: XPDL (XML Process Definition Language). The starting point for XPDL was WPDL. However, XPDL should not be considered as the XML version of WPDL. Several concepts have been added/changed and the WfMC remained fuzzy about the exact relationship between XPDL and WPDL. In October 2002, the WfMC released a "Final Draft" of XPDL [98]. The language developed over time, but before widespread adoption, XPDL was overtaken by the *Business Process Execution Language for Web Services* (BPEL) [62, 99]. BPEL builds on IBM's WSFL (Web Services Flow Language) [100] and Microsoft's XLANG (Web Services for Business Process Design) [101] and combines accordingly the features of a block-structured language inherited from XLANG with those for directed graphs originating from WSFL. BPEL received considerable support from large vendors such as IBM and Oracle. However, in practical terms also the relevance of BPEL is limited. Vendors tend to develop all kinds of extensions (e.g., for people-centric processes) and dialects

of BPEL. Moreover, the increasing popularity of BPMN is endangering the position of BPEL (several vendors allow for the direct execution of subsets of BPMN thereby bypassing BPEL). Furthermore, process models are rarely exchanged between different platforms because of technical problems (the "devil is in the details") and too few use cases.

Figure 21 shows the BPM reference architecture proposed in [1]. It is similar to the reference model of the WfMC, but the figure details the data sets used and lists the roles of the various stakeholders (management, worker, and designer). The designer uses the design tools to create models describing the processes and the structure of the organization. The manager uses management tools to monitor the flow of work and act if necessary. The worker interacts with the enactment service. The enactment service can offer work to workers and workers can search, select, and perform work. To support the execution of tasks, the enactment service may launch various kinds of applications. Note that the enactment service is the core of the system deciding on "what," "how," "when," and "by whom." Clearly, the enactment service is driven by models of the processes and the organizations using the system. By merely changing these models the system evolves and adapts. This is the ultimate promise of WFM/BPM systems.

*Service-Oriented Computing* (SOC) has had an incredible impact on the architecture of process enactment infrastructures. The key idea of service orientation is to *subcontract work to specialized services in a loosely coupled fashion*. In SOC, functionality provided by business applications is encapsulated within web services, that is, software components described at a semantic level, which can be invoked by application programs or by other services through a stack of Internet standards including HTTP, XML, SOAP, WSDL, and UDDI [102–107]. Once deployed, web services provided by various organizations can be interconnected in order to implement business collaborations, leading to composite web services. Although service-orientation does not depend on a particular technology, it is often associated with standards such as HTTP, XML, SOAP, WSDL, UDDI, and BPEL. Figure 22 shows an overview of the "web services technology stack" and its relation to BPMN and BPEL.

In a *Service-Oriented Architecture* (SOA) services are interacting, for example, by exchanging messages. By combining basic services more complex services can be created [103, 107]. *Orchestration* is concerned with the composition of services seen from the viewpoint of single service (the "spider in the web"). *Choreography* is concerned with the composition of services seen from a global viewpoint focusing on the common and complementary observable behavior. Choreography is particularly relevant in a setting where there is no single coordinator. The terms orchestration and choreography describe two aspects of integrating services to create end-to-end business processes. The two terms overlap somewhat and their distinction has been heavily discussed over the last decade.

SOC and SOA can be used to realize process enactment infrastructures. Processes may implement services and, in turn, may use existing services. All modern BPM/WFM systems provide facilities to expose defined processes as services and to implement activities in a process by simply calling

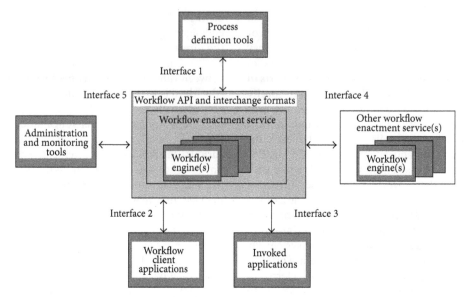

FIGURE 20: Reference model of the Workflow Management Coalition (WfMC).

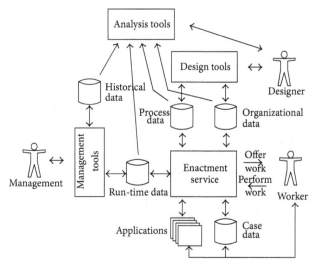

FIGURE 21: BPM reference architecture.

other services. See, for example, the YAWL architecture [38] which completely decouples the invocation of an activity from the actual execution of the activity.

Interactions between different processes and applications may be more involved as illustrated by the *service interaction patterns* by Barros et al. [93] and the *enterprise integration patterns* by Hohpe and Woolf [108].

For the implementation of process enactment infrastructures, *cloud computing* and related technologies such as *Software as a Service* (SaaS), *Platform as a Service* (PaaS), and *Infrastructure as a Service* (IaaS) are highly relevant. SaaS, often referred to as "on-demand software," is a software delivery model in which the software and associated data are centrally hosted on the cloud. The SaaS provider takes care of all hardware and software issues. A well-known example is the collection of services provided by Safesforce. In the PaaS

delivery model, the consumer creates the software using tools and libraries from the provider. The consumer also controls software deployment and configuration settings. However, the provider provides the networks, servers, and storage. The IaaS delivery model, also referred to as "hardware as a service," offers only computers (often as virtual machines), storage, and network capabilities. The consumer needs to maintain the operating systems and application software.

The above discussion of different technologies illustrates that there are many ways to implement the functionality shown in Figure 21. There are both *functional* and *nonfunctional requirements* that need to be considered when implementing a process-aware information system. The different collections of workflow patterns can be used to elicit functional requirements. For example, the control-flow-oriented workflow patterns [9] can be used to elicit requirements with respect to the ordering of activities. An example is the "deferred choice" pattern [9], that is, a choice controlled by the environment rather than the WFM/BPM system. An organization needs to determine whether this pattern is important and, if so, the system should support it. The workflow resource patterns [24], workflow data patterns [25], and exception handling patterns [92] can be used in a similar fashion. However, architectural choices are mostly driven by nonfunctional requirements related to costs, response times, and reliability.

Several BPM research groups are concerned with the performance of WFM/BPM systems. Although the core process management technology by itself is seldom the bottleneck, some process-aware information systems need to deal with millions of cases and thousands of concurrent users. Note that process-related data are typically small compared to the data needed to actually execute activities. The process state can be encoded compactly and the computation of the next state is typically very fast compared to application-related processing. However, since WFM/BPM systems needs to

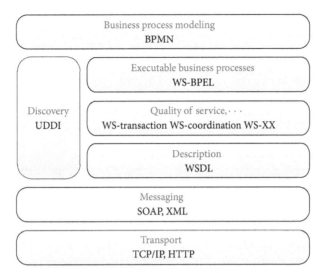

FIGURE 22: Web services technology stack linking business process modeling (e.g., using the BPMN notation) to technologies to realize a SOA.

control other applications, architectural considerations are important for the overall system's performance. For example, when the number of cases handled per hour grows over time, there is a need to reconfigure the system and to distribute the work over more computing nodes. Cloud computing and SaaS provide the opportunity to outsource such issues. Load balancing and system reconfiguration are then handled by the service provider.

Another concern addressed by BPM research is the *reliability* of the resulting information system. WFM/BPM systems are often the "spider in the web" connecting different technologies. For example, the BPM system invokes applications to execute particular tasks, stores process-related information in a database, and integrates different legacy and web-based systems. Different components may fail resulting in loss of data and parts of the systems that are out of sync. Ideally, the so-called *ACID properties* (Atomicity, Consistency, Isolation, and Durability) are ensured by the WFM/BPM system; *atomicity*: an activity is either successfully completed in full (commit) or restarted from the very beginning (rollback), *consistency*: the result of an activity leads to a consistent state, *isolation*: if several tasks are carried out simultaneously, the result is the same as if they had been carried out entirely separately, and *durability*: once a task is successfully completed, the result must be saved persistently to ensure that work cannot be lost. In the second half of the nineties many database researchers worked on the so-called workflow transactions, that is, long-running transactions ensuring the ACID properties at a business process level [40, 109–113]. Business processes need to be executed in a partly uncontrollable environment where people and organizations may deviate and software components and communication infrastructures may malfunction. Therefore, the BPM system needs to be able to deal with failures and missing data. Research on workflow transactions [40, 109–113] aims to gracefully handle exceptions and maintain system integrity at all times.

Related to reliability are *security* concerns. WFM/BPM systems should ensure that only authorized people can execute activities and access data [114]. Role-Based Access Control (RBAC, [115]) techniques can be applied in this setting. The workflow resource patterns [24] also incorporate RBAC functionalities. Moreover, process-specific security patterns such as the "four-eyes principle" (the same person may not execute two dependent tasks for the same case even if the person has the appropriate role for both tasks) are incorporated. Cloud computing and SaaS technologies fuel new security-related anxieties. Multi-tenancy, that is, multiple organizations using the same system, is interesting from a cost perspective. Costs are shared by different organizations using economies of scale. Moreover, load balancing and reconfiguration can be supported in a better manner when many tenants are sharing a large common infrastructure. For example, smaller organizations may share a workflow engine, whereas larger organizations use many engines at the same time. This is all handled by the service provider. For the service consumer these system (re)configurations are invisible. However, multi-tenancy implies that different, possibly competing, organizations are using the same cloud or SaaS system. Therefore, the process infrastructure should ensure that information from one tenant cannot leak to another tenant.

*5.3. Process Model Analysis.* There are two mainstream approaches for model-based analysis: *verification* and *performance analysis*. Verification is concerned with the correctness of a system or process. Performance analysis focuses on flow times, waiting times, utilization, and service levels. Unlike process mining, these approaches do not use event data and perform analysis using just the model.

A typical correctness property used for verification is the *soundness* notion [13, 52]. Soundness was originally defined for *workflow nets* (WF-nets) but it applies to all modeling techniques. A WF-net is a Petri net with a dedicated source place where the process starts and a dedicated sink place where the process ends. Moreover, all nodes are on a path from source to sink. A token on the source place denotes the initial state. The state with just a token on the sink place denotes the desired end state. Such a WF-net models the *life cycle of cases* of a given kind. Examples of cases are insurance claims, job applications, customer orders, replenishment orders, patient treatments, and credit applications. The process model is instantiated once for each case. Each of these process instances has a well-defined start (case creation) and end (case completion). In-between these points, activities are conducted according to a predefined procedure. One model may be instantiated many times. For example, the process of handling insurance claims may be executed for thousands or even millions of claims. These instances can be seen as copies of the same WF-net; that is, tokens of different cases are not mixed.

Not every WF-net represents a correct process. The modeled process may exhibit errors such as deadlocks, activities that can never become active, livelocks, and improper termination (i.e., garbage being left in the process after completion). Consider, for example, the WF-net shown in Figure 23 exhibiting several problems.

A WF-net is *sound* if and only if (a) from any reachable state it is possible to reach a state with a token in the sink place (*option to complete*), (b) any reachable state having a token in the sink place does not have a token in any of the other places (*proper completion*), and (c) for any transition there is a reachable state enabling it (*absence of dead parts*) [13, 52]. The WF-net shown in Figure 23 obviously violates all three properties. For subclasses of WF-nets, soundness can be analyzed without constructing the state space. For example, for free-choice Petri nets, that is, processes where choice and synchronization can be separated, soundness can be checked by analyzing the rank of the corresponding incidence matrix [13, 116]. Hence, soundness can be checked in polynomial time for free-choice WF-nets. Invariants can often be used to diagnose soundness problems; for example, the absence of particular place and transition invariants for the short-circuited WF-net provides possible causes for nonsoundness. However, most of the more interesting verification questions require the exploration of (a part of) the state space. See [13, 52, 55, 65, 68, 117–131] for examples of verification techniques analyzing soundness-related properties for workflows and business processes

Soundness is a generic property, but sometimes a more specific property that needs to be investigated; for example, "the ticket was checked for all rejected requests." Such properties can be expressed in *temporal logic* [72, 73]. As mentioned earlier Linear Temporal Logic (LTL) is an example of a temporal logic that, in addition to classical logical operators, uses temporal operators such as always ($\square$), eventually ($\lozenge$), until ($\sqcup$), weak until ($W$), and next time ($\bigcirc$). The expression $\lozenge b \Rightarrow \lozenge g$ means that for all cases in which $b$ (*skip extra insurance*) is executed also $g$ (*add extra insurance*) is executed. Another example is $\square(e \Rightarrow \lozenge l)$ that states that any occurrence of $e$ will eventually be followed by $l$ (after confirmation eventually a car is supplied). Model checking techniques can be used to check such properties [72].

Another verification task is the comparison of two models. For example, the implementation of a process is compared to the high-level specification of the process. There exist different equivalence notions (trace equivalence, branching bisimilarity, etc.) [132, 133]. Trace equivalence considers two transition systems to be equivalent if their execution sequences are the same. More refined notions like (branching) bisimilarity also take the moment of choice into account [132, 133]. Two process models are bisimilar if the first model can, "mimic any move" of the second, and vice versa. Consider, for example, the processes $P = a \cdot (b + c)$ and $Q = a \cdot b + a \cdot c$. Both processes can generate traces $\langle a, b \rangle$ and $\langle a, c \rangle$. However, in process $P$ the choice between $b$ and $c$ is made after the occurrence of $a$, whereas in $Q$ this choice is made upfront, that is, before the concurrence of $a$. To understand that such differences are relevant replace $a, b$, and $c$ by "take exam," "pass," and "fail," respectively.

Also in the context of services soundness-like properties have been investigated [117, 134–144]. These techniques focus on uncovering problems related to interactions between different parties or services. For example, one service is waiting for the other service to make the first move and vice versa. Note that one can easily design services that cannot interoperate with any other service. The approach using the so-called operating guidelines [144] computes a finite characterization of all partner services, that is, services that can interoperate well with a given service.

Configurable models represent families of process models [46, 47, 145–147]. A configurable model can be configured to obtain a *specific* process model that is subsequently used to handle individual cases, for instance, to process customer orders. Various configurable languages have been proposed as extensions of existing languages (e.g., C-EPCs [46], C-iEPCs [146], C-WF-nets [148], C-SAP, and C-BPEL [47]) but few are actually supported by enactment software (e.g., C-YAWL [47]). Process configuration is notoriously difficult as there may be all kinds of interdependencies between configuration decisions. In fact, an incorrect configuration may lead to behavioral issues such as deadlocks and livelocks. The approach presented in [148] derives propositional logic constraints from configurable process models that, if satisfied by a configuration step, guarantee the behavioral correctness of the configured model. The approach in [51] ensures this by using partner synthesis: for a configurable process model a finite representation of all correct configurations is generated.

There are various tools to verify process/workflow models. A classical example is Woflan that is tailored towards checking soundness [149]. Also workflow systems such as YAWL [150] provide verification capabilities [68]. The tool Wendy [151] is an example of a tool tailored towards partner synthesis. See [55, 124] for a comparative evaluation of several verification tools checking soundness-related properties.

Obviously, model-based analysis is not limited to correctness. In fact, from a management point of view, performance analysis is more relevant. The performance of a process or organization can be defined in different ways. Typically, three dimensions of performance are identified: *time, cost,* and *quality*. For each of these performance dimensions different *Key Performance Indicators* (KPIs) can be defined. When

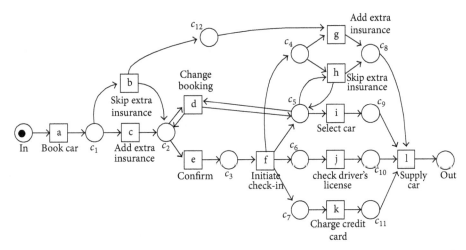

FIGURE 23: A WF-net that is not sound: activity $d$ is dead (can never be executed), cases may deadlock in the state with a token in $c4$, $c9$, $c10$, and $c11$, and a token may be left behind in place $c12$.

looking at the *time dimension* the following performance indicators can be identified.

(i) The *lead time* (also referred to as flow time) is the total time from the creation of the case to the completion of the case. In terms of a WF-net, this is the time it takes to go from source place to sink place. One can measure the average lead time over all cases. However, the degree of variance may also be important; that is, it makes a difference whether all cases take more or less two weeks or if some take just a few hours, whereas others take more than one month. The *service level* is the percentage of cases having a lead time lower than some threshold value, for example, the percentage of cases handled within two weeks.

(ii) The *service time* is the time actually worked on a case. One can measure the service time per activity (e.g., the average time needed to make a decision is 35 minutes) or for the entire case. Note that in case of concurrency the overall service time (i.e., summing up the times spent on the various activities) may be longer than the lead time. However, typically the service time is just a fraction of the lead time (minutes versus weeks).

(iii) The *waiting time* is the time a case is waiting for a resource to become available. This time can be measured per activity or for the case as a whole. An example is the waiting time for a customer who wants to talk to a sales representative. Another example is the time a patient needs to wait before getting a knee operation. Again one may be interested in the average or variance of waiting times. It is also possible to focus on a service level, for example, the percentage of patients that have a knee operation within three weeks after the initial diagnosis.

(iv) The *synchronization time* is the time an activity is not yet fully enabled and waiting for an external trigger or another parallel branch. The time the case is partially

enabled (i.e., waiting for synchronization rather than an available resource) is counted as synchronization time.

Performance indicators can also be defined for the *cost dimension*. Different costing models can be used, for example, Activity-Based Costing (ABC), Time-Driven ABC, and Resource Consumption Accounting (RCA) [152]. The costs of executing an activity may be fixed or depend on the type of resource used, its utilization, or the duration of the activity. Resource costs may depend on the utilization of resources. A key performance indicator in most processes is the *average utilization* of resources over a given period; for example, an operating room in a hospital has been used 85% of the time over the last two months.

The *quality dimension* typically focuses on the "product" or "service" delivered to the customer. Like costs, this can be measured in different ways. One example is customer satisfaction measured through questionnaires. Another example is the average number of complaints per case or the number of product defects.

Whereas verification focuses on the (logical) correctness of the modeled process, performance analysis aims at improving processes with respect to time, cost, or quality. Within the context of operations' management many analysis techniques have been developed [153–156]. Some of these techniques "optimize" the model given a particular performance indicator. For example, integer programming or Markov decision problems can be used to find optimal policies. For typical BPM problems "what if" analyses using simulation, queueing models, or Markov models are often most appropriate. Analytical models typically require many assumptions and can only be used to answer particular questions. Therefore, one often needs to resort to *simulation*. Most BPM tools provide simulation capabilities.

Although many organizations have tried to use simulation to analyze their business processes at some stage, few are using simulation in a structured and effective manner. This may be caused by a lack of training and limitations of existing tools. However, there are also several additional and more fundamental problems. First of all, simulation models tend to *oversimplify* things. In particular the behavior of resources is often modeled in a rather naïve manner. People do not work at constant speeds and need to distribute their attention over multiple processes. This can have dramatic effects on the performance of a process and, therefore, such aspects should not be "abstracted away" [157, 158]. Second, various *artifacts readily available are not used as input for simulation*. Modern organizations store events in logs and some may have accurate process models stored in their WFM/BPM systems. Also note that in many organizations, the state of the information system accurately reflects the state of the business processes supported by this system. Nevertheless, such information (i.e., event logs and status data) is rarely used for simulation or a lot of manual work is needed to feed this information into the model. Third, the focus of simulation is mainly on "design" whereas managers would also like to use simulation for "*operational decision making*," that is, solving the concrete problem at hand rather than some abstract future problem. Fortunately, *short-term simulation* [157] can provide answers for questions related to "here and now." The key idea is to start all simulation runs from the current state and focus on the analysis of the transient behavior. This way, a "fast forward button" into the future, is provided [8, 157].

Verification and performance analysis heavily rely on the availability of high-quality models. When the models and reality have little in common, model-based analysis does not make much sense. For example, some process model may be internally consistent and satisfy all kinds of desirable properties. However, if the model describes a highly idealized version of reality, it may be useless for governance and auditing purposes as in reality all kinds of deviations may take place. Similar comments hold for simulation models. It may be that the model predicts a significant improvement, whereas in reality this is not the case because the model is based on flawed assumptions. All of these problems stem from *a lack of alignment between handmade models and reality*. Process mining, discussed next, aims to address these problems by establishing a direct connection between the models and actual low-level event data about the process.

*5.4. Process Mining.* As information systems are becoming more and more intertwined with the operational processes they support, multitudes of events are recorded by these systems. The goal of *process mining* is to use such event data to extract process-related information, for example, to automatically discover a process model by observing events recorded by some system or to check the conformance of a given model by comparing it with reality [8, 159]. This provides new means to improve processes in a variety of application domains. There are two main drivers for this new technology. On the one hand, more and more events are being recorded thus providing detailed information about the history of processes. On the other hand, vendors of Business Process Management (BPM) and Business Intelligence (BI) software have been promising miracles. Although BPM and

BI technologies received lots of attention, they did not live up to the expectations raised by academics, consultants, and software vendors. Hence, despite the omnipresence of event data, most organizations diagnose problems based on fiction rather than facts.

Process mining is an emerging discipline providing comprehensive sets of tools to provide fact-based insights and to support process improvements [8, 160]. This new discipline builds on process model-driven approaches and data mining. However, process mining is much more than an amalgamation of existing approaches. For example, existing data mining techniques are too data centric to provide a comprehensive understanding of the end-to-end processes in an organization. BI tools focus on simple dashboards and reporting rather than clear-cut business process insights. BPM suites heavily rely on experts modeling idealized to-be processes and do not help the stakeholders to understand the as-is processes.

Figure 24 shows the *process mining framework* described in [8]. The top of the diagram shows an external "world" consisting of business processes, people, and organizations supported by some information system. The information system records information about this "world" in such a way that events logs can be extracted. The term *provenance* used in Figure 24 emphasizes the systematic, reliable, and trustworthy recording of events. The term provenance originates from scientific computing, where it refers to the data that is needed to be able to reproduce an experiment [42, 161]. *Business process provenance* aims to systematically collect the information needed to reconstruct what has actually happened in a process or organization [162]. When organizations base their decisions on event data it is essential to make sure that these describe history well. Moreover, from an auditing point of view it is necessary to ensure that event logs cannot be tampered with. Business process provenance refers to the set of activities needed to ensure that history, as captured in event logs, "cannot be rewritten or obscured" such that it can serve as a reliable basis for process improvement and auditing.

As shown in Figure 24, event data can be partitioned into "*premortem*" and "*postmortem*" event logs. "Postmortem" event data refer to information about cases that have completed; that is, these data can be used for process improvement and auditing, but not for influencing the cases they refer to. "Premortem" event data refer to cases that have not yet completed. If a case is still running, that is, the case is still "alive" (premortem), then it may be possible that information in the event log about this case (i.e., current data) can be exploited to ensure the correct or efficient handling of this case.

"Postmortem" event data are most relevant for *offline process mining*, for example, discovering the control flow of a process based on one year of event data. For *online process mining* mixtures of "premortem" (current) and "postmortem" (historic) data are needed. For example, historic information can be used to learn a predictive model. Subsequently, information about a running case is combined with the predictive model to provide an estimate for the remaining flow time of the case.

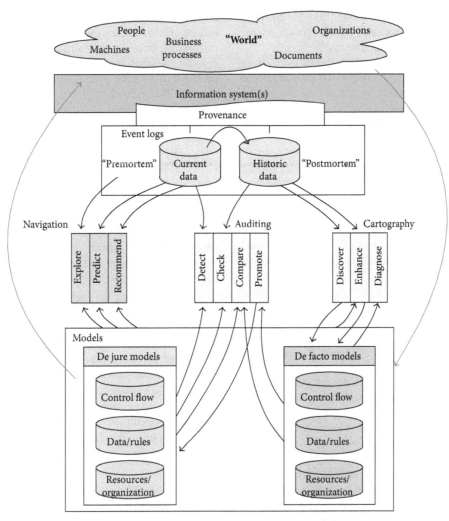

FIGURE 24: Overview of the process mining spectrum.

The process mining framework described in [8] also distinguishes between two types of models: "*de jure models*" and "*de facto models*." *A de jure model is normative*; that is, it specifies how things should be done or handled. For example, a process model used to configure a BPM system is normative and forces people to work in a particular way. *A de facto model is descriptive* and its goal is not to steer or control reality. Instead, de facto models aim to capture reality. As shown in Figure 24 both de jure and de facto models may cover multiple perspectives including the *control-flow perspective* ("How?"), the *organizational perspective* ("Who?"), and the *case perspective* ("What?"). The control-flow perspective describes the ordering of activities. The organizational perspective describes resources (worker, machines, customers, services, etc.) and organizational entities (roles, departments, positions, etc.). The case perspective describes data and rules.

In the middle of Figure 24 ten process mining-related activities are depicted. These ten activities are grouped into three categories: *cartography*, *auditing*, and *navigation*. The activities in the cartography category aim at making "process maps." The activities in the auditing category all involve a de jure model that is confronted with reality in the form of event data or a de facto model. The activities in the navigation category aim at improving a process while it is running.

Activity *discover* in Figure 24 responds to use case DiscM (discover model from event data) described earlier. Lion's share of process mining research has been devoted to this activity [8, 163]. A discovery technique takes an event log and produces a model without using any additional a priori information. An example is the $\alpha$-algorithm [44] that takes an event log and produces a Petri net explaining the behavior recorded in the log. If the event log contains information about resources, one can also discover resource-related models, for example, a social network showing how people work together in an organization.

Since the mid-nineties several groups have been working on techniques for process discovery [44, 160, 164–169]. In [170] an overview is given of the early work in this domain. The idea to apply process mining in the context of workflow management systems was introduced in [164]. In parallel, Datta [166] looked at the discovery of business process models. Cook and Wolf investigated similar issues in the context of software engineering processes [165]. Herbst [171] was one of the first to tackle more complicated processes, for example, processes containing duplicate tasks.

Most of the classical approaches have problems dealing with concurrency. The $\alpha$-algorithm [44] is an example of a simple technique that takes concurrency as a starting point. However, this simple algorithm has problems dealing with complicated routing constructs and noise (like most of the other approaches described in the literature). Process discovery is very challenging because techniques need to balance four criteria: *fitness* (the discovered model should allow for the behavior seen in the event log), *precision* (the discovered model should not allow for behavior completely unrelated to what was seen in the event log), *generalization* (the discovered model should generalize the example behavior seen in the event log), and *simplicity* (the discovered model should be as simple as possible). This makes process discovery a challenging and highly relevant research topic.

Activity *enhance* in Figure 24 corresponds to use cases RepM (repair model) and ExtM (extend model). When existing process models (either discovered or handmade) can be related to events logs, it is possible to enhance these models. The connection can be used to repair models [53] or to extend them [172–175].

Activity *diagnose* in Figure 24 does not directly use event logs and focuses on classical model-based process analysis as discussed in Section 5.3.

Activity *detect* compares de jure models with current "premortem" data (events of running process instances) with the goal to detect deviations at run time. The moment a predefined rule is violated, an alert is generated [176–178].

Activity *check* in Figure 24 refers to use case ConfED (check conformance using event data). Historic "postmortem" data can be cross-checked with de jure models. The goal of this activity is to pinpoint deviations and quantify the level of compliance. Various conformance checking techniques have been proposed in the literature [179–188]. For example, in [187] the fitness of a model is computed by comparing the number of missing and remaining tokens with the number of consumed and produced tokens during replay. The most sophisticated technique described in [179–181] creates the so-called *alignment* which relates a trace in the event log to an execution sequence of the model that is as similar as possible. Ideally, the alignment consists of steps where log and model agree on the activity to be executed. Steps where just the model "makes a move" or just the log "makes a move" have a predefined penalty. This way the computation of fitness can be turned into an optimization problem: for each trace in the event log an alignment with the lowest costs is selected. The resulting alignments can be used for all kinds of analysis since any trace in the event log is related to an execution sequence of the model. For example, timestamps in the model can be used to compute bottlenecks and extend the model with performance information (see activity *enhance* in Figure 24).

Activity *compare* highlights differences and commonalities between a de jure model and a de facto model. Traditional equivalence notions such as trace equivalence, bisimilarity, and branching bisimilarity [132, 133] can only be used

to determine equivalence using a predefined equivalence notion; for example, these techniques cannot be used to distinguish between very similar and highly dissimilar processes. Other notions such a graph-edit distance tend to focus on the syntax rather than the behavior of models. Therefore, recent BPM research explored various alternative similarity notions [56, 189–193]. Also note the *Greatest Common Divisor* (GCD) and *Least Common Multiple* (LCM) notions defined for process models in [194]. The GCD captures the common parts of two or more models. The LCM embeds all input models. We refer to [189] for a survey and empirical evaluation of some similarity notions.

Activity *promote* takes (parts of) de facto models and converts these into (parts of) de jure models; that is, models used to control or support processes are improved based on models learned from event data. By promoting proven "best practices" to de jure models, existing processes can be improved.

The activities in the cartography and auditing categories in Figure 24 can be viewed as "backward looking." The last three activities forming the navigation category are "forward-looking" and are sometimes referred to as *operational support* [8]. For example, process mining techniques can be used to make predictions about the future of a particular case and guide the user in selecting suitable actions. When comparing this with a car navigation system from TomTom or Garmin, this corresponds to functionalities such predicting the arrival time and guiding the driver using spoken instructions.

Activity *explore* in Figure 24 visualizes running cases and compares these cases with similar cases that were handled earlier. The combination of event data and models can be used to explore business processes at run time and, if needed, trigger appropriate actions.

By combining information about running cases with models (discovered or handmade), it is possible to make predictions about the future, for example, predicting the remaining flow time or the probability of success. Figure 24 shows that activity *predict* uses current data and models (often learned over historic data). Various techniques have been proposed in BPM literature [195–197]. Note that already a decade ago Staffware provided a so-called "prediction engine" using simulation [198].

Activity *recommend* in Figure 24 aims to provide functionality similar to the guidance given by car navigation systems. The information used for predicting the future can also be used to recommend suitable actions (e.g., to minimize costs or time) [176, 199]. Given a set of possible next steps, the most promising step is recommended. For each possible step, simply assume that the step is made and predict the resulting performance (e.g., remaining flow time). The resulting predictions can be compared and used to rank the possible next steps.

The ten activities in Figure 24 illustrate that process mining extends far beyond process discovery. The increasing availability and growing volume of event data suggest that the importance of process mining will continue to grow in the coming years.

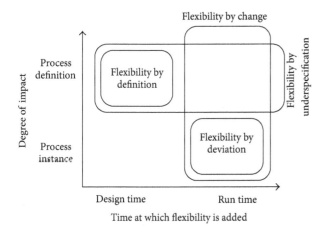

FIGURE 25: Taxonomy of process flexibility identifying four main flexibility types: flexibility by *definition*, flexibility by *deviation*, flexibility by *underspecification*, and flexibility by *change*.

*5.5. Process Flexibility.* Effective business processes must be able to accommodate changes in the environment in which they operate, for example, new laws, changes in business strategy, or emerging technologies. The ability to encompass such changes is termed *process flexibility* and is definitely a key concern of BPM as reflected by various publications [200–207]. Modern processes and information systems need to be able to deal with both foreseen and unforeseen changes. This quality of a process—termed flexibility—reflects its ability to deal with such changes, by varying or adapting those parts of the business process that are affected by them, whilst retaining the essential format of those parts that are not impacted by the variations. Indeed, flexibility is as much about what should stay the same in a process as what should be allowed to change [208, 209].

In [209] a taxonomy of process flexibility is presented. The taxonomy identifies four main flexibility types: flexibility by *definition*, flexibility by *deviation*, flexibility by *underspecification*, and flexibility by *change* (cf. Figure 25).

*Flexibility by definition* is the ability to incorporate alternative execution paths within a process definition at design time such that selection of the most appropriate execution path can be made at runtime for each process instance. For example, an XOR-split defined at design time adds the ability to select one or more activities for subsequent execution from a set of available activities. Parallelism defined at design time leaves the actual ordering of activities open and thus provides more flexibility than sequential routing. All WFM/BPM systems support this type of flexibility. However, declarative languages make it easier to defer choices to runtime.

The classical workflow patterns mentioned earlier [9, 91] can be viewed as a classification of "flexibility by definition" mechanisms for procedural languages. For example, the "deferred choice" pattern [9] leaves the resolution of a choice to the environment at runtime. Note that a so-called "flower place" in a Petri net, that is, a place with many transitions that have this place as only input and output place, provides a lot of flexibility. Also declarative languages like Declare [70, 71] can be used to provide a lot of flexibility at runtime. (As discussed

in Section 5.1, declarative models use an "outside-to-inside" approach: anything is possible unless explicitly forbidden).

*Flexibility by deviation* is the ability for a process instance to deviate at runtime from the execution path prescribed by the original process without altering the process definition itself. The deviation can only encompass changes to the execution sequence for a specific process instance and does not require modifications of the process definition. Typical deviations are *undo*, *redo*, and *skip*.

The BPM|one system of Perceptive/Lexmark (based on the FLOWer system developed by Pallas Athena) is a system that provides various mechanisms for deviations at runtime. The case handling paradigm [200] supported by BPM|one allows the user to skip or redo activities (if not explicitly forbidden and assuming the user is authorized to do so). Moreover, data can be entered earlier or later because the state is continuously recomputed based on the available data.

*Flexibility by underspecification* is the ability to execute an incomplete process specification, that is, a model that does not contain sufficient information to allow it to be executed to completion. An incomplete process specification contains one or more so-called *placeholders*. These placeholders are nodes which are marked as underspecified (i.e., "holes" in the specification) and whose content is specified during the execution of the process. The manner in which these placeholders are ultimately enacted is determined by applying one of the following approaches: *late binding* (the implementation of a placeholder is selected from a set of available process fragments) or *late modeling* (a new process fragment is constructed in order to complete a given placeholder). For late binding, a process fragment has to be selected from an existing set of fully predefined process fragments. This approach is limited to selection and does not allow a new process fragment to be constructed. For late modeling, a new process fragment can be developed from scratch or composed from existing process fragments.

In the context of YAWL [150], the so-called *worklets* approach [201] has been developed which allows for late binding and late modeling. Late binding is supported through the so-called "ripple-down rules," that is, based on context information the user can be guided to selecting a suitable fragment. In [210] the term "pockets of flexibility" was introduced to refer to the placeholder for change. In [211] an explicit notion of "vagueness" is introduced in the context of process modeling. The authors propose model elements such as arc conditions and task ordering to be deliberately omitted from models in the early stages of modeling. Moreover, parts of the process model can be tagged as "incomplete" or "unspecified."

*Flexibility by change* is the ability to modify a process definition at run time such that one or all of the currently executing process instances are migrated to a new process definition. Changes may be introduced both at the process instance and the process type levels. A *momentary change* (also known as change at the instance level) is a change affecting the execution of one or more selected process instances. An example of a momentary change is the postponement of registering a patient that has arrived to the hospital emergency center: treatment is started immediately rather than spending time on formalities first. Such a momentary change performed on a given process instance does not affect any future instances. An *evolutionary change* (also known as change at the type level) is a change caused by modification of the process definition, potentially affecting all new process instances. A typical example of the evolutionary change is the redesign of a business process to improve the overall performance characteristics by allowing for more concurrency. Running process instances that are impacted by an evolutionary or a momentary change need to be handled properly. If a running process instance is transferred to the new process, then there may not be a corresponding state (called the "dynamic change bug" in [203]).

Flexibility by change is very challenging and has been investigated by many researchers. The ability to adapt the structure of running workflow was investigated in the context of the WASA system [207]. In the context of the ADEPT system, flexibility by change has been examined in detail [205, 206]. This work shows that changes can introduce all kinds of anomalies (missing data, deadlocks, double work, etc.). For example, it is difficult to handle both momentary changes and evolutionary changes at the same time, for instance, an ad hoc change made for a specific instance may be affected by a later change at the type level. The declarative workflow system Declare has been extended to support both evolutionary and momentary changes [204] thus illustrating that a declarative style of model simplifies the realization of all kinds of flexibility support.

See also [40, 208, 210, 212–215] for other classifications of flexibility.

*5.6. Process Reuse.* BPM initiatives within larger organizations resulted in collections of hundreds or even thousands of process models. Such large collections of process models provide new challenges, sometimes referred to as "BPM-in-the-large" [216]. A recent survey [217] shows that since 2005 there has been a growing research interest in the management of large collections of business process models. The survey also refers to examples of large collections, for example, Suncorp's process model repository containing more than 6,000 insurance-related processes. Organizations having hundreds or thousands of process models often have problems maintaining these models. Some models may be outdated, parts of models may have been duplicated, and due to mergers there may be different models for similar or even identical processes. Reuse is limited; that is, even though many processes share activities, subprocesses, and organizational entities, processes are often modeled from scratch. BPM research aims to support the reuse of process modeling efforts.

Process model repositories allow for the storage and retrieval of process models. Most business process modeling tools, for example, tools like ARIS [218, 219], provide such facilities. The well-known SAP reference model consisting of over 600 nontrivial process models (expressed in terms of EPCs) has been distributed with the ARIS toolset. A more recent initiative is APROMORE [220, 221], an advanced process model repository providing a rich set of features for the analysis, management, and usage of large sets of process models.

Figure 26 shows various activities related to the management of large collections of business process models stored in some repository.

Activity *search* in Figure 26 refers to use case SelM (select model from collection). Given a query, a set of models is returned. The returned models are often ranked based on some metric (e.g., similarity or popularity). The query may refer to *syntax* (i.e., structure and labels) or *behavior*. Example queries referring to only the syntax are "Find all process models that contain both activities $X$ and $Y$," "Find all process models containing activities executed by people having role $R$," and "Find all process models containing activities accessing data element $D$." An example of a query that also refers to behavior is "Find all process models where activity $X$ is always followed by $Y$." Sometimes behavior can be derived from the syntax, for example, for free-choice nets [116, 130]. Queries referring to behavior typically use some temporal logic, for example, LTL with standard temporal operators such as always ($\Box$), eventually ($\Diamond$), until ($\sqcup$), weak until ($W$), and next time ($\circ$) [72, 73]. Such queries can be formulated graphically using a language like Declare [70, 71]. Another query language is the Business Process Model Notation Query (BPMN-Q) language [222]. BPMN-Q can be used to define patterns using an extension of the BPMN syntax. Both Declare and BPMN-Q can also be used for compliance checking.

A *model similarity search* [56, 189–191] is a particular query looking for the model most similar to a given model. For model similarity searches both syntax and behavior can be used. For example, given one model one may want to find another model that has the smallest edit distance (i.e., the number of atomic edit operation to convert one model into another model). However, two behavioral equivalent models may have many different syntactical differences. Therefore, various approaches consider (an abstraction of) behavior. Since it is often intractable to compare state spaces or execution sequences, these approaches use abstractions of models such as direct succession [8] or eventual succession [189, 223].

Queries can refer to multiple perspectives. However, current research seems to focus on control-flow-related queries.

Activity *merge* in Figure 26 corresponds to use cases MerM (merge models) and MerCM (merge models into configurable model). A set of models is merged into a single model that captures (most of) the behavior of the original models. For example, in [224] models of ten Dutch municipalities are merged into configurable process models [46, 47, 146]. Different techniques for process model merging have been proposed in the literature [145, 225–227]. When merging process models it is interesting to analyze commonalities and differences. In the context of inheritance of dynamic behavior, notions such as the Greatest Common Divisor (GCD) and Least Common Multiple (LCM) of process model variants have been defined [194]. When merging models it is often not sufficient to just consider the syntax of the model. Also behavioral issues need to be considered. For example, a

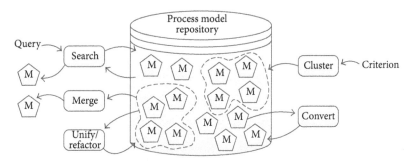

FIGURE 26: Overview of the main activities related to the management of large process model collections.

sequential process may be embedded in a more concurrent model.

In [227] three requirements are listed for model merging. First of all, the behavior of the merged model should subsume the behaviors of all input models. Any execution sequence possible in one of the original models should be possible according to the merged model (possibly after configuration). Second, it should be possible to trace back each element in the merged model. For example, for each activity in the merged model it should be indicated from which of the input models it originated. Third, given the merged model it should be possible to reconstruct each of the input models; that is, each of the input models should correspond to a configuration of the resulting merged model. For example, in Figure 9 the two input models can be reconstructed from the configurable model by selecting appropriate configurations.

The approaches described in [145, 224–227] produce configurable process models [46, 47, 146]. In [228, 229] an approach is presented that does not produce a configurable model and does not aim to address the three requirements listed in [227]. This approach produces a model that has the smallest edit distance to all original models; that is, modification rather than configuration is used to create process model variants.

Activity *cluster* in Figure 26 aims to identify a set of related process models. For example, models may be clustered in groups based on similarity search [189]. Clusters of related models may be used as input for merging, unification, or refactoring.

Activity *unify/refactor* in Figure 26 takes a set of models as input and aims to improve these models by aligning them, removing redundancies, and applying modeling conventions consistently. Note that large collections of process models often have overlapping process fragments without explicitly reusing parts. Shared subprocesses may be modeled differently, models may use different conventions, and there may be different versions of the same processes. Model similarity search can be used to identify possible redundancies before adding a new model.

Activity *convert* in Figure 26 refers to the various mappings from one notation to another notation. As described in use case RefM (refine model) a conceptual model may be converted into an executable model. It may also be converted into a formal model that allows for analysis. Often a repository contains models using different formats

while referring to the same process. It is far from trivial to keep all of these models consistent, for example, changes in the conceptual model should be reflected in the executable model.

A general problem affecting all activities in Figure 26 is the use for informal text. The same activity may be labeled "approve claim" in one process and "evaluate insurance claim" in another. As a result the correspondence between both activities may be missed and redundancies and inconsistencies remain unnoticed. To determine the similarity between activity names in different models one can use naïve approaches such as the string edit distance [230] or linguistic similarity (e.g., similarity based on WordNet [231]). However, it is better to use a common ontology. Semantic technologies [232] aim to address obvious problems related to string edit distance and linguistic similarity. However, in practice, few process model collections use a common ontology. Therefore, in most cases, semantical annotations still need to be added to process models before being able to use semantic technologies.

*5.7. Evolution of Key Concerns in BPM Conference Proceedings.* As for the use cases, the papers in [26–34, 36] were tagged with one, or sometimes more, key concerns [54]. A total of 342 tags were assigned to the 289 papers (1.18 tag per paper on average). The tags were used to determine the relative frequencies listed in Table 2. For example, for BPM 2010 four papers were tagged with key concern *process reuse*. The total number of tags for BPM 2010 is 25. Hence, the relative frequency is 4/25 = 0.16. The bottom row gives the average relative frequency of each concern over all 10 years.

Figure 27 shows the average relative frequency of each concern in a graphical manner. As expected, the first three concerns are most frequent. The fourth and sixth concern (process mining and process reuse) are gaining importance, whereas the relative frequency of the process flexibility concern seems to decrease over time (see Figure 28).

It should be noted that the tagging of the 289 papers with use cases and key concerns is highly subjective. It is unlikely that two BPM experts would use precisely the same tags for all papers. For example, to tag a paper one needs to decide what the key contribution of the paper is. Many papers are rather broad and difficult to classify. For example, papers on topics such as "Social BPM," "BPM Maturity," "BPM in Healthcare," and "BPM Security" cannot be tagged easily, because these

TABLE 2: Relative importance of concerns over the years.

| Year | Process modeling languages | Process enactment infrastructures | Process model analysis | Process mining | Process flexibility | Process reuse |
|---|---|---|---|---|---|---|
| 2000 | 0.355 | 0.161 | 0.290 | 0.000 | 0.161 | 0.032 |
| 2003 | 0.325 | 0.200 | 0.250 | 0.050 | 0.075 | 0.100 |
| 2004 | 0.286 | 0.238 | 0.238 | 0.143 | 0.048 | 0.048 |
| 2005 | 0.288 | 0.231 | 0.212 | 0.058 | 0.096 | 0.115 |
| 2006 | 0.154 | 0.308 | 0.288 | 0.096 | 0.077 | 0.077 |
| 2007 | 0.387 | 0.097 | 0.194 | 0.194 | 0.065 | 0.065 |
| 2008 | 0.324 | 0.108 | 0.297 | 0.135 | 0.081 | 0.054 |
| 2009 | 0.148 | 0.111 | 0.370 | 0.222 | 0.037 | 0.111 |
| 2010 | 0.240 | 0.240 | 0.200 | 0.160 | 0.000 | 0.160 |
| 2011 | 0.143 | 0.171 | 0.200 | 0.314 | 0.000 | 0.171 |
| Average | 0.265 | 0.187 | 0.254 | 0.137 | 0.064 | 0.093 |

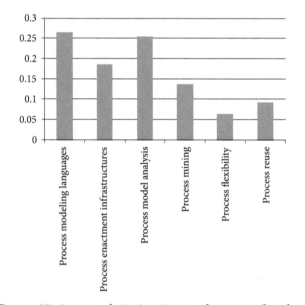

FIGURE 27: Average relative importance of concerns (based on Table 2).

topics seem orthogonal to the use cases and key concerns. This explains why broad use cases like *design model* (DecM) and *enact model* (EnM) score relatively high.

The key concerns were identified before tagging the papers [54]. In hindsight there seem to be at least three potentially missing concerns: *process integration*, *patterns*, and *collaboration*. Many papers are concerned with web services and other technologies (e.g., SaaS, PaaS, clouds, and grids) to integrate processes. These are now tagged as *process enactment infrastructures* (second concern). In the BPM proceedings there are various papers proposing new patterns collections or evaluating existing languages using the well-known workflow patterns [9, 24]. These are now tagged as *process modeling languages* (first concern). Another recurring concern seems to be collaboration, for example, collaborative modeling or system development.

Given a process, different *perspectives* can be considered. the *control-flow* perspective ("What activities need to be executed and how are they ordered?"), the *organizational* perspective ("What are the organizational roles, which activities can be executed by a particular resource, and how is work distributed?"), the *case/data* perspective ("Which characteristics of a case influence a particular decision?"), and the *time* perspective ("What are the bottlenecks in my process?"), and so forth. The use cases and key concerns are neutral/orthogonal with respect to these perspectives. Although most papers focus on the control-flow perspective, there are several papers that focus on the organizational perspective, for example, papers dealing with optimal resource allocations or role-based access control. It would have been useful to add additional tags to papers based on the perspectives considered.

Despite these limitations, Tables 1 and 2 provide a nice overview of developments in the BPM discipline. Comparing papers published in the early BPM proceedings with papers published in more recent BPM proceedings clearly shows that the BPM discipline progressed at a remarkable speed. The understanding of process modeling languages improved and analysis techniques have become much more powerful.

## 6. Outlook

Over the last decade there has been a growing interest in Business Process Management (BPM). Practitioners have been using BPM technologies to model, improve, and enact business processes. Today, a plethora of BPM systems and tools is available. Academics have been developing new techniques and approaches to support more advanced forms of BPM. This survey describes the state-of-the-art in BPM. The BPM discipline has been structured in various ways and developments have been put in their historic context. The core of the survey is based on a set of twenty BPM use cases and six BPM key concerns. The use cases show "how, where, and when" BPM techniques can be used. The six key concerns highlight important research areas within the BPM discipline.

TABLE 3: Relation between the twenty use cases and six key concerns (+ = related and ++ = strongly related).

| Use case | Process modeling languages | Process enactment infrastructures | Process model analysis | Process mining | Process flexibility | Process reuse |
|---|---|---|---|---|---|---|
| Design model (DesM) | ++ | | + | | + | |
| Discover model from event data (DiscM) | | | | ++ | | |
| Select model from collection (SelM) | | | | | | ++ |
| Merge models (MerM) | | | | | | ++ |
| Compose model (CompM) | | | | | | + |
| Design configurable model (DesCM) | + | | | | | ++ |
| Merge models into configurable model (MerCM) | | | | | | ++ |
| Configure configurable model (ConCM) | | | | | | ++ |
| Refine model (RefM) | + | + | | | | + |
| Enact model (EnM) | + | ++ | | | + | |
| Log event data (LogED) | | + | | ++ | | |
| Monitor (Mon) | | + | | + | | |
| Adapt while running (AdaWR) | | + | | | ++ | |
| Analyze performance based on model (PerfM) | | | ++ | | | |
| Verify model (VerM) | | | ++ | | | + |
| Check conformance using event data (ConfED) | | | | ++ | | |
| Analyze performance using event data (PerfED) | | | | ++ | | |
| Repair model (RepM) | | | | ++ | | |
| Extend model (ExtM) | | | | ++ | | |
| Improve model (ImpM) | | | ++ | + | | |

Table 3 relates the BPM use cases and BPM key concerns. As shown, the six key concerns cover the twenty use cases well.

The BPM discipline has developed at an amazing speed. However, a careful analysis of BPM literature also reveals some weaknesses.

Many papers introduce a new modeling language. The need for such new languages is often unclear, and, in many cases, the proposed language is never used again after publication. A related problem is that many papers spend more time on presenting the context of the problem rather than the actual analysis and solution. For example, there are papers proposing a new verification technique for a language introduced in the same paper. Consequently, the results cannot be used or compared easily.

Many papers cannot be linked to one of the twenty use cases in a straightforward manner. Authors seem to focus on originality rather than relevance and show little concern for real-life use cases. One could argue that some of these papers propose solutions for rather exotic or even nonexisting problems.

Our use-case-based analysis of existing literature shows that various use cases are neglected by both BPM researchers and BPM software. For example, use cases related to improving the performance of processes seem to be neglected. It is remarkable that there are hardly any tools that provide suggestions for redesigning processes. Simulation tools just provide "what-if" analysis without suggesting better alternatives. Moreover, business "intelligence" tools do not use event data to suggest better process designs. The active classification of tools and publications using the use cases may simulate academics and practitioners to focus on process improvement scenarios.

Many papers describe implementation efforts; however, frequently the software is not available for the reader. Moreover, regrettably, many of the research prototypes seem to "disappear" after publication. As a result, research efforts get lost.

Many papers include case studies, for example, to test a new technique or system, which is good. Unfortunately, most case studies seem rather artificial. Often the core contribution of the paper is not really evaluated or the case study is deliberately kept vague.

To address the weaknesses just mentioned, authors and tool developers are encouraged to clearly state which of the BPM use cases their results (algorithms, procedures, tools, etc.) aim to support. The twenty use cases presented in this paper can serve as the starting point for a commonly agreed-upon taxonomy of BPM use cases. The current use cases could be subdivided in more specific ones. Such a structuring would hopefully result in collections of benchmark problems, comparable to the datasets used in data mining and model checking competitions. Practitioners and academics are encouraged to share open-source software and

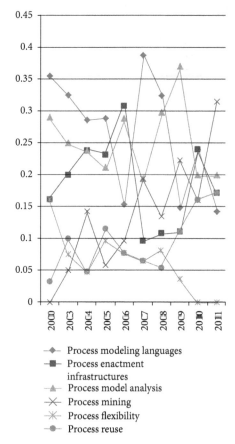

FIGURE 28: The importance of each concern plotted over time thus showing changes in the relative attention for each concern over time (based on Table 2).

data sets (collections of process models, event logs, etc.). Currently, many prototypes are developed from scratch and "fade onto oblivion" when the corresponding research project ends. Moreover, it is often impossible to compare different approaches in a fair manner as experiments are incomparable or cannot be reproduced. Given the importance of BPM, these weaknesses need to be tackled urgently. This survey is a modest attempt to guide BPM research towards the real key challenges in our field.

# References

[1] W. M. P. van der Aalst, "Business process management demystified: a tutorial on models, systems and standards for workflow management," in *Lectures on Concurrency and Petri Nets*, J. Desel, W. Reisig, and G. Rozenberg, Eds., vol. 3098 of *Lecture Notes in Computer Science*, pp. 1–65, Springer-Verlag, Berlin, Germany, 2004.

[2] M. Weske, *Business Process Management: Concepts, Languages, Architectures*, Springer-Verlag, Berlin, Germany, 2007.

[3] W. M. P. van der Aalst, A. H. M. ter Hofstede, and M. Weske, "Business process management: a survey," in *Proceedings of the International Conference on Business Process Management (BPM '03)*, W. M. P. van der Aalst, A. H. M. ter Hofstede, and M. Weske, Eds., vol. 2678 of *Lecture Notes in Computer Science*, pp. 1–12, Springer-Verlag, Berlin, 2003.

[4] W. M. P. van der Aalst and K. M. van Hee, *Workflow Management: Models, Methods, and Systems*, MIT press, Cambridge, Mass, USA, 2004.

[5] S. Jablonski and C. Bussler, *Workflow Management: Modeling Concepts, Architecture, and Implementation*, International Thomson Computer Press, London, UK, 1996.

[6] F. Leymann and D. Roller, *Production Workflow: Concepts and Techniques*, Prentice-Hall, Upper Saddle River, NJ, USA, 1999.

[7] M. Dumas, W. M. P. van der Aalst, and A. H. M. ter Hofstede, *Process-Aware Information Systems: Bridging People and Software through Process Technology*, Wiley & Sons, New York, NY, USA, 2005.

[8] W. M. P. van der Aalst, *Process Mining: Discovery, Conformance and Enhancement of Business Processes*, Springer-Verlag, Berlin, Germany, 2011.

[9] W. M. P. van der Aalst, A. H. M. ter Hofstede, B. Kiepuszewski, and A. P. Barros, "Workflow patterns," *Distributed and Parallel Databases*, vol. 14, no. 1, pp. 5–51, 2003.

[10] M. Zur Muehlen and J. Recker, "How much language is enough? Theoretical and practical use of the business process modeling notation," in *Proceedings of the 20th International Conference on Advanced Information Systems Engineering (CAISE '08)*, Z. Bellahsene and M. L. Leonard, Eds., vol. 5074 of *Lecture Notes in Computer Science*, pp. 465–479, Springer-Verlag, Berlin, Germany, 2008.

[11] E. F. Codd, "A relational model for large shared data banks," *Communications of the ACM*, vol. 13, no. 6, pp. 377–387, 1970.

[12] P. P. Chen, "The entity-relationship model: towards a unified view of data," *ACM Transactions on Database Systems*, vol. 1, pp. 9–36, 1976.

[13] W. M. P. van der Aalst, "The application of Petri nets to workflow management," *Journal of Circuits, Systems and Computers*, vol. 8, no. 1, pp. 21–66, 1998.

[14] C. A. Ellis, "Information control nets: a mathematical model of office information flow," in *Proceedings of the Conference on Simulation, Measurement and Modeling of Computer Systems*, pp. 225–240, ACM Press, Boulder, Colo, USA, 1979.

[15] C. A. Ellis and G. Nutt, "Workflow: The process spectrum," in *Proceedings of the NSF Workshop on workflow and Process Automation in Information Systems*, A. Sheth, Ed., pp. 140–145, Athens, Ga, USA, May 1996.

[16] C. A. Ellis and G. J. Nutt, "Office information systems and computer science," *Computing surveys*, vol. 12, no. 1, pp. 27–60, 1980.

[17] A. W. Holt, "Coordination technology and Petri Nets," in *Advances in Petri Nets*, G. Rozenberg, Ed., vol. 222 of *Lecture Notes in Computer Science*, pp. 278–296, Springer-Verlag, Berlin, Germany, 1985.

[18] A. W. Holt, H. Saint, R. Shapiro, and S. Warshall, "Final report on the information systems theory troject," Tech. Rep. RADC-TR-68-305, Griffiss Air Force Base, New York, NY, USA, 1968.

[19] M. zur Muehlen, *Workflow-Based Process Controlling: Foundation, Design and Application of workflow-driven Process Information Systems*, Logos, Berlin, Germany, 2004.

[20] M. D. Zisman, *Representation, specification and automation of office procedures [Ph.D. thesis]*, University of Pennsylvania, Warton School of Business, Pennsylvania, Pa, USA, 1977.

[21] M. D. Zisman, "Office automation: revolution or evolution," *Sloan Management Review*, vol. 19, no. 3, pp. 1–16, 1978.

[22] M. D. Zisman, "Use of production systems for modeling asynchronous concurrent processes," *Pattern-Directed Inference Systems*, pp. 53–68, 1978.

[23] C. A. Ellis and G. J. Nutt, *Computer Science and Office Information Systems*, Palo Alto Research Center Xerox, Palo Alto, Calif, USA, 1979.

[24] N. Russell, W. M. P. van der Aalst, A. H. M. ter Hofstede, and D. Edmond, "Workflow resource patterns: identification, representation and tool support," in *Proceedings of the 17th International Conference on Advanced Information Systems Engineering (CAiSE '05)*, pp. 216–232, June 2005.

[25] N. Russell, A. H. M. ter Hofstede, D. Edmond, and W. M. P. van der Aalst, "Workflow data patterns: identification, representation and tool support," in *Proceedings of the 24nd International Conference on Conceptual Modeling (ER '05)*, L. Delcambre, C. Kop, H. C. Mayr, J. Mylopoulos, and O. Pastor, Eds., vol. 3716 of *Lecture Notes in Computer Science*, pp. 353–368, Springer-Verlag, Berlin, Germany, 2005.

[26] W. M. P. van der Aalst, A. H. M. ter Hofstede, and M. Weske, Eds., *International Conference on Business Process Management (BPM 2003)*, vol. 2678 of *Lecture Notes in Computer Science*, Springer-Verlag, Berlin, Germany, 2003.

[27] J. Desel, B. Pernici, and M. Weske, Eds., *International Conference on Business Process Management (BPM 2004)*, vol. 3080 of *Lecture Notes in Computer Science*, Springer-Verlag, Berlin, Germany, 2004.

[28] W. M. P. van der Aalst, B. Benatallah, F. Casati, and F. Curbera, Eds., *International Conference on Business Process Management (BPM 2005)*, vol. 3649 of *Lecture Notes in Computer Science*, Springer-Verlag, Berlin, Germany, 2005.

[29] S. Dustdar, J. L. Fiadeiro, and A. Sheth, Eds., *International Conference on Business Process Management (BPM 2006)*, vol. 4102 of *Lecture Notes in Computer Science*, Springer-Verlag, Berlin, Germany, 2006.

[30] G. Alonso, P. Dadam, and M. Rosemann, Eds., *International Conference on Business Process Management (BPM 2007)*, vol. 4714 of *Lecture Notes in Computer Science*, Springer-Verlag, Berlin, Germany, 2007.

[31] M. Dumas, M. Reichert, and M. C. Shan, Eds., *International Conference on Business Process Management (BPM 2008)*, vol. 5240 of *Lecture Notes in Computer Science*, Springer-Verlag, Berlin, Germany, 2008.

[32] U. Dayal, J. Eder, J. Koehler, and H. Reijers, Eds., *International Conference on Business Process Management (BPM 2009)*, vol. 5701 of *Lecture Notes in Computer Science*, Springer-Verlag, Berlin, Germany, 2009.

[33] R. Hull, J. Mendling, and S. Tai, Eds., *International Conference on Business Process Management (BPM 2010)*, vol. 6336 of *Lecture Notes in Computer Science*, Springer-Verlag, Berlin, Germany, 2010.

[34] S. Rinderle, F. Toumani, and K. Wolf, Eds., *International Conference on Business Process Management (BPM 2011)*, vol. 6896 of *Lecture Notes in Computer Science*, Springer-Verlag, Berlin, Germany, 2011.

[35] A. Barros, A. Gal, and E. Kindler, Eds., *International Conference on Business Process Management (BPM 2012)*, vol. 7481 of *Lecture Notes in Computer Science*, Springer-Verlag, Berlin, Germany, 2012.

[36] W. M. P. van der Aalst, J. Desel, and A. Oberweis, Eds., *Business Process Management: Models, Techniques, and Empirical Studies*, vol. 1806 of *Lecture Notes in Computer Science*, Springer-Verlag, Berlin, Germany, 2000.

[37] H. Smith and P. Fingar, *Business Process Management: The Third Wave*, Meghan Kiffer Press, Tampa, Fla, USA, 2006.

[38] A. H. M. ter Hofstede, W. M. P. van der Aalst, M. Adams, and N. Russell, *Modern Business Process Automation: YAWL and its Support Environment*, Springer-Verlag, Berlin, Germany, 2010.

[39] M. Reichert and B. Weber, *Enabling Flexibility in Process-Aware Information Systems: Challenges, Methods, Technologies*, Springer-Verlag, Berlin, Germany, 2012.

[40] D. Georgakopoulos, M. Hornick, and A. Sheth, "An overview of workflow management: from process modeling to workflow automation infrastructure," *Distributed and Parallel Databases*, vol. 3, no. 2, pp. 119–153, 1995.

[41] R. Medina-Mora, T. Winograd, R. Flores, and F. Flores, "Action workflow approach to workflow management technology," in *Proceedings of the Conference on Computer-Supported Cooperative Work (CSCW '92)*, pp. 281–288, 1992.

[42] B. Ludäscher, I. Altintas, C. Berkley et al., "Scientific workflow management and the Kepler system," *Concurrency Computation Practice and Experience*, vol. 18, no. 10, pp. 1039–1065, 2006.

[43] J. Manyika, M. Chui, B. Brown et al., *Big Data: The Next Frontier for Innovation, Competition, and Productivity*, McKinsey Global Institute, 2011.

[44] W. van der Aalst, T. Weijters, and L. Maruster, "Workflow mining: discovering process models from event logs," *IEEE Transactions on Knowledge and Data Engineering*, vol. 16, no. 9, pp. 1128–1142, 2004.

[45] F. Gottschalk, W. M. P. van der Aalst, and H. M. Jansen-Vullers, "Configurable process models: a foundational approach," in *Reference Modeling: Efficient Information Systems Design Through Reuse of Information Models*, J. Becker and P. Delfmann, Eds., pp. 59–78, Physica-Verlag, Springer, Germany, 2007.

[46] M. Rosemann and W. M. P. van der Aalst, "A configurable reference modelling language," *Information Systems*, vol. 32, no. 1, pp. 1–23, 2007.

[47] F. Gottschalk, W. M. P. van der Aalst, M. H. Jansen-Vullers, and M. La Rosa, "Configurable workflow models," *International Journal of Cooperative Information Systems*, vol. 17, no. 2, pp. 177–221, 2008.

[48] T. Curran and G. Keller, *SAP R/3 Business Blueprint: Understanding the Business Process Reference Model*, Prentice Hall, Upper Saddle River, NJ, USA, 1997.

[49] J. Becker, P. Delfmann, and R. Knackstedt, "Adaptive reference modeling: integrating configurative and generic adaptation techniques for information models," in *Reference Modeling: Efficient Information Systems Design through Reuse of Information Models*, J. Becker and P. Delfmann, Eds., pp. 27–58, Physica; Springer, Heidelberg, Germany, 2007.

[50] P. Fettke and P. Loos, "Classification of reference models-a methodology and its application," *Information Systems and e-Business Management*, vol. 1, no. 1, pp. 35–53, 2003.

[51] W. M. P. van der Aalst, N. Lohmann, and M. La Rosa, "Ensuring correctness during process configuration via partner synthesis," *Information Systems*, vol. 37, no. 6, pp. 574–592, 2012.

[52] W. M. P. van der Aalst, K. M. van Hee, A. H. M. ter Hofstede et al., "Soundness of workflow nets: classification, decidability, and analysis," *Formal Aspects of Computing*, vol. 23, no. 3, pp. 333–363, 2011.

[53] D. Fahland and W. M. P. van der Aalst, "Repairing process models to reflect reality," in *Proceedings of the International Conference on Business Process Management (BPM '12)*, A. Barros, A. Gal, and E. Kindler, Eds., vol. 7481 of *Lecture Notes in Computer Science*, pp. 229–245, Springer-Verlag, Berlin, Germany, 2012.

[54] W. M. P. van der Aalst, "A decade of business process management conferences: personal reflections on a developing discipline," in *Proceedings of the International Conference on Business Process Management (BPM '12)*, A. Barros, A. Gal, and E. Kindler, Eds., vol. 7481 of *Lecture Notes in Computer Science*, pp. 1–16, Springer-Verlag, Berlin, Germany, 2012.

[55] D. Fahland, C. Favre, B. Jobstmann et al., "Instantaneous soundness checking of industrial business process models," in *Proceedings of the Business Process Management (BPM '09)*, U. Dayal, J. Eder, J. Koehler, and H. Reijers, Eds., vol. 5701 of *Lecture Notes in Computer Science*, pp. 278–293, Springer-Verlag, Berlin, Germany, 2009.

[56] R. Dijkman, M. Dumas, and L. Garcia-Banuelos, "Graph matching algorithms for business process model similarity search," in *Proceedings of the Business Process Management (BPM '09)*, U. Dayal, J. Eder, J. Koehler, and H. Reijers, Eds., vol. 5701 of *Lecture Notes in Computer Science*, pp. 48–63, Springer-Verlag, Berlin, Germany, 2009.

[57] OMG, *Business Process Model and Notation (BPMN)*, Object Management Group, Needham, Mass, USA, 2011.

[58] S. A. White, A. Agrawal, and M. Anthony, Business Process Modeling Notation (BPML), Version 1.0, 2004.

[59] G. Keller, M. Nüttgens, and A. W. Scheer, *Semantische Process-modellierung auf der Grundlage Ereignisgesteuerter Processketten (EPK). Veröffentlichungen des Instituts für Wirtschaftsinformatik, Heft 89*, University of Saarland, Saarbrücken, Germany, 1992.

[60] G. Keller and T. Teufel, *SAP R/3 Process Oriented Implementation*, Addison-Wesley, Reading, Mass, USA, 1998.

[61] A. W. Scheer, *Business Process Engineering: Reference Models for Industrial Enterprises*, Springer-Verlag, Berlin, Germany, 1994.

[62] A. Alves, A. Arkin, S. Askary et al., Web Services Business Process Execution Language Version 2.0 (OASIS Standard). WS-BPEL TC OASIS http://docs.oasisopen.org/wsbpel/2.0/wsbpel-v2.0.html, 2007.

[63] C. Ouyang, E. Verbeek, W. M. P. van der Aalst, S. Breutel, M. Dumas, and A. H. M. ter Hofstede, "Formal semantics and analysis of control flow in WS-BPEL," *Science of Computer Programming*, vol. 67, no. 2-3, pp. 162–198, 2007.

[64] C. Ouyang, M. Dumas, W. M. P. van der Aalst, A. H. M. ter Hofstede, and J. Mendling, "From business process models to process-oriented software systems," *ACM Transactions on Software Engineering and Methodology*, vol. 19, no. 1, pp. 1–37, 2009.

[65] W. M. P. van der Aalst, "Formalization and verification of event-driven process chains," *Information and Software Technology*, vol. 41, no. 10, pp. 639–650, 1999.

[66] E. Kindler, "On the semantics of EPCs: resolving the vicious circle," *Data and Knowledge Engineering*, vol. 56, no. 1, pp. 23–40, 2006.

[67] H. Völzer, "A new semantics for the inclusive converging gateway in safe processes," in *Proceedings of the Business Process Management (BPM '10)*, R. Hull, J. Mendling, and S. Tai, Eds., vol. 6336 of *Lecture Notes in Computer Science*, pp. 294–309, Springer-Verlag, Berlin, Germany, 2010.

[68] M. T. Wynn, H. M. W. Verbeek, W. M. P. van der Aalst, A. H. M. ter Hofstede, and D. Edmond, "Business process verification: finally a reality!," *Business Process Management Journal*, vol. 15, no. 1, pp. 74–92, 2009.

[69] W. M. P. van der Aalst, J. Desel, and E. Kindler, "On the semantics of EPCs: a vicious circle," in *Proceedings of the EPK 2002: Business Process Management Using EPCs*, M. Nüttgens and F. J. Rump, Eds., pp. 71–80, Gesellschaft fürInformatik, Bonn, Trier, Germany, November 2002.

[70] W. M. P. van der Aalst, M. Pesic, and H. Schonenberg, "Declarative workflows: balancing between flexibility and support," *Computer Science: Research and Development*, vol. 23, no. 2, pp. 99–113, 2009.

[71] M. Montali, M. Pesic, W. M. P. van der Aalst, F. Chesani, P. Mello, and S. Storari, "Declarative specification and verification of service choreographiess," *ACM Transactions on the Web*, vol. 4, no. 1, p. 3, 2010.

[72] E. M. Clarke, O. Grumberg, and D. A. Peled, *Model Checking*, The MIT Press, London, UK, 1999.

[73] Z. Manna and A. Pnueli, *The Temporal Logic of Reactive and Concurrent Systems: Specification*, Springer, New York, NY, USA, 1991.

[74] W. M. P. van der Aalst, P. Barthelmess, C. A. Ellis, and J. Wainer, "Proclets: a framework for lightweight interacting workflow processes," *International Journal of Cooperative Information Systems*, vol. 10, no. 4, pp. 443–481, 2001.

[75] ACSI, Artifact-Centric Service Interoperation (ACSI) Project Home Page, http://www.acsi-project.eu/ .

[76] K. Bhattacharya, C. Gerede, R. Hull, R. Liu, and J. Su, "Towards formal analysis of artifact-centric business process models," in *Proceedings of the International Conference on Business Process Management (BPM '07)*, G. Alonso, P. Dadam, and M. Rosemann, Eds., vol. 4714 of *Lecture Notes in Computer Science*, pp. 288–304, Springer-Verlag, Berlin, Germany, 2007.

[77] D. Cohn and R. Hull, "Business artifacts: a data-centric approach to modeling business operations and processes," *IEEE Data Engineering Bulletin*, vol. 32, no. 3, pp. 3–9, 2009.

[78] D. Fahland, M. De Leoni, B. van Dongen, and W. M. P. van der Aalst, "Many-to-many: some observations on interactions in artifact choreographies," in *Proceedings of the 3rd Central-European Workshop on Services and their Composition (ZEUS '11)*, D. Eichhorn, A. Koschmider, and H. Zhang, Eds., CEUR Workshop Proceedings, 2011, http://ceur-ws.org/.

[79] N. Lohmann, "Compliance by design for artifact-centric business processes," in *Business Process Management BPM*, S. Rinderle, F. Toumani, and K. Wolf, Eds., vol. 6896 of *Lecture Notes in Computer Science*, pp. 99–115, Springer, Berlin, Germany edition, 2011.

[80] A. Nigam and N. S. Caswell, "Business artifacts: an approach to operational specification," *IBM Systems Journal*, vol. 42, no. 3, pp. 428–445, 2003.

[81] J. Mendling, H. A. Reijers, and W. M. P. van der Aalst, "Seven process modeling guidelines (7PMG)," *Information and Software Technology*, vol. 52, no. 2, pp. 127–136, 2010.

[82] M. La Rosa, A. H. M. ter Hofstede, P. Wohed, H. A. Reijers, J. Mendling, and W. M. P. van der Aalst, "Managing process model complexity via concrete syntax modifications," *IEEE Transactions on Industrial Informatics*, vol. 7, no. 2, pp. 255–265, 2011.

[83] M. La Rosa, P. Wohed, J. Mendling, A. H. M. ter Hofstede, H. A. Reijers, and W. M. P. van der Aalst, "Managing process model complexity via abstract syntax modifications," *IEEE Transactions on Industrial Informatics*, vol. 7, no. 4, pp. 614–629, 2011.

[84] A. A. Abdul, G. K. T. Wei, G. M. Muketha, and W. P. Wen, "Complexity metrics for measuring the understandability and maintainability of business process models using goal-

question-metric (GQM)," *International Journal of Computer Science and Network Security*, vol. 8, no. 5, pp. 219–225, 2008.

[85] K. B. Lassen and W. M. P. van der Aalst, "Complexity metrics for workflow nets," *Information and Software Technology*, vol. 51, no. 3, pp. 610–626, 2009.

[86] J. Mendling, H. A. Reijers, and J. Cardoso, "What makes process models understandable?" in *Proceedings of the International Conference on Business Process Management (BPM '07)*, G. Alonso, P. Dadam, and M. Rosemann, Eds., vol. 4714 of *Lecture Notes in Computer Science*, pp. 48–63, Springer-Verlag, Berlin, Germany, 2007.

[87] J. Recker, M. zur Muehlen, K. Siau, J. Erickson, and M. Indulska, "Measuring method complexity: UML versus BPMN," in *Proceedings of the Americas Conference on Information Systems (AMCIS '09)*, pp. 1–12, AIS, 2009.

[88] V. Gruhn and R. Laue, "Reducing the cognitive complexity of business process models," in *2009 8th IEEE International Conference on Cognitive Informatics, ICCI 2009*, pp. 339–345, hkg, June 2009.

[89] A. Streit, B. Pham, and R. Brown, "Visualization support for managing large business process specifications," in *3rd Internaional Conference on Business Process Management, (BPM '05)*, pp. 205–219, 2005.

[90] B. Weber, M. Reichert, J. Mendling, and H. A. Reijers, "Refactoring large process model repositories," *Computers in Industry*, vol. 62, no. 5, pp. 467–486, 2011.

[91] Workflow Patterns, http://www.workflowpatterns.com/.

[92] N. Russell, W. M. P. van der Aalst, and A. H. M. ter Hofstede, "Workflow exception patterns," in *Proceedings of the 18th International Conference on Advanced Information Systems Engineering (CAiSE '06)*, E. Dubois and K. Pohl, Eds., vol. 4001 of *Lecture Notes in Computer Science*, pp. 288–302., Springer-Verlag, Berlin, Germany, 2006.

[93] A. Barros, M. Dumas, and A. ter Hofstede, "Service interaction patterns," in *International Conference on Business Process Management (BPM' 05)*, W. M. P. van der Aalst, B. Benatallah, F. Casati, and F. Curbera, Eds., vol. 3649 of *Lecture Notes in Computer Science*, pp. 302–318, Springer-Verlag, Berlin, Germany, 2005.

[94] B. Weber, M. Reichert, and S. Rinderle-Ma, "Change patterns and change support features: enhancing flexibility in process-aware information systems," *Data and Knowledge Engineering*, vol. 66, no. 3, pp. 438–466, 2008.

[95] L. Fischer, Ed., *Workflow Handbook*, Workflow Management Coalition. Future Strategies, Lighthouse Point, Fla, USA, 2003.

[96] P. Lawrence, Ed., *Workflow Handbook 1997, Workflow Management Coalition*, John Wiley & Sons, New York, NY, USA, 1997.

[97] WFMC, "Workflow management coalition Workflow standard: interface 1-process definition interchange process model," Tech. Rep. WFMC-TC-1016, Workflow Management Coalition, Lighthouse Point, Fla, USA, 1999.

[98] WFMC, "Workflow management coalition Workflow standard: Workflow process definition interface-XML process definition language (XPDL)," Tech. Rep. WFMC-TC-1025, Workflow Management Coalition, Lighthouse Point, Fla, USA, 2002.

[99] T. Andrews, F. Curbera, H. Dholakia et al., Business Process Execution Language for Web Services, Version 1.1. Standards proposal by BEA Systems, International Business Machines Corporation, and Microsoft Corporation, 2003.

[100] F. Leymann, *Web Services Flow Language, Version 1. 0*, 2001.

[101] S. Thatte, *XLANG Web Services for Business Process Design*, 2001.

[102] W. M. P. van der Aalst, "Don't go with the flow: web services composition standards exposed," *IEEE Intelligent Systems*, vol. 18, no. 1, pp. 72–76, 2003.

[103] G. Alonso, F. Casati, H. Kuno, and V. Machiraju, *Web Services Concepts, Architectures and Applications*, Springer-Verlag, Berlin, Germany, 2004.

[104] B. Benatallah, F. Casati, and F. Toumani, "Representing, analysing and managing Web service protocols," *Data and Knowledge Engineering*, vol. 58, no. 3, pp. 327–357, 2006.

[105] F. Casati, E. Shan, U. Dayal, and M. C. Shan, "Business-oriented management of Web services," *Communications of the ACM*, vol. 46, no. 10, pp. 55–60, 2003.

[106] M. P. Papazoglou, P. Traverso, S. Dustdar, and F. Leymann, "Service-oriented computing: a research roadmap," *International Journal of Cooperative Information Systems*, vol. 17, no. 2, pp. 223–255, 2008.

[107] L. J. Zhang, J. Zhang, and H. Cai, *Services Computing, Core Enabling Technology of the Modern Services Industry*, Springer-Verlag, Berlin, Germany, 2007.

[108] G. Hohpe and B. Woolf, *Enterprise Integration Patterns*, Addison-Wesley Professional, Reading, Mass, USA, 2003.

[109] G. Alonso, D. Agrawal, A. El Abbadi, M. Kamath, R. Gunthor, and C. Mohan, "Advanced transaction models in workflow contexts," in *Proceedings of the 12th International Conference on Data Engineering*, IEEE Computer Society, New Orleans, La, USA, March 1996.

[110] D. Kuo, M. Lawley, C. Liu, and M. E. Orlowska, "A general model for nested transactional workflows," in *Proceedings of the International Workshop on Advanced Transaction Models and Architecture (ATMA '96)*, pp. 18–35, Bombay, India, 1996.

[111] A. Reuter and F. Schwenkreis, "ConTracts- a low-level mechanism for building general-purpose workflow management-systems," *Data Engineering Bulletin*, vol. 18, no. 1, pp. 4–10, 1995.

[112] G. Vossen, "Transactional Workflows," in *Proceedings of the 5th International Conference on Deductive and Object-Oriented Databases (DOOD '97)*, F. Bry, R. Ramakrishnan, and K. Ramamohanarao, Eds., vol. 1341 of *Lecture Notes in Computer Science*, pp. 20–25, Springer-Verlag, Berlin, Germany, 1997.

[113] G. Weikum and G. Vossen, *Transactional Information Systems: Theory, Algorithms, and the Practice of Concurrency Control and Recovery*, Morgan Kaufmann Publishers, San Francisco, Calif, USA, 2002.

[114] E. Bertino, E. Ferrari, and V. Atluri, "The specification and enforcement of authorization constraints in workflow management systems," *ACM Transactions on Information and System Security*, vol. 22, no. 1, pp. 65–104, 1999.

[115] D. F. Ferraiolo, R. Sandhu, S. Gavrila, D. R. Kuhn, and R. Chandramouli, "Proposed NIST standard for role-based access control," *ACM Transactions on Information and System Security*, vol. 4, no. 3, pp. 224–274, 2001.

[116] J. Desel and J. Esparza, *Free Choice Petri Nets*, vol. 40 of *Cambridge Tracts in Theoretical Computer Science*, Cambridge University Press, Cambridge, UK, 1995.

[117] W. M. P. van der Aalst, "Loosely coupled interorganizational workflows: modeling and analyzing workflows crossing organizational boundaries," *Information and Management*, vol. 37, no. 2, pp. 67–75, 2000.

[118] W. M. P. van der Aalst, "Workflow verification: finding control-flow errors using Petri-net-based techniques," in *Business Process Management: Models, Techniques, and Empirical Studies*, W. M. P. van der Aalst, J. Desel, and A. Oberweis, Eds., vol. 1806 of

*Lecture Notes in Computer Science*, pp. 161–183, Springer-Verlag, Berlin, Germany, 2000.

[119] W. M. P. van der Aalst and A. H. M. ter Hofstede, "Verification of workflow task structures: a Petri-net-based approach," *Information Systems*, vol. 25, no. 1, pp. 43–69, 2000.

[120] A. Basu and R. W. Blanning, "A formal approach to workflow analysis," *Information Systems Research*, vol. 11, no. 1, pp. 17–36, 2000.

[121] H. H. Bi and J. L. Zhao, "Applying propositional logic to workflow verification," *Information Technology and Management*, vol. 5, no. 3-4, pp. 293–318, 2004.

[122] Y. Choi and J. Zhao, "Decomposition-based verification of cyclic workflows," in *Proceedings of the Automated Technology for Verification and Analysis (ATVA '05)*, D. A. Peled and Y.-K. Tsay, Eds., vol. 3707 of *Lecture Notes in Computer Science*, pp. 84–98, Springer-Verlag, Taipei, Taiwan, 2005.

[123] R. Eshuis, "Symbolic model checking of UML activity diagrams," *ACM Transactions on Software Engineering and Methodology*, vol. 15, no. 1, pp. 1–38, 2006.

[124] D. Fahland, C. Favre, J. Koehler, N. Lohmann, H. Völzer, and K. Wolf, "Analysis on demand: instantaneous soundness checking of industrial business process models," *Data and Knowledge Engineering*, vol. 70, no. 5, pp. 448–466, 2011.

[125] S. Fan, W. C. Dou, and J. Chen, "Dual workflow nets: mixed control/data-flow representation for workflow modeling and verification," in *Proceedings of the Advances in Web and Network Technologies, and Information Management (APWeb/WAIM '07)*, vol. 4537 of *Lecture Notes in Computer Science*, pp. 433–444, Springer-Verlag, Berlin, Germany, 2007.

[126] X. Fu, T. Bultan, and J. Su, "Formal verification of e-services and workflows," in *Proceedings of the CAiSE 2002 International Workshop on Services, E-Business, and the Semantic Web (WES '02)*, C. Bussler, R. Hull, S. McIlraith, M. Orlowska, B. Pernici, and J. Yang, Eds., vol. 2512 of *Lecture Notes in Computer Science*, pp. 188–202, Springer-Verlag, Berlin, Germany, 2002.

[127] K. M. van Hee, N. Sidorova, and M. Voorhoeve, "Soundness and separability of workflow nets in the stepwise refinement approach," in *Proceedings of the Application and Theory of Petri Nets 2003*, W. M. P. van der Aalst and E. Best, Eds., vol. 2679 of *Lecture Notes in Computer Science*, pp. 335–354, Springer-Verlag, Berlin, Germany, 2003.

[128] K. M. van Hee, N. Sidorova, and M. Voorhoeve, "Generalised soundness of workflow nets is decidable," in *Proceedings of the Application and Theory of Petri Nets 2004*, J. Cortadella and W. Reisig, Eds., vol. 3099 of *Lecture Notes in Computer Science*, pp. 197–215, Springer-Verlag, Berlin, Germany, 2004.

[129] A. H. M. ter Hofstede, M. E. Orlowska, and J. Rajapakse, "Verification problems in conceptual workflow specifications," *Data and Knowledge Engineering*, vol. 24, no. 3, pp. 239–256, 1998.

[130] B. Kiepuszewski, A. H. M. ter Hofstede, and W. M. P. van der Aalst, "Fundamentals of control flow in workflows," *Acta Informatica*, vol. 39, no. 3, pp. 143–209, 2003.

[131] W. Sadiq and M. E. Orlowska, "Applying graph reduction techniques for identifying structural conflicts in process models," in *Proceedings of the 11th International Conference on Advanced Information Systems Engineering (CAiSE '99)*, M. Jarke and A. Oberweis, Eds., vol. 1626 of *Lecture Notes in Computer Science*, pp. 195–209, Springer-Verlag, Berlin, Germany, 1999.

[132] R. J. van Glabbeek and W. P. Weijland, "Branching time and abstraction in bisimulation semantics," *Journal of the ACM*, vol. 43, no. 3, pp. 555–600, 1996.

[133] R. Milner, *Communication and Concurrency*, Prentice-Hall, New York, NY, USA, 1989.

[134] W. M. P. van der Aalst, "Interorganizational workflows: an approach based on message sequence charts and Petri nets," *Systems Analysis Modelling Simulation*, vol. 34, no. 3, pp. 335–367, 1999.

[135] W. M. P. van der Aalst, "Inheritance of interorganizational workflows: how to agree to disagree without loosing control?" *Information Technology and Management Journal*, vol. 4, no. 4, pp. 345–389, 2003.

[136] W. M. P. van der Aalst, N. Lohmann, P. Massuthe, C. Stahl, and K. Wolf, "From public views to private views: correctness-by-design for services," in *Proceedings of the 4th International Workshop on Web Services and Formal Methods (WSFM '07)*, M. Dumas and H. Heckel, Eds., vol. 4937 of *Lecture Notes in Computer Science*, pp. 139–153, Springer-Verlag, Berlin, Germany, 2008.

[137] W. M. P. van der Aalst, N. Lohmann, P. Massuthe, C. Stahl, and K. Wolf, "Multiparty contracts: agreeing and implementing interorganizational processes," *Computer Journal*, vol. 53, no. 1, pp. 90–106, 2010.

[138] J. A. Fisteus, L. S. Fernández, and C. D. Kloos, "Formal verification of BPEL4WS business collaborations," in *Proceedings of the 5th International Conference on Electronic Commerce and Web Technologies (EC-Web '04)*, K. Bauknecht, M. Bichler, and B. Proll, Eds., vol. 3182 of *Lecture Notes in Computer Science*, pp. 79–94, Springer-Verlag, Berlin, Germany, 2004.

[139] H. Foster, S. Uchitel, J. Magee, and J. Kramer, "Model-based verification of web service composition," in *Proceedings of 18th IEEE International Conference on Automated Software Engineering (ASE '03)*, pp. 152–161, Montreal, Canada, October 2003.

[140] X. Fu, T. Bultan, and J. Su, "WSAT: a tool for formal analysis of web services," in *Proceedings of the 16th International Conference on Computer Aided Verification (CAV '04)*, vol. 3114 of *Lecture Notes in Computer Science*, pp. 510–514, Springer-Verlag, Berlin, Germany, 2004.

[141] E. Kindler, A. Martens, and W. Reisig, "Inter-operability of workflow applications: local criteria for global soundness," in *Business Process Management: Models, Techniques, and Empirical Studies*, In W.M.P. van der Aalst, J. Desel, and A. Oberweis, Eds., vol. 1806 of *Lecture Notes in Computer Science*, pp. 235–253, Springer-Verlag, Berlin, Germany, 2000.

[142] M. Koshkina and F. van Breugel, "Verification of business processes for web services," Tech. Rep. CS-2003-11, York University, Toronto, Canada, 2003.

[143] N. Lohmann, P. Massuthe, C. Stahl, and D. Weinberg, "Analyzing interacting BPEL processes," in *International Conference on Business Process Management (BPM '06)*, S. Dustdar, J. L. Fiadeiro, and A. Sheth, Eds., vol. 4102 of *Lecture Notes in Computer Science*, pp. 17–32, Springer-Verlag, Berlin, Germany, 2006.

[144] N. Lohmann and P. Massuthe, "Operating guidelines for finite-state services," in *Proceedings of the 28th International Conference on Applications and Theory of Petri Nets and Other Models of Concurrency (ICATPN '07)*, J. Kleijn and A. Yakovlev, Eds., pp. 25–29, Siedlce, Poland, June 2007.

[145] F. Gottschalk, T. Wagemakers, M. H. Jansen-Vullers, W. M. P. van der Aalst, and M. La Rosa, "Configurable process models: experiences from a municipality case study," in *Proceedings of the 21st International Conference on Advanced Information Systems Engineering (CAiSE '09)*, P. van Eck, J. Gordijn, and R.

Wieringa, Eds., vol. 5565 of *Lecture Notes in Computer Science*, pp. 486–500, Springer-Verlag, 2009.

[146] M. La Rosa, M. Dumas, A. H. M. ter Hofstede, and J. Mendling, "Configurable multi-perspective business process models," *Information Systems*, vol. 36, no. 2, pp. 313–340, 2011.

[147] A. Schnieders and F. Puhlmann, "Variability mechanisms in E-business process families," in *Proceedings of the 9th International Conference on Business Information Systems (BIS '06)*, W. Abramowicz and H. C. Mayr, Eds., vol. 85 of *LNI*, pp. 583–601, 2006.

[148] W. M. P. van der Aalst, M. Dumas, F. Gottschalk, A. H. M. ter Hofstede, M. La Rosa, and J. Mendling, "Preserving correctness during business process model configuration," *Formal Aspects of Computing*, vol. 22, no. 3-4, pp. 459–482, 2010.

[149] H. M. W. Verbeek, T. Basten, and W. M. P. van der Aalst, "Diagnosing workflow processes using Woflan," *Computer Journal*, vol. 44, no. 4, pp. 246–279, 2001.

[150] W. M. P. van der Aalst and A. H. M. ter Hofstede, "YAWL: Yet Another Workflow Language," *Information Systems*, vol. 30, no. 4, pp. 245–275, 2005.

[151] N. Lohmann and D. Weinberg, "Wendy: a tool to synthesize partners for services," in *Applications and Theory of Petri Nets*, J. Lilius and W. Penczek, Eds., vol. 6128 of *Lecture Notes in Computer Science*, pp. 279–307, Springer, Berlin, Germany, 2010.

[152] B. D. Clinton and A. van der Merwe, "Management accounting: approaches, techniques, and management processes," *Cost Management*, vol. 20, no. 3, pp. 14–22, 2006.

[153] J. A. Buzacott, "Commonalities in reengineered business processes: models and issues," *Management Science*, vol. 42, no. 5, pp. 768–782, 1996.

[154] J. J. Moder and S. E. Elmaghraby, *Handbook of Operations Research: Foundations and Fundamentals*, Van Nostrand Reinhold, New York, NY, USA, 1978.

[155] H. Reijers, *Design and Control of Workflow Processes: Business Process Management for the Service Industry*, vol. 2617 of *Lecture Notes in Computer Science*, Springer-Verlag, Berlin, Germany, 2003.

[156] R. Wild, *Production and Operations Management : Principles and Techniques*, Cassell, London, UK, 1989.

[157] W. M. P. van der Aalst, "Business process simulation revisited," *Lecture Notes in Business Information Processing*, vol. 63, pp. 1–14, 2010.

[158] W. M. P. van der Aalst, J. Nakatumba, A. Rozinat, and N. Russell, "Business process simulation," in *Handbook on Business Process Management, International Handbooks on Information Systems*, J. vom Brocke and M. Rosemann, Eds., pp. 313–338, Springer-Verlag, Berlin, Germany, 2010.

[159] IEEE Task Force on Process Mining, "Process mining manifesto," in *Business Process Management Workshops*, F. Daniel, K. Barkaoui, and S. Dustdar, Eds., vol. 99 of *Lecture Notes in Business Information Processing*, pp. 169–194, Springer-Verlag, Berlin, Germany, 2012.

[160] W. M. P. van der Aalst, H. A. Reijers, A. J. M. M. Weijters et al., "Business process mining: an industrial application," *Information Systems*, vol. 32, no. 5, pp. 713–732, 2007.

[161] S. Davidson, S. Cohen-Boulakia, A. Eyal et al., "Provenance in scientific workflow systems," *Data Engineering Bulletin*, vol. 30, no. 4, pp. 44–50, 2007.

[162] F. Curbera, Y. Doganata, A. Martens, N. Mukhi, and A. Slominski, "Business provenance: a technology to increase traceability of end-to-end operations," in *Proceedings of the 16th*

International Conference on Cooperative Information Systems (CoopIS-OTM '08) Part I*, R. Meersman and Z. Tari, Eds., vol. 5331 of *Lecture Notes in Computer Science*, pp. 100–119, Springer-Verlag, Berlin, Germany, 2008.

[163] B. F. van Dongen, A. K. Alves de Medeiros, and L. Wenn, "Process mining: overview and outlook of Petri net discovery algorithms," in *Proceedings of the Transactions on Petri Nets and Other Models of Concurrency II*, K. Jensen and W. M. P. van der Aalst, Eds., vol. 5460 of *Lecture Notes in Computer Science*, pp. 225–242, Springer-Verlag, Berlin, Germany, 2009.

[164] R. Agrawal, D. Gunopulos, and F. Leymann, "Mining process models from workflow logs," in *Proceedings of the 6th International Conference on Extending Database Technology*, vol. 1377 of *Lecture Notes in Computer Science*, pp. 469–483, Springer-Verlag, Berlin, 1998.

[165] J. E. Cook and A. L. Wolf, "Discovering models of software processes from event-based data," *ACM Transactions on Software Engineering and Methodology*, vol. 7, no. 3, pp. 215–249, 1998.

[166] A. Datta, "Automating the discovery of AS-IS business process models: probabilistic and algorithmic approaches," *Information Systems Research*, vol. 9, no. 3, pp. 275–301, 1998.

[167] B. F. Van Dongen and W. M. P. van der Aalst, "Multi-phase process mining: building instance graphs," in *Proceedings of the International Conference on Conceptual Modeling (ER '04)*, P. Atzeni, W. Chu, H. Lu, S. Zhou, and T. W. Ling, Eds., vol. 3288 of *Lecture Notes in Computer Science*, pp. 362–376, Springer-Verlag, Berlin, Germany, 2004.

[168] B. F. van Dongen and W. M. P. van der Aalst, "Multi-phase mining: aggregating instances graphs into EPCs and Petri Nets," in *Proceedings of the 2nd International Workshop on Applications of Petri nets to Coordination, Workflow and Business Process Management*, D. Marinescu, Ed., pp. 35–58, Florida International University, Miami, Fla, USA, 2005.

[169] A. J. M. M. Weijters and W. M. P. van der Aalst, "Rediscovering workflow models from event-based data using little thumb," *Integrated Computer-Aided Engineering*, vol. 10, no. 2, pp. 151–162, 2003.

[170] W. M. P. van der Aalst, B. F. van Dongen, J. Herbst, L. Maruster, G. Schimm, and A. J. M. M. Weijters, "Workflow mining: a survey of issues and approaches," *Data and Knowledge Engineering*, vol. 47, no. 2, pp. 237–267, 2003.

[171] J. Herbst, "A machine learning approach to workflow management," in *Proceedings of the 11th European Conference on Machine Learning*, vol. 1810 of *Lecture Notes in Computer Science*, pp. 183–194, Springer-Verlag, Berlin, Germany, 2000.

[172] A. Rozinat and W. M. P. van der Aalst, "Decision mining in ProM," in *Proceedings of the International Conference on Business Process Management (BPM '06)*, S. Dustdar, J. L. Fiadeiro, and A. Sheth, Eds., vol. 4102 of *Lecture Notes in Computer Science*, pp. 420–425, Springer-Verlag, Berlin, Germany.

[173] A. Rozinat, R. S. Mans, M. Song, and W. M. P. van der Aalst, "Discovering colored Petri nets from event logs," *International Journal on Software Tools for Technology Transfer*, vol. 10, no. 1, pp. 57–74, 2008.

[174] A. Rozinat, R. S. Mans, M. Song, and W. M. P. van der Aalst, "Discovering simulation models," *Information Systems*, vol. 34, no. 3, pp. 305–327, 2009.

[175] A. Rozinat, M. T. Wynn, W. M. P. van der Aalst, A. H. M. ter Hofstede, and C. J. Fidge, "Workflow simulation for operational decision support," *Data and Knowledge Engineering*, vol. 68, no. 9, pp. 834–850, 2009.

[176] W. M. P. van der Aalst, M. Pesic, and M. Song, "Beyond process mining: from the past to present and puture," in *Proceedings of the 22nd International Conference on Advanced Information Systems Engineering (CAiSE '10)*, B. Pernici, Ed., vol. 6051 of *Lecture Notes in Computer Science*, pp. 38–52, Springer-Verlag, Berlin, Germany, 2010.

[177] F. M. Maggi, M. Montali, and W. M. P. van der Aalst, "An operational decision support framework for monitoring business constraints," J. de Lara and A. Zisman, Eds., vol. 7212 of *Lecture Notes in Computer Science*, pp. 146–162, Proceedings of the International Conference on Fundamental Approaches to Software Engineering (FASE '12).

[178] F. M. Maggi, M. Westergaard, M. Montali, and W. M. P. van der Aalst, "Runtime verification of LTL-based declarative process models," in *Proceedings of the Runtime Verification (RV '11)*, S. Khurshid and K. Sen, Eds., vol. 7186 of *Lecture Notes in Computer Science*, pp. 131–146, Springer, 2012.

[179] W. M. P. van der Aalst, A. Adriansyah, and B. van Dongen, "Replaying history on process models for conformance checking and performance analysis," *WIREs Data Mining and Knowledge Discovery*, vol. 2, no. 2, pp. 182–192, 2012.

[180] A. Adriansyah, B. van Dongen, and W. M. P. van der Aalst, "Conformance checking using cost-based fitness analysis," in *IEEE International Enterprise Computing Conference (EDOC '11)*, C. H. Chi and P. Johnson, Eds., pp. 55–64, IEEE Computer Society, 2011.

[181] A. Adriansyah, B. F. van Dongen, and W. M. P. van der Aalst, "Towards robust conformance checking," *Lecture Notes in Business Information Processing*, vol. 66, pp. 122–133, 2011.

[182] T. Calders, C. W. Günther, M. Pechenizkiy, and A. Rozinat, "Using minimum description length for process mining," in *24th Annual ACM Symposium on Applied Computing, SAC 2009*, pp. 1451–1455, usa, March 2009.

[183] J. E. Cook and A. L. Wolf, "Software process validation: quantitatively measuring the correspondence of a process to a model," *ACM Transactions on Software Engineering and Methodology*, vol. 8, no. 2, pp. 147–176, 1999.

[184] S. Goedertier, D. Martens, J. Vanthienen, and B. Baesens, "Robust process discovery with artificial negative events," *Journal of Machine Learning Research*, vol. 10, pp. 1305–1340, 2009.

[185] J. Munoz-Gama and J. Carmona, "A fresh look at precision in process conformance," in *Business Process Management (BPM 2010)*, R. Hull, J. Mendling, and S. Tai, Eds., vol. 6336 of *Lecture Notes in Computer Science*, pp. 211–226, Springer-Verlag, Berlin, Germany, 2010.

[186] J. Munoz-Gama and J. Carmona, "Enhancing precision in process conformance: stability, confidence and severity," in *Proceedings of the IEEE Symposium on Computational Intelligence and Data Mining (CIDM '11)*, pp. 184–191, Paris, France, April 2011.

[187] A. Rozinat and W. M. P. van der Aalst, "Conformance checking of processes based on monitoring real behavior," *Information Systems*, vol. 33, no. 1, pp. 64–95, 2008.

[188] J. De Weerdt, M. De Backer, J. Vanthienen, and B. Baesens, "A robust F-measure for evaluating discovered process models," in *Proceedings of the IEEE Symposium on Computational Intelligence and Data Mining (CIDM '11)*, pp. 148–155, Paris, France, April 2011.

[189] R. Dijkman, M. Dumas, B. Van Dongen, R. Krik, and J. Mendling, "Similarity of business process models: metrics and evaluation," *Information Systems*, vol. 36, no. 2, pp. 498–516, 2011.

[190] T. Jin, J. Wang, and L. Wen, "Efficient retrieval of similar workflow models based on structure," in *OTM 2011*, vol. 7044 of *Lecture Notes in Computer Science*, pp. 56–63, Springer-Verlag, Berlin, Germany, 2011.

[191] T. Jin, J. Wang, and L. Wen, "Efficient retrieval of similar workflow models based on behavior," in *APWeb 2012*, vol. 7235 of *Lecture Notes in Computer Science*, pp. 677–684, Springer-Verlag, Berlin, Germany, 2012.

[192] J. Mendling, B. F. van Dongen, and W. M. P. van der Aalst, "On the degree of behavioral similarity between business process models," in *Proceedings of 6th Workshop on Event-Driven Process Chains (WI-EPK '07)*, M. Nuettgens, F. J. Rump, and A. Gadatsch, Eds., pp. 39–58, Gesellschaft für Informatik, St. Augustin, Fla, USA, November 2007.

[193] M. Weidlich, R. Dijkman, and M. Weske, "Behavioral equivalence and compatibility of business process models with complex correspondences," *Computer Journal*. In press.

[194] W. M. P. van der Aalst and T. Basten, "Identifying commonalities and differences in object life cycles using behavioral inheritance," in *Application and Theory of Petri Nets*, J. M. Colom and M. Koutny, Eds., vol. 2075 of *Lecture Notes in Computer Science*, pp. 32–52, Springer-Verlag, Berlin, Germany, 2001.

[195] W. M. P. van der Aalst, M. H. Schonenberg, and M. Song, "Time prediction based on process mining," *Information Systems*, vol. 36, no. 2, pp. 450–475, 2011.

[196] B. F. van Dongen, R. A. Crooy, and W. M. P. van der Aalst, "Cycle time prediction: when will this case finally be finished," in *Proceedings of the 16th International Conference on Cooperative Information Systems (CoopIS-OTM '08) Part I*, R. Meersman and Z. Tari, Eds., vol. 5331 of *Lecture Notes in Computer Science*, pp. 319–336, Springer-Verlag, Berlin, 2008.

[197] H. A. Reijers, "Case prediction in BPM systems: a research challenge," *Journal of the Korean Institute of Industrial Engineers*, vol. 33, pp. 1–10, 2006.

[198] Staffware, *Staffware Process Suite Version 2-White Paper*, Staffware PLC, Maidenhead, UK, 2003.

[199] H. Schonenberg, B. Weber, B. F. van Dongen, and W. M. P. van der Aalst, "Supporting flexible processes through recommendations based on history," in *International Conference on Business Process Management (BPM '08)*, M. Dumas, M. Reichert, and M. C. Shan, Eds., vol. 5240 of *Lecture Notes in Computer Science*, pp. 51–66, Springer-Verlag, Berlin, Germany, 2008.

[200] W. M. P. van der Aalst, M. Weske, and D. Grünbauer, "Case handling: a new paradigm for business process support," *Data and Knowledge Engineering*, vol. 53, no. 2, pp. 129–162, 2005.

[201] M. Adams, A. H. M. ter Hofstede, W. M. P. van der Aalst, and D. Edmond, "Dynamic, extensible and context-aware exception handling for workflows," in *Proceedings of the OTM Conference on Cooperative information Systems (CoopIS '07)*, F. Curbera, F. Leymann, and M. Weske, Eds., vol. 4803 of *Lecture Notes in Computer Science*, pp. 95–112, Springer-Verlag, Berlin, Germany, 2007.

[202] S. Dustdar, "Caramba-a process-aware collaboration system supporting ad hoc and collaborative processes in virtual teams," *Distributed and Parallel Databases*, vol. 15, no. 1, pp. 45–66, 2004.

[203] C. A. Ellis, K. Keddara, and G. Rozenberg, "Dynamic change within workflow systems," in *Proceedings of the Conference on Organizational Computing Systems*, N. Comstock, C. Ellis, R. Kling, J. Mylopoulos, and S. Kaplan, Eds., pp. 10–21, ACM SIGOIS, ACM Press, Milpitas, Calif, USA, August 1995.

[204] M. Pesic, M. H. Schonenberg, N. Sidorova, and W. M. P. van der Aalst, "Constraint-based workflow models: change made easy," in *Proceedings of the OTM Conference on Cooperative information Systems (CoopIS '07)*, F. Curbera, F. Leymann, and M. Weske, Eds., vol. 4803 of *Lecture Notes in Computer Science*, pp. 77–94, Springer-Verlag, Berlin, Germany, 2007.

[205] M. Reichert and P. Dadam, "ADEPTflex-Supporting dynamic changes of workflows without losing control," *Journal of Intelligent Information Systems*, vol. 10, no. 2, pp. 93–129, 1998.

[206] S. Rinderle, M. Reichert, and P. Dadam, "Correctness criteria for dynamic changes in workflow systems: a survey," *Data and Knowledge Engineering*, vol. 50, no. 1, pp. 9–34, 2004.

[207] M. Weske, "Formal foundation and conceptual design of dynamic adaptations in a workflow management system," in *Proceedings of the 34th Annual Hawaii International Conference on System Science (HICSS-34)*, R. Sprague, Ed., IEEE Computer Society Press, Los Alamitos, Calif, USA, 2001.

[208] W. M. P. van der Aalst and S. Jablonski, "Dealing with workflow change: identification of issues and solutions," *Computer Systems Science and Engineering*, vol. 15, no. 5, pp. 267–276, 2000.

[209] H. Schonenberg, R. Mans, N. Russell, N. Mulyar, and W. van der Aalst, "Process flexibility: a survey of contemporary approaches," *Lecture Notes in Business Information Processing*, vol. 10, pp. 16–30, 2008.

[210] S. Sadiq, W. Sadiq, and M. Orlowska, "Pockets of flexibility in workflow specification," in *Proceedings of the 20th International Conference on Conceptual Modeling (ER '01)*, vol. 2224 of *Lecture Notes in Computer Science*, pp. 513–526, Springer-Verlag, Berlin, Germany, 2001.

[211] T. Herrmann, M. Hoffmann, K. U. Loser, and K. Moysich, "Semistructured models are surprisingly useful for user-centered design," in *Proceedings of the Designing Cooperative Systems (Coop '00)*, G. De Michelis, A. Giboin, L. Karsenty, and R. Dieng, Eds., pp. 159–174, IOS Press, 2000.

[212] M. Adams, *Facilitating dynamic flexibility and exception handling for workflows [Ph.D. thesis]*, Queensland University of Technology, Queensland, Ga, USA, 2007.

[213] P. Heinl, S. Horn, S. Jablonski, J. Neeb, K. Stein, and M. Teschke, "A comprehensive approach to flexibility in workflow management systems," G. Georgakopoulos, W. Prinz, and A. L. Wolf, Eds., Work Activities Coordination and Collaboration (WACC '99), pp. 79–88, ACM press, San Francisco, Calif, USA, 1999.

[214] M. Pesic, *Constraint-based Workflow management systems: shifting control to users [Ph.D. thesis]*, Eindhoven University of Technology, Eindhoven, The Netherlands, 2008.

[215] S. Rinderle, M. Reichert, and P. Dadam, "Evaluation of correctness criteria for dynamic workflow changes," in *Proceedings of the International Conference on Business Process Management (BPM '03)*, W. M. P. van der Aalst, A. H. M. ter Hofstede, and M. Weske, Eds., vol. 2678 of *Lecture Notes in Computer Science*, pp. 41–57, Springer-Verlag, Berlin, Germany.

[216] C. Houy, P. Fettke, P. Loos, W. M. P. van der Aalst, and J. Krogstie, "Business process management in the large," *Business and Information Systems Engineering*, vol. 3, no. 6, pp. 385–388, 2011.

[217] R. Dijkman, M. La Rosa, and H. A. Reijers, "Managing large collections of business process models: current techniques and challenges," *Computers in Industry*, vol. 63, no. 2, pp. 91–97, 2012.

[218] A. W. Scheer, *Business Process Engineering: ARIS-Navigator for Reference Models for Industrial Enterprises*, Springer-Verlag, Berlin, Germany, 1995.

[219] A. W. Scheer, *ARIS: Business Process Modelling*, Springer-Verlag, Berlin, Germany, 2000.

[220] M. C. Fauvet, M. La Rosa, M. Sadegh et al., "Managing process model collections with APROMORE," in *Proceedings of the Service-Oriented Computing (ICSOC '10)*, P. Maglio, M. Weske, J. Yang, and M. Fantinato, Eds., vol. 6470 of *Lecture Notes in Computer Science*, pp. 699–701, Springer-Verlag, Berlin, Germany, 2010.

[221] M. La Rosa, H. A. Reijers, W. M. P. van der Aalst et al., "APROMORE: an advanced process model repository," *Expert Systems with Applications*, vol. 38, no. 6, pp. 7029–7040, 2011.

[222] A. Awad, M. Weidlich, and M. Weske, "Visually specifying compliance rules and explaining their violations for business processes," *Journal of Visual Languages and Computing*, vol. 22, no. 1, pp. 30–55, 2011.

[223] M. Weidlich, A. Polyvyanyy, N. Desai, J. Mendling, and M. Weske, "Process compliance analysis based on behavioural profiles," *Information Systems*, vol. 36, no. 7, pp. 1009–1025, 2011.

[224] J. J. C. L. Vogelaar, H. M. W. Verbeek, B. Luka, and W. M. P. van der Aalst, "Comparing business processes to determine the feasibility of configurable models: a case study," in *Proceedings of the International Workshop on Process Model Collections on Business Process Management (PMC '11)*, F. Daniel, K. Barkaoui, and S. Dustdar, Eds., vol. 100 of *Lecture Notes in Business Information Processing*, pp. 50–61, Springer-Verlag, Berlin, Germany, 2012.

[225] F. Gottschalk, W. M. P. van der Aalst, and M. H. Jansen-Vullers, "Merging event-driven process chains," in *Proceedings of the 16th International Conference on Cooperative Information Systems (CoopIS-OTM '08) Part I*, R. Meersman and Z. Tari, Eds., vol. 5331 of *Lecture Notes in Computer Science*, pp. 418–426, Springer-Verlag, Berlin, Germany, 2008.

[226] M. La Rosa, M. Dumas, R. Uba, and R. M. Dijkman, "Merging business process models," in *Proceedings of the International Conference on Cooperative Information Systems (CoopIS '10)*, R. Meersman, T. Dillon, and P. Herrero, Eds., vol. 6426 of *Lecture Notes in Computer Science*, pp. 96–113, Springer-Verlag, Berlin, Germany, 2010.

[227] M. La Rosa, M. Dumas, R. Uba, and R. M. Dijkman, "Business process model merging:an approach to business process consolidation," *ACM Transactions on Software Engineering and Methodology*. In press.

[228] C. Li, M. Reichert, and A. Wombacher, "Discovering reference models by mining process variants using a heuristic approach," in *Proceedings of the Business Process Management (BPM '09)*, U. Dayal, J. Eder, J. Koehler, and H. Reijers, Eds., vol. 5701 of *Lecture Notes in Computer Science*, pp. 344–362, Springer-Verlag, Berlin, Germany, 2009.

[229] C. Li, M. Reichert, and A. Wombacher, "The MINADEPT clustering approach for discovering reference process models out of process variants," *International Journal of Cooperative Information Systems*, vol. 19, no. 3-4, pp. 159–203, 2010.

[230] V. Levenshtein, "Binary codes capable of correcting deletions, insertions, and reversals," *Soviet Physics-Doklady*, vol. 10, no. 8, pp. 707–710, 1966.

[231] G. Miller, "WordNet: a lexical database for English," *Communications of the ACM*, vol. 38, no. 11, pp. 39–41, 1995.

[232] M. Hepp, F. Leymann, J. Domingue, A. Wahler, and D. Fensel, "Semantic business process management: a vision towards using semantic web services for business process management," in *Proceedings of the IEEE International Conference on e-Business Engineering (ICEBE '05)*, pp. 535–540, 2005.

# 5

# Web Services Conversation Adaptation Using Conditional Substitution Semantics of Application Domain Concepts

**Islam Elgedawy**

*Computer Engineering Department, Middle East Technical University, Northern Cyprus Campus, Guzelyurt, Mersin 10, Turkey*

Correspondence should be addressed to Islam Elgedawy; elgedawy@metu.edu.tr

Academic Editors: A. Lastovetsky, G. Petrone, and G. Saake

Internet of Services (IoS) vision allows users to allocate and consume different web services on the fly without any prior knowledge regarding the chosen services. Such chosen services should automatically interact with one another in a transparent manner to accomplish the required users' goals. As services are chosen on the fly, service conversations are not necessarily compatible due to incompatibilities between services signatures and/or conversation protocols, creating obstacles for realizing the IoS vision. One approach for overcoming this problem is to use conversation adapters. However, such conversion adapters must be automatically created on the fly as chosen services are only known at run time. Existing approaches for automatic adapter generation are syntactic and very limited; hence they cannot be adopted in such dynamic environments. To overcome such limitation, this paper proposes a novel approach for automatic adapter generation that uses conditional substitution semantics between application domain concepts and operations to automatically generate the adapter conversion functions. Such conditional substitution semantics are captured using a concepts substitutability enhanced graph required to be part of application domain ontologies. Experiments results show that the proposed approach provides more accurate conversation adaptation results when compared against existing syntactic adapter generation approaches.

## 1. Introduction

Internet of Services (IoS) vision enables users (i.e. people, businesses, and systems) to allocate and consume the required computing services whenever and wherever they want in a context-aware seamless transparent manner. Hence, chosen services automatically interact with one another in a transparent manner to accomplish the required users' goals. Middleware software plays an essential role in supporting such interactions, as it hides services heterogeneity and ensures their interoperability. Middleware enables services to locate one another without a priori knowledge of their existences and enables them to interact with one another even though they are running on different devices and platforms [1]. Services interactions are conducted via exchanging messages. A conversation message indicates the operation to be performed by the service receiving the message. A sequence of messages exchanged between services to achieve a common goal constitutes what is known by a conversation pattern. A set of conversation patterns is referred to as a service conversation. However, services may use different concepts, vocabularies, and semantics to generate their conversation messages, raising the possibility for having conversation incompatibilities. Such incompatibilities must be automatically resolved in order to enable services conversations on the fly. This should be handled by a conversation adapter created on the fly by the middleware, please refer to Section 2.2 for more information about conversation adapters.

In general, in order to create a conversation adapter, first we have to identify the possible conversation incompatibilities and then try to resolve the incompatibilities using the available conversation semantics, which are constituted from service semantics (such as service external behavior, encapsulated business logic, and adopted vocabulary) and application domain semantics (such as concepts relations and domain rules). If solutions are found, the adapter can be created; otherwise the conversations are labelled as unadaptable, and the corresponding services cannot work together. Hence, we argue that in order to automatically generate conversation adapters the following prerequisites must be fulfilled.

(i) First, we require substitution semantics of application domain concepts and operations to be captured in application domain ontologies in a context-sensitive manner, as such semantics differ from one context to another in the same application domain, for example, the concepts Hotel and Resort could be substitutable in some contexts and not substitutable in others. Hence, capturing substitution semantics and its corresponding conversion semantics in a finite context-sensitive manner is mandatory to guarantee the adapter functional correctness, as these conversion semantics provide the basic building blocks for generating converters needed for building the required adapters.

(ii) Second, we require services descriptions to provide details about the supported conversation patterns (that is the exchanged messages sequences), such as the conversation context, the supported operations, and the supported invocation sequences. Such information must be captured in a machine-understandable format and must be based on the adopted application-domain ontology vocabulary.

(iii) Finally, as different conversation patterns could be used to accomplish the same business objective, different types of mappings between the conversation patterns operations must be automatically determined (whether it is many-to-many, or one-to-one, and etc). Such operations mappings are essential for determining the required adapter structure.

Unfortunately, existing approaches for adapter generation (such as the ones discussed in [2–9]) do not fulfill the mentioned prerequisites; hence they are strictly limited and cannot be adopted in dynamic environments implied by the IoS vision. More details and discussion about these approaches are given in the related work section (Section 3).

To overcome the limitations of the existing adaptation approaches, this paper proposes a novel approach for automatic adapter generation that is able to fulfill the above prerequisites by adopting and integrating different solutions from our previous research endeavors discussed in [10–16]. The proposed approach successfully adapts both signature and protocol conversation incompatibilities in a context-sensitive manner. First, we adopt the metaontology proposed in [13, 14, 16] to capture the conversion semantics between application domain concepts in a context-sensitive manner using the Concepts Substitutability Enhanced Graph (CSEG) (details are given in Section 4). Second, we adopt the $G^+$ model [10, 16] to semantically capture the supported service conversation patterns using concepts and operations defined in CSEG (details are given in Section 5). Third, we adopt the context matching approach proposed in [12] to match conversation contexts and adopt a Sequence Mediation Procedure (SMP) proposed in [10, 15] to mediate between different exchanged messages sequences (details are given in Section 2). Fourth, the proposed approach generates the conversation patterns from the services $G^+$ model then matches these patterns using context matching and SMP procedures to find the operations mappings, which determine the required

adapter structure, and then generates converters between different operations using the concepts substitution semantics captured in the CSEG. Finally, it builds the required adapter from the generated converters between conversation operations (i.e. messages). Each couple of conversation patterns should have their own corresponding adapter. Experiments results show that the proposed approach provides more accurate conversation adaptation results when compared against existing syntactic adapter generation approaches. We believe the proposed automated approach helps in improving business agility and responsiveness and of course establishes a solid step towards achieving the IoS vision.

*1.1. Contributions Summary.* We summarize paper contributions as follows.

(i) We propose a novel approach for automatic service conversation adapter generation that uses conditional substitution semantics between application domain concepts and operations in order to resolve conversation conflicts on the fly, in a context-aware manner.

(ii) We propose to use a complex graph data structure, known as the Concepts Substitutability Enhanced Graph (CSEG), which is able to capture the aggregate concept substitution semantics of application domain concepts in a context-sensitive manner. We believe CSEG should be the metaontology for every application domain.

(iii) We propose a new way for representing a service behavior state that helps us to improve the matching accuracy and propose a new behavior matching procedure known as Sequence Mediator Procedure (SMP) that can match states in a many-to-many fashion.

(iv) We propose an approach for service operation signature adaptation using CSEG semantics.

(v) We propose an approach for service conversation adaptation using CSEG semantics and SMP.

The rest of the paper is organized as follows. Section 2 provides some background regarding service conversation management, conversation adaptation, application domain representation, and concepts substitutability graph. Section 3 provides the related work discussions in the areas of conversation adaptation and ontology mapping. Section 4 provides an overview on the adopted metaontology and its evolution. Section 5 proposes the adopted conversation model and describes how to extract the corresponding behavior model. Section 6 proposes the adopted approach for signature adaptation, while Section 7 proposes the adopted approach for conversation protocol adaptation. Section 8 proposes the adopted approach and algorithms for automatic adapter generation. Section 9 shows the various verification experiment and depicts results. Finally, Section 11 concludes the paper and discusses future work.

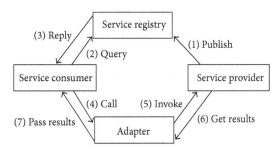

FIGURE 1: Service-Oriented Architecture with Adapters.

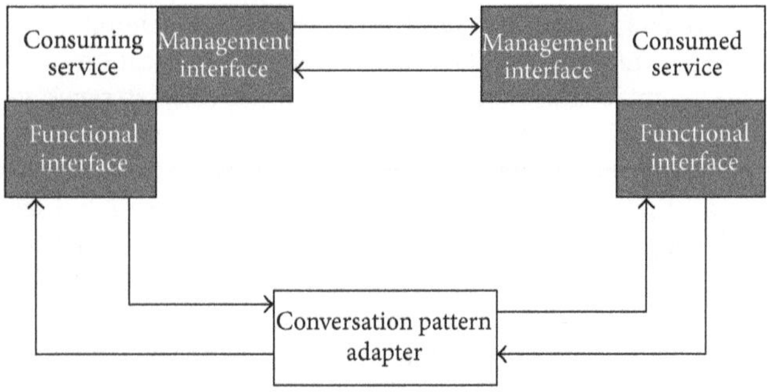

FIGURE 2: Conversation Management Architecture.

## 2. Background

This section provides some basic principles regarding conversation management and application domain representation needed to understand the proposed automatic adapter generation approach.

*2.1. Service Conversation Management.* Basically, we require each web service to have two types of interfaces: a functional interface and a management interface [17, 18]. The functional interface provides the operations others services can invoke to accomplish different business objectives, while the management interface provides operations to other services in order to get some information about the service internal state that enables other services to synchronize their conversations with the service, such as operations for conversation start and end, supported conversation patterns, and supported application domain ontologies. However, to generate the right adapters, we need first to know which conversation patterns will be used before the conversation started. Therefore, we require from the consuming service to specify which conversation pattern it will use and which conversation pattern required from the consumed service before starting the conversation. This information is provided to the consuming service via the matchmaker or the service discovery agent, as depicted in Figure 1. Figure 1 indicates consuming services call conversation adapters to accomplish the required operations, and in turn the adapter invokes the corresponding operations from the service providers side and does the suitable conversions between exchanged messages.

Once the consuming service knows which conversation patterns are required, it needs to communicate this information with the consumed service in order to build the suitable adapter. This could be achieved by invoking the conversation management operations defined in the management interface of the consumed service, as depicted in Figure 2. The figure indicates that the consuming service calls the consumed service management interface to specify the required conversation pattern; once it gets the confirmation, it starts the conversation and performs the conversation interactions via the conversation adapter. The adapter in turn will invoke the needed operations from the functional interface of the consumed service. This forms what we define as the *conversation management architecture*, in which each service is capable of monitoring and controlling its

conversations and can synchronize with other services via management interfaces.

Specifying the required conversation patterns in advance has another benefit that services could determine the correctness of the interactions during the conversation and that if a service received any operation invocation request not in the specified conversation pattern or even in the wrong order, it could reject the request and reset the conversation. It is important to note that management interfaces should be created according to a common standard such as Web Services Choreography Interface (WSCI) [19].

*2.2. Conversation Adaptation.* Conversations incompatibilities are classified into signature incompatibilities and protocol incompatibilities [20, 21]. Signature incompatibilities arise when the operation to be performed by the receiving service is either not supported or not described using the required messaging schema (such as using a different number of input and output concepts, different concepts names, and different concepts types). On the other hand, protocol incompatibilities arise when interacting services expect a different ordering for the exchanged message sequences. An example for signature incompatibility occurs when one service needs to perform an online payment via operation `PayOnline` that has input concepts `CreditCard`, `Amount`, and `Currency`, and the output concept `Receipt`. The `CreditCard` concept contains the card information such as card holder name, card number, card type, and card expiration date while the `Receipt` concept contains the successful transaction number. Continuing with our example, another service performs online payment by invoking operation `PaymentRequest` that has one input concept `Payment` (which contains all the payment details) and one output concept `Confirmation`, which contains the transaction number. With purely syntactical matching between operations signatures, the first service cannot invoke the second service in spite of its ability to perform the required payment operation. An example for protocol incompatibility occurs when one service needs to perform a purchase operation and expects to send a message containing user details first and then another message containing purchase-order details, while the other interacting service is receiving the purchase-order details first and then the user details. One well-known approach for handling conversation incompatibilities is through the use of conversation

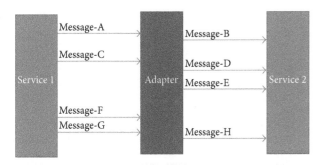

FIGURE 3: Conversation customization via an adapter.

adapters [2–6, 11]. A conversation adapter is the intermediate component between the interacting services that facilitates service conversations by converting the exchanged messages into messages "understandable" by the interacting services, as indicated in Figure 3.

Figure 3 shows an example of interactions between two incompatible services via a conversation adapter. Figure 3 shows that mapping between messages could be of different types (i.e. one-to-one, one-to-many, many-to-one, and many-to-many). For example, the adapter converts Message-A into Message-B, while it converts Message-C into the sequence consisting of Message-D and Message-E, and finally it converts the sequence consisting of Message-F and Message-G into Message-H. In other words, the adapter performs conversation customization and translation. The adapter can convert one message into another message or into another sequence of messages. It can also convert a sequence of messages into a single message or into another sequence of messages. Creating conversation adapters manually is a very time-consuming and costly process, especially when business frequently changes its consumed services, as in the IoS vision. This creates a need for automatic generation for web services conversations adapters, in order to increase business agility and responsiveness, as most of the business services will be discovered on the fly.

Automatic conversation adaptation is a very challenging task, as it requires understanding of many types of semantics including user semantics, service semantics, and application-domain semantics. All of these types of semantics should be captured in a machine-understandable format so that the middleware can use them to generate the required conversation adapters. One way of capturing different types of semantics in a machine-understandable format is using ontologies. Ontologies represent the semantic web architecture layer concerned with domain conceptualization. They are created to provide a common shared understanding of a given application domain that can be communicated across people, applications, and systems [10]. Ontologies play a very important role in automatic adapter generation, as they provide the common reference for resolving any appearing semantic conflicts. Therefore, we argue that the adopted application domain ontologies must be rich enough to capture different types of semantics in order to be able to resolve different conversation conflicts in a context-aware semantic manner. We argued in our previous work [10, 12, 13]

that ontologies defined as a taxonomy style are not rich enough to capture complex types of semantics; hence more complex ontology models must be adopted. Therefore, we proposed in [10, 13, 14] to capture relationships between application domain concepts as a multidimensional hypergraph rather than a simple taxonomy; more details will be given in Section 4.

*2.3. Application Domain Representation.* Business systems use application domain ontologies in their modelling and design in order to standardize their models and to facilitate systems interaction, integration, evolution, and development. This is because application domain ontologies provide a common shared understanding of application domains that can be communicated across people, applications, and systems. Ontologies represent the semantic web architecture layer concerned with domain conceptualization; hence application domain ontology should include descriptions of the domain entities and their semantics, as well as specify any attributes of domain entities and their corresponding values. An ontology can range from a simple taxonomy to a thesaurus (words and synonyms), to a conceptual model (where more complex relations are defined), or to a logical theory (where formal axioms, rules, theorems, and theories are defined) [22, 23].

It is important to note the difference between application-domain ontologies and service modelling ontologies. In Application-domain ontologies the vocabulary are needed for describing the domain concepts, operations, rules, and so forth. Application-domain ontologies could be represented by existing semantic web standards, such as Web Ontology Language (OWL 2.0) [24]. On the other hand, service modelling ontologies provide constructs to build the service model in a machine-understandable format; such constructs are based on the vocabulary provided by the adopted application domain ontologies. Web Services Modelling Ontology (WSMO) [25], Web Ontology Language for Services (OWL-S) [26], and Semantic Annotations for Web Services Description Language (SAWSDL) [27] are examples of existing service modelling ontologies. The conversation modelling problem has attracted many research efforts in the areas of SOC and agent communication (such as in [28–30]). Additionally, there are some industrial standards for representing service conversations, such as Web Services Choreography Interface (WSCI) [19] for modelling service choreography and Web Services Business Process execution Language (WS-BPEL) [31] for modelling service orchestration. In this paper, we preferred to conceptually describe our conversation and applications-domain models without being restricted to any existing standards. However, any existing standard that is sufficiently rich to capture the information explained below will be suitable to represent our models.

In general, there are two approaches that can be adopted for application domain conceptualization: the single-ontology approach and the multiple-ontology approach. The single-ontology approach requires every application domain to be described using only one single ontology, and everyone in the world has to follow this ontology. The multiple-ontology approach allows the application domain to be

The consensus approach          The multiontology approach

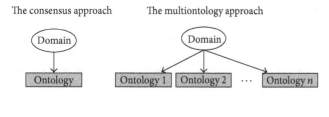

The proposed metaontology approach

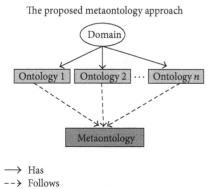

$\longrightarrow$ Has
$--\rightarrow$ Follows

FIGURE 4: Approaches for application domain conceptualization.

described by different ontologies such that everyone can use a different preferred ontology. As we can see both approaches have serious practicality concerns if adopted, the single-ontology approach requires reaching world consensus for every application domain conceptualization, which is far from feasible. On the other hand, the multiple-ontology approach requires determining the mappings between different ontologies in order to be able to resolve any appearing incompatibilities, which is not feasible approach when the number of ontologies describing a given application domain is big. Ontologies incompatibilities result due to many reasons. For example, two different concepts could be used to describe the same entity, or the same concept could be used to represent different entities. An entity could appear as an attribute in a given ontology and appear as a concept in other ontology, and so forth [32].

The ontology mapping process is very complex, and it requires identification of semantically related entities and then resolving their appearing differences. We argued before in [10] that any appearing conflicts should be resolved according to the defined semantics of involved application domains as well as the semantics of the involved usage contexts. When services in the same domain adopt different ontologies, ontology mapping becomes crucial for resolving conversation incompatibilities. To maintain the flexibility of application domain representation without complicating the ontology-mapping process, we propose to adopt a metaontology approach, which is a compromise between the consensus and multiple-ontology approaches, as depicted in Figure 4. Figure 4 shows the difference between the single-ontology, multiple-ontology, and metaontology approaches. Adopting a metaontology approach for application domain conceptualization provides users with the flexibility to use multiple ontologies exactly as in the multiple-ontology approach, but it requires ontology designers to follow a common structure

indicating the entities and the types of semantics to be captured, which indeed simplifies the ontology mapping process. Furthermore, having a common structure ensures that all application domain ontologies capture the same types of semantics; hence we can systematically resolve any appearing conflicts; more details are given in Section 4.

*2.4. Concepts Substitutability Graph (CSG).* As we indicated before that we adopt a metaontology approach for describing application domain ontologies. Following the separation of concerns design principle, we argue that the metaontology should consist of two layers: a schematic layer and a semantic layer [10, 13, 14]. The schematic layer defines which application domain entities need to be captured in the ontology, which will be used to define the systems models and their interaction messages. The semantic layer defines which entities semantics need to be captured in the ontology.

In the metaontology schematic layer, we propose to capture the application domain concepts and operations. *An application domain concept* is represented as a set of features defined in an attribute-value format. *An application domain operation* is represented as a set of features defined in an attribute-value format. In addition it has a set of input concepts, a set of output concepts, a set of preconditions and a set of postconditions. The preconditions are over the input concepts and must be satisfied before the operation invocation. The postconditions are over the output concepts and guaranteed to be satisfied after the operation finishes its execution.

A *conversation message* is basically represented by an application domain operation. A sequence of conversation messages constitutes a *conversation pattern*, which describes an interaction scenario supported by the service. Each conversation pattern has a corresponding *conversation context* that is represented as a set of preconditions and a set of postconditions. The context preconditions are the conditions that must be satisfied in order to be able to use the conversation pattern, while the context postconditions are the conditions guaranteed to be satisfied after the conversation pattern finishes its execution. A set of conversation patterns constitutes the *service conversation model*. In general, service conversation models are not necessarily linear. However, linear models (in which interactions are described as a sequence of operations) could be extracted from the nonlinear models (in which interactions are described as a graph of operations) by tracing all possible paths in the nonlinear model. During runtime, having linear conversation patterns provides faster performance than subgraph matching approaches, as graph paths are analyzed and enumerated (which could be performed offline) only once when a service is published and not repeated every time a matching process is needed as in subgraph matching approaches; additional details about this approach may be found in [10].

In our previous work [10, 12, 15, 16], we argued that concept substitutability should be used for concept matching that our approach maps a concept A to a concept B only if the concept A can substitute the concept B in the involved context without violating any conditions in the involved context

TABLE 1: A Part of CSG segment for `CargoTransportation` operation, adapted from [10].

| From scope | To scope | Conversion function | Substitution constraints |
|---|---|---|---|
| Cargo.Det | Freight.Det | Freight.Det = Cargo.Det | |
| Freight.Det | Cargo.Det | Cargo.Det = Freight.Det | |
| Credit.Period | Payment.Type | IF (Credit.Period > 0) THEN<br>Payment.Type = Credit<br>ELSE<br>Payment.Type = Cash<br>END IF | Credit.Period $\geq$ 0 |
| Payment.Type | Credit.Period | IF (Payment.Type = Credit) THEN<br>Credit.Period $\in$ {15, 30, 45, 60}<br>ELSE<br>Credit.Period = 0<br>END IF | Payment.Type $\in$ {Credit, Cash} |

or any rule defined in the application domain ontology. Matching concepts based on their conditional substitutability is not a straightforward process due to many reasons. First, there exist different types of mappings between concepts such as one-to-one, one-to-many, many-to-one, and many-to-many mappings, which require taking concept aggregation into consideration. For example, the `Address` concept could be substituted by a composite concept constituted from the `Country`, `State`, `City`, and `Street` concepts, as long as the usage context allows such substitution. Second, concept substitution semantics could vary according to the logic of the involved application domain operation; hence substitution semantics should be captured for each operation separately. Third, concept substitutability should be determined in a context-sensitive manner and not via generic schematic relations in order to be able to check if such concept substitution violates the usage context or not. In order to fulfill these requirements and capture the concept conditional substitution semantics in a machine-understandable format, we propose to use a complex graph data structure, known as the Concepts Substitutability Enhanced Graph (CSEG), which is able to capture the aggregate concept substitution semantics in a context-sensitive manner with respect to every application domain operation. Hence, we propose the metaontology semantic layer to include CSEG as one of its basic constructs.

CSEG extends the Concept Substitutability Graph (CSG) previously proposed in [10], which captures only the bilateral conditional substitution semantics between concepts. CSEG captures both bilateral as well as aggregate conditional substitution semantics of application domain concepts. Hence, we first summarize CSG graph depicted in Figure 5 and then discuss CSEG in more details. Figure 5 indicates that CSG consists of segments, where each segment captures the substitution semantics between application domain concepts with respect to a given application domain operation. For every pair of concepts the following are defined: substitutable attributes and their substitution constraints, conversion functions, and operator mapping matrices. The substitution context is represented by a set of substitution constraints that must be satisfied during substitution in order to have a valid substitution. A CSG captures the concepts functional

substitution semantics at the scope level (a scope is defined by a combination of concept $C_i$ and attribute $attr_k$ with the form $C_i.attr_k$), and not at the concept level only. This is needed because attributes with similar names could have different semantics when they are used to describe different concepts.

The proposed concept matching approach maps a concept A to a concept B only if the concept A can substitute the concept B in the involved context without violating any conditions in the involved context or any rule defined in the application domain ontology. This is done by defining the conditional substitution semantics of application domain concepts in application domain ontologies and then using such conditional semantics to resolve appearing incompatibilities by checking if the conditions representing the involved context satisfy the required substitution conditions between concepts before performing any concepts substitutions. In other words, concept mapping is conditional and not generic that concept mapping will be only valid in the contexts satisfying the required substitution conditions. Table 1 shows an example of a segment of a CSG in the logistics application domain that corresponds to the *CargoTransportation* operation. A row represents an edge in a segment in the substitutability graph. For example, the first row indicates the existence of an edge in the CSG going from the scope `Cargo.Det` (the cargo details) into the scope `Freight.Det` (the freight details). This edge has also the corresponding substitution constraint as well as conversion function. Substitutability semantics defined in CSG can be seen as conditional conversion semantics, as it allows conversion only when the substitution constraints are valid. Also it provides the details of how to perform such conversion via conversion functions and operator mapping matrices.

CSG managed to provide a conditional ontology mapping approach that is able to resolve appearing concepts incompatibilities in a context-sensitive manner (more details will be given later in Section 4.1). Unfortunately, this approach cannot resolve cases requiring concept aggregation, in which one concept can substitute for a group of concepts and vice versa. For example, in the signature incompatibilities example given before, this proposed approach can resolve the conflict between the `Confirmation` and `Receipt` concepts but it cannot resolve the conflict between the input concepts, as the

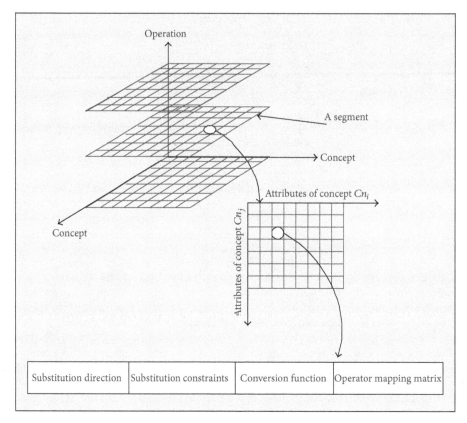

FIGURE 5: Concepts substitutability graph.

CreditCard, Amount, and Currency concepts need to be aggregated in order to substitute the Payment concept. To overcome such a limitation, our work in [13, 14] extended CSG graph to capture aggregate conditional substitution semantics of application domain concepts. The new graph is known as the Concepts Substitutability Enhanced Graph (CSEG). CSEG uses the notion of substitution patterns that indicate the mapping types (such as one-to-one, one-to-many, many-to-one, and many-to-many) between application domain concepts with respect to every application domain operation. More details about CSEG are given in Section 4.

## 3. Related Work

This section discusses two main related areas for our work. First, we discuss related work in the area of conversation adaptation and then discuss the related work in the area of ontology mapping that shows different approaches for resolving conflicts.

*3.1. Conversation Adaptation.* The problem of synthesizing adapters for incompatible conversations has been studied by many researchers in the area of SOC such as the work described in [2–8, 11] and earlier in the area of component-based software engineering such as the work described in [9]. We can broadly classify these efforts into three categories:

manual such as work in [2, 3, 7, 8], semiautomated such as work in [4, 9], and fully automated solutions such as work in [5, 6, 11].

The manual approaches provide users with guidelines to identify conversation incompatibilities and propose templates to resolve identified mismatches. for example, work in [7] tries to mediate between services based on signatures without taking into consideration services behavior, while work in [8] requires adapter specification to be defined manually. On the other hand, work in [3] proposes a method for creating adapters based on mismatch patterns in service composition; however they adopt a syntactic approach for comparing patterns operations, which of course cannot work if different operations sequences or different operation signatures are used.

The semiautomated approaches generate the adapters after receiving some inputs from the users regarding conversation incompatibilities resolution. The fully automated approaches generate the adapters without human intervention provided that conversation models are created according to some restrictions to avoid having signature incompatibilities and protocol deadlocks. Manual and semiautomated approaches are not suitable for dynamic environments due to the following reasons. First, they require experts to analyze the conversation models and to design solutions for incompatibilities resolution, resulting in high financial costs and time barriers for adapter development. This creates obstacles for achieving on-demand customizations and minimizes users' flexibility and agility, especially when users tend to use services for a short term and to change services frequently. Second, the number of services and users in dynamic environments is rapidly growing, which diminishes any chances for having predefined manual customizations policies. Therefore, to have on-demand conversation customizations, adapters should be created automatically. To achieve such a vision, we argue that the middleware should be enabled to automatically create such adapters to avoid any human intervention and to ensure smooth services interoperability. Unfortunately, existing automatic adapter generation approaches are strictly limited [11, 20] as they require no mismatch at the services interface level; otherwise the conversations are considered unadaptable. We argue that such syntactic approaches are not suitable for dynamic environments as service heterogeneity is totally expected in dynamic environments. Hence, conversation incompatibilities should be semantically resolved without any human intervention. Therefore, in this paper, we capture both service conversations and application domain semantics in a machine-understandable format such that we can automatically resolve appearing conflicts without human intervention; more details are given in Sections 5, 6, 7, and 8.

*3.2. Ontology Mapping.* Concepts incompatibilities arise when business systems adopt different application domain ontologies during their interactions. One approach for resolving such incompatibilities is using an intermediate ontology mapping approach that transforms the exchanged concepts into concepts understandable by the interacting systems. Unfortunately, existing approaches for ontology mapping are known for having limited accuracy. This is because such approaches are basically based on generic schematic relations (such as Is-a and Part-of) and ignore the involved usage context as well as the logic of the involved operation.

We argue that the ontology mapping process could be tolerated if the number of ontologies representing a given application domain is small and if there exists a systematic straightforward approach in finding the mappings between semantically related entities. Indeed, in real life, we are expecting the number of ontologies describing a given application domain to be small, as people tend to cluster and unify their understanding. Of course, we are not expecting them to cluster into one group that uses a single ontology; however it is more likely they will cluster into few groups using different ontologies. To fulfil the second requirement, many research efforts have been proposed to provide systematic straightforward approaches for ontology mapping such as [33–37]. A good survey about existing ontology mapping approaches could be found in [22]. For example, work in [33] proposed a language for specifying correspondence rules between data elements adopting a general structure consisting of general ordered labelled trees. Work in [34] developed a translation system for symbolic knowledge. It provides a language to represent complex syntactic transformations and uses syntactic rewriting (via pattern-directed rewrite rules) and semantic rewriting (via partial semantic models and some supported logical inferences) to translate different

statements. Its inferences are based on generic taxonomic relationships. Work in [35] provides an ontology mapping approach based on tree structure grammar. They try to combine between internal concept structure information and rules provided by similarity languages. Work in [36] proposed a metric for determining objects similarity using hierarchical domain structure (i.e. Is-a relations) in order to produce more intuitive similarity scores. work in [37] determines the mapping between different models without translating the models into a common language. Such mapping is defined as a set of relationships between expressions over the given model, where syntactical inferences are used to find matching elements. As we can see, existing ontology mapping approaches try to provide a general translation model that can fit in all contexts using generic schematic relations (such as Is-a and Part-of relations), or depending on linguistic similarities to resolve conflicts. We argue that such approaches cannot guarantee high accuracy mapping results in all contexts [10]. Simply because such generic relations and linguistic rules could be sources of ambiguities, which are resulting from the actual domain semantics themselves. For example, the concept Islam could be a name of a religion or a name of a person and could be applied for both males and females. Another example, the Resort concept could be related to the Hotel concept using the *Is-a* relation, however, we cannot substitute the concept Resort by the concept Hotel in all context. Such ambiguities can be resolved only by taking the involved contexts into consideration. Hence, we argue that in order to guarantee the correctness of the mapping results, ontology mappings should be determined in a customized manner according to the usage context as well as the logic of the involved application domain operation (i.e. the transaction needs to be accomplished by interacting systems or users). Next section provides our approach for fulfilling these requirements.

# 4. A Context-Sensitive Metaontology for Applications Domains

Unlike CSG only capturing bilateral substitution semantics between application domain concepts, CSEG is able to capture the aggregate concept conditional substitution semantics in a context-sensitive manner to allow a concept to be substituted by a group of concepts and vice versa. This is achieved by introducing the notion of substitution patterns. CSEG consists of a collection of segments, such that each segment is corresponding to one of the application domain operations. Each segment consists of a collection of substitution patterns corresponding to the operation input and output concepts. Each substitution pattern consists of a scope, a set of substitution conditions, and a conversion function, as depicted in Figure 6.

Figure 6 indicates the substitution patterns corresponding to a given operation input and output concepts. For example, the input concept C1 has three substitution patterns. The first pattern indicates that the concepts C5, C6, and C7 can substitute the concept.

TABLE 2: An example for operation substitution patterns.

| Operation | Concepts | Scope | Conversion function | Substitution condition |
|-----------|----------|-------|---------------------|------------------------|
| PayOnline | Input: CreditCard<br>Input: Amount<br>Input: Currency | Payment | Payment.Method = Credit<br>Payment.Details = CreditCard.Details<br>Payment.Currency = Currency<br>Payment.CreditAmt = Amount | CreditCard.Details ≠ NULL<br>Amount >0<br>Currency ≠ NULL |
| | Output: Receipt | Confirmation | Receipt = Confirmation | Confirmation ≠ NULL |

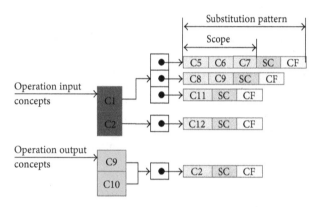

SC: Substitution conditions
CF: Conversion function

FIGURE 6: An example for a CSEG segment.

A substitution pattern scope is a set of concepts that contains at least one application domain concept. A substitution condition is a condition that must be satisfied by the conversation context in order to consider such substitution as valid. A conversion function indicates the logic needed to convert the scope into the corresponding operation concepts or vice versa. Of course, instead of writing the conversion function code, we could refer to a service or a function that realizes it using its corresponding Uniform Resource Identifier (URI). A substitution pattern could correspond to a subset of concepts. For example, a substitution pattern for a subset of input concepts represents the set of concepts (i.e. the pattern scope) that can substitute such subset of input concepts, while a substitution pattern for a subset of output concepts represents the set of concepts that can be substituted by such subset of output concepts.

Table 2 shows an example of an input and an output substitution patterns for PayOnline operation. The input pattern indicates that CreditCard, Amount, and Currency concepts can be replaced by the Payment concept only if credit card details and the currency are not null and the amount is greater than zero. The output pattern indicates we can substitute the concept Confirmation by the concept Receipt only when conformation is not null. As we can see, substitution patterns are valid only in the contexts satisfying their substitution conditions. Of course instead of writing the conversion function code, we could refer to the URI of its realizing web service. Another advantage of using CSEG

is that it systemizes the ontology mapping process, as all that needs to be done is to add the suitable substitution patterns between the ontologies concepts with respect to every domain operation. The mappings between the operations will be automatically determined based on the satisfiability of their pre- and postconditions (details are given later). In the next section, we will show how CSEG substitution patterns are used to resolve concepts incompatibilities.

Indeed CSEG could be represented in many different ways differing in their efficiency. However, we prefer to represent it in an XML format as XML is the industrial de facto standard for sharing information. In case the XML file becomes very large, it should be compressed with a query-aware XML compressor and then accessed in its compressed format; more details about this approach could be found in [38]. For example, the substitution patterns depicted in Table 2 could be represented in XML format as shown in Listing 1.

*4.1. Resolving Concepts Conflicts via Substitutability Semantics.* CSEG contains the information indicating which concepts are substitutable with respect to every application domain and also indicates the corresponding conversion functions. Hence, concepts mapping is determined by checking if there exists a sequence of transformations (i.e. substitution patterns) that can be carried out to transform a given concept or a group of concepts into another concept or group of concepts. This is done by checking if there exists a path between the different concepts in the CSEG segment corresponding to the involved application domain operation. Having no path indicates there is no mapping between such concepts according to the logic of the involved operation. We identify the concepts as reachable if such path is found. However, in order to consider reachable concepts as substitutable, we have to make sure that the usage context is not violated by such transformations. This is done by checking if the conditions of the usage context satisfy the substitution conditions defined along the identified path between the concepts. The concepts are considered substitutable only when the usage context satisfies such substitution conditions. Determining condition satisfiability is a tricky process, as conditions could have different scopes (i.e. concepts appearing in the conditions) and yet could be satisfiable; for example, the condition (Capital.Name = Cairo) satisfies the condition (Country.Name = Egypt) in spite of having a different scope. Unfortunately, such cases cannot be resolved by existing condition satisfiability approaches [39, 40] as they

```
<Root>
    <Operation name = "PayOnline">
        <Inputs>
            <Concepts names = {"CreditCard, Amount, Currency"} >
                <SubstitutionPattern>
                    <Scope>
                        <Concepts names = {"Payment"}/>
                    </Scope>
                    <Condition>
                        (CreditCard.Details ≠ NULL) and (Amount >0)
                        and (Currency ≠ NULL)
                    </Condition>
                    <ConversionFunction>
                        "http://example.org/URI/path/convert1.java"
                    </ConversionFunction>
                </SubstitutionPattern>
            </Concepts>
        </Inputs>
        <Outputs>
            <Concepts names = {"Receipt"} >
                <SubstitutionPattern>
                    <Scope>
                        <Concepts names = {"Confirmation"}/>
                    </Scope>
                    <Condition>
                        (Confirmation ≠ NULL)
                    </Condition>
                    <ConversionFunction>
                        "http://example.org/URI/path/convert2.java"
                    </ConversionFunction>
                </SubstitutionPattern>
            </Concepts>
        </Outputs>
    </Operation>
    -
</Root>
```

LISTING 1: An XML representation for a CSEG segment.

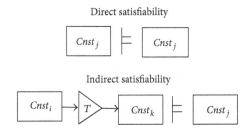

FIGURE 7: Direct versus indirect condition satisfiability.

are syntactic and require the conditions to have the same scope in order to be examined.

To handle such cases, first we differentiate between the two cases as follows. When satisfiable conditions have the same scope, we identify this case as *"condition direct satisfiability"* which should be determined using existing condition satisfiability approaches. When satisfiable conditions have different scopes, we identify such case as *"condition indirect satisfiability"* which should be determined via generation of intermediate condition, as depicted in Figure 7. The figure indicates that conditions indirect satisfiability implies transforming the first condition into another intermediate condition via a transformation (T) such that the intermediate condition directly satisfies the second condition. Transformation (T) must not violate any condition in the usage context. We determine conditions indirect satisfiability between two different conditions as follows. First, we check if the conditions scopes are reachable. Second, if the scopes are reachable, we use the conversion functions defined along the path to convert the first scope into the second scope and use the obtained values to generate another intermediate condition with the same scope of the second condition. Third, we check if the intermediate condition satisfies the second condition using existing syntactic condition satisfiability approaches. Finally, if the intermediate condition satisfies the second condition, we check if the conditions of the usage context

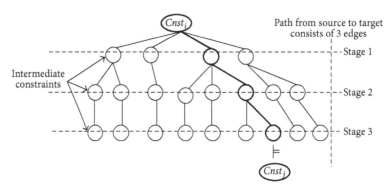

FIGURE 8: Generated intermediate conditions.

TABLE 3: Interaction context.

| Goal | Freight movement |
|---|---|
| Preconstraints | {Freight.Det ≠ Null, Origin.Det ≠ Null, Dest.Det ≠ Null, IncoTerm.Type ∈ {FOB, EXW, CIF}} |
| Desc-Constraints | {Credit.Period = 15, Speciality.Type ⊆ {Motor-Vehicles}} |
| Postconstraints | {ShippingOrder.Status = Fulfilled, Payment.Status = Received} |

satisfy the substitution conditions defined along the path to accept such transformation. More theoretical details and proofs regarding indirect satisfiability could be found in [10]. As a conversion function could have multiple finite output values, the first condition could be transformed into a finite number of intermediate constraints at a given stage (i.e., a path edge). This forms a finite tree of the possible intermediate constraints that can be obtained from the first condition using the defined finite conversion function. When one of the intermediate constraints of the final stage directly satisfies the second condition, this implies that the first condition can indirectly satisfy the second condition, as indicated in Figure 8. More details about the condition indirect satisfiability approach and the techniques for intermediate conditions generation as well as the corresponding theoretical proofs could be found in [10].

## 5. Service Conversation Model: $G^+$ Model

Services interactions are captured via the $G^+$ model [10, 12, 16, 41]. $G^+$ model captures services goals and interaction contexts as well as the expected interaction scenarios (depicted in Figure 9). A goal is represented by an application domain operation, a scenario is represented by a sequence of application domain operations, and a context is represented by different sets of constraints over application domain concepts (that is pre, post, and capability describing constraints), as in Table 3.

A Goal Achievement Pattern (GAP) is a global (end-to-end) snapshot of how the service's goal is expected to be

accomplished, representing one given way to achieve a goal. A GAP is determined by following the path from the goal node to a leaf operation node, as depicted in Figure 9.

At the point where a branch starts, a group of constraints must be valid in order to visit that branch. This group of constraints acts as a *subcontext* for the GAP. This subcontext will be added to the preconstraints of the context of the $G^+$ model to form the GAP interaction context, forming what we define as a *conversation context*, and the GAP formulates what we define as a *conversation pattern*. In order to be able to semantically match conversation patterns, we need to generate their corresponding behavior models. A behavior model corresponding to a given conversation pattern is a sequence of conversation states representing the transition point between its operations. The first transition point is the point before invoking the first operation in the pattern, and the final transition point is the point after finishing the execution of the last operation in the pattern. Intermediate transition points are the points located between each pair of consecutive operation. A conversation state is represented by a set of conditions that are guaranteed to be satisfied at the corresponding transition point. For example, the conditions at the first transition point are the preconditions of the conversation context, while the conditions at a given transition point $x$ are the ones constituted from the postconditions of the preceding operations as well as the preconditions of the conversation context that are still satisfied at $x$. Table 4 shows a simplified example for a sequence of operations and its corresponding state sequence. We propose a new way for representing a behavior state that helps us to improve the matching accuracy. Instead of representing the state as a set of conditions or constraints holding at a given transition point, we differentiate between these constraints based on their effect on the next operation to be executed. As we can see in Table 4, we classify state conditions in two classes: effective conditions and idle conditions. Effective conditions are the minimal subset of the state conditions that satisfies the preconditions of the following operation, while the idle conditions are the maximal subset of the state conditions that are independent from the preconditions of the following operation. This differentiation is important as states will be matched according to their effective conditions only, as including idle conditions in the state matching process just

TABLE 4: An example of a conversation pattern and its corresponding state sequence.

| Conversation pattern | Preconditions | Postconditions |
|---|---|---|
| Conversation context | $C.a = 10$ <br> $C.b = 20$ | |
| OP1 | $C.a \neq$ NULL | $C.a < 0$ <br> $C.x = 5$ |
| OP2 | $C.b \neq$ NULL <br> $C.x \neq$ NULL | $C.b > 0$ |

| State | Effective conditions | Idle conditions |
|---|---|---|
| $S_0$ | $C.a = 10$ | $C.b = 20$ |
| $S_1$ | $C.b = 20, C.x = 5$ | $C.a < 0$ |
| $S_2$ | $C.a < 0, C.b > 0$ | |

adds unnecessary restrictions as idle conditions have no effect on the invocation of the following operation [10].

The first row in Table 4 contains the conversation context. The preconditions of the conversation context are divided into an effective condition ($C.a = 10$) and an idle condition ($C.b = 20$) to form the first state $S_0$, as only the condition ($C.a = 10$) is satisfying the pre-condition of operation OP1. After OP1 finishes its execution, three conditions are still satisfied ($C.b = 20$), ($C.x = 5$), and ($C.a < 0$), which in turn are divided into effective and idle conditions according to the preconditions of OP2 to form the state $S_1$. The process is repeated at every transition point to compute the corresponding state. We consider all the conditions of the final state as effective. Such behavior models could be constructed offline as well as on the fly, and they will be used to determine the mappings between conversation patterns to create the conversation adapter.

## 6. Signature Adaptation

This section discusses the proposed approach for signature adaptation. It is based on the context-sensitive conditional concept substitutability approach discussed before to resolve concepts conflicts using CSEG semantics. As a conversation message is formulated according to the vocabulary of the sending service, a chance for signature incompatibility may arise if such a vocabulary is not supported by the receiving service or the receiving service is adopting a different messaging schema. It is fortuitous that a signature incompatibility may be resolved using converters if the operations are substitutable with respect to the involved conversation context [10].

Operations mapping is determined based on their substitutability status. Operations substitutability is determined according to the satisfiability status between their pre- and postconditions, respectively, that an operation OP1 can be substituted by an operation OP2 when the preconditions of OP1 satisfy the preconditions of OP2 and the postconditions of OP2 satisfy the postconditions of OP1, as indicated in Figure 10. The figure shows that operation OP2 can substitute operation OP1 with respect to a given conversation context. OP2 is adapted to OP1 by generating an input converter (which converts OP1 inputs to OP2 inputs) and an output

converter (which converts OP2 outputs to OP1 outputs). Converters consist of a set of conversion functions determined according to the mapping types between involved concepts. Operations substitutability is determined according to the satisfiability status between their pre- and postconditions, respectively. An operation OP1 can be substituted by an operation OP2 when the preconditions of OP1 satisfy the preconditions of OP2 and the postconditions of OP2 satisfy the postconditions of OP1. Operations substitutability is not necessarily bidirectional, as it depends on the satisfiability directions between their conditions. When we have two operations OP1 and OP2 with different signatures, we check if the preconditions of OP1 satisfy the preconditions of OP2 and the postconditions of OP2 satisfy the postconditions of OP1 with respect to the conversation context as discussed above. When such conditions are satisfied, the input and output converters are generated from the conversation functions defined along the identified paths. We summarize the steps needed to generate a converter that transforms a set of concept A to a set of concepts B in Algorithm 1. Generating concepts converters is not a trivial task, as it requires to capture the conversion semantics between application domain concepts, in a context-based finite manner and requires use of these semantic to determine conversion validation with respect to the conversation context. Luckily, concept substitutability graph captures concepts functional substitutability semantics in a context-based manner and provides the conversion semantics and the substitutability constraints that must be satisfied by the conversation context, in order to have a valid conversion. It is important to note that one concept can be converted to another concept in one context, and the same two concepts cannot be converted in other contexts. In order to determine whether two concepts are convertible or not, first we check if the there is a path between the two concepts in the CSEG. If there is no path this means that they cannot be convertible; otherwise, we check the satisfiability of the substitution constraints along the path with respect to the conversation context. If all the constraints are satisfied, this means that the concepts are convertible; otherwise, they are not. Details about this process are in given [10, 16].

To convert a list of concepts to another list, first we construct a concepts mapping matrix ($\Gamma$) between the two lists (one list is represented by the columns, and the other is represented by the rows). A matrix cell has the value 1 if the corresponding concepts are convertible in the direction needed otherwise the cell will have the value 0. When concepts are convertible, we perform the conversion process by invoking the conversion functions defined along with the edges of the path between them. So the invocation code of such conversion functions forms the source code of the needed converter. Steps of generating such converter are indicated in Algorithm 1.

The converter class will have a CONVERT method to be invoked to perform the conversion process. Of course conversion functions along the path are cascaded, so there is no need for adaptation. The converter is represented as a class with different methods corresponding to conversion functions to be invoked. Algorithm 1 requires the converter class to have a CONVERT method, which is invoked to apply

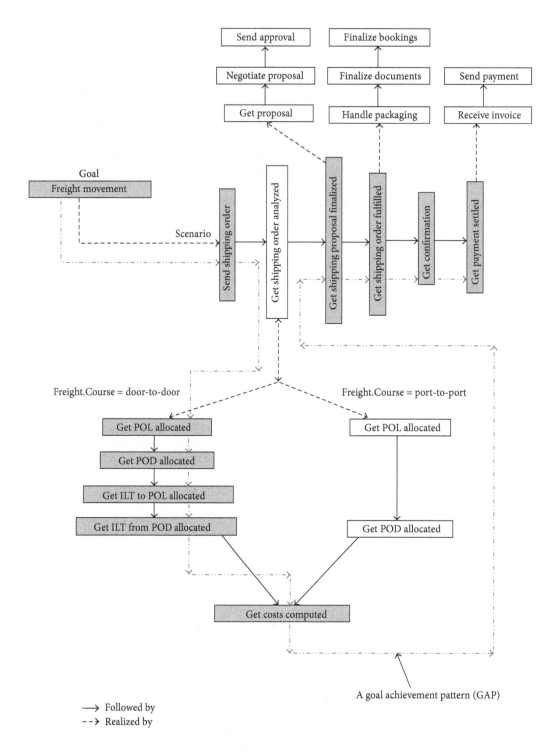

FIGURE 9: Interaction scenarios.

the conversions. The algorithm indicates that each element in B should be reachable to a subset of A (i.e., the subset appeared as a scope in a given substitution pattern) and also indicates that the conversation context should satisfy all the substitution conditions defined along the identified path; otherwise such concept substitution is considered invalid and cannot be used. Once substitutions validity is confirmed, the determined concepts mappings are accepted, and the converter is generated. Figure 11 shows an example for a converter consisting of six conversion functions resulting from different types of concept mappings. For example, the conversion function *CF4* is responsible for converting the concepts C6

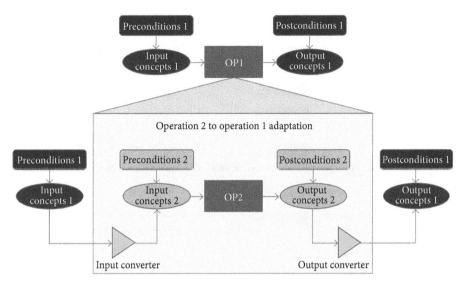

FIGURE 10: Signature adaptation.

and C7 into the concept C8. In the next section, we show how the substitutability between two different sequences of operations (conversation patterns) is determined. More details about adapter generation will be given later.

## 7. Conversation Protocol Adaptation

One approach for semantically resolving conversation incompatibilities involves the use of the substitutability rule [10, 42] in which two conversation patterns are considered compatible when one pattern can substitute for the other without violating any condition in the corresponding conversation context. In order to determine the substitutability between two conversation patterns, we must check the substitutability of their messages (representing the operations to be performed), which in turn requires checking the substitutability of their input and output concepts. Hence, the first step needed to resolve conversation incompatibilities involves the ability to automatically determine concepts substitutability, as indicated before.

Every service supports a specific number of conversation patterns and requires other services to follow the supported patterns during their interactions. However, protocol incompatibilities could arise when the interacting services expect different ordering for the exchanged message sequences. Protocol incompatibilities may be resolved if there exists a mapping pattern between the operations appeared in the conversation patterns [10]. Conversation adapter structure is decided according to the determined operations mappings, as they specify which messages should be generated by the adapter when a given message or a sequence of messages is received. Operations mappings could be of different types such as one-to-one, one-to-many, many-to-one, and many-to-many mappings and guaranteed to exist if the conversation patterns are substitutable with respect to the conversation context [10]. Hence, to resolve protocol incompatibilities, first we must check the substitutability of the involved

conversation patterns, and then find their corresponding operations mappings. Conversation patterns substitutability is determined according to the satisfiability status between their pre and postconditions corresponding to the pre and postconditions of their contexts, respectively, that a conversation pattern $CP1$ can be substituted by a conversation pattern $CP2$ when the preconditions of $CP1$ satisfy the preconditions of $CP2$ and the postconditions of $CP2$ satisfy the postconditions of $CP1$. Conversation patterns substitutability is not necessarily bidirectional, as it depends on the satisfiability directions between their conditions. To find the operation mappings between two substitutable conversation patterns, we must analyze their corresponding behavior models as operations are matched semantically not syntactically. To find the operation mappings between two substitutable conversation patterns, we must find the mappings between their corresponding behavior states by grouping adjacent states in both models into matching clusters. A state $S_x$ matches a state $S_y$ only when the effective conditions of $S_x$ satisfy the effective conditions of $S_y$. A cluster $CL_x$ matches another cluster $CL_y$ when the state resulting from merging $CL_x$ states matches the state resulting from merging $CL_y$ states, as depicted in Figure 12.

The figure shows the initial state sequences, the state clusters, and the final state sequences. Merging two consecutive states $S_x, S_{x+1}$ in a given behavior model to form a new expanded state $S_m$ means that we performed a virtual operation merge between $OP_{x+1}, OP_{x+2}$ to obtain a coarser operation $OP_m$, as depicted in Figure 13. The figure indicates that the input of $OP_m$ is formulated from the sets of concepts A and B, and its output is formulated from the sets of concepts C and E. As we can see, the set of concepts D does not appear in $OP_m$ signature and consequently will not appear in $S_m$ conditions. Such information hiding provides a chance for having matching states. $S_m$ is computed by reclassifying the effective and idle conditions of $S_x$ into new sets of effective and idle conditions according to the preconditions of $OP_m$. For example, by merging states $S_0, S_1$ shown in

Converter structure

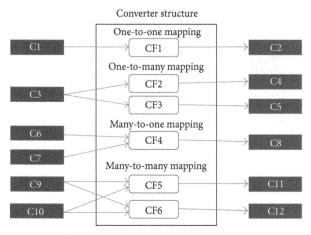

FIGURE 11: Converter structure.

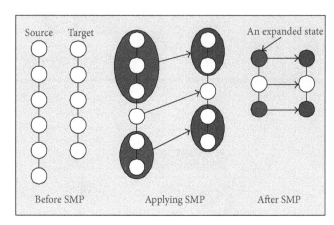

FIGURE 12: State clustering effect.

Table 4, the resulting $S_m$ will have the set ($C.a$ = 10), ($C.b$ = 20) as its effective conditions, and the set ($C.a$ < 0), ($C.b$ > 0) as its idle conditions. As we can see, conditions on $C.x$ do not appear in $S_m$. We use a Sequence Mediation Procedure (SMP) (discussed in the next subsection) to find such matching clusters. SMP starts by examining the initial states in both sequences, then moves forward and backward along the state sequences until matching clusters are formed and the corresponding operations mappings are determined. The highest level of abstraction that could be reached occurs when all the conversation pattern operations are merged into one operation. As the number of the states is quite small, the backtracking approach does not diminish the performance.

*7.1. Conversation Pattern Matching.* Sequence Mediator Procedure (SMP) is a procedure used to match different state sequences. Such state sequences are generated from the GAPs (conversation patterns) to be matched. Each transition point $x$ between two consecutive operations $Op_x$ and $Op_{x+1}$ in a given GAP is represented by a behavior state. Such state is captured via constraints active at this transition point $x$. A constraint at a transition point $x$ is considered effective if it needs to be true in order to invoke $Op_{x+1}$. A state $S_x$ matches a state $S_y$ when its effective constraints subsume the effective constraints of $S_y$ (theoretical models and proofs could be found in [10]). SMP does not require the state sequences to have the same number of states in order to be matched; however, it applies different state expansion operations to reach to a matching case if possible. When a state is expanded, it could be merged with either its successor states (known as *Down Expansion* and denoted as $\Downarrow_G$) or its predecessor states (known as *Reverse Expansion* and denoted as $\Uparrow_G$), where $G$ is the conversation goal, setting the conversation context. SMP uses these different types of state expansions to recluster unmatched state sequences to reach a matching case. This reclustering operation could happen on both state sequences, as indicated in Figure 12. Merging two consecutive states in a given state sequence means that their successor operations are merged to form a new operation, as depicted in Figure 13.

Figure 13 shows that the states $S_x$ and $S_{x+1}$ are merged forming a new state $S_m$, which is computed as if there is a new operation $Op_m$ in the sequence replacing the operations $Op_{x+1}$ and $Op_{x+2}$. The input of $Op_m$ is the union between the sets of concepts A and B, its output is the union between the sets of concepts C and E, while the set of concepts D will not appear neither in $Op_m$ input nor in $Op_m$ output.

SMP tries to recluster both state sequences until it reached into an organization that has both sequences matched; if such organization is reached, SMP announces that it found a match and provides the mappings between the resulting clusters. Such mappings are provided in the form of an Operations Mapping Matrix (denoted as $\Theta$) that indicated which operations in a source sequence are mapped to which operations in a target sequence, as indicated in Table 5.

Once obtaining the operations mapping matrix from SMP, only matched GAPs that require no change in the requested conversation pattern will be chosen, and therefore their corresponding adapters could be generated. SMP starts by examining the first state of the "source target" against the first state of the "target sequence." When the source state matches the target state, SMP applies Algorithm 2 to handle the matching case. When a source state matches a target state, SMP checks the target down expansion to match as many target states as possible with the source state (lines 2 and 3).

In Algorithm 3, SMP aims to find a matching source cluster for every target state. However, when a source state fails to match a target state, SMP checks if the source state could be down expandable (lines 5–7). If this checking fails too, SMP checks whether the source state could be reverse expanded with respect to the target state (lines 9–11). When a source state cannot be expanded in either directions, SMP tries the successor source states to match the target state using the down and reverse source expansion scenarios (line 16). It stores the unmatched source state for backtracking purposes (line 13). When a target state cannot be matched to any source state, SMP tries reverse expanding the target state to find a match for it (lines 18–20); when that fails this target state is considered unmatched, and the next target state will be examined (lines 22-23). The algorithm continues even if unmatched target state is reached, as this unmatched state

```
Input: Set of concepts A, B, Conversation Context CC,
and The CSEG segment S.
Output: Source code of converting A to B with respect
to CC.
  Begin
  Get Concepts Mapping Matrix Γ between A and B.
  Create an empty class CONVERTER.
  Create a method CONVERT with A as its input, and
  B as its output.
  for each concept cᵢ in A do
      Get corresponding mapping concept cⱼ using Γ.
      if There exists a path from cᵢ to cⱼ in S then
          for each edge e₍w,z₎ in the path do
              Create a method in CONVERTER with same
              signature and body of the edge conversion function Ψ₍w,z₎.
              Add Ψ₍w,z₎ invocation code to CONVERT body.
          end for
      else
          Return Error.
      end if
  end for
  Return CONVERTER generated code.
  End
```

ALGORITHM 1: Converter generator.

could be merged with any of its successors if they are going to be reversely expanded.

## 8. Automatic Adapter Generation

Each service has different conversation patterns (generated from its $G^+$ model) that could use to interact with other services. Such conversation patterns could be matched by one service or by many different services, as depicted in Figure 14.

Figure 14 indicates that each conversation pattern should have its own adapter. Once the required conversation patterns are specified via the management interfaces (as indicated in Section 2.1), the adapter generation process is started. The outcome of the adapter generation process is the source code for the adapter class that consists of the methods to be invoked by the consuming services. The body of these methods consists of the invocation code for the consumed service operations and the invocation code for the corresponding converters. First, we determine the required adapter structure then generate the source code for the adapter and the needed converters. Once the class adapter is generated, it is compiled, and the corresponding WSDL file is generated, in order to expose the adapter class as a service, which could be easily invoked by the consuming service. The details are discussed in the following subsections.

Once two services "decide" to interact with each other, they notify the middleware such that it identifies their substitutable conversation patterns and generates the corresponding conversation adapters. The middleware notifies back the services with the identified substitutable patterns such that each service knows which patterns should be used

TABLE 5: Example of a conversation patterns mapping matrix $\Theta$.

| Mapping type | $CP_x$ | $CP_y$ |
|---|---|---|
| 1 to 1 | $OP_{(x,1)}$ | $OP_{(y,1)}$ |
| 1 to many | $OP_{(x,2)}$ | $OP_{(y,2)}, OP_{(y,3)}$ |
| Many to 1 | $OP_{(x,3)}, OP_{(x,4)}$ | $OP_{(y,4)}$ |
| Many to many | $OP_{(x,5)}, OP_{(x,6)}$ | $OP_{(y,5)}, OP_{(y,6)}, OP_{(y,7)}$ |

during the conversation [11]. Once a conversation pattern $CP_x$ is identified as substitutable with a conversation pattern $CP_y$, the middleware performs the following steps (similar to Algorithm 1) to generate their corresponding conversation adapter, which transforms $CP_x$ incoming messages into $CP_y$ outgoing messages. First, it generates an adapter class with methods corresponding to $CP_x$ operations (incoming messages), such that each method consists of a signature (similar to the signature of the corresponding incoming message) and an empty body (which will be later containining the code for generating the corresponding $CP_y$ outgoing messages). Second, it determines the operations mappings between $CP_x$ and $CP_y$ and then uses these mappings to construct the generation code for the outgoing message. Table 5 provides an example for a $CP_x$ conversation pattern that is substituted by a conversation pattern $CP_y$, showing the corresponding operations mappings.

Figure 15 shows the corresponding adapter structure. Signature incompatibilities are handled by generating the suitable input and output converters. The outgoing message generation code is constructed as follows.

In one-to-one operations mappings, one $CP_x$ operation matches one $CP_y$ operation. The input converter is created

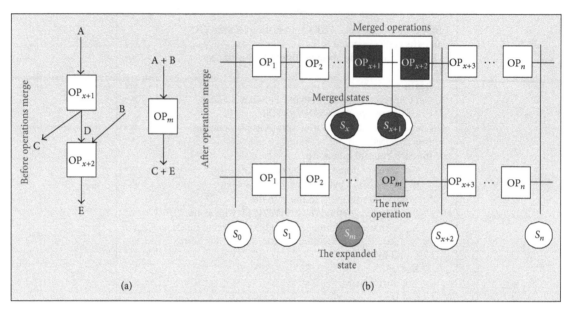

FIGURE 13: Consecutive states merge.

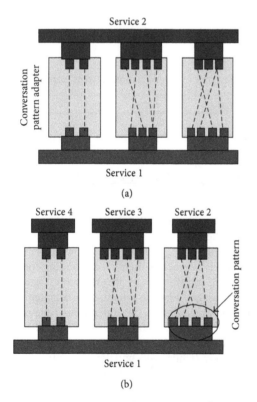

FIGURE 14: Service conversation patterns adapters.

between the inputs of the $CP_x$ operation and the inputs of $CP_y$ operation. The output converter is created between the outputs of the $CP_y$ operation and the outputs of $CP_x$ operation. The outgoing message generation code consists of the invocation code for the input converter, the $CP_y$ operation, and the output converter, as depicted for $OP_{x+1}$ in Figure 15.

In one-to-many operations mappings, one $CP_x$ operation matches subsequence of $CP_y$ operations. An input converter is created between the inputs of the $CP_x$ operation and the inputs of the $OP_{my}$ operation (resulting from merging the $CP_y$ subsequence). An output converter is created between the outputs of the $OP_{my}$ operation and the outputs of the $CP_x$ operation. The outgoing message generation code consists of the invocation code for the input converter, the $CP_y$ subsequence (multiple messages), and the output converter, as depicted for $OP_{(x,2)}$ in Figure 15.

In many-to-one operation mapping, a subsequence of $CP_x$ operations matches one $CP_y$ operation. The outgoing message cannot be generated unless all the operations of the $CP_x$ subsequence are received. Hence, before generating the outgoing message, all the incoming messages should be buffered until the last message is received. This is achieved by using a message buffer handler. An input converter is created between the inputs of $OP_{mx}$ (resulting from merging the $CP_x$ subsequence) and the inputs of the $CP_x$ operation. An output converter is created between the outputs of $CP_y$ operation and the outputs of the $OP_{mx}$ operation. The outgoing message generation code consists of the invocation code for the input converter, the $CP_y$ operation, and the output converter, as depicted for $OP_{(x,3)}$, $OP_{(x,4)}$ in Figure 15.

In many-to-many operation mapping, a subsequence of $CP_x$ operations matches a subsequence of $CP_y$ operations. Incoming messages are buffered as indicated earlier. An input converter is created between the inputs of $OP_{mx}$ and the inputs of $OP_{my}$. An output converter is created between the outputs of $OP_{my}$ and the outputs of $OP_{mx}$. The outgoing message generation code consists of the invocation code for the input converter, the $CP_y$ subsequence (multiple messages), and the output converter, as depicted for $OP_{(x,5)}$, $OP_{(x,6)}$ in Figure 15.

Once the adapter class is successfully generated, the middleware can reroute the conversation messages to the

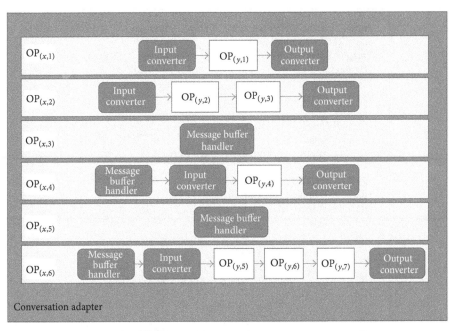

FIGURE 15: Conversation adapter structure for patterns in Table 5.

**Input:** $S[i]$ (the $i$th source state), $T[j]$ (the $j$th target state), $G$ (the required goal)
**Output:** Return true when sequences re-clustering is finished.
(1) **Begin**
(2)   **if** $(T[j] \Downarrow_G S[i])$ **then**
(3)     Expand $T[j]$
(4)   **end if**
(5)   Mark $T[j]$, $S[i]$ as matching peers
(6)   **if** $(j < \|T[]\|)$ **then**
(7)     **if** $(i < \|S[]\|)$ **then**
(8)       Apply Algorithm 4 over $(S[i+1], T[j+1], G)$
(9)     **else**
(10)      Apply Algorithm 4 over $(S[i], T[j+1], G)$
(11)     **end if**
(12) **else**
(13)     Return true
(14) **end if**
(15) **End**

ALGORITHM 2: SMP matching case handling.

adapter service (corresponding to the generated class) to perform the needed conversation customizations. Invoking operations from existing services is a straightforward simple task, however generating the inputs and outputs converters is not, as we need to find the mappings between the concepts and their conversion functions. Steps of generating such adapter class are indicated in Algorithm 4. Algorithm 4 simply starts by creating an empty class then adds methods to this class with the same signatures of the consuming service conversation pattern. For each created method, it gets the sequence of operations realizing the method with the help of the operation mapping matrix($\Theta$). Then, it creates the concepts converters by calling the `ConverterGenerator`

function (depicted in Algorithm 1) with the proper parameters. Finally, it adds the converter generated code to the adapter if no error resulted during the generation.

In case the algorithm returns error, this means conversation adaptation cannot be performed; therefore, these services cannot talk to each other on the fly, and a manual adapter needs to be created to enable such conversation.

## 9. Experiments

This section provides simulation experiments used for verifying the proposed approaches. First, we start by the verifying

---

**Input**: $S[i]$ (the $i$th source state), $T[j]$ (the $j$th target
state), $G$ (the required goal)
**Output**: Return true when sequences re-clustering is finished.
(1)  **Begin**
(2)   **if** $(S[i] \trianglerighteq_G T[j])$ **then**
(3)       Apply Algorithm 3 over $(S[i], T[j], G)$
(4)   **else**
(5)       **if** $(S[i] \Downarrow_G T[j])$ **then**
(6)           Expand $S[i]$
(7)           Apply Algorithm 3 over $(S[i], T[j], G)$
(8)       **else**
(9)           **if** $(S[i] \Uparrow_G T[j])$ **then**
(10)              Apply CRO over $S[i]$
(11)              Apply Algorithm 3 over $(S[i], T[j], G)$
(12)          **else**
(13)              BackTrack $= S[i]$
(14)              **if** $(j < \|T[\,]\|)$ **then**
(15)                  **if** $(i < \|S[\,]\|)$ **then**
(16)                      Apply Algorithm 4 over $(S[i + 1], T[j], G)$
(17)                  **else**
(18)                      **if** $(T[j] \Uparrow_G S[i])$ **then**
(19)                          Apply CRO over $T[j]$
(20)                          Apply Algorithm 3 over $(S[i], T[j], G)$
(21)                      **else**
(22)                          Mark $T[j]$ as Unmatched
(23)                          Apply Algorithm 4 over (BackTrack,
                             $T[j + 1], G)$
(24)                      **end if**
(25)                  **end if**
(26)              **else**
(27)                  Merge unmatched source states with their
                     predecessors.
(28)                  Return true
(29)              **end if**
(30)          **end if**
(31)      **end if**
(32)  **end if**
(33) **End**

---

ALGORITHM 3: Sequence mediator procedure (SMP).

experiments for the proposed signature adaptation approach; then we introduce the verifying experiments for the proposed conversation adaptation approach.

*9.1. Signature Adaptation.* To verify the proposed signature adaptation using conditional ontology mapping approach, we use a simulation approach to compare between the proposed approach and the generic mapping approach that adopts only Is-a relations to match signature concepts (both input and output concepts). The used comparison metric is the F-measure metric.

F-measure metric combines between the retrieval precision and recall metrics and is used as an indicator for accuracy that approaches with higher values which means that they are more accurate. F-measure is computed as $(2 * Precision * Recall)/(Recall + Precision)$. The experiment starts by generating two random sets of independent concepts (representing two different ontologies). One set will be used as the original dataset, and the second one will be used as a query set. For each concept in the query set, we randomly generate an Is-a relation to a corresponding concept in the original dataset (i.e., mapping using Is-a relation). For each pair of concepts having an Is-a relation, we generate a corresponding substitution pattern in the CSEG. For simplicity, the substitution pattern is generated as follows. The scope is equal to the original dataset concept. The substitution condition is generated as greater than condition with a randomly generated integer number (e.g., C1 >10). The conversion function is just an equality function (e.g., C1 = C2). From the generated set of concepts, we generate a random signature (i.e., a random operation) by randomly choosing a set of input concept and a set of output concepts. For each generated signature in the query set, we generate a corresponding context. For simplicity, the context will consist of one equality condition with a randomly generated integer number (e.g., C1 = 20).

**Input**: $CP_x$ (consuming GAP), $CP_y$, Operations Mapping
Matrix $\Theta$.
**Output**: Source code of the adapter between $CP_x$ and
$CP_y$.
  **Begin**
  Create an empty class ADAPTER.
  **for each** operation $Op_{(x,i)}$ in $GAP_x$ **do**
    Create a method in ADAPTER with same signature
    as $Op_{(x,i)}$.
    Get realizing operations subsequence $OPSeq$ from
    $CP_y$ using $\Theta$.
    Call ConverterGenerator ($Op_{(x,i)}$ Inputs, $OPSeq$ Inputs).
    // Algorithm 2
    **if** Converter Code generated successfully **then**
      Add Inputs Converter Code to method body.
      Add invocation Code for $OPSeq$ to method body.
      Call ConverterGenerator ($OPSeq$ Output, $Op_{(x,i)}$
      Outputs).
      **if** Converter Code generated successfully **then**
        Add Outputs Converter Code to method body.
      **else**
        Return Error.
      **end if**
    **else**
      Return Error.
    **end if**
  **end for**
  Return ADAPTER generated code.
  **End**

ALGORITHM 4: Adapter automatic generator.

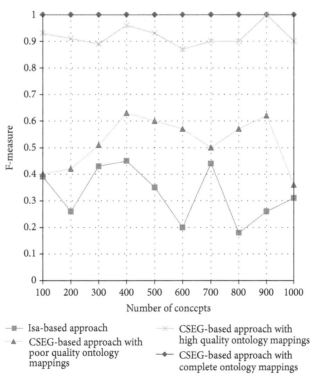

FIGURE 16: Signature adaptation approaches comparison.

TABLE 6: An example of two matching GAPs

|  | $S_2$ GAP | $S_1$ GAP |
|---|---|---|
| Preconstraints | {Cargo.Det = 1000 cars, Cargo.POL = Melbourne-Australia, Cargo.POD = Alexandria-Egypt, Cargo.Course = Port-To-Port, IncoTerm.Type = CIF} | {Freight.Det ≠ Null, Origin.Det ≠ Null, Dest.Det ≠ Null, Freight.Course = Port-To-Port, IncoTerm.Type ∈ {FOB, EXW, CIF}} |
| Desc-Constraints | {Payment.type = Credit, Speciality.Type = Motor-Vehicles} | {Credit.Period = 15, Speciality.Type ⊆ {Motor-Vehicles, Dangerous-Cargo}} |
| Postconstraints | {Cargo.Status = Accomplished} | {ShippingOrder.Status = Fulfilled, Payment.Status = Received} |
| Goal | Cargo transportation | Freight movement |
| Operation sequence | (1) Send-Cargo-Details<br>(2) Get-Offer<br>(3) Negotiate-Offer<br>(4) Accept-Offer<br>(5) Execute-Offer<br>(6) Send-Payment | (1) Send-Shipping-Order<br>(2) Get-POL-Allocated<br>(3) Get-POD-Allocated<br>(4) Get-Costs-Computed<br>(5) Get-Proposal<br>(6) Negotiate-Proposal<br>(7) Send-Approval<br>(8) Handle-Packaging<br>(9) Finalize-Documents<br>(10) Finalize-Bookings<br>(11) Get-Confirmation<br>(12) Receive-Invoice<br>(13) Send-Payment |

TABLE 7: Part of the ontology operations' definitions adopted by $S_2$.

| Operation | Preconstraints | Postconstraints |
|---|---|---|
| Send-Cargo-Details | {Cargo.Det ≠ Null, Cargo.POL ≠ Null, Cargo.POD ≠ Null, IncoTerm.Type ≠ Null} | {Cargo.Status = Received} |
| Get-Offer | {Cargo.Status = Received, Cargo.Course ≠ Null} | {Offer.Status = Sent} |
| Negotiate-Offer | {Offer.Status = Sent} | {Offer.Status = Approved} |
| Accept-Offer | {Offer.Status = Approved} | {Offer.Status = Accepted} |
| Execute-Offer | {Offer.Status = Accepted} | {Offer.Status = Executed} |
| Send-payment | {Offer.Status = Executed} | {Cargo.Status = Accomplished} |

Hence, not all the substitution patterns defined in the CSEG will be valid according to the generated contexts. We submit the query set to the two approaches to find matches in the original dataset, and based on the retrieved concepts the F-measure is computed. Figure 16 depicts the results. As we can see, the generic approach ignores the contexts and retrieves the whole original dataset as answers, which results in low F-measure values, while the proposed approach succeed to reach 100%.

However, this result could be misleading, as the experiment is done with complete CSEG patterns. In practice, an ontology designer may skip some substitution patterns when defining CSEG patterns. Therefore, the proposed approach will not be able to resolve the cases with missing patterns. In other words, the accuracy of the proposed approach mainly depends on the quality of the defined ontology mappings. To show such effect, we repeated the experiment except that we store only a portion of the generated substitution patterns. A high-quality ontology mapping means that up to 25% of the generated patterns are missing. A low-quality ontology mapping means that from 50% to 80% of the generated patterns are missing. Then, we compute the F-measure values for each case. Results are depicted in Figure 16. As we can see, when low-quality mappings are used, the proposed approach

TABLE 8: Part of the ontology operations' definitions adopted by $S_1$.

| Operation | Preconstraints | Postconstraints |
|---|---|---|
| Send-Shipping-Order | {Freight.Det ≠ Null,<br>Origin.Det ≠ Null,<br>Dest.Det ≠ Null,<br>Freight.Course ≠ Null,<br>IncoTerm.Type ≠ Null} | {ShippingOrder.Status = Created} |
| Get-Shipping-Order-Analyzed | {ShippingOrder.Status = Created} | {ShippingOrder.Status = Analyzed} |
| Get-POL-Allocated | {ShippingOrder.Status = Created} | {POL.Status = Allocated} |
| Get-POD-Allocated | {POL.Status = Allocated} | {POL.Status = Allocated,<br>POD.Status = Allocated} |
| Get-ILT-To-POL-Allocated | {POL.Status = Allocated} | ILT.ToStatus = Allocated |
| Get-ILT-From-POD-Allocated | {POD.Status = Allocated} | ILT.FromStatus = Allocated |
| Get-Costs-Computed | {POL.Status = Allocated,<br>POD.Status = Allocated} | {ShippingOrder.Status = Analyzed} |
| Get-Shipping-Proposal-Finalized | {ShippingOrder.Status = Analyzed} | {ShippingOrder.Status = Approved} |
| Get-Proposal | {ShippingOrder.Status = Analyzed} | {Proposal.Status = Sent} |
| Negotiate-Proposal | {Proposal.Status = Sent} | {Proposal.Status = Approved} |
| Send-Proposal | {Proposal.Status = Approved} | {ShippingOrder.Status = Approved} |
| Get-Shipping-Order-Fulfilled | {ShippingOrder.Status = Approved} | {ShippingOrder.Status = Executed} |
| Handle-Packaging | {ShippingOrder.Status = Approved} | {Packaging.Status = Accomplished} |
| Finalize-Documents | {Packaging.Status = Accomplished} | {Documentation.Status = Accomplished} |
| Finalize-Bookings | {Documentation.Status = Accomplished} | {ShippingOrder.Status = Executed} |
| Get-Confirmation | {ShippingOrder.Status = Executed} | {ShippingOrder.Status = Confirmed} |
| Get-Payment-Settled | {ShippingOrder.Status = Confirmed} | {ShippingOrder.Status = Fulfilled,<br>Payment.Status = Received} |
| Receive-Invoice | {ShippingOrder.Status = Confirmed} | {ShippingOrder.Status = Pending} |
| Send-Payment | {ShippingOrder.Status = Pending} | {ShippingOrder.Status = Fulfilled,<br>Payment.Status = Received} |

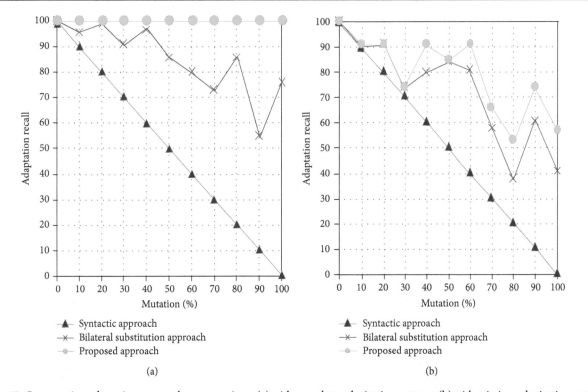

FIGURE 17: Conversation adaptation approaches comparison: (a) with complete substitution patterns (b) with missing substitution patterns.

TABLE 9: $S_1$ and $S_2$ behavior models.

| $S_1$ Behavior model | |
| --- | --- |
| $S_0$ | $\langle\{$*Freight.Det* $\neq$ Null, *Origin.Det* $\neq$ Null, *Dest.Det* $\neq$ Null, *Freight.Course* = Port-to-Port, IncoTerm.Type $\in$ {FOB, EXW, CIF}}, {}$\rangle$ |
| $S_1$ | $\langle\{$*ShippingOrder.Status* = Created}, {}$\rangle$ |
| $S_2$ | $\langle\{$*POL.Status* = Allocated}, {}$\rangle$ |
| $S_3$ | $\langle\{$*POL.Status* = Allocated, *POD.Status* = Allocated}, {}$\rangle$ |
| $S_4$ | $\langle\{$*ShippingOrder.Status* = Analyzed}, {}$\rangle$ |
| $S_5$ | $\langle\{$*Proposal.Status* = Sent}, {}$\rangle$ |
| $S_6$ | $\langle\{$*Proposal.Status* = Approved}, {}$\rangle$ |
| $S_7$ | $\langle\{$*ShippingOrder.Status* = Approved}, {}$\rangle$ |
| $S_8$ | $\langle\{$*Packaging.Status* = Accomplished}, {}$\rangle$ |
| $S_9$ | $\langle\{$*Documentation.Status* = Accomplished}, {}$\rangle$ |
| $S_{10}$ | $\langle\{$*ShippingOrder.Status* = Executed}, {}$\rangle$ |
| $S_{11}$ | $\langle\{$*ShippingOrder.Status* = Confirmed}, {}$\rangle$ |
| $S_{12}$ | $\langle\{$*ShippingOrder.Status* = Pending}, {}$\rangle$ |
| $S_{13}$ | $\{$*ShippingOrder.Status* = Fulfilled, *Payment.Status* = Received}, {}$\rangle$ |

| $S_2$ Behavior model | |
| --- | --- |
| $S_0$ | $\langle\{$*Cargo.Det* = 1000 Cars, *Cargo.POL* = Melbourne-Australia, *Cargo.POD* = Alexandria-Egypt, IncoTerm.Type = FOB}, {*Cargo.Course* = Port-to-Port}$\rangle$ |
| $S_1$ | $\langle\{$*Cargo.Course* = Port-to-Port, *Cargo.Status* = Received}, {}$\rangle$ |
| $S_2$ | $\langle\{$*Offer.Status* = Sent}, {}$\rangle$ |
| $S_3$ | $\langle\{$*Offer.Status* = Approved}, {}$\rangle$ |
| $S_4$ | $\langle\{$*Offer.Status* = Accepted}, {}$\rangle$ |
| $S_5$ | $\langle\{$*Offer.Status* = Executed}, {}$\rangle$ |
| $S_6$ | $\langle\{$*Cargo.Status* = Accomplished}, {}$\rangle$ |

accuracy is negatively affected. The worst case complexity of the proposed approach is $O(n * m^{\|p\|})$, where $n$ is the average number of substitution patterns of domain operations, $m$ is average number of possible outputs generated from conversion functions, and $\|p\|$ is the length of the path $p$ linking between mapped concepts (details could be found in [10]). The factor $m^{\|p\|}$ is the cost endured to find a sequence of generated intermediate conditions to indirectly match two conditions. However, in practice, $n, m$, and $p$ are expected to be small; hence, we argue that the performance of the proposed approach is acceptable.

*9.2. Conversation Adaptation.* Currently, there is no standard datasets for service conversations. Hence, to verify the proposed approach for automated adapter generation, we follow a simulation approach similar to the one used in [10]. The proposed simulation approach compares three approaches for automated adapter generation. The first approach is a syntactic approach that requires no changes at the services interface level of the operations. It cannot resolve any semantic differences. We use this approach as a benchmark for our works. The second approach is our approach proposed in [11] that uses bilateral concept substitution to resolve signatures incompatibilities. We use this approach to show the effect of not supporting concept aggregation. The third approach is the approach proposed in this paper that uses aggregate concept conditional substitution semantics to resolve signature incompatibilities. The used comparison metric is the adaptation recall metric. It is similar to the retrieval recall metric and is computed as the percentage of the number of adapted conversation patterns (i.e., the ones that have a successfully generated conversation adapter) with respect to the actual number of the adaptable conversation patterns in the dataset.

The experiment starts by generating a random set of independent conversation patterns, for which each pattern has a unique operation, and each operation has different input and output concepts. A query set is generated as a copy of the original set. The query set is submitted to the three adaptation approaches in order to generate the adapters between the query set patterns and the original set patterns. As the two sets are identical and the conversation patterns are independent, each pattern in the query set will have only one substitutable pattern in the original set (i.e., its copy). The second phase of the experiment involves the gradual mutation of the query set and submission of the mutated query set to the three approaches, and then we check the number of adapters generated by each approach to compute the adaptation recall metric. The mutation process starts by mutating 10% of the query set and then continues increasing the percentage by 10% until the query set is completely mutated. The value of 10% is an arbitrary percentage chosen to show the effect of semantic mutations on the approach. At each step, the adaptation recall metric is computed for the three approaches. The mutation process is performed by changing the signatures of the operations with completely new ones. Then the corresponding substitution patterns are added between the old concepts and the new concepts in the CSEG. The number of concepts in a substitution pattern is randomly chosen between 1 (to ensure having cases of bilateral substitution) and 5 (an arbitrary number for concept aggregation). For simplicity, conversion functions are generated by assigning the old values of the concepts to the new values of the concepts, and the substitution conditions are generated as not null conditions.

The experiment results are depicted in Figure 17(a). The figure shows that the syntactic approach could not handle any mutated cases, as it cannot resolve signature incompatibilities. Hence, its corresponding adaptation recall values drops proportionally to the mutation percentage. The bilateral substitution approach only solved the cases with substitution patterns having one concept in their scopes, while it could not solve the cases with substitution patterns having more than one concept in their scopes (i.e., cases representing concept aggregation). Hence, its corresponding adaptation

TABLE 10: CSG segment for `CargoTransportation` operation.

| Source | Destination | Conversion Fn | Substitution Cond. |
|---|---|---|---|
| Cargo.Det | Freight.Det | Freight.Det = Cargo.Det | |
| Freight.Det | Cargo.Det | Cargo.Det = Freight.Det | |
| Cargo.POL | Origin.Det | Origin.Det = Cargo.POL | |
| Origin.Det | Cargo.POL | Cargo.POL = Origin.Det | |
| Cargo.POD | Dest.Det | Dest.Det = Cargo.POD | |
| Dest.Det | Cargo.POD | Cargo.POD = Dest.Det | |
| Cargo.Type | Freight.Type | Freight.Type = Cargo.Type | |
| Freight.Type | Cargo.Type | Cargo.Type = Freight.Type | |
| Credit.Period | Payment.Type | IF (Credit.Period > 0) THEN Payment.Type = Credit ELSE Payment.Type = Cash END IF | $Credit.Period \geq 0$ |
| Payment.Type | Credit.Period | IF (Payment.Type = Credit) THEN Credit.Period ∈ {15, 30, 45, 60} ELSE Credit.Period = 0 END IF | Payment.Type ∈ {Credit, Cash} |
| Order.Stat | Cargo.Stat | SWITCH (Order.Stat) CASE Fulfilled: Cargo.Stat = Done CASE Created: Cargo.Stat = Received END CASE | Order.Stat ∈ {Fulfilled, Created} |
| Cargo.Stat | Order.Stat | SWITCH (Cargo.Stat) CASE Done: Order.Stat = Fulfilled CASE Received: Order.Stat = Created END CASE | Cargo.Stat ∈ {Done, Received} |
| Proposal.Stat | Offer.Stat | Offer.Stat = Proposal.Stat | Proposal.Stat ∈ {Sent, Approved} |
| Offer.Stat | Proposal.Stat | Proposal.Stat = Offer.Stat | Offer.Stat ∈ {Sent, Approved} |
| Order.Stat | Offer.Stat | IF (Order.Stat = Approved) THEN Offer.Stat = Accepted ELSE Offer.Stat = Executed END IF | Order.Stat ∈ {Approved, Executed} |
| Offer.Stat | Order.Stat | IF (Offer.Stat = Accepted) THEN Order.Stat = Approved ELSE Order.Stat = Executed END IF | Offer.Stat ∈ {Accepted, Executed} |
| Payment.Stat | Cargo.Stat | IF (Payment.Stat = Received) THEN Cargo.Stat = Done END IF | Payment.Stat = Received |
| Cargo.Stat | Payment.Stat | IF (Cargo.Stat = Done) THEN Payment.Stat = Received END IF | Cargo.Stat = Done |

recall values are higher than the values of the syntactic approach (as it solved bilateral substitution cases) and lower than the values of the proposed approach (as it could not resolve cases require concept aggregation). On the other hand, the proposed approach managed to generate adapters for all the mutated cases, providing a stable adaptation recall value of one.

However, these results could be misleading, as the experiment is performed with complete CSEG patterns. In practice, an ontology designer may skip some substitution patterns when defining CSEG patterns, depending on his/her domain knowledge and modelling skills. Therefore, the proposed approach will not be able to resolve the cases with missing patterns. In other words, the accuracy of the proposed

TABLE 11: Matching behavior models using SMP.

| $S_1$ behavior model | $S_2$ behavior model |
| --- | --- |
| $S_0, S_1, S_2, S_3, S_4$ | $S_0, S_1$ |
| $S_5$ | $S_2$ |
| $S_6$ | $S_3$ |
| $S_7, S_8, S_9$ | $S_4$ |
| $S_{10}, S_{11}, S_{12}$ | $S_5$ |
| $S_{13}$ | $S_6$ |

approach mainly depends on the quality of the defined ontology mappings. To show such effects, we repeated the previous experiment except that we store only a random portion (0%–100%) of the generated substitution patterns. The results are depicted in Figure 17(b). The figure shows that the proposed approach could not resolve all the mutation cases due to missing substitution patterns; however, it succeeds in adapting more cases than the other approaches.

The worst case complexity of the proposed approach is $O(n^3)$, where $n$ is the number of operations in a conversation pattern (a theoretical proof can be found in [10]). In practice, n is expected to be small; hence, we argue that the performance of the proposed approach is acceptable, especially when compared to the time needed for manually developing conversation adapters (which could require several days). We will focus our future research efforts to optimize the proposed algorithms and apply them to real-life application domains, which require involvement of application-domain experts to precisely define the needed CSEG.

## 10. Case Study

Given a service $S_1$ and $S_2$ with GAPs depicted in Table 6. In order to find wether these GAPs are matching or not, we have to extract the behavior models of each GAP. Let us assume the operations definitions as in Tables 7 and 8. Hence, extracted behavior models will be as listed in Table 9. Assuming that we have a CSG segment as depicted in Table 10, and applying the SMP procedure, we will find the matching behavior models states as indicated in Table 11. We can see from the table that $S_1$ operations *Send—Shipping—Order*, *Get—POL—Allocated*, *Get—POD—Allocated*, and *Get—Costs—Computed* are matching the operation *Send—Cargo—Details* of $S_2$. Hence, the corresponding adapter method is created; accordingly, the rest of the adapter methods is created by the mappings given in Table 11.

## 11. Conclusion

In this paper, we have proposed an automated approach for generating service conversation adapters on the fly in dynamic smart environments, where services interact with each other in seamless transparent manner without human intervention. The proposed approach customizes service conversations in a context-sensitive manner by resolving conversation conflicts (signature and/or protocol) using aggregate concept conditional substitution semantics captured by the proposed concepts substitutability extended graph (CSEG) that required to be a part of the adopted application domain ontology. We illustrated how such semantics are used to resolve signature and protocol incompatibilities. We provided the algorithms needed for automatic adapter generation and presented the verifying simulation experiments. Finally, we indicated how the adapter structure is determined and provided the algorithms needed for adapter source code generation. The proposed approach enables services in dynamic environments to smoothly interact with one another without having semantic interoperability concerns, thus increasing the chances for service reuse, and consequently improving the efficiency of dynamic environments. We believe that the proposed approach helps in improving business agility and responsiveness and of course resembles an important step toward achieving the IoS vision.

## References

[1] M. Papazoglou and D. Georgakopoulos, "Service oriented computing," *Communications of the ACM*, vol. 46, no. 10, pp. 24–28, 2003.

[2] M. Dumas, M. Spork, and K. Wang, "Adapt or perish: algebra and visual notation for service interface adaptation," in *Business Process Management*, vol. 4102 of *Lecture Notes in Computer Science*, pp. 65–80, 2006.

[3] B. Benatallah, F. Casati, D. Grigori, H. R. Motahari Nezhad, and F. Toumani, "Developing adapters for web services integration," in *Proceedings of the 17th International Conference on Advanced Information Systems Engineering (CAiSE '05)*, pp. 415–429, June 2005.

[4] H. R. Motahari Nezhad, B. Benatallah, A. Martens, F. Curbera, and F. Casati, "Semi-automated adaptation of service interactions," in *Proceedings of the 16th International World Wide Web Conference (WWW '07)*, pp. 993–1002, May 2007.

[5] R. Mateescu, P. Poizat, and G. Salaün, "Behavioral adaptation of component compositions based on process algebra encodings," in *Proceedings of the 22nd IEEE/ACM International Conference on Automated Software Engineering (ASE '07)*, pp. 385–388, November 2007.

[6] A. Brogi and R. Popescu, "Automated generation of BPEL adapters," in *Proceedings of the 4th International Conference on Service-Oriented Computing (ICSOC '06)*, vol. 4294 of *Lecture Notes in Computer Science*, pp. 27–39, 2006.

[7] J. Hau, W. Lee, and S. Newhouse, "The ICENI semantic service adaptation framework," in *UK e-Science All Hands Meeting*, pp. 79–86, 2003.

[8] A. Brogi and R. Popescu, "Service adaptation through trace inspection," *International Journal of Business Process Integration and Management*, vol. 2, no. 1, pp. 9–16, 2007.

[9] D. M. Yellin and R. E. Strom, "Protocol specifications and component adaptors," *ACM Transactions on Programming Languages and Systems*, vol. 19, no. 2, pp. 292–333, 1997.

[10] I. Elgedawy, Z. Tari, and J. A. Thom, "Correctness-aware high-level functional matching approaches for semantic Web services," *ACM Transactions on the Web*, vol. 2, no. 2, article 12, 2008.

[11] I. Elgedawy, "Automatic generation for web services conversations adapters," in *Proceedings of the 24th International Symposium on Computer and Information Sciences (ISCIS '09)*, pp. 616–621, Guzelyurt, Turkey, September 2009.

[12] I. Elgedawy, Z. Tari, and M. Winikoff, "Exact functional context matching for Web services," in *Proceedings of the Second International Conference on Service Oriented Computing (ICSOC '04)*, pp. 143–152, New York, NY, USA, November 2004.

[13] I. Elgedawy, "A context-sensitive approach for ontology mapping using concepts substitution semantics," in *Proceedings of the 25th International Symposium on Computer and Information Sciences (ISCIS '10)*, vol. 62 of *Lecture Notes in Electrical Engineering*, pp. 323–328, London, UK, 2010.

[14] I. Elgedawy, "Conditional ontology mapping," in *Proceedings of the 36th IEEE International Conference on Computer Software and Applications (COMPSAC '12), the 7th IEEE International Workshop on Engineering Semantic Agent Systems (ESAS '12)*, Izmir, Turkey, 2012.

[15] I. Elgedawy, Z. Tari, and M. Winikoff, "Scenario matching using functional substitutability in web services," in *Proceedings of the 5th International Conference on Web Information Systems Engineering (WISE '04)*, Brisbane, Australia, 2004.

[16] I. Elgedawy, Z. Tari, and M. Winikoff, "Exact functional context matching for Web services," in *Proceedings of the 2nd International Conference on Service Oriented Computing (ICSOC '04)*, pp. 143–152, Amsterdam, Netherlands, November 2004.

[17] F. Casati, E. Shan, U. Dayal, and M.-C. Shan, "Business—oriented management of Web services," *Communications of the ACM*, vol. 46, no. 10, pp. 55–60, 2003.

[18] M. P. Papazoglou and W.-J. van den Heuvel, "Web services management: a survey," *IEEE Internet Computing*, vol. 9, no. 6, pp. 58–64, 2005.

[19] W3C, "Web service choreography interface," 2002, http://www.w3.org/TR/wsci/.

[20] M. Dumas, B. Benatallah, and H. R. M. Nezhad, "Web service protocols: compatibility and adaptation," *IEEE Data Engineering Bulletin*, vol. 31, no. 3, pp. 40–44, 2008.

[21] M. Nagarajan, K. Verma, A. P. Sheth, J. Miller, and J. Lathem, "Semantic interoperability of Web services—challenges and experiences," in *Proceedings of the 4th IEEE International Conference on Web Services (ICWS '06)*, pp. 373–380, September 2006.

[22] Y. Kalfoglou and M. Schorlemmer, "Ontology mapping: the state of the art," *Knowledge Engineering Review*, vol. 18, no. 1, pp. 1–31, 2003.

[23] N. Shadbolt, W. Hall, and T. Berners-Lee, "The semantic web revisited," *IEEE Intelligent Systems*, vol. 21, no. 3, pp. 96–101, 2006.

[24] B. C. Grau, I. Horrocks, B. Motik, B. Parsia, P. Patel-Schneider, and U. Sattler, "OWL 2: the next step for OWL," *Web Semantics*, vol. 6, no. 4, pp. 309–322, 2008.

[25] D. Roman, U. Keller, and H. Lausen, "Web service modeling ontology (WSMO)," Feburary 2005, http://www.wsmo.org/TR/d2/v1.1/20050210/.

[26] "OWL-Services-Coalition, OWL-S: semantic markup for web services," 2003, http://www.daml.org/services/owl-s/1.0/owl-s.pdf.

[27] J. Kopecký, T. Vitvar, C. Bournez, and J. Farrell, "SAWSDL: semantic annotations for WSDL and XML schema," *IEEE Internet Computing*, vol. 11, no. 6, pp. 60–67, 2007.

[28] M. Kova, J. Bentahar, Z. Maamar, and H. Yahyaoui, "A formal verification approach of conversations in composite web services using NuSMV," in *Proceedings of the Conference on New Trends in Software Methodologies, Tools and Techniques*, 2009.

[29] L. Ardissono, A. Goy, and G. Petrone, "Enabling conversations with web services," in *Proceedings of the 2nd International Joint Conference on Autonomous Agents and Multiagent Systems (AAMAS '03)*, pp. 819–826, July 2003.

[30] M. T. Kone, A. Shimazu, and T. Nakajima, "The state of the art in agent communication languages," *Knowledge and Information Systems*, vol. 2, no. 3, 2000.

[31] M. B. Juric, *Business Process Execution Language for Web Services BPEL and BPEL4WS*, Packt Publishing, Birmingham, UK, 2nd edition, 2006.

[32] V. Kashyap and A. Sheth, "Semantic and schematic similarities between database objects: a context-based approach," *The VLDB Journal*, vol. 5, no. 4, pp. 276–304, 1996.

[33] S. Abiteboul, S. Cluet, and T. Milo, "Correspondence and translation for heterogeneous data," *Theoretical Computer Science*, vol. 275, no. 1-2, pp. 179–213, 2002.

[34] H. Chalupksy, "Ontomorph: a translation system for symbolic knowledge," in *Proceedings of the 17th International Conference on Knowledge Representation and Reasoning*, Breckenridge, Colo, USA, 2000.

[35] S. Li, H. Hu, and X. Hu, "An ontology mapping method based on tree structure," in *Proceedings of the 2nd International Conference on Semantics Knowledge and Grid (SKG '06)*, November 2006.

[36] P. Ganesan, H. Garcia-Molina, and J. Widom, "Exploiting hierarchical domain structure to compute similarity," *ACM Transactions on Information Systems*, vol. 21, no. 1, pp. 64–93, 2003.

[37] J. Madhavan, P. A. Bernstein, P. Domingos, and A. Y. Halevy, "Representing and reasoning about mappings between domain models," in *Proceedings of the 18th National Conference on Artificial Intelligence (AAAI '02)*, pp. 80–86, August 2002.

[38] I. Elgedawy, B. Srivastava, and S. Mittal, "Exploring queriability of encrypted and compressed XML data," in *Proceedings of the 24th International Symposium on Computer and Information Sciences (ISCIS '09)*, pp. 141–146, Guzelyurt, Turkey, September 2009.

[39] J. Pearson and P. Jeavons, A survey of tractable constraint satisfaction problems CSD-TR-97-15, Oxford University, Computing Laboratory, Oxford, UK, 1997, http://citeseerx.ist.psu.edu/viewdoc/summary?doi=10.1.1.43.9045.

[40] P. G. Jeavons and M. C. Cooper, "Tractable constraints on ordered domains," *Artificial Intelligence*, vol. 79, no. 2, pp. 327–339, 1995.

[41] I. Elgedawy, "A conceptual framework for web services semantic discovery," in *Proceedings of On The Move (OTM) to Meaningful Internet Systems*, Catania, Italy, 2003.

[42] Y. Taher, D. Benslimane, M.-C. Fauvet, and Z. Maamar, "Towards an approach for web services substitution," in *Proceedings of the 10th International Database Engineering and Applications Symposium (IDEAS '06)*, pp. 166–173, December 2006.

# 6

# Foundations and Technological Landscape of Cloud Computing

**Nattakarn Phaphoom, Xiaofeng Wang, and Pekka Abrahamsson**

*Faculty of Computer Science, Free University of Bolzano-Bozen, Piazza Domenicani 3, 39100 Bolzano, Italy*

Correspondence should be addressed to Nattakarn Phaphoom; phaphoom@inf.unibz.it

Academic Editors: M. Meringer and R. J. Walker

The cloud computing paradigm has brought the benefits of utility computing to a global scale. It has gained paramount attention in recent years. Companies are seriously considering to adopt this new paradigm and expecting to receive significant benefits. In fact, the concept of cloud computing is not a revolution in terms of technology; it has been established based on the solid ground of virtualization, distributed system, and web services. To comprehend cloud computing, its foundations and technological landscape need to be adequately understood. This paper provides a comprehensive review on the building blocks of cloud computing and relevant technological aspects. It focuses on four key areas including architecture, virtualization, data management, and security issues.

## 1. Introduction

Cloud computing technology has attracted significant attention from both academic and industry in recent years. It is perceived as a shift in computing paradigm in which computing services are offered and acquired on demand over the global-scaled network [1]. In this paradigm, cloud service providers manage a pool of computing resources, generally by means of virtualization, and offer services in terms of infrastructure, platform, and software to consumers using a multitenancy model [2]. Consumers can provision and release such computing capabilities as needed through self-service interfaces. Service usages are automatically metered, allowing consumers to pay for the services only for what they use. In this ecosystem, cloud service providers gain an opportunity to maximize their profit through the economies of scale, while consumers gain access to (seemingly) unlimited resources to address their changing demands without requiring an upfront investment on cost and effort to set up an IT infrastructure.

Cloud computing has the potential to transform IT industry and change the way Enterprise IT is operated [3]. The adoption of cloud services, that is, provisions of data center, hosted deployment environment or on demand software, leads to different degrees of impacts on an enterprise. Focusing on a technical perspective, the potential benefits of cloud services include (a) an ability to shorten the cycle from ideas to profitable products; (b) an ability to address volatile workload without service interruptions or slowing down system performance; (c) simplified processes of establishing environments for application development and deployment; (d) decreased run time for backend jobs by using temporarily acquired resource; (e) an efficient solution for business continuity; (f) minimized software maintenance activities due to a shift of work to the cloud provider; and (g) centralized quality assurance as responsibility on quality control such as security and performance are transferred to the provider [4–7].

However, cloud services and security concerns inherited from their underlying technologies might negatively impact an enterprise if they are not properly managed. Technical and security risks identified in this context include (a) data lock-in and system lock-in; (b) unreliable system performance due to many uncontrollable factors such as network traffic, load balancing, and context switching cost; (c) decreased performance due to virtualization; (d) complex integration between legacy and cloud-based systems; (e) incompatibility of user behaviors and enterprise process over a new version of cloud software, as software upgrade is controlled by the provider; (f) information leakage in a multitenant model; (g) data interception during the transfer over public networks; and (h) security breach in a virtualization monitoring layer [3, 8–10].

One of the core aspects of cloud computing is that it hides IT complexity under service offering models. While it is evident that components in the building blocks of cloud services introduce a certain degree of impacts on service characteristics, it is less evident how different the impacts would be in different configurations. This knowledge is essential for service consumers. Software developers working on cloud platforms need to understand it to apply appropriate software designs and properly configure their deployment environments, in order to ensure certain characteristics of resulting software. Enterprise consumers need this knowledge during service level agreement (SLA) negotiation and to determine the line of responsibility. End users also need it to adjust their usage behavior.

This paper aims to provide a better understanding over cloud computing technology as well as its associated foundations. The knowledge serves as a basis for the in-depth analysis and assessment of cloud services. For software developers, this paper adds new aspects to consider when developing software in-the-cloud and for-the-cloud. For researchers, it identifies the landscape of the underlying technology of cloud computing, especially virtualization, data management, and security.

The remainder of the paper is organized into five sections. In the next section, we explain what cloud computing is and what it is not through reviewing various definitions, service models, deployment models, and relevant concepts. An in-depth comparison between grid and cloud computing is also presented in this section. Section 3 provides a review on existing cloud computing reference architectures and relevant quality attributes of cloud services. Virtualization technology is captured in Section 4, with a focus on the approaches to hardware system virtualization and its use scenarios. Section 5 is focused on data management in distributed environments and the design considerations of selected services from leading providers. Cloud security issues are discussed in Section 6 by considering the vulnerabilities associated to the key architectural components of cloud computing. The paper ends with the conclusions in the last section.

## 2. Cloud Computing Basics

The semantic of cloud computing is identified by its definition, service models, and deployment models.

*2.1. Definition.* The standard definition of "cloud computing" is on the way of reaching its consensus [11]. Among many interpretations of this term, its general objective and view are agreeable. The term "cloud computing" refers to the fact that computing services of any form—IT infrastructure, platforms, or applications—could be provisioned and used through the Internet. Cloud is built upon a large-scaled distributed infrastructure in which a pool of resources is generally virtualized, and offered services are distributed to clients in terms of a virtual machine, deployment environment, or software. In this way cloud services could be scaled dynamically according to requirements and current workloads. The usage of resources is measured, and the payment is made on a consumption basis.

Foster et al. provide a definition of cloud computing as they compare cloud with grid computing. According to their definition [12], cloud computing is "*a large-scale distributed computing paradigm that is driven by economies of scale, in which a pool of abstracted, virtualized, dynamically-scalable, managed computing power, storage, platforms, and services are delivered on demand to external customers over the Internet.*"

Vaquero et al. identify more than 20 existing definitions of cloud computing and propose their own definition. As it is perceived in the end of 2008 [13], cloud computing is "*a large pool of easily usable and accessible virtualized resources (such as hardware, development platforms and/or services). These resources can be dynamically re-configured to adjust to a variable load (scale), allowing also for an optimum resource utilization. This pool of resources is typically exploited by a pay- per-use model in which guarantees are offered by the Infrastructure Provider by means of customized SLAs.*"

The most cited definition of cloud computing is the one proposed by The US National Institute of Standards and Technology (NIST). NIST provides the following definition [2]: "*Cloud computing is a model for enabling convenient, on demand network access to a shared pool of configurable computing resources (e.g., networks, servers, storage, applications, and services) that can be rapidly provisioned and released with minimal management effort or service provider interaction.*"

These definitions reveal three characteristics of the clouds. First of all, cloud services are massively scalable, and the acquisition and release of these services could be done dynamically with minimum operational supports required. Secondly, the cost is charged on a usage basis and the quality of services is guaranteed by a providers based on a service level agreement. Lastly, the quality of cloud services, such as security and performance, relies primarily on availability of Internet and how underlying resources are managed and distributed to clients.

*2.2. Service Models.* A service model determines the types of computer resources offered to consumers. Three main types of cloud services are infrastructure (IaaS), platform (PaaS), and software (SaaS). However, new service models are continuously emerging.

*2.2.1. Infrastructure-as-a-Service (IaaS).* A provider provides a virtual infrastructure where computing resources including processing units, storage, and network could be provisioned in order to set up a deployment environment for their software system. A customer has flexibility to manage and control a software stack to be deployed ranging from an operating system, middleware, and applications. Examples of IaaS are Amazon Elastic Compute Cloud (EC2) (http://aws.amazon.com/), Eucalyptus (http://open.eucalyptus.com/), Openstack (http://openstack.org/projects/compute/), and OpenNebula (http://www.opennebula.org/).

*2.2.2. Platform-as-a-Service (PaaS).* PaaS provides customers with the capability to develop and deploy applications based on tools and programming languages supported by the providers. This hosted platform is configurable in a limited manner based on a provided set of APIs. Examples of this class of services include Google AppEngine (http://code.google.com/appengine/), Windows Azure Platform (http://www.microsoft.com/windowsazure/), Force.com (http://developer.force.com/), and Rackspace (http://www.rackspace.com/).

*2.2.3. Software-as-a-Service (SaaS).* SaaS provides the capability to use the applications which run on cloud infrastructure. These applications are accessible through standard interfaces such as a web browser or an email client. SaaS offers the experience of getting to work on applications and data from anywhere at any time by using various form of devices. Examples of widely used SaaS are Facebook, Gmail, and OfficeLive (http://www.officelive.com/en-us/). Enterprise SaaS exist in many domains such as accounting, customer relationship management, content management, and enterprise resource planning.

*2.2.4. Human-as-a-Service (HuaaS).* HuaaS relies on information aggregation techniques to extract meaningful information or prediction from massive-scale data [24]. The services make use of information provided by large cyber communities, such as Digg (http://digg.com/), which aims to be the first source of news in any topic. A concept of Crowdsourcing [25, 26] and Crowdservicing [27], which gathers a group of people to solve complex problems or to contribute with innovative ideas, belongs to this model. Examples of Crowdsourcing include community-based design and human-based computation.

*2.2.5. Everything-as-a-Service (XaaS).* A computing paradigm is moving toward a XaaS concept in which everything could be acquired as a service. Cloud computing and aforementioned service models are in support of XaaS [24]. XaaS implies a model of dynamic environments in which clients have a full control to customize the computing environment to best fit their unique demands by composing varieties of cloud-based services.

These examples are fairly well-known cloud services. OpenCrowd taxonomy [16] presents a collection of cloud service providers for each of the defined models.

*2.3. Deployment Models.* Different deployment models are designed to support a variation of consumers' privacy requirements for cloud adoption. NIST defines cloud deployment models as public, private, community, and hybrid [2]. Virtual private cloud is introduced by Amazon as an alternative solution that balances flexibility of public clouds and security of private clouds [28, 29].

    (i) *Public cloud.* The cloud infrastructure is owned and managed by a provider who offers its services to public.

    (ii) *Private cloud.* The cloud infrastructure is built for a specific organization, but might be managed by a third party under a service level agreement.

    (iii) *Virtual private cloud (VPC).* Virtual private cloud removes security issues caused by resource sharing of public clouds by adding a security platform on top of the public clouds. It leverages virtual private network (VPN) technology and provides some dedicated resources allowing consumers to customize their network topology and security settings.

    (iv) *Community cloud.* The infrastructure is shared among several organizations that have common requirements or concerns.

    (v) *Hybrid cloud.* Several types of clouds are composed together through data portability technology and federated authentication mechanism.

*2.4. History of Computing Paradigms.* Cloud computing introduces a shift in a computing paradigm. Voas and Zhang in their article [1] illustrate the computing evolution through six distinct phases. In the first phase people use a powerful *mainframe* which is designed to multiplex its computing cycle to support multiple applications. A *personal computer* has become a convenient mean to perform a daily work in the next phase, responding to a drop of hardware costs and its sufficient computational power. A *computer network* in a form of local area network (LAN) or wide area network (WAN) is flourished in the third phases as a mean for resource sharing. The *Internet* has introduced after that as a global network that allows people to utilize remote services. The fifth phase has brought a concept of *grid computing* which utilizes distributed systems and parallel computing to serve high throughput and high performance computing. Finally, in a current phase *cloud computing* provides a convenient way to acquire any form of computing services through the Internet as another utility.

*2.5. Relevant Concepts.* The concept of cloud computing is not a revolution. In fact, it introduces an overlap with many concepts and technologies, such as grid computing, utility computing, and virtualization. This subsection gives an overview to these concepts and points out common angles that each of these concepts share with cloud computing.

*2.5.1. Grid Computing.* Grid computing is a distributed computing paradigm that enables resource sharing among multivirtual organizations in order to solve a common computational problem [30]. Grid has been developed originally to serve scientific applications that require tremendous computational power. The grid composes of heterogeneous and physically distributed resources. To unify a computing environment from such diversity, grid frameworks provide standard protocols and middleware that mediate accesses to a range of physical resources, as well as organizing basic functionalities such as resource provisioning, catalogue, job scheduling, monitoring, and security assurance. Compared to cloud computing, grid shares a common objective of achieving optimization of resource usage. The difference is that cloud infrastructure is owned and managed by a single organization, resulting in a homogenous platform by nature. The management of cloud, as a consequence, focuses on utilizing a resource pool, rather than coordinating resources. An example of grid framework is Globus (http://www.globus.org/).

*2.5.2. Utility Computing.* Utility computing presents a model that enables the sharing of computing infrastructure in which the resources from a shared pool are distributed to clients upon requests, and the cost of acquiring services are charged based on the usage [31]. Cloud computing realizes the concept of utility computing by offering computing power which could be acquired over the Internet under a fixed or on demand pricing model. In addition to resource optimization, achieving a satisfactory level of service quality is a main goal for both environments.

*2.5.3. Virtualization.* Virtualization is an abstraction of a computing system that provides interfaces to hardware including a processing unit and its register, storages, and I/O devices [32–34]. These physical resources are visible to processes or devices in a higher abstraction level as virtualized resources. Virtualization at a system level allows multiple virtual machines to operate on the same physical platform. Virtualization at a process level is managed by an operating system, multiplexing processing cycles and resources to support multiple processes. Cloud computing providers in general use system virtualization to provide the capability of resource pooling by allocating and deallocating virtualized resources in terms of a virtual machine to a client's system on demand. Examples of virtualization solutions are VMWare (http://www.vmware.com/) (commercial), Xen (http://www.citrix.com/) (open source), and KVM (http://www.linux-kvm.org/) (open source).

*2.5.4. Service Oriented Architecture.* Architectural patterns are used to create designs that are standardized, well understood, and predictable. These patterns are proven solutions to recurring common problems in software design [35]. Service oriented architecture (SOA) is a widely adopted architectural pattern for designing distributed and loosely couple systems. It is designed to help organizations to achieve business goals including easy integration with legacy systems, remove inefficient business processes, and reduce cost, agile adaptation, and fast responses in competitive markets [36].

Varieties of architectures could be derived from SOA. Erl, in his book "SOA design patterns" [37] and a community site (http://www.soapatterns.org/), introduces more than eighty patterns for service oriented systems. The following are examples of categories and corresponding designs.

(i) *Patterns for creating service inventory.* Enterprise Inventory (to maximize recomposition), Service Normalization (to avoid redundant service logic), and Service Layer (to organize logics based on a common functional type).

(ii) *Patterns for organizing logical service layers.* Utility Abstraction (to govern common nonbusiness centric logics), Entity Abstraction (to organize agonistic business processes), and Process Abstraction (to organize nonagonistic business processes).

(iii) *Patterns for enhancing interoperability.* Data Model Transformation (to convert data of different schemas), Data Format Transformation (to allow services to interact with programs that use different data formats), and Protocol Bridging (to allow services that use different communication protocol to exchange data).

(iv) *Patterns for infrastructure.* Enterprise Service Bus, Orchestration, and Service Broker.

(v) *Patterns for enhancing security.* Exception Shielding (to prevent disclosure of internal implementation when exceptions occur), Message Screening (to protect a service for malformed and malicious input), and Service Perimeter Guard (to make internal services available to external users without exposing other internal resources).

SOA is considered as a basic for cloud computing, as it provides software architecture that addresses many quality attributes required for cloud services, such as component composibility, reusability, and scalability. The concept of SOA is leveraged to construct extensible cloud solution architecture, standard interfaces, and reusable components [22].

*2.6. A Comparison of Grid and Cloud Computing.* Grid and cloud computing have been established based on a particular common ground of distributed and parallel computing, targeting at a common goal of resource sharing. Both technologies offer a similar set of advantages such as flexibility of acquiring additional resources on demand and optimizing the usage of infrastructure. However, they pose differences especially from a point of view of resource management. This section provides such comparisons based on the work of Foster et al. presented in [12]. In their work cloud and grid are compared in terms of business models, architecture, resource management, and programming models.

*2.6.1. Business Models.* A business model captures a flow in which services are created and delivered to clients in order to generate incomes to a service provider and to serve clients' requirements. In cloud computing a role of providers is to provide computing services as a basic utility. Cloud generally offers a fixed or on demand pricing model. In either case, clients benefit from a reduction on upfront IT investments and flexibility in scaling its applications. In grid environments, an incentive to join the community is to get access to additional computing utilities, with the price of sharing one's own resources. The whole community benefits from optimization.

*2.6.2. Architecture.* In terms of infrastructure cloud is designed to serve as an internet-scale pool of resources. The whole infrastructure is managed by a single provider. Thus, a single unit of resource is conformed to a common governance

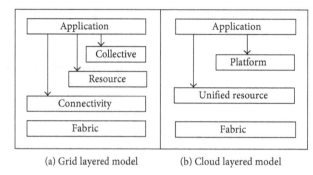

(a) Grid layered model          (b) Cloud layered model

FIGURE 1: An architecture comparison: (a) grid model that provides connectivity to heterogeneous resources and (b) cloud model that manages a pool of resources by means of virtualization [12].

model. In contrast, grid has been developed to integrate distributed, dynamic, and heterogeneous resources. A set of open standard protocols and facilities is established to allow those resources to be interoperated. The differences are reflected in their reference models (Figure 1). Composing of four layers, distributed resources residing at a cloud fabric layer are encapsulated (generally by means of virtualization), so that they can be used by platform and application layers as integrated resources. Grid composes of five layers. Instead of depending on virtualization, grid defines standard protocols at a connectivity layer which allows communications among distributed nodes. A resource layer defines protocols for publication, discovery, negotiation, and payment. A collective layer controls interactions across collections of resources such as scheduling and monitoring. Applications exploit services provided at the lower layer through APIs.

*2.6.3. Resource Management.* Resource management targets at the mechanisms to control resource pooling, to achieve effective resource allocation and a satisfactory level of service quality. It covers four main areas including computing model, data model and locality, virtualization, and monitoring.

*Computing Model.* A computing model concerns with how resources are distributed for computational work. Cloud resources are distributed in terms of a virtual machine. A new instance of a virtual machine is created and placed to a physical location which is unknown to clients. The placement algorithm is customized to maintain a balance of platform utilization, relevant costs, and a guaranteed quality of services. In contrast, grid uses queuing system to manage jobs and resource allocations. Job stays in queue until the required amount of resources are available. Once allocated, resources are dedicated only for that job. Due to such scheduling policy, interactive applications which require short latency time could not operate natively on the grid.

*Data Model and Locality.* In both grid and cloud, data are distributed and replicated into a number of nodes to minimize the cost of communication between data and processors. Cloud uses a MapReduce framework to handle data locality. MapReduce runs on top of the file system, where data files are partitioned into chunks and replicated in many nodes. When

a file needs to be processed, the storage service schedules a processor at the node hosting each chunk of the data to process the job. However, data locality cannot be easily exploited in grid, as the resource is allocated based on availability. One technique to tackle this issue is to consider data locality information, while a processor is schedule for computation. This approach is implemented in a data-aware scheduler.

*Virtualization.* Virtualization is a mechanism to provide abstraction to resources in the fabric layer, allowing administrative work (e.g., configuring, monitoring) to be performed more effectively in the cloud. Grid does not rely on virtualization as much as cloud does. This is due to the scale and the fact that each organization in grid community has ultimate control over their resources.

*Monitoring.* In cloud environment, client's capability for monitoring is restricted to a type of services employed. A model that provides infrastructure-as-a-service (IaaS) gives more flexibility for clients to monitor and configure lower level resources and middleware. Monitoring inside grid environment could be done in a more straightforward manner through user's credential which defines the right of users to access resources at different grid sites.

*2.6.4. Programming Model.* On top of Google's MapReduce, a number of programming models have been created to facilitate the development of distributed and parallel programming [38]. These include Sawzall (http://code.google.com/p/szl/), Hadoop (http://hadoop.apache.org/), and Pig (http://pig.apache.org/). Microsoft provides DryadLINQ framework to serve the similar purpose [39]. A main concern of programming model in grid is due to a large number of heterogeneous resources. Programming models which are generally used are Message Passing Interfaces (MPI), Grid Remote Procedural Call, and Web Service Resource Framework which allows applications to be stateful.

In brief, cloud and grid share similarity in terms of their goal and underlining technologies that serve as a building block. They are different from a point of view of resource management. These differences are caused by the fact that (1) clouds and grids build upon resources of different nature;

(2) clouds are operated for larger target group and serve a wider range of applications which put emphasis on different aspects of service quality.

*2.7. Summary.* The most respected definition of cloud is the one given by NIST. Cloud embraces the following characteristics: (a) it provides on demand computing capability which is accessible through the internet; (b) the computing capability could be provisioned and scaled with a minimum operational effort; (c) the usage of resources is metered and charged accordingly; (d) provider's resources are pooled to serve multiple clients; (e) it inherits benefits and risks from IT outsourcing. In terms of computing paradigm, clouds are considered as an evolution of grid computing. Both technologies share a common goal of optimizing resource usage and offer a similar set of advantages. However, clouds and grid are significantly different from a perspective of resource management.

## 3. Architecture and Quality of Cloud Services

Cloud computing architecture is partly represented through service and deployment models described in the previous section. Its complete architecture must capture relationship and dependency among relevant entities and activities in that environment.

*3.1. Existing Cloud Computing Reference Architecture.* A reference model is an abstract view of an environment of interest. It presents relationships and dependencies among entities in that environment, while abstracting away the standard, technology, and implementation underneath. It is particularly useful to identify an abstract solution to a given issue and to determine the scope of influence.

A report by the US National Institute of Standards and Technology (NIST) gathers cloud reference architecture models proposed by known organizations [40]. Architectural elements that are consistently presented in these models are (a) *a layered model*, that combines key components and their relationship; (b) *actors*, including their role and responsibilities; and (c) *management domains*, which facilitate basic operations of data centers and services on top of it.

This subsection summarizes main components of reference models list in the NIST report and proposed models found in the literatures.

*3.1.1. Distributed Management Task Force, Inc.* DMTF (http://dmtf.org/) proposes the cloud conceptual architecture integrating actors, interfaces, data artifacts, and profiles [14]. It focuses on a provider interface layer which offers specific services, standards, and environments to different users according to their registered profiles.

*3.1.2. IBM.* IBM's view on cloud management architecture combines actor's roles, services, virtualized infrastructure, and provider management platforms [15]. It offers Business-Process-as-a-Service (BPaaS) on to top of software capability which allows an automated customization of business workflows. The management platforms are customized for business-related services and technical-related services.

*3.1.3. Cloud Security Alliance.* CSA (https://cloudsecurityalliance.org/) introduces a seven-layer stack model that captures relationship and dependency of resources and services [16]. The model is customized for security analysis by separating a layer of resource management to an abstraction sublayer and a core connectivity and delivery sublayer. Elements of cloud applications (or SaaS) are presented through four sublayers comprising data, metadata, contents, applications, APIs, modality, and a presentation platform.

*3.1.4. Cisco.* Instead of focusing on a service model representation, Cisco explicitly puts security architecture and service orchestration into the frame [17]. Cisco framework consists of five layers: data center architecture, security, service orchestration, service delivery and management, and service customer. A security framework is built across the whole infrastructure. An orchestration layer maps a group of technological components to a services component for delivery.

*3.1.5. Open Security Architecture.* OSA (http://www.opensecurityarchitecture.org/) publishes a collection of cloud security patterns for more than 25 usage contexts such as client-server modules, identity management patterns, and SOA internal service usages [18]. These patterns combine actors, systems, activities, and features of related entities. They could be used as a high level use cases that capture cloud service interfaces for each of the actor's activities.

*3.1.6. The Federal Cloud Computing Initiative.* FCCI (http://www.info.apps.gov/) targets at government-wide adoption of cloud computing [19]. FCCI defines eight service components for the government to be addressed to deliver online user interfaces. These components consist of customizable user pages, application library, online storage, collaboration enabler widgets, connectivity, interoperability, provisioning and administrative tools, and the security mechanism that apply for the entire system. FCCI also provides a drafted layered service framework that outlines main service components for each layer of the government cloud.

*3.1.7. The Storage Networking Industry Association.* SNIA (http://www.snia.org/) proposes Cloud Data Management Interface (CDMI) as standard interfaces to access cloud storage and to manage the data stored [20]. CDMI comprises three main interfaces to increase interoperability among cloud storages: (1) data management interfaces that allow application to add, retrieve, update, and delete data elements stored in the cloud; (2) storage management interfaces that support legacy system, scalable nonrelational database (NoSQL), and object storages; and (3) the Resource Domain Model which describes how requirements and quality of services could be achieved.

*3.1.8. Youseff et al.* The authors propose cloud ontology based on composibility of service [21]. A cloud layer is higher

TABLE 1: Cloud computing reference models.

| Name | Objective | Key components | References |
| --- | --- | --- | --- |
| Distributed management task force | To achieve interoperability | Actors, service interfaces, and profile | [14] |
| IBM | General purpose | Actors and roles, cloud services, and management activities to support business-related services and technical-related services | [15] |
| Cloud security alliance | Security assessment | Stack model, cloud services | [16] |
| Cisco | General purpose | Stack model for service composition | [17] |
| Open security architecture | Security assessment | Actors, flow of traffic and information in the cloud, security policy implemented by each actors, and servers to secure cloud operations | [18] |
| Federal cloud computing initiative | Standard for government clouds | Stack model representing cloud core capabilities and their associated management domain, actors, and cloud services | [19] |
| Cloud data management interfaces | Standard interfaces for cloud storage | Interfaces to data storage and associated metadata | [20] |
| Cloud ontology | General purpose | Stack model representing basic cloud resources and services | [21] |
| Cloud computing open architecture | Open standard and cloud ecosystem | Stack model integrating cloud virtual resources, common reusable services, core services, offerings, unified architecture interfaces, quality and governance, and ecosystem management | [22] |

in stack if its services are composed of other services of underlying layers. Services belong to the same layer if they have the same level of abstraction. The concept results in a simple five-layered cloud ontology, consisting of hardware, software kernel, cloud software infrastructure, cloud software environment, and cloud applications.

### 3.1.9. Zhang and Zhou.

The authors present a cloud open architecture (CCOA) aiming to assist strategic planning and consultancy of cloud computing services [22]. Their architecture illustrates seven principles of cloud and their correlations. These principles include virtualization, service orientation for reusable services, provision and subscription, configurable cloud services, unified information representation and exchange framework, quality and governance, and ecosystem management. Cloud actors are integrated to related principles.

Table 1 summarizes key details of aforementioned models.

The existence of multiple cloud computing architectures, even though serving different purposes, reflects a lack of standardization and interoperability in this field. In fact, the views of cloud represented by each model are not disrupted. They rather reflect cloud environments at different levels of abstraction and put a focus on different aspects. However, having a uniformed model would enhance collaborations among stakeholders and help to prevent a vendor lock-in problem.

### 3.2. Cloud Computing Layered Models.

The objective of the first focus area is to understand the relationship and dependency of basic cloud components, actors, and management activities. A multilayer stack model allows us to put in place the technology associated to each layer, without being interfered by management activities. Figure 2 compares three models which depict cloud components at the different levels of abstraction.

Model (a) is introduced by Foster et al. to identify the differences between grid and cloud computing [12]. This four-layer model separates the fabric layer and the unified resource layer to present the distributed and resource-sharing nature of cloud, as well as to identify the need of a virtualization tool to simulate isolated environment for each consumer. In Figure 2(b), Youseff et al. design a five-layer model to capture different types of cloud services [21]. It distinguishes three types of service models (i.e., IaaS, PaaS, and SaaS) which are built upon one another, as well as three types of virtualized resources (computing, storage, and network) under cloud infrastructure. Interfaces to virtual resources and operating system are not explicit in this model. Model (c) proposed by CSA explicitly defines APIs layer which mediates communication between an operation system and integrated virtual resources. It also illustrates dependency of relevant SaaS components. This model is probably most appropriate for a security assessment.

### 3.2.1. Facilities and Hardware Layer.

The bottom layer consists of physical computing resources, storages, network devices, data centers, and a mean to provide access to physical resources from other networks. CSA separates the hardware and facility layer to identify different kinds of security concerns associated to hardware and data centers. Relevant technologies in this layer include green data center, distributed system, cluster system, and firewall.

### 3.2.2. Abstraction Layer.

The abstraction layer provides a unified view of distributed and heterogeneous physical resources generally by mean of virtualization. The abstract infrastructure composes of the view of servers (processor, memory, and node), storages, network, and other facilities. Relevant technologies include virtualization and virtual machine monitor.

### 3.2.3. Core Connectivity and Delivery Layer.

This layer provides necessary tools to perform basic cloud operations

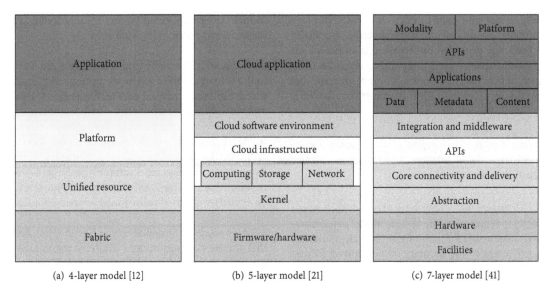

| (a) 4-layer model [12] | (b) 5-layer model [21] | (c) 7-layer model [41] |

FIGURE 2: Cloud computing stacked models.

such as resource provision, orchestra, utilization, monitoring, and backup. It allows providers to manage load balancing, optimization of resource, and security in multitenant environments. Relevant technologies include resource pooling, multitenancy, distributed storages, NoSQL, virtual machine, virtual network, load balancing, cloud service bus, and Map-Reduce.

*3.2.4. APIs Layer.* The API layer provides interfaces for consumers to access, manage, and control their provision resources. Relevant technologies include web services, virtual machine, virtual data center, authentication and authorization mechanisms, multitenancy, and Infrastructure-as-a-Service.

*3.2.5. Integration and Middleware Layer.* This layer provides a customizable development environment on top of a virtualized platform for the development and deployment of cloud software. Relevant technologies include hardened pared-down operating system, development environment, deployment environment, and Platform-as-a-Service.

*3.2.6. Application Layer.* This layer offers web applications and services running on cloud infrastructure which are accessible through standard interfaces and devices. Relevant technologies include web services (e.g., WSDL, SOAP, and REST), web technology (e.g., HTML, CSS, JavaScript, DOM, AJAX, and mash-up), authentication and authorization (public-key cryptography), federated identity management (OpenID, Oauth), secured web browsers, data format (e.g., XML, HTML, and JSON), and Software-as-a-Service.

*3.3. Cloud Actors and Roles.* Four types of cloud actors are defined in the reference models and literature. These include *consumer, provider, facilitator, and developer.* A consumer refers to an end-user or an organization that use cloud

services. It could be further categorized into three subclasses including end users of SaaS, users of PaaS, and users of IaaS. A provider offers services to consumers at agreed quality levels and prices. SaaS providers maintain cloud software which is offered as a web application or a service. PaaS providers maintain virtualized platforms for development and deployment of cloud software. IaaS providers maintain hosted data centers. A facilitator interacts with consumers, providers, and other facilitators to provide a requirement-specific cloud solution by integrating and customizing standard cloud services. Facilitators could be seen as a cloud carrier or broker. A developer develops, tests, deploys, maintains, and monitors cloud services.

*3.4. Cloud Management Domain.* Several models (i.e., IBM, GSA, NIS, and GSA) identify groups of management activities required to maintain cloud production environments. We derive five cloud management domains based on management activities outlined in reviewed reference models.

*3.4.1. Management of Physical Resources and Virtualization.* This domain is primarily used by providers to maintain physical and virtualized cloud infrastructure. It allows basic operation including resource monitoring, optimization, load balancing, metering the usage, and providing isolation over multitenancy environment.

*3.4.2. Management of Service Catalogues.* The objective of this domain is to make cloud services and applications available to consumers. It allows services to be found, requested, acquired, managed, and tested.

*3.4.3. Management of Operational Supports.* This domain concerns with technical-related services. The responsibilities are threefold. First of all, it provides management of service instances. This includes deployment, configure, testing, debugging, and performance monitoring. Second, it provides transparency and control over an isolated deployment environment. From consumer perspective, especially for IaaS and PaaS, the provided information is sufficient for SLA management, capacity planning, and analysis security concerns. Lastly, it provides management over resources. This includes provisioning, configuration management, backup, and recovery.

*3.4.4. Management of Business Supports.* This domain concerns with business-related services, for instance, invoice, billing, and customer management.

*3.4.5. Security Management.* Every layer of cloud stack needs different security mechanisms. The service model determines an actor who is responsible for maintaining security concerns for each layer. Generally the security of virtualized infrastructure (facility, hardware, abstraction, and connectivity) is managed by the provider. Consumers of IaaS have to manage the integration of an operating system and virtualized infrastructure. Consumers of PaaS have to manage the configuration of deployment environments and application security. Security concerns, including user authentication and authorization, are all handled by the providers in SaaS.

*3.5. Quality of Cloud Computing Services.* Cloud computing is considered as a form of outsourcing where the ultimate management and control over acquired services are delegated to an external provider [6, 42]. A needed level for services is defined through a formal contract between the provider and its consumers. This contract is known as service level agreement (SLA). For the consumers, it is important to ensure that the agreed level of service is respected, and any violation is reported accordingly. For the providers, it is important to manage dynamic infrastructure to meet SLA and to maximize the profit and resource utilization [43].

SLA is defined in terms of quality of services such as performance and availability. Dynamic nature of clouds caused by virtualization, resource pooling, and network directly impacts service characteristics. Quality attributes relevant to cloud services are given in this subsection.

*3.5.1. Scalability and Elasticity.* Scalability refers to capability to scale up or down the computing resources including processing units, memory, storages, and network to response to volatile resource requirements [2]. Elasticity refers to ability to scale with minimum overheads in terms of time and operation supports [2, 38]. Providers offer this characteristic to IaaS and PaaS through automatic resource provisions. For SaaS, scalability means ability to address changing workload without significantly downgrading other relevant quality attributes [42, 44].

*3.5.2. Time Behavior.* Time behaviors (e.g., performance, response time) are critical of latency sensitive applications and introduce high impact for user experiences. As cloud applications are operated on virtual distributed platform, time behaviors touch upon various area such as a quality of network, virtualization, distributed storage, and computing

model. Aforementioned factors cause unreliable time behavior for cloud services [3, 9, 45].

*3.5.3. Security.* Security and trust issues are early challenges to the introduction of a new technology. As cloud infrastructure is built upon several core technologies, the security relies on every of these components. Trust requires portions of positive experiences and provider's reputation. Common threats to cloud security include abuse of cloud services, insecure APIs, malicious insiders, shared technology vulnerabilities, data loss and leakage, and service hijacking [41]. Mechanisms to handle such issues and other cloud vulnerabilities should be explicitly clarified prior to the service adoption.

*3.5.4. Availability.* Availability refers to a percentage of time that the services are up and available for use. SLA contracts might use a more strict definition of availability by counting on uptime that respects at the quality level specified in the SLA [46].

*3.5.5. Reliability.* Reliability is capability of services to maintain a specific level of performance overtime (adapted from ISO/IEC 9126 [ISO/IEC 9126-1]). Reliability is influenced directly by a number of existing faults, a degree of fault tolerance, and recoverable capability of services in case of failures. Cloud infrastructure is built upon a number of clusters of commodity servers, and it is operated on the internet scale. Partial network failures and system malfunction need to be taken as a norm, and such failures should not impact availability of services.

*3.5.6. Portability.* Portability is an ability to move cloud artifacts from one provider to another [47]. Migration to the cloud introduces a certain degree of dependency between client systems and the service providers. For instance, clients might rely on proprietary features and versions of hardware supported by a certain provider. Such dependency needs to be minimized to facilitate future migrations and to reduce a risk of system lock-in and data lock-in. A lack of standardization for virtual machines, hypervisors, and storage APIs causes similar issue [3].

*3.5.7. Usability.* Usability refers to capability of services to be understood, learned, used, and attractive to users (adapted from ISO/IEC 9126 [ISO/IEC 9126-1]). IaaS and PaaS providers should offer sufficient APIs to support resource provisions, management, and monitoring activities. Usability is particularly important for SaaS to retain customers due to a low cost of switching.

*3.5.8. Customizability.* Capability of services to be customized to address individual user preferences is important for services that serve internet-scale users [48]. As it is impossible for providers to offer unique solution for each user, the service should be designed in a way that it allows a sufficient degree of customizability.

*3.5.9. Reusability.* Reusability is capability of software service components to serve for construction of other software.

Cloud computing amplifies the possibility of service reuse through broad Internet access.

*3.5.10. Data Consistency.* Consistency characteristic is relevant for SaaS. If the data is consistent, then all clients will always get the same data regardless of which replicas they read from. However, it is costly to maintain strong consistency in distributed environments [49], and this is the case for clouds. Many cloud storage solutions compromise a strong degree of consistency for higher availability and network partition tolerance [38, 50, 51].

*3.6. Summary.* In this section we reviewed existing cloud computing reference architectures proposed by different enterprises and researchers for different purposes. Some intend to initiate an open standard to enhance interoperability among providers; some aim to understand the dependencies of relevant components for effective security assessment; others are for general proposes. Three entities are generally presented in the reference models. These include a stack model, actors, and management domains. The most abstract model of cloud consists of four-layers fabric, unified resource, platform, and application. One of the most descriptive models is proposed by CSA. It separates the fabric layer into facility and hardware sublayers. The unified resource layer is separated into abstraction and core connectivity sublayers; the platform layer is separated into infrastructure's APIs and middleware sublayers; the application layer is further divided into a number application components. Cloud actors might take more than one role at a time; for instance, an enterprise could be a customer of IaaS provided by Amazon and develop SaaS for its customers. The responsibilities of each actor are explicitly defined in service level agreement. Management and operational activities to maintain cloud production environments could be grouped into five domains including physical resources and virtualization, service catalogues, operational supports, business supports, and security. Essential quality attributes relevant to cloud service are availability, security, scalability, portability, and performance. Cloud underlying technologies, such as virtualization, distributed storages, and web services, directly affect these quality attributes. Fault tolerance is taken as a mandatory requirement as partial network failures, and occasional crashes of commodity servers are common for systems of the internet scale. Usability is one of the most important characteristics for SaaS due to a low cost of switching.

# 4. Virtualization

Cloud computing services offer different types of computing resources over the internet as a utility service. A cloud service provider manages clusters of hardware resources and dynamically allocates these resources for consumers in terms of a virtual machine. Consumers acquire and release these virtual resources according to current workloads of their applications. The provider ensures a secure compartment for each of the consumer's environments, while trying to utilize the entire system at the lowest cost. Virtualization is an enabler technology behind this scenario.

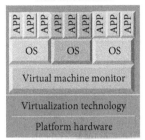

FIGURE 3: A comparison of a computer system with and without virtualization [53].

*4.1. Virtualization Basics.* Virtualization is an abstraction of a computer system which allows multiple guest systems to run on a single physical platform [52]. Host's physical resources (e.g., processor, registers, memory, and I/O devices) are shared and accessible through standard virtualization interfaces. Virtualization software creates an isolated environment for each of the guest systems by multiplexing host's computing cycles and virtualizing hardware resources. It mediates communications between guest and host systems and manipulates their messages and instructions if necessary to maintain the guest's illusion of having an ultimate control over the system.

Virtualization could be done at a process or system level. The software for system virtualization is broadly known as a hypervisor or a virtual machine monitor (VMM). The term VMM is used in this document, but they are semantically interchangeable.

Figure 3 compares a computing system with and without virtualization. Virtualized systems have a layer of VMM running on top of the hardware. A VMM allows multiple and possible different guest VMs to run simultaneously on the same physical system, while maintaining their illusions of having a sole control over the resources. To achieve this transparency the VMM operates in a higher privilege level than guest VMs. It intercepts guest's privilege instructions and executes them differently at the hardware level when necessary. It also maintains a secure confinement for each of the VM instances. Thus, resources allocated to one VM could not be interfered by other VMs running on the same physical block. This mechanism helps to promote security, as any compromise to system security is confined within an original VM.

Three immediate advantages of virtualization that could be derived from this model include: (1) *hardware independence*, as it allows different operating systems to run on the same platform; (2) *easy migration*, as the state of the system and applications is kept inside the VM; and (3) *resource optimization*, as the physical resources are shared to serve multiple virtual systems.

*4.2. History of Virtualization Technology.* The evolution of virtualization technology is explained by Rosenblum and Garfinkel [34]. Virtualization has been a solution to different issues during the evolution of computing trend. Its introduction dates back in '60 in the age of mainframe computing.

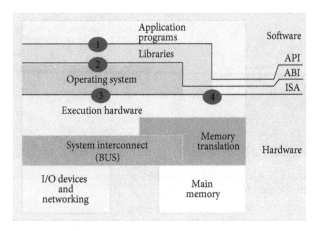

FIGURE 4: Interfaces of a computer system at different levels of abstraction [32].

IBM found a way to multiplex the usage of expensive hardware resources to support multiple applications in the same time. VMM was implemented as an abstraction layer that partitions a mainframe system to one or more virtual machines. Each of the machines held similar architecture as the hardware platform. A decrease of hardware cost and an emergence of multitasking OS during '80 caused in a drop of VMM necessity, until the point that the design of hardware no longer supported an efficient implementation of VMM.

The rule of polarity took place at the flourish age of microcomputers and complex OS. The drop in hardware cost has led to a variation of machines. Over-complex and large operating systems compromised its reliability. The OS became fragile and vulnerable, that the system administrator deployed one application per machine. Clearly, these machines were underutilized and resulted in maintenance overheads. In '05, virtualization became a solution to this problem. It was used as a mean to consolidate servers. Nowadays, virtualization is used for security and reliability enhancements.

*4.3. Computer Architecture.* Understanding of virtualization requires knowledge on computer architecture. Architecture could be seen as a formal specification of interfaces at a given abstraction level. A set of the interfaces provides a control over the behaviors of resources implemented at that level. Implementation complexity is hidden underneath. Smith and Nair describe the computer architecture at three abstraction levels: a hardware level, an operating system level, and an operating system library level [32]. Figure 4 illustrates the dependency among each level of interfaces. Virtualization exposes these interfaces and interacts with virtual resources they provide.

The interfaces at three abstraction level of computer systems are defined as follows.

*4.3.1. Instruction Set Architecture (ISA).* As an interface to hardware, ISA is a set of low level instructions that interact directly with hardware resources. It describes a specification of instructions supported by a certain model of processor. This includes an instruction's format, input, output, and the

semantic of how the instruction is interpreted. While most of these instructions are only visible to the OS, some can be called directly by applications.

*4.3.2. Application Binary Interface (ABI).* At a higher level ABI provides indirect accesses to hardware and I/O devices through OS system calls. The OS executes necessary validation and perform that operation on behalf of the caller. In contrast to ISA ABI is platform independent, as the OS handles the actual implementation on different platforms.

*4.3.3. Application Programming Interface (API).* At the application level functionality is provided to application programs in terms of libraries. API is independent from the model of platform and OS, given that the variations are implemented at the lower abstraction levels (ABI and ISA).

*4.4. Hardware Virtualization Approaches.* As mentioned, a virtualized system contains an addition software layer called VMM or hypervisor. The main functionality of VMM is to multiplex hardware resources to support multiple guest VMs and to maintain its transparency. To achieve this VMM needs to handle the virtualization of a processor unit and registers, memory space, and I/O devices [34]. This subsection summarizes an implementation approach for virtualizing these resources.

*4.4.1. CPU Virtualization.* There are several techniques to allow multiple guest systems to share similar processing units. We summarize three main approaches for CPU virtualization that are largely discussed in the literature. The first technique requires a hardware support; the second relies on a support from an operating system; the last uses a hybrid approach.

*Direct Execution.* CPU is virtualizable if it supports VMM's direct execution [34]. Through direct execution, guest's privileged and unprivileged instructions are executed in a CPU's unprivileged mode, while VMM's instructions are executed in a privileged mode. This architecture allows a VMM to trap guest's privileged instructions (kernel instructions) and CPU's responses and emulate them in order to let VMM run transparently.

Figure 5 compares a CPU privileged ring that supports the direct execution with a tradition system. In tradition system (Figure 5(a)) operating system has the highest privilege. VMM uses a deprivileging technique (Figures 5(b) and 5(c)) to facilitate its operations. For example, through a 0/3/3 model (Figure 5(c)) guest's privileged and unprivileged instructions are executed in a CPU's unprivileged mode, while VMM's instructions are executed in a CPU's privileged mode.

*Paravirtualization.* Paravirtualization technique is introduced by Denali [54, 55] and is used by Xen [56]. It is one of the most common techniques to support an implementation of VMM on nonvirtualizable CPUs [34]. Through paravirtualization, the operating systems are ported to a specific CPU architecture. A nonvirtualizable part of ISA is replaced with virtualized and efficient code. This allows most of typical applications to run unmodified. This technique results in a

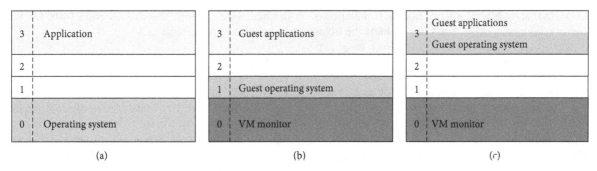

FIGURE 5: Privileged ring options for virtualizing CPU [33].

better system performance due to a reduction of trapping and instruction emulating overheads. However, it requires support from operating system vendors.

*Binary Translation.* This technique combines direct execution with on-the-fly binary translation. Typical applications running under CPU unprivileged mode can run using direct execution, while nonvirtualizable privileged code is run under control of the binary translator. The traditional binary translator was later improved for better performance. Instead of using a line-based translation, this translator translates the privileged code into an equivalent block with a replacement of problematic code and stores the translated block in the cache for future uses.

*4.4.2. Memory Virtualization.* A software technique for virtualizing memory which is to have VMM maintains a shadow version of a guest's page table and to force CPU to use the shadow page table for address translation [34]. The page table contains mappings of virtual addresses (used by processes) and physical addresses of the hardware (RAM). When a virtual address is translated to a physical address, CPU first searches for a corresponding address in a translation lookaside buffer (TLB). If a match is not found, it then searches in a page table. If a match is found, the mapping is written into TLB for a future translation. In case the lookup fail, a page fault interruption is generated.

To maintain a valid shadow page table, VMM must keep track of the guest's page table and update corresponding changes to the shadow page table. Several mechanisms are designed to ensure the consistency of page tables [57].

*Write Protect.* One technique is to write protect the physical memory of the guest's page table. Any modification by the guest to add or remove a mapping, thus, generates a page fault exception, and the control is transferred to VMM. The VMM then emulates the operation and updates the shadow page table accordingly.

*Virtual TLB.* Another technique is Virtual TLB. It relies on CPU's page fault interruptions to maintain the validity of shadow page table. VMM allows new mapping to be added to the guest's page table without any intervention. When the guest tries to access the address using that mapping, the page fault interruption is generated (as that mapping does not exist in the shadow page table). The interruption allows VMM

to add new mapping to the shadow page. In the case that the mapping is removed from the guest' page table, VMM intercepts this operation and removes the similar mapping from the shadow page table.

In addition, VMM needs to distinguish the general page fault scenario from the one associated to inconsistency of the shadow page table. This could result in significant VMM overhead.

*4.4.3. I/O Virtualization.* The goal of virtualizing I/O devices is to allow multiples VM to share a single host's hardware. Challenges in this area include scalability, performance, and hardware independence [58]. Existing approaches are as follows.

*Device Emulation.* Through device emulation, VMM intercepts an I/O operation and performs it at the hardware devices [59]. This technique does not require changes in an operating system and device drivers, but it generates significant overhead of context switching between VM and VMM.

*Paravirtualization.* Paravirtualization is introduced to reduce the limitation of device emulation. To achieve better performance, a guest operating system or device drivers is modified to support VMM interfaces and to speed up I/O operations [60, 61]. The performance of paravirtualization is better than the pure emulation approach, but it is significantly slower as compared to the direct access to the device.

*Direct Access.* An intermediate access through VMM is bypassed when using a direct access. VMs and I/O devices communicate directly through a separate channel processor. It results in significant elimination of virtualization overhead. However, the advantage of hardware independence is lost by having VMs tie with a specific hardware.

*4.5. System Virtualization.* When considering computing architecture, virtualization is generally implemented at two levels: at the application level (process virtualization) and at the bottom of software stack (system virtualization). Smith and Nair summarize the mechanism behind these basic types of virtualization [32].

*Process virtualization* is a basic mechanism used in multitasking operating systems. The OS virtualizes processing unit, registers, memory address space, and I/O resources for each process, so that multiple processes can run simultaneous without intervening each other. The OS maintains the isolation for each process instance (no intervention), maintains the state and context for each process instance, and ensures that each process receives a fair share of processing cycles.

This process is executed through scheduling and context switching. Through context switching, the OS switch in the value of CPU registers for the current process, so that it starts from the previous processing state. CPU is virtualized by scheduling algorithm and context switching. The memory is virtualized by giving an individual memory page table for each process. Interactions between a process and virtual resources are through ABI and API. In short, the goal of process virtualization is to allow multiple processes to run in the same hardware, while getting a fair share of CPU times and preventing intervention, such as access to memory, from other processes.

In *system virtualization* the whole computer system is virtualized. This enables multiple virtual machines to run isolated on the same physical platform. Each virtual machine can be either different or similar to the real machine. System virtualization is known as virtual machine monitor (VMM) or hypervisor. VMM operates above the physical resource layer. VMM divides the resources among VMs using static or dynamic allocation. In a static allocation, a portion of resources allocated to a specific VM is solely dedicated for that VM. For instance, each core of CPU might be fixedly allocated to each of the client VMs. Dynamic allocation manages entire resource as a pool. A portion of resources is dynamically allocated to a VM when needed and is deallocated to the pool when the job is done. Static allocation results in higher degree of isolation and security, while dynamic allocation helps to achieve better performance and utilization.

As mentioned, VMM provides system virtualization and facilitates the operations of VMs running above it. Several types of VMM could be found in the literature. In general they provide similar functionalities, but implementation details underneath are different, for instance, how the I/O resources are shared or how ISA translations are performed. Different approaches to system virtualization are as follows.

### 4.5.1. Bare-Metal or Native VMM.
Native VMM runs on bare hardware and provides device drivers to support multiple VMs placed on top. Guest VMs might use similar or different ISA as an underlying platform. VMM runs in the highest privileged mode and gains an ultimate control over the resources. VMM needs to maintain its transparency to guest VMs, while providing them secured compartment. To achieve this, it intercepts and emulates guest privileged instructions (kernel related). Most of the guest applications could be run unmodified under this architecture. Examples of traditional VMM include XEN (http://xen.org/) and VMWare ESX (http://www.vmware.com/products/vsphere/esxi-and-esx/index.html).

Traditional VMM may virtualize a complete ISA to support guest VMs that use different ISA than the host platform. XEN uses paravirtualization, while VMWare ESX uses binary translation. Other VMMs might use a combination of both techniques or their improvement or neither. This depends on the hardware support, the collaboration from OS vendors, and system requirements [52].

### 4.5.2. Hosted VMM.
An alternative to native VMM places VMM on top of the host operating system. The hosted VMM could be installed as an application. Another advantage of hosted VMM is that it relies on components and services provided by the host OS and virtualizes them to support multiple guest VMs. For instance, in contrast to traditional VMMs, hosted VMM uses device driver from host OS. This results in a smaller-size and less complex VMM. However, host VMM does not support different ISA guest VMs. Example of this type of VMM are Oracle VirtualBox (https://www.virtualbox.org/) and VMWare workstation (http://www.vmware.com/products/workstation/).

### 4.5.3. Codesigned VMM.
Codesigned VMMs target at improving performance by compromising portability. It implements a proprietary ISA that might be completely new or is an extension of an existing ISA. To achieve performance, a binary translator translates guest's instruction to an optimized sequence of host ISA and caches the translation for future use. Codesigned VMM is placed in a hidden part of memory inaccessible by guest systems. Examples include Transmeta Crusoe and IBM iSeries.

### 4.5.4. Microkernel.
Microkernel is a thin layer over the hardware that provides basic system services, for instance isolated address space to support multiple processes [52]. Microkernel serves as a base for virtualization, in which provisioning application could be deployed upon to provide a complete system virtualization. The OS could also be paravirtualized and run directly on the microkernel to increase the performance.

### 4.6. Use Scenarios and Benefits.
The benefits of virtualization could be derived from its usage model. Uhlig et al. identify three main use scenarios of virtualization and their respective benefits as follows.

*Workload Isolation.* Main benefits as virtualization is used for workload isolation (Figure 6(a)) are as follows: (a) security enhancement, as compromise to security is limited to a specific compartment; (b) reliability enhancement, a fault in one module that might generate a system failure in one VM does not affect others VM running on the same physical block; (c) fault tolerance, as virtualization allows control over the state of VM through suspend, resume, mark a checkpoint, and roll back.

*Workload Consolidation.* In many cases virtualization is used for server consolidation (Figure 6(b)). Its benefits for this use case are (a) *reduction of server maintenance cost*. One solution to increase system reliability is to run single-OS and single application on a server. It leads to a situation that a company needs to maintain a proliferation of underutilized servers to support different types of applications. Virtualization could be used to consolidate individual server into a single platform, increasing utilization and reducing maintenance cost.

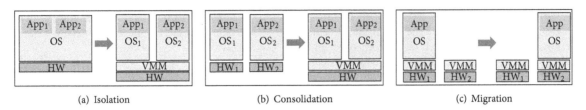

(a) Isolation       (b) Consolidation       (c) Migration

FIGURE 6: Three usage models of virtualization [33].

(b) *Supporting incompatible legacy systems*, as virtualization enable legacy and updated OS to run concurrently on the same platform.

*Workload Migration.* Figure 6(c) illustrates a case that virtualization supports system migration. It allows hot migrations and load balancing to be performed easily and effectively, as the state of the entire system is encapsulated within the VM and decoupled from the physical platform.

*4.7. Summary.* This section gives a review on virtualization technology, especially on system-level virtualization which is used to manage a resource pool in cloud computing environments. Virtualization has been used since 1960 in mainframe environments for a system isolation purpose. Before the introduction of cloud computing, virtualization provides an efficient solution to consolidate underutilized servers. The benefits of server consolidation, including resource optimization, a reduction of energy consumption, and a maintenance cost reduction, drive its large adoption. System virtualization software, known as a virtual machine monitor (VMM), allows multiple guest systems to share a similar hardware system. To enable this sharing, three main hardware elements, that is, CPU, memory, and I/O devices, are virtualized. Based on architecture and supports from operating system vendors, CPU virtualization could be done in several ways. Its goal is to multiplex CPU cycles and to remain invisible to guest systems. VMM direct execution requires VMM to run in a higher privileged level than the guest's OS and applications, in order to trap guest's instructions and emulate CPU responses when necessary. Paravirtualization ports an OS directly to a specific CPU architecture, resulting in better performance. The direct execution could be combined with line-based or block-based binary translation to remove the dependency on OS vendors. I/O virtualization appears to be the most problematic one that causes significant performance overhead.

## 5. Cloud Data Management

The goal of this section is to explore cloud storage solutions and understand impacts of their design decisions to system characteristics. Scalable storages known as NoSQL are becoming popular, as it solves performance problems of relation databases when dealing with big data. The differences between NoSQL and relational databases including their implementation details are analyzed in this section.

*5.1. Data Management Basis.* For several decades traditional ways of storing data persistently have been through relational databases or file systems [38]. An alternative to the traditional approaches has been introduced in recent years under the name of NoSQL [62]. A number of cloud storage solutions, for instance, Google Bigtable [63], Yahoo's PNutts [50], Amazon's SimpleDB (http://aws.amazon.com/simpledb/), Cassandra [64], and CouchDB (http://couchdb.apache.org/) belong to this category. This section summarizes the characteristics of relational and NoSQL databases.

*5.1.1. Relational Databases.* Relational database is a common term for relational database management systems (RDBMS). RDBMS represents a collection of relations and mechanisms that force a database to conform to a set of policies such as constrains, keys, and indices. A relation (table) consists a number of tuples (rows) that have a similar set of attributes (columns). In other words, a relation represents a class and tuples represent a set of objects which belong to the same class. The relation is defined using data schema which describes a name and a data type for each of the attributes.

RDBMS provides operations to define and adjust a schema for table and enforces that data stored in the relation are strictly conformed to the schema. Relations can be modified through *insert*, *delete*, and *update* operations. Operations across relations are provided based on set operations including *union*, *intersection*, and *difference*. *Selections* of tuples from relations with a specific criterion, *projection*, *join* of multiple relations could be done through query languages. RDBMS supports *data indexing* to improve query performance. It also provides a concept of *foreign keys* to maintain data integrity.

*Characteristics and Limitations.* RDBMS was designed primarily for business data processing [65]. It supports a concept of *transactional operations* to serve this purpose. This support guarantees that a unit of work (transaction) performed in a database must be done successfully, or otherwise all the executed operations in the same unit of work must be cancelled [66]. This proposition is also known as all-or-nothing. RDBMS supports flexible query languages including expensive operations such as multiple joins and range queries.

However, strong data consistency and complex queries supported by RDBMS cause several limitations in terms of scalability, performance, and inflexibility of data schema.

   (a) *Scalability.* Automatic partitioning which is a key for performance scalability could not be done naturally in RDBMS due to the guarantee on transactional consistency and complex data access operations it provides [67, 68].

(b) *Performance.* As RDBMS was not originally designed for distributed environments, the way to improve its performance is through architectural changes and reducing operational overheads on a single server [62]. The performance issue of RDBMS is caused by the fact that its core architecture was designed for more than 30 years when hardware characteristics, including processor performance, memory and disk space, were much different than today [65].

(c) *Inflexibility of Schema Changes.* Current markets for data storages have evolved from business data processing to other areas, such as stream processing and text management, in which the data do not necessarily conform to a strict database schema.

*5.1.2. NoSQL Databases.* As an alternative to RDBMS, NoSQL databases offer scalable distributed data tier for large scale data management [38]. The term NoSQL was firstly used in 1998 as a name for an open-source database that does not offer SQL interfaces. It was reintroduced in 2009 referring to nonrelational distributed database model [69].

There are two categories of NoSQL databases [62, 69], as follows.

*Key-Value Stores.* Data are stored as an array of entries, where a single entry is identified through a unique key. Common operations are deletion, modification or read an entry of a given key, and insertion of a new key with associated data. Key-value stores are implemented by distributed hash tables. Examples include Amazon Dynamo and MemcacheDB.

*Document-Oriented Stores.* Document-oriented storages represent loosely structured data storages where there is no predefined schema or constrains limiting databases to conform to a set of requirements. Records can contain any number of attributes. Attributes could be added, removed, and modified in a flexible manner without interrupting ongoing operations. Examples include MongoDB and CouchDB.

NoSQL databases differ significantly at the implementation level, for instance, data models, update propagation mechanisms, and consistency scheme. However, several characteristics and features are common for NoSQL systems [62, 67, 70]. First of all, it is designed for distributed environments, where data are horizontally partitioned and replicated across multiple sites. Second, the system uses nonrelational data models, allowing flexibility over schema changes. Third, it provides a restrictive set of queries and data operations, most of which are based on a single row. Fourth, on the contrary to a strong consistency guaranteed by relation databases, NoSQL systems often tradeoff the consistency to yield higher availability and better response time.

*5.2. Foundation.* This section covers a concept of database transactions which is guaranteed through ACID properties and mechanisms to support ACID in distributed systems.

*5.2.1. ACID Properties.* The ACID is fundamental principle of database system [66]. It contains the following properties.

(i) *Atomicity.* All actions of a transaction is executed and reflected in the database, or the entire transaction is rolled back (all or nothing).

(ii) *Consistency.* A transaction reaches its normal state, committing only legal results and preserving the consistency of the database.

(iii) *Isolation.* Events within a transaction are hidden from other transactions running concurrently, allowing the transaction to be reset to the beginning state if necessary.

(iv) *Durability.* Once a transaction has been completed, results have been committed to database, and the system must guarantee that the modification is permanent even in the case of subsequent failures. The durability is ensured by the use of transaction logs that facilitate the restoration process of committed transaction if any failure occurs.

Based on the ACID properties, a transaction can be terminated in three ways. First, it successfully reaches its commit point, holding all properties true. Second, in a case that bad input or violations that prevent a normal termination has been detected, all the operations that have been executed are reset. Finally, the transaction is aborted by the DBMS in the case of session time-out or deadlock.

*5.2.2. CAP Theorem.* Web services are expected to provide strongly consistent data and to be highly available. To preserve consistency they need to behave in a transactional manner; that is, ACID properties are respected [49]. The strong consistency is particularly important for critical and financial systems. Similarly, the service should be available whenever it is needed, as long as the network on which it runs is available. For distributed network, however, it is desirable that the services could sustain through a certain level of network failures.

It is challenging in general to maintain the ACID properties for distributed storage systems, as the data are replicated over geographic distances. In practice, it is impossible to achieve three desired properties in the same time [49, 71]. We could get only two out of the three. CAP theorem describes trade-off decisions needed to be made when designing highly scalable systems. It is related to three core system requirements as follows.

(i) *Consistency (atomic consistency).* The notion of consistent services is somewhat different than consistent property of database systems, as it combines the database notion of atomicity and consistence. The consistency enforces that multiple values of the same data is not allowed.

(ii) *Availability.* Requests to a nonfailure node must result in a response, instead of a message about a service being unavailable.

(iii) *Partition tolerance.* When data and logic are distributed to different nodes, there is a chance (which is not rare) that a part of network becomes unavailable.

This property guarantees that "*no set of failures less than total network failure is allowed to cause the system to respond incorrectly.*"

To deal with CAP, the designer has an option of dropping one of three properties from system requirements or improving an architectural design. The scenarios of dropping one of the CAP are, for instance, running all components related to the services on one machine (i.e., dropping partition tolerance); waiting until data of every replicated node become consistent before continuing to provide the services (i.e., dropping availability); or accepting a notion of weaker consistency.

CAP implies that if we want a service to be highly available (minimal latency) and we want the system to be tolerant to network partition (e.g., messages lost, hardware outages), then sometimes there will be a case that the values of the data at different nodes are not consistent.

*5.2.3. Consistency Scheme.* As mentioned, dealing with the consistency across replicas is one of challenges of distributed services. A variety of consistency models have been proposed to support applications that can tolerate different levels of relaxed consistency [51]. The following defines well-known classes of consistency.

(i) *Strong consistency.* After the update is complete, subsequent accesses to any replicas will return the updated value.

(ii) *Eventual consistency.* The system guarantees that if there is no new update to the object, the subsequent accesses will eventually return the updated value. The degree of inconsistency depends on communication delay, system workload, and the number of replicas.

(iii) *Timeline consistency.* Timeline refers to a scenario in which all the replicas of a given record apply all updates to the record in the same order. This is done by using a per record mastership mechanism. With this mechanism the replica that receives the most frequent updates for each record is set as a master for that record [50]. As the updates are performed in an asynchronized manner, the system provides various data retrieval APIs that support different consistency levels. This mechanism is introduced by Yahoo!.

(iv) *Optimistic consistency (weak consistency).* The system does not guarantee that the subsequence access will return the updated value.

*5.2.4. Architectural Tradeoffs.* A number of cloud storage systems have emerged in the recent years. A lack of a standard benchmark makes it difficult to understand the design tradeoffs and quality of services; each of them provides to support different workloads. To this end, Cooper et al. summarize main tradeoffs the providers face during the architectural design which impact the CAP property of the system and applications relying on it [72].

*Read Performance versus Write Performance.* Different types of applications (i.e., latency sensitive applications at one end and throughput oriented applications at another end) needs different tradeoffs between optimizing for read and write operations. Several design decisions for these operation exists. An *update* could be written to a target file for each single operation or could be written later as a group update. A *log* could be recorded on a row basis where a complete row is written, or it could be stored as a log-structured system where only an update delta is recorded. The structured log can be inefficient for reads as all the updated must be merged to form a consistent record but it provides a lower cost on updates. An *access mechanism*, that is, sequential and random access, should also be suitable for a specific nature of applications.

*Latency versus Durability.* Updates could be written to disk before it returns success to users, or it could be buffered for a group write. In cases that multiple updates could be merge to a single I/O operation, the group write results in a lower latency and higher throughput. This advantage comes with a risk of losing recent updates when a server crashes.

*Synchronous versus Asynchronous Replication.* The purpose of synchronization is to ensure that data stored in all replicas are updated and consistent. An algorithm for synchronizing replicas determines a level of consistency, availability (through a locking mechanism), and response time.

*Data Partitioning.* A storage could be strictly row-based structured or allows for a certain degree of column storage. Row-based storage is efficient for accessing a few records for their entirely content, while column-based storage is efficient for accessing multiple records for their certain details.

The concept of "one-architecture-fits-all" does not suit for distributed storage systems. However, the ultimate goal for each design is to maximize key properties of storage system: performance, availability, consistency, and durability. Different design decisions reflect in the features and quality of services provided by different storage providers which are discussed in the next section.

*5.3. Selected Cloud-Based Data Management Services.* Cloud providers offer a number of solutions for very large data storages. It is necessary to understand the mechanisms that each solution applies to enforce system requirements. This includes, for instance, how the data are partitioned across machines (elasticity), how the updates are routed (consistency), how the updates are made persistent (durability), and what and how failures are handled (availability).

*5.3.1. Google Bigtable.* Google Bigtable is a distributed data storage designed to scale to a very large size, to be fault tolerant, and to support a wide range of applications. It is designed to support applications which require different workload and performance. Bigtable is used by more than 60 products of Google, such as search engine, Google Docs, and Google Earth. Chang et al. describe architecture of Bigtable as summarized in this subsection [63].

(1) *Data Model.* Bigtable is a sparse, distributed, and multidimensional sorted map. The map is indexed by a combination

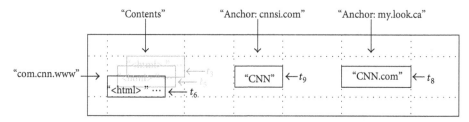

FIGURE 7: An example a Bigtable that stores a webpage [63].

of row key, column key, and timestamp. This design makes it convenient to store a copy of a large collection of web pages into a single table Figure 7.

*Row.* Read or write of data is atomic under a single row key disregard of a number of columns involved. A row range of the table is partitioned into a *tablet* which represents a unit of distribution and load balancing. A read of short row ranges is sufficient and requires communications only with few machines.

*Column Family.* A column key is formed by a syntax *family (qualifier)*. A column family is a group of associated column keys. A table can have unbounded number of columns, but generally a number of column families are in hundreds at most. An access control is performed at the column family level.

*Timestamp.* Each cell of Bigtable can contain multiple versions of the same data, indexed by a timestamp.

(2) *System Model.* Bigtable is built on top of several components of Google infrastructure.

*Distributed File System (DFS).* Bigtable uses DFS to store logs and data files. A cluster of Bigtable is controlled by a cluster management system which performs job scheduling, failure handlings, consistency controls, and machine monitoring.

*Google SSTable.* SSTable is an immutable sorted map from keys to values used by DFS to store chucks of data files and its index. It provides look up services for key/value pairs of a specific key range. Figure 8 depicts how a tablet is chucked under SSTable.

*Chubby Distributed Lock Service.* Chubby is a highly available persistent distributed lock service. It consists of five active replicas, one of which is assigned to be a master to handle service requests. The main task of Chubby is to ensure that there is at most at a time only one active master which is responsible for storing a bootstrap location of Bigtable data, discovering tablet servers and storing Bigtable schemas and access control lists.

A structure of Bigtable consists three main components: a master server, tablet servers, and a library that is stored at the client-side. The master server assigns a range of tablets to be stored at each tablet server, monitors servers' status, controls load balancing, and handles changes of the table

schema. The tablet servers could be added or removed with response to the current workload under the control of the master. Read and write of records are performed by the tablet server. Thus, clients communicate directly to a tablet server to access their data. This architecture eliminates a bottleneck at the master server, as clients do not rely on it for tablet location information. Instead, this information is cached in a library at the client side.

(3) *Consistency and Replication Mechanism.* A large number of Google products rely on Google File System (GFS) for storing data and replication. While sharing the same goals as other distributed storage systems (such as fault tolerance, performance, and availability), GFS are optimized for the following use scenarios [23]: (a) component failures are treated as a norm rather than exceptions; (b) files are large and consist in a large number of application objects; (c) in most occasions files are changed by appending new data rather than changing existing details; and (d) GFS APIs are accustomed to suit application requirements.

GFS uses a relaxed consistency model which implies the following characteristics [23].

*Atomicity and Correctness.* File namespace mutations are atomic and are exclusively handled by the master server. A global order of operations is recorded in the master's operation log, enforcing the correct execution order for concurrent operations. Possible states of mutated file are summarized in Table 2. A file region is *consistent* if clients get the same data regardless of which replica has been accessed. A file region is *defined* if after the mutation it is consistent and clients see the changes from all replicas. A file region is *inconsistent* if different clients see different data when reading from different locations.

A mutation could be a write or a record append. A write mutation writes data at an application-specific file offset. An append mutation appends the data atomically at least once at the offset determined by GFS and returns that offset to the client. When the write mutation succeeds without interferences from concurrent writes, the file region is defined. In existence of concurrent writes, successful write mutations leave the region consistent but undefined; that is, data are consistent across replicas, but they might not contain the data written by the last mutation. Failed write mutations result in an inconsistent file region. With regards to an append mutation, GFS guarantees that the data must have been written at the same offset on all replicas before the operation reports success. The region in which the data

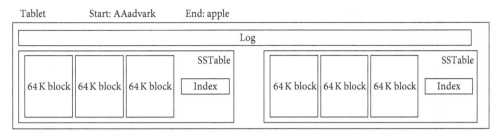

Tablet Start: AAadvark End: apple

FIGURE 8: Tablet.

TABLE 2: File region state after mutation [23].

|  | Write | Record append |
| --- | --- | --- |
| Serial success | Defined | Defined interspersed with inconsistent |
| Concurrent success | Consistent but undefined | |
| Failure | Inconsistent | |

have been written successfully is defined, while intervening regions are inconsistent.

*Updates for Replicas.* GFS guarantees that a file region is defined after successful mutations by using the following update sequence: (1) mutations are applied to a file region in the same order on all replicas; (2) stale replicas (the ones have missed mutation updates during the time that chunkserver is down) is not involved during the update, thus their locations are not given to clients.

*5.3.2. Yahoo PNUTS.* Yahoo PNUTS is a massively parallel distributed storage system that serves Yahoo's web applications. The data storage is organized as an ordered table or hash table. PNUTS is designed based on an observation that a web application mostly manipulates a single data record at a time, and activities on a particular record are initiated mostly at a same replica. This design decision reflects on its guaranteed consistency and replication process. Cooper et al. describe the architecture of PNUTS as explained in this subsection [50].

(1) *Data Model.* PNUTS presents a simplified relational model in which data are organized into a table of records (row) with multiple attributes (column). In addition to typical data types, it allows arbitrary and possibly large structured data, which is called *bulb*, to be stored in a record. Examples of bulb objects include pictures and audio files. Schema changes are flexible, such that new attributes can be added without interrupting ongoing activities. The system does not enforce referential constraints, and some of the attributes could be left unfilled.

The query language of PNUTS is more restrictive than those supported by relation models. It allows selections and projections over a single table. A primary key is required for updates and deletes of records. In addition, it provides a multiget operation which retrieves up to a few thousand records in parallel based on a given set of primary keys.

Currently the system does not support complex and multi-table queries such as join and group by operations.

(2) *System Model.* PNUTS system is divided into multiple regions, each of which represents a complete system and contain a complete copy of tables. It relies on a pub/submechanism for replication and update propagations. The architecture of PNUT with two regions is illustrated in Figure 9. Each region contains three main components: storage units, tablet controller, and routers. Message brokers control replications and consistency among different regions.

*Storage Unit.* In terms of storage, tables are partitioned horizontally into a number of tablets. A tablet size varies from hundred megabytes to few gigabytes. A server contains thousands of tablets. The assignments of tablets to servers are optimized for load balancing. PNUT supports two types of storage structures: ordered tables and hash tables.

*Router.* In order to localize a record to be read or written, a router determines a tablet that contains the requested record and a server that stores that tablet. For ordered tables, the router stores an interval mapping which defines boundaries of tablets and a map from tablets to a storage unit. For hash tables, the hash space is divided into intervals, each of which corresponds to a single tablet. Tablet boundaries are defined by a hash function of a primary key.

*Tablet Controller.* Although the process of record localization is performed by the router, it stores only a cached copy of the mapping. The whole mappings are maintained by the tablet controller. It controls load balancing and division of records over tablets. Changes of record locations cause the router to misroute the requests and trigger the new mapping retrieval.

(3) *Consistency and Replication Mechanism.* A consistency model of PNUTS comes from an observation that web applications often changes one record at a time, and different records have activities with different locality. PNUTS proposes *per record timeline consistency*, in which all replicas of a given record apply a series of update to that record in the same order. It also supports a range of APIs for various degrees of consistency guarantees. To implement this mechanism, one of the replicas is appointed as the master independently for each record. The updates to that record are sent to the master. The record master is automatically adjusted to the replica that receives the majority of write requests.

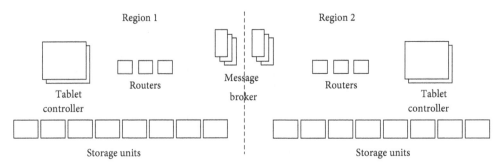

FIGURE 9: PNUTS's architecture.

The system currently provides three variations of data accesses: *read any* (no consistency guaranteed), *read critical* (guarantee that the returned record is at least as new as a given version), and *read latest* (strong consistency guaranteed). It provides two variations of write operations: *write* (transactional ACID guaranteed), *test-and-set-write* (the write is performed if and only if the record holds the same version as the given one).

*5.3.3. Amazon Dynamo.* Amazon has developed a number of solutions for large scale data storages, such as Dynamo, Simple Data Storage S3, SimpleDB, and Relational Database Service (RDS). We focus on the architecture of Dynamo because it has served a number of core e-commerce services of Amazon that need a tight control over the trade-offs between availability, consistency, performance, and cost effectiveness. The architecture of Dynamo is described by DeCandia et al. [73].

(1) *Data Model.* Dynamo is classified as a distributed key-value storage optimized for high availability for write operations. It provides read and write operations to an object which is treated as an array of bytes uniquely identified by a primary key. The write operation requires that a context of the object is specified. The object's context encodes system metadata, such as a version which is necessary for validity checks before write requests could be performed.

(2) *System Model.* Dynamo uses consistent hashing to distribute workloads across multiple storage hosts. Consistent hashing is a solution for distributed systems in which multiple machines must agree on a storage location for an object without communication [74]. Through this partitioning mechanism, the hash space is treated as a ring in which a largest hash value is connected to the smallest one. Each storage node receives a random value which determines its position on a ring. An assignment of an object to a storage node is done by hashing an object's key which results in a position in the ring and walking the ring clockwise to the first larger node than the hash value.

Dynamo replicates objects into multiple nodes. Once a storage node is determined, that node (known as *coordinator*) is responsible for replicating all data items that fall into its range to the successor nodes in the ring. Figure 10 illustrates a storage ring in which workloads are partitioned among node

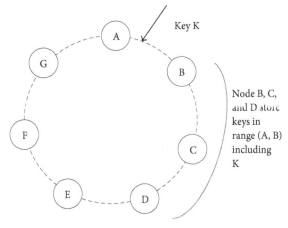

FIGURE 10: Partitioning and replication model of Amazon Dynamo.

A to G. Suppose that the hash function of key K of an object falls between a location of node A and B, leading the object to be stored at node B. Node B is in charge of replicating this object to node C, D. In other words, node D will store copies of data that their key falls between A and D.

(3) *Consistency and Replication Mechanism.* Dynamo provides eventual consistency, as updates are propagated to replicas in an asynchronous manner. A write request responses to the caller before the update is successfully performed at all the replicas. As a result, a read request might not return the latest update. However, applications that rely on this system can tolerate the cost of relaxed consistency for the better response time and higher availability.

Dynamo uses a vector clock to handle different versions of the object during the update reconciliation. A write request is attached with object's context metadata which contains the vector clock information. This data is received from the earlier read. Read and write operations are handles by the coordinator node. To complete a write operation, the coordinator generates the vector clock for the new version, writes the object locally, and propagates the update to highest-ranked nodes which are preferable locations for storing that object. In addition, the system allows clients to define a minimum number of nodes that must participate in a successful write. Each write request is successful when the coordinator receives at least that minimum number of responses from the target nodes.

*5.4. Summary.* Cloud storage solutions are reviewed in this section. We begin the section by clarifying the fundamental differences between relational and scalable NoSQL databases. The name NoSQL comes from its lack of supports on complex query languages and data integrity checks. NoSQL works well with big data because the data are partitioned and stored in distributed nodes. It generally maintains better performance as compared to relation databases by compromising strong data consistency and complex query supports. CAP theorem explains the dependencies between three desired properties-consistency, availability, and partition tolerance. To deal with CAP, one property needs to be dropped from a system property, resulting in having a CA, CP, or AP as a main architectural driver. Consistency schemes ordered from the strongest to and weakest one are strong, eventual, timeline, and optimistic accordingly. While strong consistency guarantees that accesses to any replica return a single most updated value, optimistic consistency does not guarantee whether or not an access to a certain replica returns an updated value at all. Three scalable storage models used by leading cloud providers, that is, Google Bigtable, Yahoo PNUTS, and Amazon Dynamo, are distributed key value stores that supports relaxed consistency and provide low level APIs as query interfaces. They are in fact significantly different in architecture and implementation details. The diversity of data management interfaces among providers might result in data lock-in which is one of the primary concern of its adoption.

# 6. Security

The objective of this section is to provide an insight to security concerns associated to cloud computing. To achieve it, first of all, we point out security vulnerabilities associated to the key architectural components of cloud computing. Guidance to reduce the probability that vulnerabilities would be exploited is described. In the end we present a mapping of cloud vulnerabilities and prevention mechanisms.

*6.1. Vulnerabilities to Cloud Computing.* The architecture of cloud computing comprises an infrastructure and a software operating on the cloud. Physical locations of the infrastructure (computing resources, storages, and networks) and its operating protocol are managed by a service provider. A virtual machine is served as a unit of application deployment. Underneath a virtual machine lies an additional software layer, that is, virtualized hypervisor, which manages a pool of physical resources and provides isolated environments for clients' virtual machines.

Vulnerability, threat, and risk are common terms in the context of security which are used interchangeably, regardless of their definitions. To remain consistent we provide the definition of these terms as follows: (i) Vulnerability is defined by NIST as "*a flaw or weakness in system security procedures, design, implementation, or internal controls that could be*

*exercised and result in security breach or a violation of the system' security policy.*" (ii) Threat is defined by ENISA as "*a circumstance or event with potential to adversely impact an asset through unauthorized access, destruction, disclosure, modification, and/or denial of services.*" (iii) Risk is defined in ISO27005 based on the previous terms as "*the potential that a given threat will exploit vulnerability of an asset or group of assets and thereby cause harm to an organization.*"

Vulnerabilities to cloud computing arise from flaws or weaknesses of its enabling technologies and architectural components [10]. A simplified cloud stack model provides a good basic for vulnerability identifications. As Section 2 explains, clouds are abstracted into five layers including: a software layer, a platform layer, an infrastructure layer, a unified resource layer, and a fabric layer. We explain cloud security by discussing the vulnerabilities associated to system procedure, design and implementation, and controls of each component at each layer.

Vulnerabilities and security requirements of cloud services are identified in a number of literatures. In the work of Grobauer et al. the influences of cloud computing on established security issues are analyzed [10]. Cloud specific vulnerabilities are identified in association to the core technologies, essential characteristics, and architecture of cloud computing. The discussion on the last area is based on a reference architecture proposed by University of California and IBM [21]. The mapping to those architectural components, in turn, points out the relevant vulnerabilities to specific cloud services' consumers.

Through his work "Monitoring Cloud Computing by Layer," Spring presents a set of restrictions and audits to facilitate cloud security [75, 76]. The discussion is organized around a seven-layer cloud model proposed by the cloud security alliance. These layers are either controlled by cloud providers or consumers. The line of responsibility is generally clarified in terms of SLA. The list of security controls by layer assist SLA formation and security monitoring.

Iankoulova and Daneva performed a systematic review to address requirements of SaaS security and propose solutions to deal with it [77]. Their selection criterion leads to identifying 55 papers for a detailed analysis. The discussion is organized into nine areas following the taxonomy of security quality factors. These include access control, attack/harm detection, nonrepudiation, integrity, security auditing, physical protection, privacy, recovery, and prosecution. Top areas for cloud security research include integrity, access control, and security auditing, while the issues related to physical protection, nonrepudiation, recovery, and prosecution are not broadly discussed.

In this subsection we shortly review the functionalities and components at each cloud layer and point out a number of vulnerabilities and subvulnerabilities related to them.

*6.1.1. Application Layer.* At the highest layer, SaaS is offered to consumers based on web technologies. The reliability of web services (backend), web browsers (frontend), and authentication and authorization mechanisms influences service security.

*Vulnerabilities of Web Services (v1).* The vulnerabilities of web services are associated to the implementation of a session handler and the mechanism to detect inputs which creates erroneous executions.

(i) *Session-handling vulnerability (v1a).* Http is a stateless protocol, while a majority of nontrivial applications and transactions require the notion of state. The state is handled by a session-handling mechanism. An inappropriate implementation of the session-handler might introduce vulnerabilities on session riding and session hijacking, where the credential of the message originator is stolen and misused [10].

(ii) *Injection vulnerability (v1b).* This vulnerability is exploited by manipulating service requests or input to an application with an intension to create an erroneous execution at the backend. Injections occur in three forms: SQL injection (targeting at backend database), command injection (targeting at backend operating system), and cross-site scripting (targeting at a victim's web browser) [10].

*Vulnerabilities of Client-Side Data Manipulation (v2).* Client-side data manipulation vulnerability is caused by inappropriate permissions given to web browser components such as plug-ins and mash-ups, allowing these components to read and modify data sent from the web application to the server [10, 78]. Attacks targeting at this vulnerability impact information confidentiality and integrity.

*Vulnerabilities of Authentication and Authorization (v3).* The vulnerability of authentication and authorization refers to the weaknesses in a credential verification process and the management of credential information from both provider and user sides. A variety of consumer population increases the complexity in managing the controls in this area [79]. Moreover, an enterprise authentication and authorization framework does not generally cover the integration of SaaS [80].

(i) *Authentication vulnerability (v3a).* It includes insecure user behaviors (for instance, reused credentials, weak password), the usage of one-factor authentication, and a weak credential changing and resetting process.

(ii) *User authorization scheme vulnerabilities (v3b).* It is caused by insufficient authorization checks on programming interfaces, coarse authorization scheme which does not support delegation of user privileges (to access only required resources).

*Vulnerabilities of Encryption and Keys (v4).* The use of a weak encryption algorithm, an insufficient key length, or an inappropriate key management process introduces encryption vulnerability.

(i) *Weak cryptography vulnerability (v4a).* Keys and encryption are crucial to protect confidentiality and integrity of data in shared environment. The use of

insecure and obsolete cryptography is vulnerable in cloud environments especially for public clouds.

(ii) *Key management vulnerability (v4b).* Key management concerns how the encryption keys are created, stored, transferred, backed up, and recovered. Compromise in this process results in information leakage and a loss of data those keys protect.

*6.1.2. Platform Layer.* A virtualized cloud platform is composed of a layer of development and deployment tools, middleware, and operating system (OS) which are installed on a virtual machine. The security of platforms relies on the robustness of each component, their integration, the platform management portal, and provided management APIs.

*Vulnerabilities of Cloud Operating Systems (v5).* An OS arranges communications (system calls) between applications and hardware, therefore it has access to all data stored in the virtual machine. Data leakage could occur when an OS contains malicious services running on the background. For PaaS, a common practice of providers to secure cloud OS is to deploy single, harden, pared-down OS, and monitor binary changes on the OS image [75]. However, this mechanism is not applied to IaaS where an OS monitoring process is performed individually by each client.

*Vulnerabilities of Access to Platform Administrative and Management Interfaces (v6).* PaaS providers must provide a portal which allows system administrators to manage and control their environments. These administrative and management accesses share a similar set of web services vulnerabilities and the vulnerabilities of identity authentication and authorization control [10].

*6.1.3. Infrastructure Layer.* Cloud infrastructure is transferred to consumers in terms of a virtual machine (VM) that provides computing capability, memory, storages, and connectivity to a global network. Vulnerabilities to cloud infrastructure are caused by traditional VM weaknesses, management of VM images, untraceable virtual network communications, data sanitization in shared environments, and access to infrastructure administrative and management APIs.

*Vulnerabilities of a Virtual Machine and Its Interfaces (v7).* Apart from the vulnerability residing in a VM image itself, this issue is concerned with the common practice of a provider to offer cloned VM images for IaaS and PaaS consumers and the management of these images.

(i) *Traditional VM vulnerability (v7a).* Data centers are traditionally protected by perimeter-security measures such as firewalls, security zone, intrusion prevention and detection tools, and network monitoring. In contrast, security controls in virtual environments must be implemented also at the VM level. Vulnerable areas of VM include the remote access to administrative interfaces, the ease of reconfiguration that might propagate unknown configuration errors, and *patch management* which is difficult, if not impossible, to maintain by the providers to ensure the compatibility for all VMs' configuration [81].

(ii) *Cloned VM image vulnerability (v7b).* This vulnerability is concerned with how VM images are handled. The usage of cloned VM and OS images as an abstract platform is a common practice for PaaS consumers [78]. As attackers could easily register for IaaS and gain access to the image, they could track useful knowledge related to the drawbacks and limitations of that type of VM such as determining the channel of data leakage and might be able to attack consumers using the same product [10, 81].

(iii) *Insecure VM image vulnerability (v7c).* Another issue is that an IaaS consumer might obtain and use manipulated VM images from a notorious source. In this case, attackers gain a back-door access to the victim's platform to conduct their malicious activities [10].

*Vulnerabilities of Virtual Network Communications (v8).* Virtual communication channel vulnerability is concerned with the communications between VMs on the same physical resources. Generally a VM provides the capability for users to configure virtual network channels in order to directly communicate with another VM running on the same physical platform. The messages sent through such channels are invisible to network monitoring devices and therefore untraceable [78].

*Vulnerabilities of Data Sanitization (v9).* As previously mentioned, data in use, in transit and at rest must be secured. Access control and encryption are employed to protect data at rest. Secure network protocol, encryption, and public key are used to protect data in transit. However, the mechanism of freeing resources and removing sensitive data is overlooked, even though it is equally important in a shared environment. *Data sanitization vulnerability* is related to deletion of data, applications, and platform instances in the end of their life cycle, which is more difficult to perform when the physical resources are shared with other tenants [10, 78]. Flaws in data sanitization could result in data leakage.

*Vulnerabilities of Access to Infrastructure Administrative and Management Interfaces (v10).* IaaS must provide interfaces allowing administrators to perform their administrative and management activities. This includes remote accesses to utilize and configure computing services, storages, and network. These accesses share a similar set of web services vulnerabilities and the vulnerabilities of identity authentication and authorization control [10].

### 6.1.4. Unified Resource Layer.

Multitenancy is a core mechanism of cloud computing to achieve the economies of scale. A virtualized hypervisor is designed to operate multiple VMs on a shared platform and therefore leads to resource optimization, decreased energy consumption, and cost reduction.

There are, however, a number of vulnerabilities associated to hypervisors and the multitenancy architecture.

*Vulnerabilities of a Virtualized Hypervisor and Its Interfaces (v11).* An insecure implementation of a hypervisor causes several vulnerabilities as follows.

(i) *Vulnerabilities of a complex hypervisor (v11a).* A simple, small-sized, and feature-limited hypervisor is generally more robust and easier to maintain. However, several hypervisors are adapted from an operating system and combined with advanced features. A proper tradeoff between simplicity and functionality is essential in order to maintain its robustness [78].

(ii) *Vulnerabilities of access to administrative and management interface (v11b).* A hypervisor provides APIs and web portals, allowing cloud administrators to perform their activities. These accesses share a similar set of web service vulnerabilities.

*Vulnerabilities of Multitenant Environments (v12).* The concept of multitenancy holds different definitions based on an abstraction to which it is applied [16]. It generally refers to an architectural approach that leverages shared infrastructure, data, services, and applications to serve different consumers. Achieving secure multitenancy thus requires policy driven enforcement, segmentation, service level agreement, and billing models for different use scenarios. The followings point out its vulnerabilities.

(i) *Vulnerabilities of data leakage in multitenant environments (v12a).* The leakage could occur when the process of data sanitization does not completely remove the data stored in the physical resources before returning them to the share pool.

(ii) *Vulnerabilities of cross-tenant access (v12b).* Malicious cross-tenant access refers to an attempt of malicious code to escape from its compartment and to interfere with processes of other VMs running on the same tenant.

*Vulnerabilities of Sharing Network Components (v13).* In IaaS, it is likely that several VM instances share network infrastructure components such as DNS servers and DHCP servers [10]. Attacks to such components would create a cross-tenant impact.

### 6.1.5. Fabric Layer.

This layer is concerned with physical security including servers, processors, storages, and network devices hosted in a data center.

*Vulnerabilities of Physical Resources (v14).* The physical security of cloud data centers is concerned with the following issues [78].

(i) *Malicious insider vulnerability.* Malicious insiders could introduce severe security threats, as they might gain physical access to the datacenter if a provider neglects in applying an appropriate privilege and access control.

TABLE 3: Cloud computing core technologies and associated vulnerabilities.

| Layer | Functionality | Vulnerabilities |
|---|---|---|
| (1) Application | Provide services through web applications and web services. | (v1) Vulnerabilities of web services<br>(v2) Vulnerabilities of client-side environments<br>(v3) Vulnerabilities of authentication and authorization<br>(v4) Vulnerabilities of encryption mechanisms and keys |
| (2) Platform | Provide programming interfaces and mediate communications between software and the underlining platform. | (v5) Vulnerabilities of a cloud platform<br>(v6) Vulnerabilities of access to platform administrative and management interfaces |
| (3) Infrastructure | Provide computing and storage capabilities and connectivity to a global network. | (v7) Vulnerabilities of a virtual machine<br>(v8) Vulnerabilities of virtual network communications<br>(v9) Vulnerabilities of data sanitization<br>(v10) Vulnerabilities of access to infrastructure administrative and management interfaces |
| (4) Unified resources | Three main features of hypervisors: operate multitenant virtual machine and application built up on it; provide isolation to multiple guest VMs; support administrative work to create, migrate, and terminate virtual machine instances. | (v11) Vulnerabilities of a virtualized hypervisors and its interfaces<br>(v12) Vulnerabilities of multi-tenant environments<br>(v13) Vulnerabilities of shared network components |
| (5) Fabric | Cloud physical infrastructure including servers, processors, storages, and network devices hosted in the data center. | (v14) Vulnerability of physical resources |

(ii) *Natural disaster vulnerability.* Environmental concerns impact the availability of data and the continuity of services running on the cloud. A data center must have a comprehensive continuity of services plan in place, preferably conforming to an accepted standard.

(iii) *Internet access vulnerability.* This refers to an attempt for an unauthorized outsider to gain access to a datacenter through network channels.

A summary of the vulnerabilities associated to each of the cloud enabling technologies is presented in Table 3.

*6.2. Common Threats to Cloud Security.* Having identified the associated vulnerabilities to cloud computing, we are able to analyze to which extent they cover security breaches occurred and the concerns raised by current and prospect cloud consumers. In this section we present a list of threats to cloud security based on the cloud security alliance "*Top threats to cloud computing*" report [41].

*Abuse of Cloud Computing.* Based on its simple registration process and flexible usage model, clouds attract a number of attackers to host and conduct their malicious activities. Several malicious cloud adoptions have been found in recent years. Examples include *Zeus Botnet* which steals victims' credential and credit card information, *InfoStealer Trojan horses* designed to steal personal information, and *download for Microsoft Office and Adobe exploits*. It could be prevented by enforcing a strict initial registration which allows for sufficient identity validation.

*Insecure Application Programming Interfaces.* Clouds provide interfaces for consumers to use services and perform administrative and management activities such as provision, monitoring, and controlling VM instances. These features are generally designed as web services and thus inherit

their vulnerabilities. Robust designs must ensure appropriate authentication and authorization mechanisms, a secure key management process, strong encryption, and sufficient monitoring of intrusion attempts.

*Malicious Insiders.* This threat is concerned with considerable damage that malicious insiders could create by getting an access or manipulating data in a data center. Centralization of data inside cloud servers itself creates an attractive condition for an adversary to try out fraud attempts. To reduce the risk, cloud providers must ensure strong and sufficient physical access controls, perform employee's background checks, make security process transparent to consumers, and allow for external audits.

*Shared Technology Vulnerabilities.* A virtualized hypervisor provides secure compartments and mediates communication between guest systems and physical resources underneath. Flaws in hypervisors might grant an inappropriate permission for an operating system to access or modify physical resources which belong to other tenants. The risk could be reduced by monitoring physical resources for unauthorized activities, implementing best practices for deployment and configuration, performing a vulnerability scan and configuration audits on a hypervisor, and following best practices during its installation and configuration.

*Data Loss and Data Leakage.* Data loss and leakage could be a result of unauthorized access, data manipulation, or physical damage. To protect unexpected loss and leakage, providers must implement robust access controls and secure key management process. Backup and recovery mechanisms should be put in place.

*Account and Service Hijacking.* Cloud service models put paramount importance to authentication and authorization, as the security of every service depends on its accountability and robustness. The use of two-factor authentication, secure key management process, and a careful design of web services help to reduce the damage of this attack.

While most of the common threats to cloud security are associated to its underlining technologies (web services and virtualization), some of them (abusing and malicious insiders) could be solved by better governances. This list is expected to be updated as the usage of cloud computing grows in popularity.

*6.3. Recommended Practices to Enhance Cloud Security.* This subsection presents a list of best practices to enhance cloud security as proposed by leading cloud providers and researchers. The practices are organized into five main areas including: identity and access control, data security, application security, security of virtualized environment, and physical and network security.

*6.3.1. Identity and Access Control.* The provisions of IT infrastructure offered by cloud computing extend the focus of identity and access control from the application level to the platform and virtual machine level. The goal of identity and access control is to ensure that accesses to data and applications are given only to authorized users. Associated areas include strong authentication, delegated authentication and profile management, notification, and identity federation. A set of recommended practices is relevant to both cloud providers and consumers.

*Authentication.* The challenges of authentication include the use of strong authentication methods, identity management, and federation.

(i) *Verification of users identities and access rights* is securely performed before the access to data and services is granted [82].

(ii) *Multifactor authentication* is applied before the access to highly sensitive and critical data (e.g., customer's identity, financial information) and processes (e.g., an administrative portal) is granted [82, 83]. Cloud providers should provide various authentication methods, including, for instance, biometrics, certificates, and one-time password, to support different security requirements.

(iii) *A secure communication tunnel* (e.g., VPN connections using SSL, TSL, or IPSEC) and a valid certificate are required to access highly sensitive and critical assets [16, 82].

(iv) *The use of federated identity*, that is, authenticating users through identity providers, enables a single sign-on or a single set of identities which are valid among multiple systems [82]. A privilege granted to an external user authenticated through identity federation should be limited appropriately [16].

(v) *Delegated authentication capability* is provided for enterprise consumers. Several current standards for

exchanging authentication (and authorization) are Security Assertion Markup Language (SAML) and WS-federation [16].

*Authorization.* The goal of authorization is to ensure adequacy and appropriateness of the access control to data and services. It could be achieved by matching a user's privileges to his/her job responsibilities and to the characteristics of assets to be accessed and maintaining information necessary for audits.

(i) *Least-privileged scheme.* Users are granted the access only to the data and services necessary for their job responsibilities [82–84]. A least-privileged model for authorization and role-based access model support this practice. Access to additional data and services requires a formal approval and an audit trail is recorded [84].

(ii) *Asset classification.* Assets are classified according to their sensitivity levels and criticality levels [82, 83]. This information is used to determine the strength of authentication methods and the access granted.

(iii) *Regular review and audit trails.* User access lists and granted authority need to be regularly updated and reviewed. Audit trails are maintained [16, 82–84].

*Identity Management.* Strong identity management includes the restriction of a strong password, password expiration, secure password changing, and resetting mechanisms [82–84]. A full list is provided in [82].

*Notification.* Cloud providers should implement a notification process to inform users of security breaches that (might) happen [82, 84]. Logs of activities on users' behavior and access patterns, such as the one implemented by Facebook and Google to monitor users' log-in behaviors, can be monitored for malicious attempts [76]. Unexpected behaviors are notified for user considerations.

*6.3.2. Data Security.* The security of data and information on the cloud is one of the main hindrances for prospective cloud consumers. ISO 27001 defines information security through the following six perspectives: *confidentiality*—ensuring that the information is prevented from disclosure to unauthorized parties; *integrity*—ensuring that the information is not maliciously modified during the transit; *availability*—ensuring that the denial of service is prevented so the information is available when needed; *authenticity*—ensuring that the retrieved information is genuine; *authorization*—ensuring that the information could be accessed only by authorized parties; and *nonrepudiation*—ensuring that each party could not deny their action.

The responsibility of cloud providers is to guarantee that the security is satisfied at every state of the data life cycle, that is, created, stored, used, transferred, archived, and destroyed. Data security policy and practices adopted by a provider should be explicitly declared and adhered to the quality of services agreed in the SLA.

*Data Classification and Access Control.* This practice area supports authorization. Its challenge is to define appropriate and practical data classification scheme and access controls for different classes of data.

(i) *Data owner's practices.* The data owner is responsible for determining the data category and the access control. The classification scheme should at least consider the data sensitivity, criticality, and the frequency of use [82–84]. The access control defines who (individual person, role) get access to the data, under which permission (read, write, modify, and delete) and under which circumstances. It is equally important to keep the classification scheme and the access control updated. Tools such as Digital Right Management and Content Discovery are designed to facilitate this process [16].

(ii) *Provider's support.* The providers should support different levels of protection according to the classification scheme. Necessary information is logged for audit.

*Encryption and Key Management.* Encryption is used to ensure confidentiality, integrity, authenticity, and nonrepudiation. It should be applied at all states of the data life cycle when operating in shared environments.

(i) *Strong encryption.* Encryption is done by using a trustworthy encryption algorithm and an appropriate key length. At minimum, the 128-bit key length is required for symmetric encryption, and the 2048-bit key length is required for asymmetric encryption [83].

(ii) *Key management.* A key management process ensures the protection of key storages, the appropriateness of access controls, and key backup and recoverability. IEEE1619.3 is designed to support this process [16].

(iii) *Understanding security mechanisms used by the provider.* Consumers should understand the encryption mechanisms used in the cloud storage and apply additional mechanisms when the provided features are not sufficient for a security level required.

*Backup and Recovery.* Data availability is guaranteed by an appropriate backup and recovery plan. Its challenge is to ensure that the backup is performed regularly, and data encryption is done when it is required. In addition, it is equally important to perform the recovery test. In Google, the backup is supported by a distributed file system, in which the data are segregated into chunks and replicated over many places [84].

*Data Sanitization.* Data sanitization is the process of removing data stored in memory and storage before returning such resources to the shared pool. Sanitization is more difficult in a multi-tenancy environment where physical resources are shared [75]. The challenge is to ensure that the data is completely deleted and unrecoverable, and the sanitization does not impact the availability of data resided in other tenants. Several techniques such as crypto shredding, disk wiping, and degaussing facilitate this process [16].

*6.3.3. Application Security.* People and processes are the main factors to achieve secured software. It is essential to have motivated and knowledgeable team members to adopt a development process which suits to the context and to have sufficient resources. This practice area aims to ensure that all of these factors are in place to support the development of secured software. We set the primary focus on web applications which is a general form of SaaS.

*Software Development Life Cycle.* Software quality is influenced by the whole software development life cycle. The development team ought to set quality as a priority, apart from scheduling and financial concerns. Compromise on quality impacts a company's sustainability in a long run, if not worse. The challenge in this area is to put appropriate and sufficient practices in place to ensure their compliance, to implement an appraisal program, and to provide the relevant knowledge to associated people. A list of best practices to ensure security of developed software adopted in Google [84] and Microsoft [83] is presented in this subsection.

(i) *Team and software development process.* A development team should be well trained and understand products and the context of the project. The team is equipped with sufficient knowledge on design patterns, web services, vulnerability patterns, protection strategies, and cloud computing. Quality attributes on focus are identified as a basis for design decisions. A development model is selected and customized to suit the nature of the project and the resources.

(ii) *Practices for design.* For the design, software design best practices are adopted when appropriate. The related practices are formal architecture reviews, identifications of high-level security risks, development of sufficient detailed designs, measurement programs for software security tracking, identification alternative implementation solutions, and taking associated risks to project-level decision making process, obtaining an architecture review from an external third party to assess the possible limitations of an internal review.

(iii) *Practice for coding.* For code artifacts, the related best practices are conformance to the coding standard and guidance, pair programming, test first, code inspections, peer review on critical modules, and development of reusable components which are proved to be secure for certain types of vulnerabilities for common usages. Google has implemented a database access layer which is robust for SQL injection vulnerability, and a HTML template framework designed to prevent cross-site-scripting vulnerability.

(iv) *Practices for testing.* For testing, automate tests help to detect common coding errors, especially in interfaces, application logics, and workflows. In addition to the normal test practices, fuzzing tools could be used to detect vulnerabilities. This tool generates erroneous inputs to the program and records crashes and errors that occur, so that developers could correct them before deployment [76].

*Web Services Implementation.* A web service holds certain classes of vulnerabilities when it is not appropriately implemented. In cloud, web services are one of the core technologies in which cloud applications and operations (for instance, administration, provision, and service orchestration) rely on. It is a challenge for a development team to understand vulnerability and possible attack scenarios and to adopt counter mechanisms to ensure all perspectives of security. An example of standard counter mechanisms is *WS-Security* which combines three elements to secure service communications: *security tokens*—to verify a user's identity and his/her access rights; *encryption*—to ensure confidentiality and integrity; and *signature*—to ensure integrity and non-repudiation.

*Frontend Environment.* A frontend environment, including web browsers and front front-end systems, is one area of the attack surfaces [8]. The vulnerability of web browsers mainly results from an inappropriate level of permission given to its plug-ins. To ensure the front-end security, users should allow only necessary and trustable plug-ins to be installed in web browsers, avoid saving their identity in the web browsers, and use antivirus and antispyware with updated profiles.

*6.3.4. Virtualized Environment.* Virtualization covers the layers of a virtualized hypervisor which handles compartmentalization and resource provisions, a virtual machine, and an operating system.

*Virtualized Hypervisor.* A special care should be given to a hypervisor, as it introduces a new attack surface, and its erroneous executions generate a cross-tenant impact [8]. Consumers should understand the supported features and limitations of the virtualized hypervisor used by providers, including the mechanism they employ to perform compartmentalization and provide security controls. When necessary, additional security mechanisms should be integrated to reduce the dependency on the provider [16]. A hypervisor should provide an interface to monitor the traffic crossing VM backbones through virtualized communication channels (between VMs resided in the same tenant) which are invisible to traditional network monitoring devices [16, 75].

*Virtual Machine.* A VM runs on a compartment managed by a hypervisor. The challenge for securing a VM is to verify the provided security controls, the robustness and the authenticity of an acquired VM image.

(i) *Secure image life cycle.* Providers and consumers maintain a secured life cycle of VM images. IaaS and PaaS consumers should acquire a VM image from a reliable source. Even in the case that the image is taken from the provider, the authenticity of the acquired image needs to be verified. The provider maintains a secure VM image management process from creating, storing, and cataloguing to distributing it.

(ii) *Understanding security mechanisms used by the provider.* Consumers should identify the security controls which are in place for acquired VM images and their dependencies. VM access channels and types of connection should be also identified.

(iii) *Various security zones for VM instances.* The provider segregates VMs of different classes into different security zones. VM classification considers the criticality of hosted data and processes, types of usage, and the production stage for, for example, development and production [16].

(iv) *Using tools designed for multi-tenancy.* There are several techniques to enhance VM security such as the use of bidirectional firewalls on each VM instantiation and the hypervisor-level security controls [81]. Concurrent applications of protection tools, designed for stand-alone systems on multi-tenants, might affect the performance of the whole physical platform. Cloud providers should consider performing this work at the hypervisor level.

*Cloud Operating System and Middleware.* Compromises to the security of an OS affect the security of the whole data and processes resided in the systems, therefore an OS should be highly robust and secure. The following practices are recommended to secure an OS.

(i) *Robust OS.* Rich-featured OS and complex configuration could compromise system robustness. Consumers should consider an OS which contains only necessary features and has been scanned for vulnerabilities [75]. Architecture flaws could be a result of misconfiguration of resources and policies. Maintaining a simple architecture prevent erroneous settings that might threaten security controls [76]. A strong authentication mechanism is required for an administrative access to the OS [16].

(ii) *Single hardened OS deployment.* Best practices for providers are the use of a single hardened OS and white list process monitoring. A common technique for PaaS providers to enhance security is to deploy a single hardened OS throughout the cloud and scan for its binary changes to detect security breaches [75]. Questionable changes result in a system rollback, thus keeping the system in a known good state. Walters and Petroni demonstrate this process in their paper [85]. A process-monitoring feature should run against a list of allowed processes, instead of a black list [76].

*6.3.5. Network and Physical Security*

*Robust Physical Access Control.* The centralization of data residing in a data center poses a significant security concern. Cloud consumers should be aware of a malicious insider

TABLE 4: Mapping of cloud vulnerabilities (column) and recommended security practices (row).

| | Application | | | | Platform | | | Infrastructure | | | Unified resource | | | Fabric |
|---|---|---|---|---|---|---|---|---|---|---|---|---|---|---|
| | Web service v. | Client-side data manipulation v. | Authentication & Authorization v. | Encryption & key management v. | Cloud platform v. | Access to platform admin interface v. | Traditional virtual machine v. | Virtual network communication v. | Data sanitization v. | Access to VM admin interface v. | Virtualized hypervisor & interfaces v. | Multi-tenancy v. | Shared network component v. | Physical v. |
| **Identity and access control** | | | | | | | | | | | | | | |
| Authentication | | | × | | | | | | | | | | | |
| Authorization | | | × | | | | | | | | | | | |
| Identity management | | | × | | | | | | | | | | | |
| Notification | | | × | | | | | | | | | | | |
| **Data security** | | | | | | | | | | | | | | |
| Data classification | | | × | | | | | | | | | | | |
| Encryption and key | × | | × | × | | × | | | | × | × | | | |
| Backup and recovery | | | | | | | | | | | | | | × |
| Data sanitization | | | | | | | | | × | | | × | | |
| **Application security** | | | | | | | | | | | | | | |
| Dev. life cycle | × | | × | × | × | × | × | | | × | | | | |
| Web service imp. | × | | | | | | | | | | | | | |
| Frontend environment | × | × | | | | | | | | | | | | |
| **Virtualized environment** | | | | | | | | | | | | | | |
| Virtualized hypervisor | × | | × | | | | | × | | × | | × | | |
| Virtual machine | × | | × | | | | × | | | × | | | | |
| Operating system | × | | × | | × | | | | | | | | | |
| **Network and physical security** | | | | | | | | | | | | | | |
| Robust physical access | | | | | | | | | | | | | | × |
| BCP | | | | | | | | | | | | | | × |
| Network control | | | | | | | | | | | | | | × |

threat in a cloud environment, where centralized data amplifies the motivation of malicious attempts [41]. The goal of having a robust and appropriate physical access control is to prevent insider abuse within a cloud provider.

(i) *Various security zones.* The data center should be separated to different security zones for hosting data and services which require different levels of protection. Control mechanisms are applied according to the criticality of different security zones.

(ii) *Using a least privilege policy for access controls.* A least privilege policy is applied to give only necessary permission to limited users. Employees should have limited knowledge on customers. Additional access requires a formal approval, and audit trail is always respected. Employee privilege is up-to-date and regularly reviewed. Background check on employees is performed.

*Business Continuity Plan (BCP).* The objective of this regulation is to ensure the availability of data and services hosted in cloud infrastructures. Consumers should ensure that the provider implements and respects standard Business Continuity Plan. Examples of such standard are BS25999 and ISO22301 [41].

*Network Control.* In cloud environments a provider is responsible for protecting a customer's data from accesses across the Internet. Network borders should be protected by robust mechanisms or devices. Firewalls are in place to protect each external interface, only necessary ports are open, and the default setting is denial. Intrusion detection and prevention mechanisms should be employed and kept up-to-date [41].

The mapping between the cloud vulnerabilities identified in Section 6.1 and the recommended security practices is presented in Table 4.

*6.4. Summary.* Security is one of the most critical hindrances to nontrivial adoptions of new technologies. Cloud computing inherits security issues from its enabling technologies such as web services, virtualization, multi-tenancy, and cryptography. A virtualized hypervisor which enables resource sharing leads to the economies of scale but introduces a new attack surface. We analyze the security in the cloud by understanding the weaknesses associated to system procedures, design, and implementation of the components of cloud infrastructure. These weaknesses, known as *vulnerability*, could be exploited and result in security breaches, thus requiring stakeholders to be attentive and adopt appropriate counteractions. At the application layer (SaaS), programmers need to handle the vulnerabilities of web services, authentication and authorization, and encryption and keys. End users need to prevent their frontend environments from malicious plug-ins and malware. At the platform layer in which a cloud OS and middleware are offered as a ready-made solution for development and deployment platforms, security mechanisms are generally integrated to the solution. PaaS consumers should understand which mechanisms are in place and impacts they might have on different system

configurations. The vulnerabilities at the infrastructure level (IaaS) are associated to virtual machines and virtual network communications. IaaS consumers are responsible for their own security controls from this layer up to the application layer. The vulnerabilities to the unified resource layer related to multi-tenancy and virtualized hypervisors are critical as their compromises would affect the whole cloud services. The security mechanisms and processes adopted by a provider at this level should be explicitly clarified as a part of the SLA. Physical security deals with malicious insiders, business continuity plans for natural disaster, and the preventions of unauthorized accesses through network channels. Having vulnerabilities identified, we gathered the security practices recommended by leading cloud providers, and experts and classified them into 17 practice areas.

## 7. Conclusions

In this paper we depicted a comprehensive scenery of cloud computing technology. The view of cloud computing is shaped by its definition, service model, and deployment model. The characteristic of cloud services is shaped by its architecture, service management approach, and underlying technologies. Based on its solid foundations, cloud promises significant benefits on enterprise-level cost reduction, increased agility, and better business-IT alignment. Many more benefits arise when other levels or perspectives are taken into consideration. Apart from these benefits, however, cloud services still pose a number of limitations that hinder their wider adoption. Such limitations originate in the very nature of its building blocks. An example is the instability of large-scaled network. A limited capability of network has become a main obstacle for services that require reliable response time, such as high performance computing and latency sensitive applications, to be deployed in the clouds. Security is another major hindrance of cloud adoption that touches upon many technological factors including multi-tenancy, virtualization, and federated identity management. It is further aggravated by the fact that service level agreements are generally explicit about placing security risks on consumers. As cloud computing is not the silver bullet for all circumstances, it is necessary for technology adopters to sufficiently understand its concerns and properly handle them. Without comprehending its underlying technology, finding the most appropriate adoption approach seems to be an impossible mission. Our paper can assist this endeavor by offering a comprehensive review of the fundamentals and relevant knowledge areas of cloud computing.

## References

[1] J. Voas and J. Zhang, "Cloud computing: new wine or just a new bottle?" *IT Professional*, vol. 11, no. 2, pp. 15–17, 2009.

[2] P. Mell and T. Grance, "The NIST Definition of Cloud Computing," 2011.

[3] M. Armbrust, A. Fox, R. Griffith et al., "A Berkeley view of cloud computing," Tech. Rep. UCB/EECS-2009-28, EECS Department, U.C. Berkeley, 2009.

[4] M. Creeger, "CTO roundtable: cloud computing," *Communications of the ACM*, vol. 52, no. 8, pp. 50–56, 2009.

[5] L. Herbert and J. Erickson, *The ROI of Software-As-A-Service. White Paper*, Forrester Research, Inc., 2009.

[6] A. Khajeh-Hosseini, I. Sommerville, J. Bogaerts, and P. Teregowda, "Decision support tools for cloud migration in the enterprise," in *Proceedings of the IEEE International Conference on Cloud Computing (CLOUD '11)*, pp. 541–548, 2011.

[7] N. Phaphoom, N. Oza, X. Wang, and P. Abrahamsson, "Does cloud computing deliver the promised benefits for IT industry?" in *Proceedings of the WICSA/ECSA Companion Volume(WICSA/ECSA '12)*, pp. 45–52, ACM, 2012.

[8] N. Gruschka and M. Jensen, "Attack surfaces: a taxonomy for attacks on cloud services," in *Proceedings of the 3rd IEEE International Conference on Cloud Computing (CLOUD '10)*, pp. 276–279, July 2010.

[9] P. Hofmann and D. Woods, "Cloud computing: the limits of public clouds for business applications," *IEEE Internet Computing*, vol. 14, no. 6, pp. 90–93, 2010.

[10] B. Grobauer, T. Walloschek, and E. Stöcker, "Understanding cloud computing vulnerabilities," *IEEE Security and Privacy*, vol. 9, no. 2, pp. 50–57, 2011.

[11] C. Baun, M. Kunze, J. Nimin, and S. Tai, *Cloud Computing: Web-Based Dynamic IT Services*, Springer, 2011.

[12] I. Foster, Y. Zhao, I. Raicu, and S. Lu, "Cloud Computing and Grid Computing 360-degree compared," in *Proceedings of the Grid Computing Environments Workshop (GCE '08)*, pp. 1–10, November 2008.

[13] L. M. Vaquero, L. Rodero-Merino, J. Caceres, and M. Lindner, "A break in the clouds: towards a cloud definition," *SIGCOMM Computer Communication Review*, vol. 39, pp. 50–55, 2008.

[14] DMTF, "Interoperable Clouds a white paper from the Open Cloud Standards Incubator," 2009.

[15] IBM, "IBM Cloud Computing—Service Management," 2009.

[16] Cloud Security Alliance, "Security Guidance for Critical Areas of Focus in Cloud Computing V2.1," 2009.

[17] Cisco, "Cisco Cloud Computing—Data Center Strategy, Architecture, and Solutions," 2009.

[18] Open Security Architecture, "SP-011: Cloud Computing Pattern," 2011.

[19] US General Service Administration, "Cloud Computing Initiative Vision and Strategy Document (DRAFT)," 2010.

[20] Storage Networking Industry Association, "5. Overview of Cloud Storage," 2011.

[21] L. Youseff, M. Butrico, and D. Da Silva, "Toward a unified ontology of cloud computing," in *Proceedings of the Grid Computing Environments Workshop (GCE '08)*, pp. 1–10, November 2008.

[22] L. J. Zhang and Q. Zhou, "CCOA: cloud computing open architecture," in *Proceedings of the IEEE International Conference on Web Services (ICWS '09)*, pp. 607–616, July 2009.

[23] S. Ghemawat, H. Gobioff, and S. Leung, "The Google file system," *ACM SIGOPS Operating Systems Review*, vol. 37, pp. 29–43, 2003.

[24] A. Lenk, M. Klems, J. Nimis, S. Tai, and T. Sandholm, "What's inside the cloud? An architectural map of the cloud landscape," in *Proceedings of the ICSE Workshop on Software Engineering Challenges of Cloud Computing (CLOUD '09)*, pp. 23–31, May 2009.

[25] J. Howe, "The rise of crowdsourcing," *Wired Magazine*, vol. 14, pp. 1–5, 2006.

[26] A. Kittur, E. H. Chi, and B. Suh, "Crowdsourcing user studies with Mechanical Turk," in *Proceedings of the 26th Annual CHI Conference on Human Factors in Computing Systems (CHI '08)*, pp. 453–456, ACM, New York, NY, USA, April 2008.

[27] J. G. Davis, "From crowdsourcing to crowdservicing," *IEEE Internet Computing*, vol. 15, no. 3, pp. 92–94, 2011.

[28] T. Dillon, C. Wu, and E. Chang, "Cloud computing: issues and challenges," in *Proceedings of the 24th IEEE International Conference on Advanced Information Networking and Applications (AINA '10)*, pp. 27–33, April 2010.

[29] Q. Zhang, L. Cheng, and R. Boutaba, "Cloud computing: state-of-the-art and research challenges," *Journal of Internet Services and Applications*, vol. 1, no. 1, pp. 7–18, 2010.

[30] I. Foster, "The anatomy of the grid: enabling scalable virtual organizations," in *Proceedings of the 1st IEEE/ACM International Symposium on Cluster Computing and the Grid*, pp. 6–7, 2001.

[31] A. Andrzejak, M. Arlitt, and J. Rolia, "Bounding the resource savings of utility computing models," Tech. Rep. HPL-2002-339, Hewlett Packard Labs, 2002.

[32] J. E. Smith and R. Nair, "The architecture of virtual machines," *Computer*, vol. 38, no. 5, pp. 32–38, 2005.

[33] R. Uhlig, G. Neiger, D. Rodgers et al., "Intel virtualization technology," *Computer*, vol. 38, no. 5, pp. 48–56, 2005.

[34] M. Rosenblum and T. Garfinkel, "Virtual machine monitors: current technology and future trends," *Computer*, vol. 38, no. 5, pp. 39–47, 2005.

[35] E. Gamma, R. Helm, R. Johnson, and J. Vlissides, *Design Patterns: Elements of Reusable Object-Oriented Software*, Addison-Wesley, 1994.

[36] P. Bianco, R. Kotermanski, and P. Merson, "Evaluating a Service-Oriented Architecture," Tech. Rep. CMU/SEI-2007-TR-015, Software Engineering Institute of Carnegie Mellon University, 2007.

[37] T. Erl, *SOA Design Patterns*, Prentice Hall PTR, Upper Saddle River, NJ, USA, 2009.

[38] S. Sakr, A. Liu, D. Batista, and M. Alomari, "A survey of large scale data management approaches in cloud environments," *IEEE Communications Surveys & Tutorials*, no. 99, pp. 1–26, 2011.

[39] Y. Yu, M. Isard, D. Fetterly et al., "DryadLINQ: a system for general-purpose distributed data-parallel computing using a high-level language," in *Proceedings of the 8th USENIX Conference on Operating systems design and implementation (OSDI '08)*, pp. 1–14, USENIX Association, Berkeley, Calif, USA, 2008.

[40] The US National Institute of Standards, "Cloud Architecture Reference Models," 2011.

[41] Cloud Security Alliance, "Top threats to cloud computing V1.0," 2010.

[42] J. Oriol Fitó, I. Goiri, and J. Guitart, "SLA-driven elastic cloud hosting provider," in *Proceedings of the 18th Euromicro Conference on Parallel, Distributed and Network-Based Processing (PDP '10)*, pp. 111–118, February 2010.

[43] F. Faniyi and R. Bahsoon, "Engineering proprioception in SLA management for cloud architectures," in *Proceedings of the 9th Working IEEE/IFIP Conference on Software Architecture (WICSA '11)*, pp. 336–340, 2011.

[44] J. Y. Lee, J. W. Lee, D. W. Cheun, and S. D. Kim, "A quality model for evaluating software-as-a-service in cloud computing," in *Proceedings of the 7th ACIS International Conference on Software Engineering Research, Management and Applications ( SERA '09)*, pp. 261–266, December 2009.

[45] D. Jayasinghe, S. Malkowski, Q. Wang, J. Li, P. Xiong, and C. Pu, "Variations in performance and scalability when migrating n-tier applications to different clouds," in *Proceedings of the IEEE International Conference on Cloud Computing (CLOUD '11)*, pp. 73–80, 2011.

[46] D. Bao, Z. Xiao, Y. Sun, and J. Zhao, "A method and framework for quality of cloud services measurement," in *Proceedings of the 3rd International Conference on Advanced Computer Theory and Engineering (ICACTE '10)*, pp. V5358–V5362, August 2010.

[47] S. Dowell, A. Barreto, J. B. Michael, and M.-T. Shing, "Cloud to cloud interoperability," in *Proceedings of the 6th International Conference on System of Systems Engineering (SoSE '11)*, pp. 258–263, 2011.

[48] M. Alhamad, T. Dillon, and E. Chang, "Conceptual SLA framework for cloud computing," in *Proceedings of the 4th IEEE International Conference on Digital Ecosystems and Technologies (DEST '10)*, pp. 606–610, April 2010.

[49] S. Gilbert and N. Lynch, "Brewer's conjecture and the feasibility of consistent, available, partition-tolerant web services," *SIGACT News*, vol. 33, pp. 51–59, 2002.

[50] B. F. Cooper, R. Ramakrishnan, and U. Srivastava, "PNUTS: Yahoo!'s hosted data serving platform," in *Proceedings of the VLDB Endowment*, vol. 2, pp. 1277–1288, 2008.

[51] W. Vogels, "Eventually consistent," *Communications of the ACM*, vol. 52, pp. 40–44, 2009.

[52] H. Douglas and C. Gehrmann, "Secure Virtualization and Multicore Platforms State-of-the-Art report," Swedish Institute of Computer Science, 2009.

[53] S. J. Vaughan-Nichols, "New approach to virtualization is a lightweight," *Computer*, vol. 39, no. 11, pp. 12–14, 2006.

[54] A. Whitaker, M. Shaw, and S. D. Gribble, "Denali: lightweight virtual machines for distributed and networked applications," Tech. Rep., The University of Washington, 2002.

[55] W. Chen, H. Lu, L. Shen, Z. Wang, N. Xiao, and D. Chen, "A novel hardware assisted full viralization technique," in *Proceedings of the 9th International Conference for Young Computer Scientists (ICYCS '08)*, pp. 1292–1297, November 2008.

[56] I. Pratt, K. Fraser, S. Hand, C. Limpach, and A. Warfield, "Xen 3.0 and the art of virtulization," in *Proceedings of the Ottawa Linux Symposium*, pp. 65–77, 2005.

[57] Advanced Micro Devices Inc., "AMD-V Nested Paging revision 1.0," Whitepaper, 2008.

[58] G. P. Chen and J. S. Bozman, "Optimizing I/O Virtualization: preparing the datacenter for next-generation applications," White Paper sponsored by Intel Corporation, 2009.

[59] J. Sugerman, G. Venkitachalam, and B. Lim, "Virtualizing I/O devices on VMware workstation's hosted virtual machine monitor," in *Proceedings of the General Track, USENIX Annual Technical Conference*, pp. 1–14, 2001.

[60] P. Barham, B. Dragovic, K. Fraser et al., "Xen and the art of virtualization," in *Proceedings of the 19th ACM Symposium on Operating Systems Principles (SOSP '03)*, pp. 164–177, ACM, New York, NY, USA, October 2003.

[61] A. Kivity, Y. Kamay, D. Laor, U. Lublin, and A. Liguori, "kvm:thelinux virtual machine monitor," in *Proceedings of the Ottawa Linux Symposium*, pp. 225–230, 2007.

[62] M. Stonebraker, "SQL databases v. NoSQL databases," *Communications of the ACM*, vol. 53, no. 4, pp. 10–11, 2010.

[63] F. Chang, J. Dean, S. Ghemawat et al., "Bigtable: a distributed storage system for structured data," *ACM Transactions on Computer Systems*, vol. 26, no. 2, article 4, 2008.

[64] A. Lakshman and P. Malik, "Cassandra: a decentralized structured storage system," *ACM SIGOPS Operating Systems Review*, vol. 44, pp. 35–40, 2010.

[65] M. Stonebraker, S. Madden, D. J. Abadi, S. Harizopoulos, N. Hachem, and P. Helland, "The end of an architectural era: (it's time for a complete rewrite)," in *Proceedings of the 33rd international conference on Very large data bases (VLDB '07)*, pp. 1150–1160, VLDB Endowment, 2007.

[66] T. Haerder and A. Reuter, "Principles of transaction-oriented database recovery," *Computing Surveys*, vol. 15, no. 4, pp. 287–317, 1983.

[67] Z. Wei, G. Pierre, and C.-H. Chi, "CloudTPS: scalable transactions for web applications in the cloud," *IEEE Transactions on Services Computing*, vol. 99, p. 1, 2011.

[68] B. Kemme and G. Alonso, "Don't be lazy, be consistent: postgres-r, a new way to implement database replication," in *Proceedings of the 26th International Conference on Very Large Data Bases (VLDB '00)*, pp. 134–143, Morgan Kaufmann Publishers, San Francisco, Calif, USA, 2007.

[69] A. Lith and J. Mattsson, *Investigating storage solutions for large data—a comparison of well performing and scalable data storage solutions for real time extraction and batch insertion of data [M.S. thesis]*, Chalmers Tekniska Hogskola, Sweden, 2010.

[70] B. G. Tudorica and C. Bucur, "A comparison between several NoSQL databases with comments and notes," in *Proceedings of the 10th Roedunet International Conference (RoEduNet '11)*, pp. 1–5, 2011.

[71] E. A. Brewer, "Toward robust distributed systems," Principles of distributed computing, Portland, Ore, USA, 2000.

[72] B. F. Cooper, A. Silberstein, E. Tam, R. Ramakrishnan, and R. Sears, "Benchmarking cloud serving systems with YCSB," in *Proceedings of the 1st ACM Symposium on Cloud Computing (SoCC '10)*, pp. 143–154, ACM, New York, NY, USA, June 2010.

[73] G. DeCandia, D. Hastorun, M. Jampani et al., "Dynamo: amazon's highly available key-value store," in *Proceedings of 21st ACM SIGOPS symposium on Operating systems principles (SOSP '07)*, pp. 205–220, ACM, New York, NY, USA, 2007.

[74] D. Karger, E. Lehman, T. Leighton, M. Levine, D. Lewin, and R. Panigrahy, "Consistent hashing and random trees: distributed caching protocols for relieving hot spots on the World Wide Web," in *Proceedings of the 29th Annual ACM Symposium on Theory of Computing (STOC '97)*, pp. 654–663, ACM, New York, NY, USA, May 1997.

[75] J. Spring, "Monitoring cloud computing by layer—part 1," *IEEE Security and Privacy*, vol. 9, no. 2, pp. 66–68, 2011.

[76] J. Spring, "Monitoring cloud computing by layer—part 2," *IEEE Security and Privacy*, vol. 9, no. 3, pp. 52–55, 2011.

[77] I. Iankoulova and M. Daneva, "Cloud computing security requirements: a systematic review," in *Proceedings of the 6th International Conference on Research Challenges in Information Science (RCIS '12)*, pp. 1–7, 2012.

[78] W. A. Jansen, "Cloud hooks: security and privacy issues in cloud computing," in *Proceedings of the 44th Hawaii International Conference on System Sciences (HICSS '10)*, pp. 1–10, January 2011.

[79] S. A. Almulla and C. Y. Yeun, "Cloud computing security management," in *Proceedings of the 2nd International Conference on Engineering System Management and Applications (ICESMA '10)*, pp. 1–7, April 2010.

[80] R. Chow, P. Golle, M. Jakobsson et al., "Controlling data in the cloud: outsourcing computation without outsourcing control,"

in *Proceedings of the ACM Workshop on Cloud Computing Security (CCSW '09)*, pp. 85–90, November 2009.

[81] L. M. Kaufman, "Can public-cloud security meet its unique challenges?" *IEEE Security and Privacy*, vol. 8, no. 4, pp. 55–57, 2010.

[82] IBM, "Cloud Security Guidance IBM Recommendations for the Implementation of Cloud Security," 2009.

[83] Microsoft Global Foundation Services, "Securing Microsoft's Cloud Infrastructure," 2009.

[84] Google, "Security Whitepaper: Google Apps Messaging and Collaboration Products," 2010.

[85] A. Walters and N. L. Petroni Jr., "Volatools: integrating volatile memory forensics into the digital investigation process," in *presented at Black Hat DC*, 2007.

# 7

# Extension of Object-Oriented Metrics Suite for Software Maintenance

**John Michura, Miriam A. M. Capretz, and Shuying Wang**

*Department of Electrical and Computer Engineering, Faculty of Engineering, The University of Western Ontario, London, ON, Canada N6A 5B9*

Correspondence should be addressed to Miriam A. M. Capretz; mcapretz@uwo.ca

Academic Editors: Y. Malaiya, A. Rausch, and C. Rolland

Software developers require information to understand the characteristics of systems, such as complexity and maintainability. In order to further understand and determine characteristics of object-oriented (OO) systems, this paper describes research that identifies attributes that are valuable in determining the difficulty in implementing changes during maintenance, as well as the possible effects that such changes may produce. A set of metrics are proposed to quantify and measure these attributes. The proposed complexity metrics are used to determine the difficulty in implementing changes through the measurement of method complexity, method diversity, and complexity density. The paper establishes impact metrics to determine the potential effects of making changes to a class and dependence metrics that are used to measure the potential effects on a given class resulting from changes in other classes. The case study shows that the proposed metrics provide additional information not sufficiently provided by the related existing OO metrics. The metrics are also found to be useful in the investigation of large systems, correlating with project outcomes.

## 1. Introduction

Software metrics have been used to solve different problems such as predicting testing complexity [1], identifying errors [2], and promoting modularity [3]. The metrics proposed by Chidamber and Kemerer [4], now referred to as the CK metrics, have become well known and widely accepted by the software engineering community. The CK metrics can be used to measure some characteristics of OO systems such as classes, message passing, inheritance, and encapsulation. On the other hand, the software maintenance phase requires that changes are made to the existing system. Although the existing metrics, such as the CK metrics, can be used to predict outcomes during software maintenance, such as effort and defects, they do not provide sufficient information regarding the difficulty in implementing such changes, as well as the potential effects of those changes. It would also be beneficial if information is provided regarding the interaction of classes in an OO system in order to predict behavioral changes in those classes during maintenance. Therefore, it is necessary to develop new metrics for software maintainers to better understand the complexity of classes as well as the potential effects of changing classes.

In order to develop new metrics, it is necessary to determine the weaknesses present in the existing metrics. Weaknesses include the loss of information when two classes are said to be coupled and the simultaneous measurement of multiple attributes. The coupling relationship also does not disclose information regarding its direction or magnitude. It is therefore imperative to identify attributes that are relevant in determining the difficulty in implementing changes as well as the effects of such changes. However, only identifying such attributes is not sufficient. It is important that such attributes are quantified in order for them to be effective. As a result, a suite of metrics is required to measure the relevant class attributes.

In this paper, we define the influence relationship, identify class attributes, and develop a proposed suite of metrics used for maintaining OO systems. The key contributions of the research presented in this paper are as follows.

(i) The complexity of a class has been shown to predict the effort required to test and maintain it [4].

Consequently, the difficulty in implementing changes onto a class will be determined by its complexity. Three attributes will be identified and measured by the proposed set of complexity metrics: method complexity, method diversity, and complexity density. These attributes are associated with the difficulty in implementing changes onto a class.

(ii) In addition, the effect of changes will be determined by the use of instance variables and methods of a given class in other classes. A relationship between two classes, influence, will be defined. The influence relationship will be used by a set of proposed metrics to measure the effects of making changes to particular classes. Two attributes will be defined and measured by the proposed set of metrics: impact and dependence. Impact is used to determine the potential effects of changes in a given class on the behavior of the system, while dependence is used to determine the potential change in behavior in a given class that results from changes in other classes.

(iii) The metrics proposed in this research will be used in conjunction with the CK metrics to provide additional information regarding the maintenance of OO systems.

The remainder of this paper is organized as follows. In Section 2, a literature review outlines various established metrics. The CK metrics are discussed as well as research conducted to investigate them. Section 3 identifies and defines attributes associated with classes and presents a suite of metrics intended to complement the CK metrics discussed in Section 2. Results used to determine the effectiveness of the new metrics are presented in Section 4. Section 5 presents the conclusions and future work.

## 2. Literature Review

The goal of this section is to provide an overview of well-adopted works in software metrics. Although widely used metrics already existed, the arrival of the object-oriented (OO) approach required the development of new metrics. The majority of the established metrics are not designed for the OO paradigm [5]. As a result, they are not sufficient in measuring properties of OO systems. Some established metrics, such as cyclomatic complexity, are also thought to be insufficient in desirable measurement properties [6], lack theoretical basis [7], and are implementation dependent [8]. On the other hand, the CK metrics present a suite of metrics for OO systems that are claimed to be theoretically sound, contained desired measurement characteristics, and are empirically validated [4]. The suite comprises six metrics: Weighted Methods per Class (WMC), Coupling Between Objects (CBO), Depth of Inheritance Tree (DIT), Number of Children (NOC), Response For a Class (RFC), and Lack of Cohesion in Methods (LCOM).

There have been many studies conducted to investigate the value of the CK metrics. The metrics have often been associated with product results such as fault-proneness [9, 10], quality [11–15], complexity measurement [16], and project results such as maintenance effort [17, 18]. We summarize five improvements upon the CK Metrics as follows.

(1) Improving upon WMC. A criticism directed at WMC is that the metric is ambiguously defined [19]. It is the sum of the complexities of the methods in the class. However, the complexities can either be unity (equal to one) or some static complexity measure such as cyclomatic complexity as assumed in this research [18]. The value of WMC is dependent on how complexity is defined. Li and Henry [18] solved this problem by defining a metric that counts the number of methods declared in the class, called Number of Methods (NOM). Li later modified NOM to count only methods that are accessible by other classes [20]. This metric is called Number of Local Methods (NLM). Both metrics have their advantages and disadvantages. NOM is a better measure of the size of the class while NLM is a better measure of the potential effect the given class can have on other classes. Li also proposed another metric that would measure the overall complexity of the class [20]. Class Method Complexity (CMC) is equal to the sum of the complexities of the methods in the class. This differs from WMC in that the complexities used in calculating CMC cannot be defined as unity.

(2) Improving upon coupling. CK's formulation of coupling has also been the subject of scrutiny. CK states that two classes are coupled if at least one method in one class uses a method or an instance variable of the other class. The metric they devised to measure coupling is CBO, a count of all classes the particular class is coupled to. Li and Henry's Message Passing Coupling (MPC) metric addresses both coupling strength and coupling direction [18]. The MPC of a class is equal to the number of messages sent out from the class. A possible shortcoming of MPC is that it assumes that instance variables are not accessed by other objects. Although the direct access of another class instance variables is considered questionable programming practices, it should not be ignored. It is often used to access constants defined within classes. As a result, it is possible that changes made to instance variables may affect other classes. Li's Coupling Through Message Passing (CTM) [20] also addresses both coupling strength and direction, but does not address instance variables in the count of message passing.

(3) Improving upon inheritance. Researchers have addressed the inheritance metrics. Li states that the DIT metric is flawed in that it does not consider cases where a class is inheriting from multiple roots [20]. She addresses this problem with the metric Number of Ancestor Classes (NAC). NAC is a count of all classes the given class inherits from. It is more accurate in determining the number of classes that can change the behavior of the given class. Li also states that CK's NOC is flawed by only considering classes that directly inherit from the given class. The

Number of Descendent Classes (NDC) is a count of all classes that inherit from the given class. Li's inheritance metrics are an accurate measure of a class involvement in inheritance. However, changes in ancestor classes can affect the behavior of classes not belonging to the same inheritance tree.

(4) Improving upon RFC (Response for a Class). The RFC metric can also be criticized in its measurement of multiple attributes [21] and is found to be highly correlated with CBO [22]. RFC intends to measure the number of different possible methods that can be executed by the class in response to a message. As a result, RFC is a function of the number of methods in the class as well as the number of different methods called within methods of the class. The criticism directed at the metric is resolved by instead using a combination of other metrics such as Li and Henry's NOM and MPC metrics.

(5) Improving upon LCOM (Lack of Cohesion in Methods). Hitz and Montazeri [23] have commented that values obtained from LCOM are difficult to explain as the value of the metric is influenced greatly by the number of methods the class contains. Chae et al. [24] also have commented that methods such as accessors (methods used to obtain the value of a class instance variables) and mutators (methods used to alter the value of a class instance variables) increase the value of the metric though they are considered sound programming practices. Many cohesion metrics have been developed by researchers to resolve the issues concerning LCOM [25, 26]. Such solutions include the exclusion of special methods [24] and changing the equation [14].

## 3. Software Metrics

The key contributions of this research are the definition of complexity and influence, the identification of class attributes related to maintenance, and the proposal of a suite of metrics used to measure such attributes.

*3.1. Class Complexity and Influence Relationship.* The focus of this research is on changes to an existing software during the maintenance phase of the software's life cycle. The attributes described in this research are aimed at providing an understanding of the difficulty, as well as the effects, of making changes to an existing system.

(i) *Complexity* is used to quantify the difficulty associated with implementing changes during the maintenance phase. Further, *complexity* is defined as the difficulty in understanding abstractions of software such as design documents and implementation code.

(a) *Class complexity* refers to the amount of effort required to understand a class. A class that is more complex will require more effort to maintain.

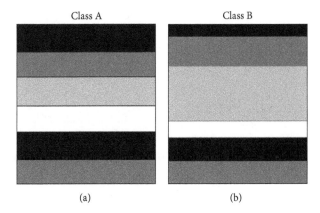

FIGURE 1: Method diversity.

(b) *Method complexity* refers to the amount of effort required to understand the method. The method complexity of a class refers to the amount of effort required to understand each of its methods.

(ii) *Complexity density* is defined as the proportion of the class complexity not resulting from methods with minimal complexity.

(iii) *Method diversity* is defined as the differences in complexities between methods within the same class. Classes with similar methods will have low method diversity while classes with very different methods will have higher method diversity. Figure 1 shows an example of two classes with different method diversities. The two classes, Class A and Class B, are represented by two rectangles. Methods are represented by subsections of the rectangles. Class complexities are represented by the areas of the rectangles. The complexities of methods are represented by the areas of the subsections. Class B is said to have more method diversity than Class A as its methods are less consistent with regard to complexity.

(iv) *Influence* is a unidirectional relationship between two classes. A class is said to have influence on the other if it contains methods or instance variables that are used in the other. The class containing the used instance variables or methods is referred to as the influencing class whereas the class using the methods or instance variables is referred to as the influenced class. Influence is measured by finding the number of instances that a method in the influenced class uses a method or instance variable declared in the influencing class. Therefore, the influence strength of a class is the average magnitude of the influences it has on other classes. The received influence strength of a class is the average magnitude of the influences other classes have on the given class. The sequence diagram in Figure 2(a) shows that the Dealership class uses two methods in the SalesAssociate class. This is shown in Figure 2(b) as the SalesAssociate class has an influence of two on the Dealership class.

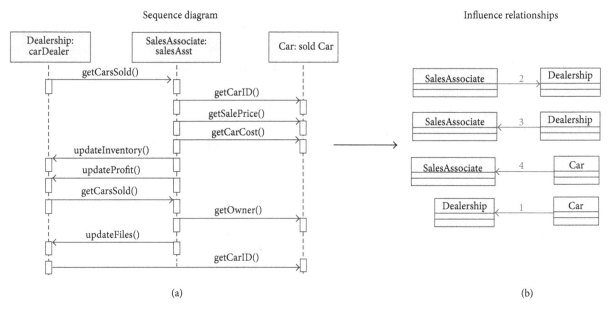

FIGURE 2: Influence relationship.

(v) *Impact* is defined as a class potential to alter the behavior of other classes when it is changed. Impact is a function of the class influence on other classes. Figure 3 shows the examples of impact of three classes: SalesAssociate, Dealership, and Car. The impact of a class can be measured by the summation of its influences. The SalesAssociate class has an impact of two since it has an influence on the Dealership class of two. The Dealership class has an impact of three since it has an influence of three on the SalesAssociate class. The Car class has an influence of four on the SalesAssociate class and one on the Dealership class. Therefore, its impact is equal to five.

(vi) *Dependence* is defined as a class potential to change in behavior when other classes are changed. It is used to quantify the possible effects associated with implementing changes during maintenance. The dependence of a class can be measured by the summation of influences on it. Figure 4 shows examples of dependence. Figure 4(b) shows the dependence of two classes: SalesAssociate and Dealership. The Dealership class has a dependence of three since the Car class has an influence on it equal to one and the SalesAssociate class has an influence on it equal to two. The SalesAssociate class has a dependence of seven since the Car class has an influence on it equal to four and the Dealership class has an influence on it equal to three. The Car class is said to have no dependence since it is not influenced by any other classes.

*3.2. Proposed Metrics.* In order to measure the attributes described in Section 3.1, a suite of metrics is developed to quantify the attributes. The suite is comprised of four subsets of metrics: complexity metrics, impact metrics, dependence metrics, and inheritance metrics.

*3.2.1. Complexity Metrics.* The purpose of the complexity metrics is to complement CK's WMC metric. Since WMC is a function of two different class attributes (number of methods and class complexity), other metrics may be required to fully understand its results. The proposed complexity metrics consist of three metrics: Mean Method Complexity (MMC), Standard Deviation Method Complexity (SDMC), and Proportion of Nontrivial Complexity (PNC).

*Definition 1. Mean Method Complexity (MMC)* is a measure of a class method complexity

$$\mathrm{MMC} = \frac{\sum c_i}{n}, \tag{1}$$

where $1 \leqslant i \leqslant n$, $c_i$ is the cyclomatic complexity of the class $i$th method, and $n$ is equal to the number of methods in the class.

MMC serves as an indicator of the complexity of the class methods. MMC is similar to Etzkorn's [27] Average Method Complexity (AMC). The difference between the two metrics is their interpretation of $c_i$. AMC specifies $c_i$ as the complexity of the method according to any static complexity measure whereas MMC specifies $c_i$ as the method's cyclomatic complexity. The purpose of this metric is to determine if a class WMC value is a result of low-complexity methods or high-complexity methods. High MMC is an indicator of classes comprised of methods with high cyclomatic complexity.

*Definition 2. Standard Deviation Method Complexity (SDMC)* is to measure the method diversity of a class. Consider

$$\mathrm{SDMC} = \sqrt{\frac{\sum \left( \mathrm{MMC} - c_i \right)^2}{n-1}}, \tag{2}$$

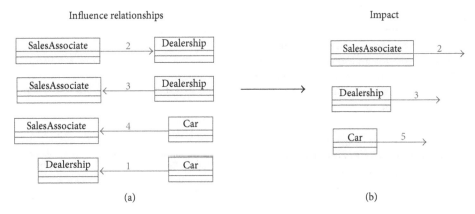

FIGURE 3: Influence relationships to impact.

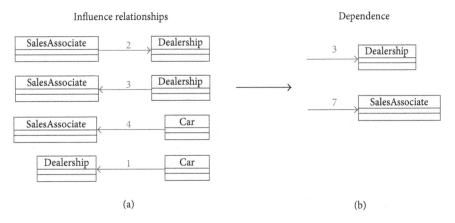

FIGURE 4: Influence relationships to dependence.

where $1 \leq i \leq n$, $c_i$ is the cyclomatic complexity of the class $i$th method, and $n$ is equal to the number of methods in the class.

A class with low SDMC implies similarly complex methods. A class with high SDMC indicates varying method complexities.

*Definition 3. Proportion of nontrivial complexity (PNC)* measures the class complexity density as

$$\text{PNC} = 1 - \frac{T}{\text{WMC}}, \tag{3}$$

where $T$ is equal to the number of trivial methods in the class, and WMC is the CK's WMC metric that is the sum of complexities of local methods in the class. A method is said to be trivial if its cyclomatic complexity is equal to one. Examples of trivial methods are accessor and mutator methods, as well as empty methods.

A low PNC implies a large proportion of trivial methods. Trivial methods require less testing and maintenance as they have the lowest possible cyclomatic complexity. Classes with high PNC indicate a higher percentage of methods that require rigorous testing.

*3.2.2. Impact Metrics.* The purpose of the impact metrics is to complement CK's CBO metric. The CBO metric is a measure of both the number of classes the given class uses and the number of classes that use the given class. The impact metrics focus on classes that use the given class in order to determine and understand the potential effect a class may have on other classes. The proposed impact metrics consist of two metrics: Class Impact (CI) and Mean Nonzero Influence (MNI).

*Definition 4. Class Impact (CI)* measures the potential effect of making changes in the given class. Consider

$$\text{CI} = \sum I_i, \tag{4}$$

where $0 \leq i \leq N$, $I_i$ is the class influence on class $I$, and $N$ is equal to the number of other classes in the system.

CI serves as an indicator of the magnitude of the potential effect that a change in the given class will have on the entire system. Classes with high CI should be tested carefully as it implies a greater potential for affecting the behavior of other classes.

*Definition 5. Mean Nonzero Influence (MNI)* is a measure of influence strength. Consider

$$\text{MNI} = \frac{\text{CI}}{M}, \tag{5}$$

where $M$ is the number of classes that the given class is influencing. If $M$ is equal to zero, then MNI is valued at zero.

Using only CI may give an incomplete view of the impact of particular classes. The class with high CI may have a large influence on a small number of classes or a small influence on a large number of classes. MNI is an indication of which case a particular class belongs to. MNI serves as an indicator of the magnitude of the effect that a change in the given class will have on the classes it is influencing.

*3.2.3. Dependence Metrics.* Like the impact metrics, the purpose of the dependence metrics is to complement CK's CBO metric. Whereas the impact metrics focus on the classes that use the given class, the dependence metrics focus on the classes that are used by the given class. The purpose of the dependence metrics is to determine and understand the potential effect other classes may have on a given class. The dependence metrics consist of two metrics: Class Dependence (CD) and Mean Nonzero Dependence (MND).

*Definition 6. Class Dependence (CD)* is a measure of dependence. Consider

$$\text{CD} = \sum D_i, \qquad (6)$$

where $0 \le i \le N$, $D_i$ is the class $i$'s influence on the given class, and $N$ is equal to the number of other classes in the system.

Class dependence measures the potential for a change in another class to create a change in behavior in the given class. CD serves as an indicator of the magnitude of the potential effect the system has on the given class. A class with high CD will likely need to be retested if changes are made to other classes.

*Definition 7. Mean Nonzero Dependence (MND)* is a measure of the influence strength on the class. Consider

$$\text{MND} = \frac{\text{CD}}{L}, \qquad (7)$$

where $L$ is the number of classes that have an influence on the given class. If $L$ is equal to zero, then MND is equal to zero.

Like CI, CD does not provide a complete view of the influence of classes on each other. A class with a high CD may be heavily influenced by a few classes or lightly influenced by a large number of classes. MND solves this by determining the average magnitude of a class influence on the given class. MND serves as an indicator of the magnitude of the effect that a change an influencing class will have on the given class. Classes with high MND will require more testing when changes are made to classes that influence it.

*3.2.4. Inheritance Metrics.* The purpose of the inheritance metrics is to complement CK's DIT and NOC metrics. The goal of the inheritance metrics is to measure impact and dependence obtained through inheritance. The inheritance metrics consist of two metrics: Inherited Dependence (ID) and Weighted Descendent Impact (WDI).

*Definition 8. Inherited Dependence (ID)* is intended to measure how easily affected the given class is to changes to classes that influence its ancestors. ID is a measure of dependence obtained through inheritance and defined as

$$\text{ID} = \sum \text{CD}_i, \qquad (8)$$

where $0 \le i \le N$, $\text{CD}_i$ is the class dependence of the class $i$th ancestor, and $N$ is equal to the number of ancestors of the given class.

A class with high ID will require more testing effort, as it is easily affected by changes made in other classes. The cause of change in behavior of this class may be more difficult to trace, as it is not found in the class itself. As a result, classes should not inherit from classes with high ID.

*Definition 9. Weighted Descendent Impact (WDI)* is a measure of a class impact obtained through inheritance. Consider

$$\text{WDI} = \sum \text{CI}_i, \qquad (9)$$

where $0 \le i \le N$, $\text{CI}_i$ is the class impact of the class $i$th descendent class, and $N$ is equal to the number of descendents of the given class.

This metric measures the class potential effect on the other classes through inheritance. Changes to a class with high WDI should be avoided as such changes made in an ancestor class may propagate to the descendent classes and other classes.

## 4. Validating Proposed Metrics

The goal of this section is to investigate and validate the proposed metrics discussed in Section 3. Section 4.1 discusses the case study used in this research. Section 4.2 discusses the validation plan used for this section, while Section 4.3 presents the results obtained from correlating the proposed metrics with existing metrics. The effectiveness of the proposed metrics is investigated in Section 4.4. Project data is correlated with the proposed metrics in Section 4.5. We also discuss the results in Section 4.6 and limitations of proposed metrics in Section 4.7.

*4.1. Case Study.* Company L provided three systems, written in Java, that required analysis. System 1 consists of 125 classes and utilizes inheritance in its design. The highest number of ancestors any given class inherited from is seven. System 2 consists of 34 classes and uses inheritance sparingly. No classes in System 2 inherit from more than one other class. System 3 consists of 12 classes and no classes in System 3 inherit from more than one other class.

*4.1.1. Metrics Collection.* The metrics are collected using a small software tool developed for this research. Values for the following existing metrics are collected:

    (i) Weighted Methods per Class (WMC);

    (ii) Number of Methods (NOM);

    (iii) Number of Local Methods (NLM);

    (iv) Coupling Between Objects (CBO);

(v) Message Passing Coupling (MPC);

(vi) Coupling Through Message Passing (CTM);

(vii) Depth in Inheritance Tree (DIT);

(viii) Number of Ancestor Classes (NAC);

(ix) Number of Children (NOC);

(x) Number of Descendent Classes (NDC).

Values for the following proposed metrics are collected:

(i) Mean Method Complexity (MMC);

(ii) Standard Deviation Method Complexity (SDMC);

(iii) Proportion of Nontrivial Complexity (PNC);

(iv) Class Impact (CI);

(v) Mean Nonzero Influence (MNI);

(vi) Class Dependence (CD);

(vii) Mean Nonzero Dependence (MND);

(viii) Weighted Descendent Impact (WDI);

(ix) Inherited Dependence (ID).

The proposed metrics are compared to values of the existing metrics. This allows for the effectiveness of the proposed metrics to be determined. It is also determined how the values of the proposed metrics correlated with project data provided by Company L in order to draw conclusions about the relationships that exist between various class attributes and project outcomes. The values obtained from the proposed metrics can also be used to obtain a better understanding regarding various characteristics of classes present in the systems.

*4.1.2. Data Collection.* The project data used in this research is collected using the Perforce software configuration management system (SCMS). The SCMS provides change histories along with the description of the changes, the classes involved in the changes, and the associated change ID number. The outputs of the SCMS provide the following project results for each class.

(i) Number of Revisions (REV): the number of revisions is investigated for multiple reasons as the number of revisions provides a clear and quantifiable measure of maintenance effort. It represents the number of times the class is changed.

(ii) Number of Defects (DEF): the number of defects is investigated for similar reasons. It is always beneficial to reduce the number of defects found in classes.

(iii) Number of Corrective Actions (COR): the number of corrections is investigated to determine the frequency to correct mistakes in the classes such as defects. Note that the number of corrections is not necessarily equal to the number of defects. It may take more than one correction to repair a defect as well as it may take only one correction to repair multiple defects. For this reason, it is determined that both defects and corrections are to be investigated. Also the number

of revisions and the number of corrective actions differ in that it may require more than one revision to complete one corrective action.

*4.2. Validation Plan.* Pearson correlations are calculated using the Statistical Package for the Social Sciences (SPSS). The correlation values are an indication of how linearly related two variables are with the lowest and highest possible values being −1.0 and 1.0, respectively. A higher magnitude indicates a stronger linear relationship between two variables. A positive correlation indicates a simultaneous increase or decrease in the values of the two variables. A negative correlation indicates that as the values of one variable increase, the values for the other variable decreased and vice versa. Correlations are considered *significant* if there is a small probability that the correlation is found due to random error. A "*" indicates that the probability that the correlation is found due to random error is less than ten percent. The explanation of random error is beyond the scope of this research. Metrics are considered to be *highly correlated* if the magnitude of the correlation is greater than 0.8.

We perform three validation tasks for the proposed metrics as follows.

(i) The introduction of new metrics requires a series of steps to determine if they are necessary. Therefore it is important to investigate how the proposed metrics correlate with similar existing CK metrics. High correlations between proposed and existing metrics imply that the proposed metrics may not be required. These correlations are investigated in Section 4.3.

(ii) The proposed metrics must also provide additional information at an acceptable frequency. The frequency at which the proposed metrics provide additional information determines their effectiveness. Section 4.4 investigates the effectiveness of the proposed metrics. The values of the proposed metrics are compared to the values of the existing metrics to determine how frequently the proposed metrics are able to provide additional information.

(iii) Once the proposed metrics are shown to provide additional information, it must be shown that such information is useful in solving problems such as the reduction of maintenance effort, identification of defect-prone classes, and reduction of necessary corrective actions. In order to do this, the values obtained from the proposed metrics are correlated with project data. The results from this investigation are discussed in Section 4.5.

*4.3. Correlating Metrics.* The values extracted from the proposed metrics are correlated with the values extracted from the existing metrics. The purpose of finding these correlations is to provide the likelihood that the proposed metrics are providing additional information. A high correlation (< −0.8 or >0.8) between two metrics implies that only one of the metrics may be necessary in providing information concerning the attribute they are measuring. As a result, high correlations between proposed and existing metrics need to be justified in order to consider the proposed metric necessary. Note that cells ("—") in Tables 1, 2, and 3 represent cases where a correlation could not be found.

### 4.3.1. Correlating Complexity Metrics.

The proposed complexity metrics MMC, SDMC, and PNC are correlated with existing related metrics WMC, NOM, and NLM as presented in Table 1(a). It shows that high correlations (>0.8) are found between MMC and WMC in System 2 and System 3. However, MMC and NLM are only highly correlated (>0.8) in System 2. The system may have been designed such that classes with a large number of methods required such methods to be more complex. No high correlations (>0.8) are found for SDMC and PNC with the existing metrics.

### 4.3.2. Correlating Impact Metrics.

The proposed impact metrics, CI and MNI, are correlated with CBO. Table 1(b) shows no high correlations between CI and CBO as well as between MNI and CBO.

### 4.3.3. Correlating Dependence Metrics.

The values for MPC and CTM were equal in all three systems provided, as methods belonging to objects created in methods were not used. As a result, only correlations concerning MPC are discussed to avoid redundancy.

Table 1(c) shows that CD was highly correlated (>0.8) with both MPC and CTM. MND was also correlated with both MPC and CTM. This is not unexpected, as CD differs from MPC and CTM mostly from its treatment of instance variables. CD counts the use of instance variables while MPC and CTM do not. Table 1(c) also shows that CD and MPC are significantly correlated (*) in all three systems. The two metrics are also highly correlated (>0.8) in all three systems as CD and MPC only differ in the use of instance variables. CD counts the use of other classes' instance variables as well as methods while MPC only counts the use of methods. The direct use of instance variables is considered as questionable programming practices and therefore does not occur often. This results in the high correlation between the two metrics. Finally, Table 1(c) shows that MND and MPC are significantly correlated (*) in all three systems. As the definitions of CD and MND show that they are proportional to each other, if CD is highly correlated to MPC, it would follow that MND is highly correlated to MPC.

### 4.3.4. Correlating Inheritance Metrics.

From Table 1(d), ID is not highly correlated (>0.8) with either DIT or NAC. This implies that there is a substantial difference between the ID and the existing metrics. Multiple inheritance has not been utilized in the first two systems and therefore the values of DIT are equal to those of NAC. Correlations for the third system could not be found, as inheritance has not been used in the development of the system. Also, Table 1(d) shows that WDI and NDC are significantly correlated (*) in System 1. That system produces a high correlation (>0.8) between the two metrics. As the number of descendents increase, so will the sum of the descendents' impacts. Also note that correlations for the third system could not be found, as inheritance has not been used in the development of the system.

### 4.4. Effectiveness of Proposed Metrics.

The effectiveness of a metric is determined by the frequency at which it provides additional information when compared to other metrics. The additional information can be detected when a case is found where an existing metric cannot correctly measure some class attributes. Therefore, the proposed metric is able to show that the existing metric leads to incorrect conclusions about the attribute. An example is using WMC to measure method complexity because more complex classes generally have more complex methods. The effectiveness of MMC is determined by the frequency at which it can show that the conclusions drawn using WMC are false. Therefore the frequency of disagreement determines the effectiveness of a proposed metric.

### 4.4.1. Effectiveness of Proposed Complexity Metrics.

Table 2(a) shows the results of investigating the effectiveness of MMC, SDMC, and PNC when compared to the existing metrics WMC, NOM, and NLM.

(i) *Effectiveness of MMC compared to WMC, NOM, and NLM—Method Complexity.* Table 2(a) shows that WMC is inaccurate in identifying which of two classes has higher method complexity in 19.1, 10.5, and 9.1 percent of cases in Systems 1, 2, and 3, respectively. It also shows that NOM is inaccurate in identifying which of two classes has higher method complexity in 28.6, 16.2, and 22.7 percent of cases in Systems 1, 2, and 3, respectively. Furthermore, Table 2(a) indicates that NLM is inaccurate in identifying which of two classes has higher method complexity in 31.2, 16.8, and 36.4 percent of cases in Systems 1, 2, and 3, respectively. Although MMC was shown to be correlated with the existing complexity metrics discussed, the results show that those metrics cannot accurately draw conclusions regarding method complexity. Therefore MMC is shown to provide additional information.

(ii) *Effectiveness of SDMC compared to WMC, NOM, and NLM—Method Diversity.* Table 2(a) shows that WMC is inaccurate in identifying which of two classes has higher method diversity in 29.6, 18.9, and 24.2 percent of cases in Systems 1, 2, and 3, respectively. Also, it is observed that NOM is inaccurate in identifying which of two classes has higher method diversity in 38.3, 22.3, and 37.9 percent of cases in Systems 1, 2, and 3, respectively. In addition, NLM is inaccurate in identifying which of two classes has higher method diversity in 40.2, 20.3, and 42.4 percent of cases in systems 1, 2, and 3 respectively. Although SDMC was correlated with the existing complexity metrics in most cases, the results show that those metrics cannot accurately draw conclusions regarding method diversity. Therefore SDMC is shown to provide additional information.

TABLE 1: Correlations between metrics.

(a) Correlations between complexity metrics

| Metric | MMC | | | SDMC | | | PNC | | |
|---|---|---|---|---|---|---|---|---|---|
| | System 1 | System 2 | System 3 | System 1 | System 2 | System 3 | System 1 | System 2 | System 3 |
| WMC | 0.794* | **0.902*** | **0.873*** | 0.490* | 0.436* | 0.647* | 0.417* | 0.500* | 0.620* |
| NOM | 0.422* | 0.796* | 0.615* | 0.113 | 0.429* | 0.315 | 0.348* | 0.545* | 0.448 |
| NLM | 0.312* | **0.888*** | 0.326 | 0.037 | 0.568* | 0.129 | 0.291* | 0.531* | 0.232 |

(b) Correlations between impact metrics

| Metric | CI | | | MNI | | |
|---|---|---|---|---|---|---|
| | System 1 | System 2 | System 3 | System 1 | System 2 | System 3 |
| CBO | 0.693* | 0.660* | 0.481 | 0.277* | 0.713* | 0.245 |

(c) Correlations between dependence metrics

| Metric | CD | | | MND | | |
|---|---|---|---|---|---|---|
| | System 1 | System 2 | System 3 | System 1 | System 2 | System 3 |
| CBO | 0.346* | 0.547* | 0.442 | 0.257* | 0.494* | 0.435 |
| MPC | **0.992*** | **0.939*** | **0.995*** | 0.797* | **0.857*** | **0.974*** |
| CTM | **0.992*** | **0.939*** | **0.995*** | 0.797* | **0.857*** | **0.974*** |

(d) Correlations between inheritance metrics

| Metric | ID | | | WDI | | |
|---|---|---|---|---|---|---|
| | System 1 | System 2 | System 3 | System 1 | System 2 | System 3 |
| DIT | 0.550* | 0.579* | — | — | — | — |
| NAC | 0.550* | 0.579* | — | — | — | — |
| NOC | — | — | — | 0.336* | 0.186 | — |
| NDC | — | — | — | **0.886*** | 0.186 | — |

(iii) *Effectiveness of PNC compared to WMC, NOM, and NLM—Method Density.* It is shown in Table 2(a) that WMC is inaccurate in identifying which of two classes has higher method density in 15.5, 18.8, and 23.6 percent of cases in Systems 1, 2, and 3, respectively. Table 2(a) also shows that NOM is inaccurate in identifying which of two classes has higher method density in 27.8, 21.3, and 17.9 percent of cases in Systems 1, 2, and 3, respectively. It indicates that NLM is inaccurate in identifying which of two classes has higher method density in 31.0, 16.3, and 27.4 percent of cases in Systems 1, 2, and 3 respectively. Although PNC was shown to be correlated with the existing complexity metrics discussed in all but two cases, the results show that those metrics cannot accurately draw conclusions regarding complexity density. Therefore PNC is shown to provide additional information.

*4.4.2. Effectiveness of the Proposed Impact Metrics.* In Table 2(b), the effectiveness of CI when compared to CBO is investigated. CBO is a measure of the number of classes that the given class is coupled to.

The percentages shown in Table 2(b) represent the percentage of classes in each system where coupling is due to the sending of messages (measured by CD) as opposed to the receiving of messages (measured by CI). The CBO metric is not able to distinguish between the sending and receiving of messages therefore drawing false conclusions regarding a class impact. CBO was shown to inaccurately determine that a class has at least some impact and thus CI provides additional information. Table 2(b) shows that CBO falsely identified a class as having at least some amount of impact in 36.0 percent of classes in System 1, 20.5 percent of classes in System 2, and 33.3 percent of classes in System 3.

In Table 2(b), MNI is used to complement CI in order to provide additional information. The definitions of CI and MNI show that MNI is more similar to CI than to CBO. Consequently, MNI is investigated with respect to CI as opposed to CBO. Table 2(b) shows that CI is inaccurate in identifying which of two classes has higher influence strength in 14.5 percent of cases in System 1, 10.6 percent of cases in System 2, and 30.0 percent of cases in System 3. The results show that CI is not sufficient in measuring influence strength. Therefore, MNI is shown to provide additional information.

*4.4.3. Effectiveness of Proposed Dependence Metrics.* Table 2(c) shows the results from investigating the effectiveness of CD when compared to CBO, MPC, and CTM. CBO measures the number of classes that the given class is coupled to. It also shows CBO can falsely conclude that the class has at least some class dependence. Note that for three investigated systems, MPC and CTM values are equal. This is not necessarily true for all systems as the systems we

TABLE 2: Effectiveness of metrics.

(a) Effectiveness of complexity metrics

| Metric | MMC | | | SDMC | | | PNC | | |
|--------|----------|----------|----------|----------|----------|----------|----------|----------|----------|
|        | System 1 | System 2 | System 3 | System 1 | System 2 | System 3 | System 1 | System 2 | System 3 |
| WMC | 19.1 | 10.5 | 9.1 | 29.6 | 18.9 | 24.2 | 15.5 | 18.8 | 23.6 |
| NOM | 28.6 | 16.2 | 22.7 | 38.3 | 22.3 | 37.9 | 27.8 | 21.3 | 17.9 |
| NLM | 31.2 | 16.8 | 36.4 | 40.2 | 20.3 | 42.4 | 31.0 | 16.3 | 27.4 |

(b) Effectiveness of impact metrics

| Metric | CI | | | MNI | | |
|--------|----------|----------|----------|----------|----------|----------|
|        | System 1 | System 2 | System 3 | System 1 | System 2 | System 3 |
| CBO | 36.0 | 20.5 | 33.3 | — | — | — |
| CI  | —    | —    | —    | 14.5 | 10.6 | 30.0 |

(c) Effectiveness of dependence metrics

| Metric | CD | | | MND | | |
|--------|----------|----------|----------|----------|----------|----------|
|        | System 1 | System 2 | System 3 | System 1 | System 2 | System 3 |
| CBO | 14.4 | 14.7 | 25.0 | — | — | — |
| MPC | 18.4 | 32.4 | 8.3 | — | — | — |
| CTM | 18.4 | 32.4 | 8.3 | — | — | — |
| CD  | —    | —    | —    | 15.8 | 11.0 | 0.0 |

(d) Effectiveness of inheritance metrics

| Metric | ID | | | WDI | | |
|--------|----------|----------|----------|----------|----------|----------|
|        | System 1 | System 2 | System 3 | System 1 | System 2 | System 3 |
| DIT | 5.6 | 8.8 | 25.0 | — | — | — |
| NAC | 5.6 | 8.8 | 25.0 | — | — | — |
| NOC | —   | —   | —    | 5.6 | 11.8 | 8.3 |
| NDC | —   | —   | —    | 5.6 | 11.8 | 8.3 |

investigated do not use methods of objects declared within methods. We also compare MND with CD. MND is used to complement CD in order to provide additional information.

*4.4.4. Effectiveness of Proposed Inheritance Metrics.* Table 2(d) shows that DIT, NAC, NOC, and NDC falsely identified a class as having at least some amount of ancestor or descendent dependence in all three systems. In addition, although ID and WDI are shown to be correlated with the related existing inheritance metrics in System 1 and System 2, the results show that those metrics cannot accurately draw conclusions regarding ancestor or descendent dependence.

*4.5. Correlating with Project Data.* In order to determine if the additional information is useful, the results from the proposed metrics are correlated with the project data described in Section 4.1. This will provide an understanding of the relationships that exist between the class attributes measured by the proposed metrics and the following project outcomes: the number of revisions (REV), number of defects (DEF), and number of corrective actions (COR).

*4.5.1. Correlating Proposed Complexity Metrics with Project Data.* The relationship between complexity and project outcomes is determined by correlating the results of the proposed complexity metrics with project data. In System 1, Table 3(a) shows that MMC, SDMC, and PNC are significantly correlated (*) to REV, DEF, and COR. This implies that, in System 1, classes with higher method diversity and complexity density are likely to require more revisions, contain more defects, and require more corrective actions. A possible explanation for the correlations is that complex methods, classes with methods that are significantly different from each other lead to mistakes which cause revisions, defects, and corrective actions.

In Systems 2 and 3, Table 3(a) shows that MMC, SDMC, and PNC are not significantly correlated (*) to REV, DEF, or COR. This implies that, in both systems, there is no relationship between complexity metrics and number of revisions, defects found, as well as required corrective actions. This could be due to the size of the systems. Systems that consist of fewer classes are less likely to require revisions than larger systems.

Table 3: Correlating metrics with project data.

(a) Correlating proposed complexity metrics with project data

| Metric | MMC | | | SDMC | | | PNC | | |
|---|---|---|---|---|---|---|---|---|---|
| | System 1 | System 2 | System 3 | System 1 | System 2 | System 3 | System 1 | System 2 | System 3 |
| REV | 0.444* | 0.218 | −0.315 | 0.190* | 0.141 | −0.369 | 0.307* | 0.154 | 0.085 |
| DEF | 0.573* | 0.218 | — | 0.394* | 0.141 | — | 0.230* | 0.154 | — |
| COR | 0.515* | 0.218 | — | 0.307* | 0.141 | — | 0.243* | 0.154 | — |

(b) Correlating proposed impact metrics with project data

| Metric | CI | | | MNI | | |
|---|---|---|---|---|---|---|
| | System 1 | System 2 | System 3 | System 1 | System 2 | System 3 |
| REV | 0.229* | 0.001 | −0.176 | 0.437* | 0.097 | −0.207 |
| DEF | 0.174 | 0.001 | — | 0.436* | 0.097 | — |
| COR | 0.200* | 0.001 | — | 0.491* | 0.097 | — |

(c) Correlating proposed dependence metrics with project data

| Metric | CD | | | MND | | |
|---|---|---|---|---|---|---|
| | System 1 | System 2 | System 3 | System 1 | System 2 | System 3 |
| REV | 0.624* | 0.031 | −0.038 | 0.495* | 0.098 | 0.070 |
| DEF | 0.745* | 0.031 | — | 0.487* | 0.098 | — |
| COR | 0.703* | 0.031 | — | 0.477* | 0.098 | — |

(d) Correlating proposed inheritance metrics with project data

| Metric | ID | | | WDI | | |
|---|---|---|---|---|---|---|
| | System 1 | System 2 | System 3 | System 1 | System 2 | System 3 |
| REV | 0.376* | −0.047 | — | −0.025 | 0.032 | — |
| DEF | 0.249* | −0.047 | — | −0.025 | 0.032 | — |
| COR | 0.256* | −0.047 | — | 0.032 | 0.032 | — |

*4.5.2. Correlating Proposed Impact Metrics with Project Data.* Table 3(b) shows the relationship between impact and project outcomes. In System 1, CI and MNI are significantly correlated (*) to REV and COR. This implies that, in System 1, classes with higher impact or influence are likely to require more revisions and require more corrective actions. A possible explanation is that classes with high impact undergo revision and corrective action in order to repair the defect in classes they influence. This would also explain why there is no significant correlation between CI and DEF.

In addition, in Systems 2 and 3, CI and MNI are not significantly correlated (*) to REV, DEF or COR. This implies that, in both systems, there is no relationship between impact and number of revisions, defects found, and required corrective actions. This could also be due to system size.

*4.5.3. Correlating Proposed Dependence Metrics with Project Data.* Table 3(c) shows that CD and MND are significantly correlated (*) to REV, DEF, and COR in System 1. This implies that, in System 1, classes with higher dependence and influence strength are likely to require more revisions, contain more defects, and require more corrective actions. A possible explanation is that classes that heavily rely on other classes, as indicated by high dependence, are more difficult to comprehend, leading to mistakes which cause revisions, defects, and corrective actions. This also supports the conclusion offered

in Section 4.5.2 regarding CI and MNI. If high dependence classes are likelier to contain defects, they are likely candidates for revisions and corrective actions. Although the classes that are influencing the high dependence classes may not contain defects, they may require revisions, as well as corrective actions, to repair the defects in the high dependence classes. This would account for the significant correlation between CI and REV as well as CI and COR. It would also explain why CI and DEF do not correlate. It is also possible that changes in other classes are introducing errors into high dependence classes. Such errors may be the cause of revisions, defects, and corrective actions.

The low correlation in Systems 2 and 3 implies that in both systems there is no relationship between dependence and number of revisions, defects found, and required corrective actions.

*4.5.4. Correlating Proposed Inheritance Metrics with Project Data.* Table 3(d) shows the dependence metrics of ID and WDI. In System 1, ID is significantly correlated (*) to REV, DEF, and COR. This implies that, in System 1, classes with higher dependence are likely to require more revisions, contain more defects, and require more corrective actions. It is possible that changes in other classes are introducing errors into high dependence classes. The errors are then inherited by subclasses leading to revisions, defects, and corrective actions. In System 2, ID is not significantly correlated (*) to REV, DEF, or COR. This implies that, in System 2, there is no relationship between inherited dependence and number of revisions, defects found, or required corrective actions. This could also be due to system size as well as a lack of inheritance in the system. There are no cases of impact or dependence through inheritance in System 3.

There was no significant correlation between WDI and REV, DEF, or COR. The lack of significant correlations may be due to system size and a lack of inheritance in System 2. However, this is not the case for System 1. System 1 consists of 125 classes and utilizes inheritance in many of its classes. This implies that there is no relationship between the impact of a class descendents and project outcomes.

*4.6. Discussion.* The investigation of the metrics in this section has two key objectives: to investigate the validity of the proposed metrics and to assess the maintainability of the three systems.

Section 4.3 discussed the correlations between the proposed metrics and related existing metrics. Although the proposed metrics are shown to be correlated with the related existing metrics, only a small subset of correlations, with the exception of the dependence metrics, are sufficiently high to raise concerns. High correlations (>0.8) raised concerns as they serve as indications that two metrics may be providing similar information. An explanation is required in cases where two metrics are highly correlated to help ensure that the proposed metrics are providing additional information. In addition, with regard to the dependence metrics, the high correlations are expected as the proposed metric CD mostly differs from MPC and CTM just in their treatment of direct access of other classes' instance variables. It was therefore necessary to investigate the frequency in which instance variables are accessed by other classes.

Section 4.4 revealed that the existing metrics are not sufficient in measuring the attributes that the proposed metrics are designed to measure. The existing metrics are inaccurate in their assessment of such attributes that it can be concluded that the proposed metrics do in fact provide additional information not otherwise available. The results from Section 4.4 show that the frequency at which CD produces different results from MPC and CTM is not negligible. This shows that instance variables are in fact accessed by other classes, although such a practice is not advised. The correlation between CD and MPC can be used as a measure to determine the level of encapsulation in the class. A higher correlation would imply that classes are being encapsulated properly with regards to hiding instance variables.

The results from Section 4.5 show that, for larger systems, the attributes measured by the proposed metrics are in fact related to the project outcomes investigated. The results supported the notion that, for large systems, method complexity, method diversity, and complexity density are related to number of revisions, defects found, and required corrective actions. The results from Section 4.5 also suggested that, in large systems, it is important to pay close attention to the complexity, impact, and dependence of classes as they can lead to revisions, defects found, and required corrective

actions. The dependence of ancestor classes is shown to be related to revisions, defects found, and required corrective actions. One point of interest is that the impact of a class descendent classes is not shown to be related to the project outcomes investigated. However, this does not mean that the metric used to measure this attribute should be discarded. It may be valuable to determine which classes have impact through inheritance. Such information may affect decisions concerning changes made during maintenance.

Another important note is that the results obtained from the values of the proposed metrics can be used to understand various attributes of classes present in the system. The values obtained from the proposed complexity metrics will allow the understanding of method complexities, method diversities, and complexity densities of the classes in systems. The values from the proposed impact and dependence metrics will allow better understanding of message passing in systems. The inheritance metrics will show how the classes interact beyond direct message passing and inheritance.

*4.7. Limitations.* We consider the limitations of proposed metrics as follows.

  (i) The attributes identified and the metrics proposed are specific in its purpose: to determine the difficulty and the effects of change. The metrics are designed to provide very specific information. The values for the metrics can only be extracted using source code or very highly detailed design documents. As a result, the attributes may not be available in early phases of a system's life cycle.

 (ii) The size of the system may be important in determining the significance of the proposed metrics [28]. The results in Section 4 imply that small systems do not benefit as readily from the metrics as larger systems. It seems advantageous to use system size in conjunction with the proposed metrics. However, the size of the system is often not determinable until implementation therefore restricting the use of metrics to the implementation phase [29]. The project data is also a determining factor in the value of the proposed metrics. A lack in project data may provide poor results and little information may be gained from using the metrics. Also, low variances have shown to cause a difficulty in finding relationships between metric values and project data [30]. More systems should be investigated to further validate the proposed metrics.

(iii) The proposed metrics do not consider the use of classes that are predefined in the programming language in their calculation. It is, however, possible to overwrite such classes and doing so may cause unpredicted changes in the system. It may be worth investigating if the use of such classes should be considered in the metrics.

# 5. Conclusion

The objective of this research was to identify the class attributes that convey information regarding the maintenance of that class in order to develop a suite of metrics that measure such attributes. A suite of metrics has been developed to provide additional information that will assist in the maintenance of object-oriented systems. The metrics have been designed to measure attributes that lead to the difficulty in maintaining classes as well as attributes that describe potential effects of class changes. The use of the proposed metrics will enable maintainers to better understand the complexity of classes as well as the potential effects of changing classes.

One possible future work is the modification of existing modeling languages in order to display values associated with the proposed metrics and convey information such as influence relationships between classes. If such work were to be completed, it may be more valuable to be able to easily visualize the influence of classes as well as their complexities. It is also possible that the metrics be applied to methods instead of classes. Further, it is possible that providing information regarding influence at a method level is as useful, if not more useful, than at a class level. An application of the proposed metrics could be the development of predictive models. Neural networks and other data mining techniques may be used to predict project outcomes by using the values obtained from the proposed metrics, such as quality and maintainability.

# References

[1] I. Bluemke, "Object oriented metrics useful in the prediction of class testing complexity," in *Proceedings of the 27th Euromicro Conference*, pp. 130–136, 2001.

[2] V. R. Basili, L. C. Briand, and W. L. Melo, "A validation of object-oriented design metrics as quality indicators," *IEEE Transactions on Software Engineering*, vol. 22, no. 10, pp. 751–761, 1996.

[3] T. J. McCabe, "Complexity Measure," *IEEE Transactions on Software Engineering*, vol. 2, no. 4, pp. 308–320, 1976.

[4] S. R. Chidamber and C. F. Kemerer, "Metrics suite for object oriented design," *IEEE Transactions on Software Engineering*, vol. 20, no. 6, pp. 476–493, 1994.

[5] M. Bundschuh and C. Dekkers, "Object-oriented metrics," in *The IT Measurement Compendium*, M. Bundschuh and C. Dekkers, Eds., pp. 241–255, Springer, Berlin, Germany, 2008.

[6] E. J. Weyuker, "Evaluating software complexity measures," *IEEE Transactions on Software Engineering*, vol. 14, no. 9, pp. 1357–1365, 1988.

[7] I. Vessey and R. Weber, "Research on structured programming: an wmpiricist's evaluation," *IEEE Transactions on Software Engineering*, vol. 10, no. 4, pp. 397–407, 1984.

[8] T. Wand and R. Weber, "Toward a theory of the deep structure of information systems," in *Proceedings of International Conference Information System*, pp. 61–71, 1990.

[9] V. R. Basili and B. T. Perricone, "Software errors and complexity: an empirical investigatio," *Communications of the ACM*, vol. 27, no. 1, pp. 42–52, 1984.

[10] M. H. Tang, M. H. Kao, and M. H. Chen, "An empirical study on object-oriented metrics," in *Proceedings of the 6th International Software Metrics Symposium*, pp. 242–249, November 1999.

[11] S. Sarkar, A. C. Kak, and G. M. Rama, "Metrics for measuring the quality of modularization of large-scale object-oriented software," *IEEE Transactions on Software Engineering*, vol. 34, no. 5, pp. 700–720, 2008.

[12] Y. Zhou, B. Xu, and H. Leung, "On the ability of complexity metrics to predict fault-prone classes in object-oriented systems," *Journal of Systems and Software*, vol. 83, no. 4, pp. 660–674, 2010.

[13] H. M. Olague, L. H. Etzkorn, S. L. Messimer, and H. S. Delugach, "An empirical validation of object-oriented class complexity metrics and their ability to predict error-prone classes in highly iterative, or agile, software: a case study," *Journal of Software Maintenance and Evolution*, vol. 20, no. 3, pp. 171–197, 2008.

[14] L. C. Briand and J. W. Daly, "A unified framework for coupling measurement in object-oriented systems," *IEEE Transactions on Software Engineering*, vol. 25, no. 1, pp. 91–121, 1999.

[15] L. C. Briand, J. Wüst, J. W. Daly, and D. Victor Porter, "Exploring the relationships between design measures and software quality in object-oriented systems," *Journal of Systems and Software*, vol. 51, no. 1, pp. 245–273, 2000.

[16] F. T. Sheldon and H. Chung, "Measuring the complexity of class diagrams in reverse engineering," *Journal of Software Maintenance and Evolution*, vol. 18, no. 5, pp. 333–350, 2006.

[17] R. Shatnawi, W. Li, J. Swain, and T. Newman, "Finding software metrics threshold values using ROC curves," *Journal of Software Maintenance and Evolution*, vol. 22, no. 1, pp. 1–16, 2010.

[18] W. Li and S. Henry, "Object-oriented metrics that predict maintainability," *The Journal of Systems and Software*, vol. 23, no. 2, pp. 111–122, 1993.

[19] N. I. Churcher and M. J. Shepperd, "'Comments on' a metrics suite for object oriented design," *IEEE Transactions on Software Engineering*, vol. 21, no. 3, pp. 263–265, 1995.

[20] W. Li, "Another metric suite for object-oriented programming," *Journal of Systems and Software*, vol. 44, no. 2, pp. 155–162, 1998.

[21] T. Mayer and T. Hall, "A critical analysis of current OO design metrics," *Software Quality Journal*, vol. 8, no. 2, pp. 97–110, 1999.

[22] S. R. Chidamber, D. P. Darcy, and C. F. Kemerer, "Managerial use of metrics for object-oriented software: an exploratory analysis," *IEEE Transactions on Software Engineering*, vol. 24, no. 8, pp. 629–639, 1998.

[23] M. Hitz and B. Montazeri, "Chidamber and kemerer's metrics suite: a measurement theory perspective," *IEEE Transactions on Software Engineering*, vol. 22, no. 4, pp. 267–271, 1996.

[24] H. S. Chae, Y. R. Kwon, and D. H. Bae, "A cohesion measure for classes in object-oriented classes," *Software*, vol. 30, no. 12, pp. 1405–1431, 2000.

[25] J. A. Dallal, "Improving the applicability of object-oriented class cohesion metrics," *The Journal of Systems and Software*, vol. 53, no. 9, pp. 914–928, 2011.

[26] K. A. M. Ferreira, M. A. S. Bigonha, R. S. Bigonha, L. F. O. Mendes, and H. C. Almeida, "Identifying thresholds for object-oriented software metrics," *The Journal of Systems and Software*, vol. 85, no. 2, pp. 244–257, 2012.

[27] L. Etzkorn, J. Bansiya, and C. Davis, "Design and code complexity metrics for OO classes," *Journal of Object-Oriented Programming*, vol. 12, no. 1, pp. 35–40, 1999.

[28] K. El Emam, S. Benlarbi, N. Goel, and S. N. Rai, "The confounding effect of class size on the validity of object-oriented metrics," *IEEE Transactions on Software Engineering*, vol. 27, no. 7, pp. 630–650, 2001.

[29] W. M. Evanco, "Comments on 'The confounding effect of class size on the validity of object-oriented metrics'," *IEEE Transactions on Software Engineering*, vol. 29, no. 7, pp. 670–672, 2003.

[30] G. Succi, W. Pedrycz, S. Djokic, P. Zuliani, and B. Russo, "An empirical exploration of the distributions of the Chidamber and Kemerer object-oriented metrics suite," *Empirical Software Engineering*, vol. 10, no. 1, pp. 81–103, 2005.

# 8

# An Assessment of Maintainability of an Aspect-Oriented System

**Kagiso Mguni and Yirsaw Ayalew**

*Department of Computer Science, University of Botswana, Private Bag 0704, Gaborone, Botswana*

Correspondence should be addressed to Yirsaw Ayalew; ayalew@mopipi.ub.bw

Academic Editors: C. Calero, R. J. Walker, and B. Yang

Software maintenance is an important activity in software development. Some development methodologies such as the object-oriented have contributed in improving maintainability of software. However, crosscutting concerns are still challenges that affect the maintainability of OO software. In this paper, we discuss our case study to assess the extent of maintainability improvement that can be achieved by employing aspect-oriented programming. Aspect-oriented programming (AOP) is a relatively new approach that emphasizes dealing with crosscutting concerns. To demonstrate the maintainability improvement, we refactored a COTS-based system known as OpenBravoPOS using AspectJ and compared its maintainability with the original OO version. We used both structural complexity and concern level metrics. Our results show an improvement of maintainability in the AOP version of OpenBravoPOS.

## 1. Introduction

Software maintenance is one of the most expensive activities that consume about 50–70 percent of the development cost [1]. Therefore, it is a very important activity that requires much attention. For this reason, people have attempted to find ways to minimize maintenance costs by introducing better development methodologies that can minimize the effects of change, simplify the understanding of programs, facilitate the early detection of faults, and so forth. In this regard, the object-oriented approach has played an important role by improving the maintainability of software using the concepts of object and encapsulation. Specifically, the OO approach has been hailed for providing constructs that minimize (i.e., localize) the impact of change. However, there are still some concerns that crosscut among a number of objects whose modification may be difficult as they are scattered across many objects. To address this issue, aspect-oriented programming (AOP) has been introduced as a way of improving the modularity of code there by facilitating maintenance. Concerns that crosscut across different components are represented by the construct aspect. A concern is a feature that a system should implement which includes all the functional, nonfunctional requirements and the design constraints in the system [2].

Aspect-oriented programming was developed to overcome the limitations of programming approaches such as OOP in handling crosscutting concerns. Therefore, it introduces several new constructs related to handling crosscutting concerns. The different constructs that are introduced by AOP are as follows.

(i) *Aspects.* Aspects are similar in nature to classes in OO. Aspects are also considered to be equivalent to the other OO constructs such as interface. Aspects are used to wrap up advices, pointcuts, and intertype declarations in a modular unit the same way classes and interfaces wrap up declarations and methods [3]. Aspects together with classes can be referred to as modules and they both represent the basic unit of modularity in AOP.

(ii) *Advices.* Advices are similar in nature to methods in OO. Aspects contain the body of the code that is executed at a given point that is captured by a join point. The advices together with their OO counterparts, methods, are referred to as operations.

(iii) *Intertype Declarations.* These are used to add new fields or methods to a class. In contrast, they are similar to static attributes in OO.

The main focus of AOP is to improve the implementation of crosscutting concerns (i.e., scattering and tangling). The question we would like to address in this paper is *"To what extent maintainability improves when an OO code is refactored using AOP?"* In other words, we want to assess the maintainability of AOP software. To answer this question, we need to understand how we measure maintainability. According to IEEE [4], maintainability can be defined as *"The ease with which a software system or component can be modified to correct faults, improve performance or other attributes, or adapt to a changed environment."* In order to measure maintainability, we need to employ appropriate metrics. There are various maintainability metrics that are geared towards the different maintainability characteristics.

Quality models such as the ISO/IEC 9126 describe maintainability using the following characteristics: analyzability, changeability, stability, testability, and maintainability compliance [5]. The new quality model, ISO25010, provides additional maintainability characteristics such as reusability and modifiability. Measures such as the maintainability index [6] have been proposed to objectively determine the maintainability of software systems based on the status of the corresponding source code. To simplify the measurement of maintainability, Heitlager et al. [7] introduced a mapping of system characteristics onto source code properties. The source code properties that were introduced include volume, complexity per unit, duplication, unit size, and unit testing. For example, it was indicated that the degree of source code duplication (also called code cloning) influences analyzability and changeability. Some metrics are used to measure the internal quality (i.e., based on source code) and others are based on the external quality (i.e., based on sources other than source code). A discussion of metrics relevant to AOP software is provided in Sections 2 and 3. The focus of this paper is on maintainability that is grounded in source code analysis. To assess the maintainability of the original code and the refactored AOP code, we have chosen open-source COTS (commercial off the shelf) components. The open source COTS components are OpenBravoPOS and Jasperreports.

The rest of the paper is organized as follows. Section 2 presents related work on maintainability of AOP software. A discussion of how we conducted the study is provided in Section 3. The results of the study and issues emanating from the study are discussed in Section 4. Section 5 provides the main points of the study and future work.

## 2. Related Works

In this section, we discuss the relevant metrics used to assess maintainability and empirical studies that were conducted to determine the effectiveness of various maintainability metrics.

*2.1. Maintainability Metrics.* Most AOP maintainability metrics were derived from the maintainability metrics of OO systems [8]. However, in some cases, some new metrics which take care of the special characteristics of AOP need to be introduced. For example, the authors in [8] have introduced specialized maintainability metrics specific to AOP.

Table 1 summarizes the different studies and the corresponding metrics used to assess maintainability of AOP software.

*2.2. Empirical Studies.* Kvale et al. [15] conducted a study to show how AOP can be used to improve the maintainability of COTS-based systems. In their study, they argue that if the code for calling the COTS libraries is scattered all over the glue code, the maintenance of the system will be difficult. They showed that if the glue code is built using AOP, then the COTS-based system can be easily maintained. They used the Java Email Server in their experiments. They showed that AOP improves the changeability of a COTS-based system as the code that has to be modified is minimal in cases where AOP is used in the glue code. They used size-based metrics in their study.

Tizzei et al. [16] undertook a study to assess the design stability of an application built using software components and aspects in the presence of changes. The components in their case study refer to components built using the Component Service Model with Semantics (COSMOS*). In their study, they compared eight releases of four different versions of a MobileMedia application: an OO version, AOP version, component-based version, and a hybrid version where both components and aspects were employed. The first two versions of the MobileMedia application already existed and the last two were refactored from the first two versions. In their study, they measured the impact of change by looking at the number of components/operations changed, added, and removed. Their study showed that the hybrid version required fewer changes as compared to the other versions.

Kumar et al. [11] undertook a study on the change impact in AOP systems. In their study, they used AOP systems that have been refactored from their OO versions. The systems that they used were refactored from 149 OO modules into 129 modules. For the OO versions, the module refers to the classes, and for the AOP version, module refers to classes and aspects. Their study used the metrics and tool for collecting metrics data as defined in [8]. In their study, they found out that the change impact is lower in AOP systems as compared to the OO systems. Also, they found out that if the concerns which are not crosscutting are moved to aspects, then the impact of change for these modules will be higher. They assessed the maintainability of the AOP based on the changeability of the system, hence their assessment was done at the module level.

Przybyek [14] compared the modularity of OO- and AOP-based systems using the GQM approach. She used several systems that have an OO and AOP versions. These systems had also been used in several other studies for studying the effect of AOP. The modularity was compared using CBO and LCOM metrics. The systems that they used in their study are Telestrada, Pet Store, CVS Core Eclipse plug-in, EImp, Health Watcher, JHotDraw, HyperCast, Prevayler, Berkely DB, and HyperSQL Database. In their study, they observed that AOP does not offer any benefits in terms of modularity.

TABLE 1: Summary of maintainability metrics.

| Study | Dependent variable | MetricstTested | Summary of result |
|---|---|---|---|
| Burrows et al. [9] | Fault-proneness | All Ceccato and Tonella metrics | In addition, they introduced a new metric base aspect coupling (BAC), which measures the coupling between base class and aspect. The study showed that the two metrics that displayed the strongest correlation to faults were CDA and BAC |
| Eaddy et al. [10] | Fault-proneness | DOSC, DOSM, CDC, CDO | Assessed the correlation between faults and crosscutting concerns. They found out that the more scattered a concern is the more faults in its implementation are. Concern metrics used to predict the scattering of a concern. These metrics are independent of the program size |
| Kumar et al. [11] | Changeability | WOM | Assessed the correlation between changeability and WOM metric. They found that the WOM can be used as an indicator of maintainability but it is a weak indicator. Change impact is less in AOP systems as compared to OO systems. Maintenance effort was measured in terms of the number of modules changed |
| Kulesza et al. [12] | Coupling, cohesion, separation of concerns | Sant'Anna metrics which includes LCOO, WOC, VS | VS and WOC cannot be used as predictors of maintainability as the increase in such metrics was always accompanied by less development effort. LCOO metric inconclusive for measuring maintainability |
| Shen et al. [13] | Changeability (coupling and maintenance tasks) | Ceccato and Tonella metrics for coupling (CFA, CMC, RFM, CAE, and CDA) | Coupling metrics correlated with maintainability. |
| Przybyek [14] | Modularity | CBO and LCOM | CBO and LCOM used to measure the modularity of a system. Aggregate coupling and cohesion should not be considered as coupling should be measured independent of the number of modules in the system. |

Lippert and Lopes [17] refactored exceptional handling using AspectJ in the JWAN framework and found out that the code was reduced by a factor of 4. The JWAN framework has been built using the design by contract; hence the refactoring was targeted towards these contracts. For example, in the JWAN framework, all methods that return an object have to ensure that the object returned is not null. This is a clear example of a feature that could be better implemented with aspects. Also, exception handling was a key design feature of the JWAN framework as about 11% of the code was targeted towards exception handling.

Our study is similar to the studies described above. However, we want our study to be wider in scope by assessing the different maintainability characteristics. For example, the authors in [11, 15] focused only on changeability. The study by Tizzei et al. [16] measured the impact of change by looking at the number of components/operations changed, added, and removed. The study by Przybyek [14] focused on assessing modularity among OO and AOP systems. Our study can complement these studies by including some additional metrics for evaluating the maintainability of the COTS-based system. These metrics include those used to measure coupling, cohesion and complexity. Most of these metrics address the different characteristics of maintainability. In addition, we want to assess maintainability at two levels:

concern level and structural level. By doing so, we want to assess their effectiveness in measuring maintainability.

## 3. Study Setup

The main aim of this research is to assess the maintainability of COTS-based systems developed using AOP. Therefore, we have formulated the following two research questions.

*Question 1: Is a COTS-Based System Built Using AOP More Maintainable Than One Built Using OO?* To answer this question, we compare the maintainability of the OO and AOP versions of OpenBravoPOS and Jasperreports. The assessment of maintainability has been carried out using structural complexity metrics and concern level metrics.

*Question 2: Which Maintainability Metrics (Structural Complexity or Concern Level) Have a Better Potential for Predicting AOP Maintainability?* To answer this question, we compare the results of the two maintenance tasks for the OpenBravo-POS and Jasperreports systems.

*3.1. Selection of COTS Components.* The COTS-based system OpenBravoPOS was selected for our study. The main reason for the selection of this system is based on our experience

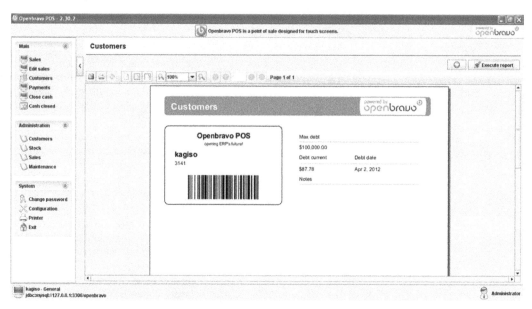

FIGURE 1. Screenshot showing OpenBravoPOS and Jasperreports in action.

on development on this system. OpenBravoPOS is a Java-based application that implements functionalities for the retail business [18]. It is an open-source system built with several components which include *Apache poi* which is used for reading and writing Microsoft Office files [19], *iText* which is used for reading and writing PDF files [20], *Commons-Logging* which is a component that provides logging features [21], and *jasperreports* which is used for the generation of reports [22]. Our study makes use of OpenBravoPOS and Jasperreports.

OpenBravoPOS is a typical example of a COTS-based system that is representative of a real world retail application. It implements common crosscutting concerns such as security, logging, persistence, and session management. The screenshot below (Figure 1) shows OpenBravoPOS and Jasperreports in action. Figure 1 shows a report running within the OpenBravoPOS. This report is generated by calling the Jasperreports component from the OpenBravoPOS.

Jasperreports is also built using several components which include *Commons-Logging, iText,* and *Apache Poi.* Jasperreports is a reporting tool and it accesses the database for retrieving data that is posted to the reports. Jasperreports implements crosscutting concerns such as persistence and transaction management in addition to the common crosscutting concerns such as logging and exceptional handling.

*3.2. Refactoring and Maintenance of OpenBravoPOS and JasperReports.* Refactoring is the process of changing the software component while leaving its functional state unchanged [10]. The COTS components OpenBravoPOS and Jasperreports were implemented using the OO programming language—Java. For the purpose of our experiment, we refactored OpenBravoPOS and Jasperreports to create equivalent implementations in AOP using the programming language AspectJ. The choice of AspectJ as the implementation language is mainly due to its popularity. In order to assess

maintainability of the original OO versions of OpenBravoPOS and Jasperreports and the refactored AOP versions, we also carried out maintenance tasks on both versions. Table 2 shows the OO versions and their corresponding AOP versions of OpenBravoPOS and Jasperreports.

Changeability in a COTS-based system refers to either replacing/removing/adding a component or replacing/removing/adding a feature of code in a component. In this study, we assess the impact of AOP in a COTS-based system where changeability is a major issue.

The maintenance tasks M1 and MJ1 refer to the addition of a feature in the OpenBravoPOS and Jasperreports components, respectively. A feature for measuring how much time is taken during the execution of SQL statements was added to both components. A top-down approach using FEAT was used for identifying the different places where the concern is implemented. It identified the different places where the calls to the database for executing select statements were implemented. A feature was then added to measure the time taken for the execution of such statements.

The maintenance task M2 refers to the replacement of the logging component within OpenBravoPOS. The original OpenBravoPOS component uses the java.util.logging library for logging. This component was replaced with the Apache commons logging component. The logging concern was refactored earlier in the experiment; hence we already had information about the different places where the logging component is called. The calls to the java.util.logging component were replaced with the calls to the Apache commons logging concerns. The information about the different places where the logging concern was implemented was already collected using FEAT.

*3.3. Aspect Mining and Concern Identification.* The components OpenBravoPOS and Jasperreports were used in our previous study [23] where the refactoring was done by starting with a list of known concerns and then looking

TABLE 2: Refactoring of the original OO version to AOP.

| OO version | AOP version | Description |
| --- | --- | --- |
| OpenBravoPOS | OpenBravoPOS-AOP | Refactored from the original |
| OpenBravoPOS-M1 | OpenBravoPOS-AOP-M1 | After applying maintenance task 1 (same maintenance to both versions) |
| OpenBravoPOS-M2 | OpenBravoPOS-AOP-M2 | After applying maintenance task 2 (same maintenance to both versions) |
| Jasperreports | Jasperreports-AOP | Re-factored from the original |
| Jasperreports-MJ1 | Jasperreports-AOP-MJ1 | After applying maintenance task 1 (same maintenance to both versions) |

for these concerns in the code. We followed the concern identification procedure used by Storzer et al. [24]. The Feature exploration and analysis (FEAT) [25] tool was also used for concern identification.

In this study, we also used an Eclipse plug-in called ConcernTagger [26] for collecting the concern level metrics which have been used in other related studies such as the one by Eaddy et al. [10]. The metrics that were implemented by ConcernTagger are CDC, CDO, DOSM, and DOSC [26]. The structural complexity metrics which are based on the Ceccato and Tonella metrics suite were collected using AOP metrics [27]. AOP metrics has been extended as an Eclipse plug-in as the developmental environment for our study has been Eclipse.

*3.4. Maintainability Metrics and Tools.* Software metrics can be classified as either product, resource, or process metrics [28]. Different researchers have proposed different metrics [8–10, 13, 29] for assessing the impact of AOP on software quality. The proposed metrics can be classified as either concern level metrics or structural complexity metrics.

*3.4.1. Concern Level Metrics.* Concern level metrics consider the lowest level of granularity of a software system to be a concern. Concerns are identified from project-related documentations and they should account for most of the source code [10]. The modules and/or operations responsible for the implementation of a given concern are grouped together and the concern level metrics collected and evaluated. Eaddy et al. [10] introduced the term *concern implementation plan*, to show the realization of concerns in the source code. Developers create concern implementation plans by creating or modifying the source code constructs in order to realize the concerns. The concerns can be mapped to different program elements in the source code such as modules, fields, operations, and statements [10]. In an ideal scenario where there are no crosscutting concerns, there would be a many-to-one relationship between the program elements and the concerns that is, several program elements mapping to one concern [30]. The concern level metrics as defined by Eaddy et al. [10] and Sant'Anna et al. [31] are as follows.

(i) *Program Element Contribution (CONT).* This is the number of lines of code associated with the implementation of a given concern.

(ii) *Concern Diffusion over Components (CDC).* This metric counts the number of classes and aspects responsible for the implementation of a concern.

(iii) *Concern Diffusion over Operations (CDO).* This metric counts the number of advices and methods responsible for the implementation of a concern.

(iv) *Degree of Scattering across Classes (DOSC).* It is the degree to which the concern code is distributed across classes. When DOSC is 0, all the code for the implementation of a concern is in one class, but when DOSC is 1, the code for the implementation is equally distributed across all classes implementing a given concern.

(v) *Degree of Scattering across Methods (DOSM).* It is the degree to which the concern code is distributed across operations.

(vi) *Lines of Concern Code (LOCC).* There are the lines of code in the implementation of a concern.

The collection of these metrics requires the assessor to construct a concern implementation plan that covers the concerns of interest in the source code of a given AOP software. There are different techniques and tools that have been proposed for identifying concerns in the source code. However, there are no widely accepted techniques and tools for locating concerns. The existing tools for measuring concern level metrics require the researcher to manually select the code associated with a given concern [32]. Such tools include ConcernTagger and AspectJ Assessment Tool (AJATO).

*3.4.2. Structural Complexity Metrics.* The AOP structural complexity metrics used in this study were defined by Ceccato and Tonella [8] which were adapted from the popular CK metrics as proposed by Chidamber and Kemerer [33]. The metrics as defined by Ceccato and Tonella and Burrows et al. [9] are as follows.

(i) *Weighted Operations per Module (WOM).* This is number of operations (methods or advices) in a module. This is equivalent to the weighted operations per class (WMC) of the CK metrics [8]. A class with a higher number of operations is considered to be more complex, and hence it is fault prone [8, 34]. The complexity of the operations is considered to be equal. Also, more effort is needed to test a class with a higher WOM value [34]. A lower value of WOM is desired per module.

(ii) *Depth of Inheritance Tree (DIT).* This is the length of the class from a given module to the class/aspect hierarchy root. This is equivalent to the DIT of the

CK metrics. The deeper a module is in the inheritance hierarchy, the more operations it will inherit and therefore the more complex the module will be thus making it fault prone [34]. Studies have also shown that a system with less inheritance can be easier to modify and understand [34]. Hence a lower value of DIT is desired as it means that the system will be easier to maintain.

(iii) *Number of Children (NOC)*. This is the number of immediate subaspects or subclasses of a given module [8]. In contrast with the DIT metric which measures the depth in the system, the NOC metric measures the breadth of the system. A lower value of NOC is desired.

(iv) *Coupling on Field Access (CFA)*. This is the number of modules that have fields that are called by a given module. This metric measures the coupling between modules based on field access [8]. A higher value of CFA implies tight coupling between the modules which indicates complexity, increase in the module being fault prone, and also decrease in the testability [34]. A lower value of CFA is desired.

(v) *Coupling on Method Calls (CMC)*. This the number of modules declaring operations that are called by a given module. Similar to the CFA metric, this measures the coupling between modules based on operation access [8]. A lower value of CMC is desired.

(vi) *Coupling between Modules (CBM)*. This is the number of operations and fields that are accessed by a given class [34–36]. This can be represented by the number of outward arrows from a given module [36]. This metric is a combination of the CMC and CFA metrics as it measures the coupling based on both the field access (CFA) and operations (CMC). HA's lower value of CBM is desired.

(vii) *Crosscutting Degree of an Aspect (CDA)*. This is the number of modules affected by *pointcuts* and *introductions* in a given aspect. This measures the number of modules that are affected by an aspect [8].

(viii) *Coupling on Advice Execution (CAE)*. This is the number of aspects containing advices triggered by the execution of operations in a given module. This is the number of inward arrows from aspects to a particular module [36]. This metric is used to measure the dependence of the operation on the advices; hence a change in the advice might impact the operation [8]. A higher value of this metric for a given module means that the module is coupled with more aspects [36].

(ix) *Response for Module (RFM)*. This is the number of operations that are executed by a given class in response to the messages received by a given class [34–36]. This includes operations that are called both implicitly and explicitly [34]. This metric can be showed pictorially in a sequence diagram [36]. Modules with a higher RFM value are more complex

and also their testing is more complicated [34, 36]. A lower value of RFM is more desired.

(x) *Lack of Cohesion of Operations (LCO)*. This metric measures the relationship between the methods in a given module [34]. High cohesion is desired in a system as it shows that the system is modularized. If a module implements several concerns, then the operations in that module will be accessing different fields and the LCO will be higher [8]. A lower value of LCO is desired for a software system.

While the concern level metrics require the developer to decompose the system into concerns (construct the concern implementation plans), the structural complexity metrics are based on already decomposed modules.

## 4. Results and Discussion

The refactoring was limited to a few concerns; therefore not all the concerns that are implemented in the components under consideration have been refactored. For the Open-BravoPOS system, the modules that were refactored are those implementing the following crosscutting concerns:

(i) session management,

(ii) logging,

(iii) exceptional handling.

For the Jasperreports component, the modules that were refactored are those implementing the following crosscutting concerns:

(i) synchronization,

(ii) object retrieval,

(iii) exceptional handling.

Tables 3 and 4 show the amount of code in OpenBravoPOS and Jasperreports components that implements the concerns that were refactored. The OpenBravoPOS component was implemented in over 53,000 lines of code and the concerns under consideration in this study were implemented in 5,313 lines of code indicating a line of code coverage of 9.94%. The concerns under consideration were also implemented in 43 modules which have a total of 625 operations. The number of operations represents all the operations in the modules implementing the concerns being considered. Alternatively, we could have reported the operations implementing the concerns under consideration, but there were some operations that implemented more than one concern being considered which would have resulted in having overlaps as the concerns were tangled.

In the Jasperreports component, 6.78% of the total lines of code which corresponded to 9,329 lines of code were assessed. This code is responsible for the concerns under consideration.

*4.1. AOP and OO Versions of OpenBravoPOS and Jasperreports.* Tables 5 and 6 show the complexity metrics for the OO and AOP versions of OpenBravoPOS and Jasperreports,

TABLE 3: Code coverage for the concerns in OpenbravoPOS.

| Code coverage: OpenBravoPOS | | | |
|---|---|---|---|
| | Total | Concern coverage | Coverage (%) |
| Lines of code | 53,433 | 5,313 | 9.94 |
| Number of modules | 978 | 43 | 4.40 |
| Number of operations (all) | 5,741 | 625 | 10.89 |

TABLE 4: Code coverage for the concerns in JasperReports.

| Code coverage: Jasperreports | | | |
|---|---|---|---|
| | Total | Concern coverage | Coverage (%) |
| Lines of code | 137,495 | 9,329 | 6.78 |
| Number of modules | 13,606 | 43 | 0.32 |
| Number of operations | 5,741 | 625 | 10.89 |

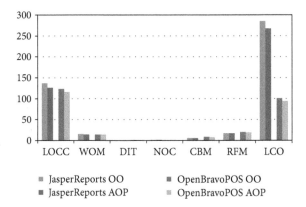

■ JasperReports OO ■ OpenBravoPOS OO
■ JasperReports AOP ■ OpenBravoPOS AOP

FIGURE 2: Comparison of the OO and AOP versions of OpenBravo-POS and Jasperreports.

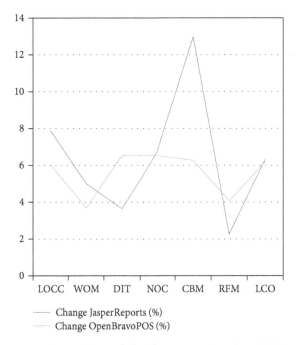

— Change JasperReports (%)
— Change OpenBravoPOS (%)

FIGURE 3: Comparison of the changes in OpenBravoPOS and Jasperreports following refactoring.

respectively. The values in Tables 5 and 6 are the average values of the metrics which are computed as the sum for the different modules divided by the number of modules under consideration.

Figures 2 and 3 indicate a comparison of structural metrics between the OO and AOP versions of OpenBravoPOS and Jasperreports.

The AOP versions of OpenBravoPOS and Jasperreports show an improvement in all the structural complexity metrics except for the CDA and CAE metrics which measure the coupling that is introduced by the aspects. CDA and CAE capture the AOP-specific coupling; hence they have a value of zero in the OO version while it shows an increase in the AOP version.

Figure 3 shows the comparison of the change in the metrics between the OpenBravoPOS and Jasperreports versions. The major improvement in the metrics is in the CBM metric for the Jasperreports component while for the OpenBravoPOS component it is for the NOC and DIT metrics. The CBM metric measures the OO coupling while the CDA metric measures the AOP-specific coupling. If the complexity of the AOP coupling is considered to be the same as the OO coupling, then the overall coupling which is obtained by adding the CBM and CDA values still shows

an overall improvement in the coupling. For example, in the OpenBravoPOS component the improvement in CBM value is the .54 in the AOP version while the AOP coupling introduces a value of −0.15; hence the overall coupling will be 0.39. Burrows et al.'s [9] study showed that AOP coupling does not result in more fault-prone modules. Also, in a study by Przybyek [14], the CBM metric was redefined so as to capture both the traditional coupling and the AOP coupling and was able to measure the overall coupling in the AOP systems using a single metric. Based on the results shown above, the AOP implementations are less structurally complex as compared to their OO counterparts.

*4.2. Concern Metrics.* Tables 7 and 8 show the concern level metrics assessment of the OO versions of the OpenBravoPOS and Jasperreports components.

TABLE 5: Structural complexity metrics for the OpenBravoPOS original and refactored versions.

| | OpenBravoPOS | OpenBravoPOS-AOP | Change | Change (%) |
|---|---|---|---|---|
| LOCC | 123.56 | 116.09 | 7.47 | 6.05 |
| WOM | 14.53 | 14.00 | 0.53 | 3.68 |
| DIT | 1.16 | 1.09 | 0.08 | 6.52 |
| NOC | 0.49 | 0.46 | 0.03 | 6.52 |
| CBM | 8.65 | 8.11 | 0.54 | 6.27 |
| CDA | 0.00 | 0.15 | −0.15 | 0.00 |
| CAE | 0.00 | 0.26 | −0.26 | 0.00 |
| RFM | 20.26 | 19.43 | 0.82 | 4.05 |
| LCO | 100.79 | 94.54 | 6.25 | 6.20 |

TABLE 6: Structural complexity metrics for the Jasperreports original and refactored versions.

| | Jasperreports | Jasperreports-AOP | Change | Change (%) |
|---|---|---|---|---|
| LOCC | 136.87 | 126.07 | 10.80 | 7.89 |
| WOM | 15.38 | 14.61 | 0.77 | 5.00 |
| DIT | 0.43 | 0.42 | 0.02 | 3.65 |
| NOC | 1.32 | 1.23 | 0.09 | 6.76 |
| CBM | 6.09 | 5.30 | 0.79 | 12.97 |
| CDA | 0.00 | 0.64 | −0.64 | 0.00 |
| CAE | 0.00 | 0.57 | −0.57 | 0.00 |
| RFM | 17.45 | 17.05 | 0.40 | 2.27 |
| LCO | 285.36 | 267.31 | 18.05 | 6.33 |

For example, if we look at the concern for contract validation during the retrieval of the object in the concern "*RetrieveObject*," it is implemented in 40 operations in 1 module. In contrast, the implementation of the concern in the AOP version shows that it has been implemented in 1 module and 1 operation over fewer lines of code; hence DOSC = 0, DOSM = 0, CDC = 1, and CDO = 1. The concern level metrics show that in the AOP implementation, the concerns are localized which is the main premise of AOP.

Table 9 shows the structural complexity metrics for the JRFillObjectFactory class in Jasperreports before and after the refactoring. After the refactoring, some parts of the code which deals with contract validation when retrieving objects was moved to the aspect and a new aspect called RetrieveObjectAspect was introduced in the AOP version. Table 9 shows that the refactoring resulted in reduction in the lines of code of this particular class which is 180 LOCC. This was in turn replaced by one module which is implemented in 12 LOCCs. In contrast, the concern level metrics shows that the concern is now implemented in 1 module and 1 operation.

*4.3. Assessment of Changeability.* To assess changeability of both the OO and AOP versions of the 2 components, we carried out 2 maintenance tasks. As mentioned earlier, maintenance task 1 refers to the introduction of a new feature to evaluate the execution time of SQL statements. Maintenance task 2 refers to the replacement of the logging component with another component of the same functionality.

*4.3.1. Results of Maintenance Task 1.* During this maintenance task, a feature was added so that the execution of the SQL statements against the database can be profiled; that is, see how long it takes for the execution of these statements. The impact of change or changeability was then assessed by counting the following code-level changes:

(i) number of modules added (MA),

(ii) number of modules removed (MR),

(iii) number of modules modified (MM),

(iv) number of operations added (OA),

(v) number of operations removed (OR),

(vi) number of operations modified (OM),

(vii) number of lines of code added (LA),

(viii) number of lines of code removed (LR),

(ix) number of lines of code modified (LM).

The results show that the change affected all the modules implementing a given concern (Table 10 and Figure 4). In the OpenBravoPOS implementation, the change affected 3 operations in 5 modules while the change affected 2 operations in 1 module in the AOP implementation. For the Jasperreports OO implementation, the change affected 10 operations in 2 modules while in the AOP implementation the change affected only 1 operation in 1 module.

The results indicate that the change impact is higher on the OO version as compared to the AOP version.

TABLE 7: Concern level metrics for the OpenbravoPOS component.

| Concern name | OpenBravoPOS | | | | |
| --- | --- | --- | --- | --- | --- |
| | DOSC | DOSM | CDC | CDO | SLOC |
| Session | 0.903 | 0.96 | 34 | 62 | 518 |
| SQLException | 0.884 | 0.944 | 12 | 43 | 582 |
| Logging | 0.856 | 0.852 | 10 | 10 | 362 |

TABLE 8: Concern level metrics for the Jasperreports component.

| Concern name | Jasperreports | | | | |
| --- | --- | --- | --- | --- | --- |
| | DOSC | DOSM | CDC | CDO | SLOC |
| CloneNotSupportedException | 0.965 | 0.964 | 37 | 36 | 779 |
| RetrieveObject | 0 | 0.974 | 1 | 40 | 494 |
| Synchronization | 0.977 | 0.977 | 43 | 43 | 473 |

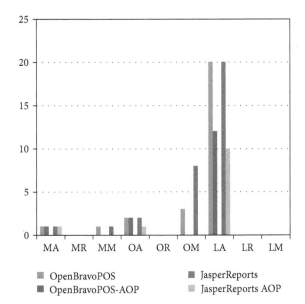

FIGURE 4: Comparison of the impact of change in OO and AOP versions of OpenBravoPOS and Jasperreports.

*4.3.2. Results of Maintenance Task 2.* A second maintenance task was carried out in the OpenBravoPOS to supplement the results of the first maintenance task. During this maintenance task, the implementation of the logging concern in Open-BravoPOS which uses java.util.logging was replaced with the Apache commons logging. The Jasperreports component also uses the commons logging component for implementing its logging features. The implementations that were used in carrying out this task were the original unmodified Open-BravoPOS component and its AOP counterpart. The logging concern had been refactored in the AOP implementation. The changeability results are in Table 11.

Table 11 shows that the impact of the change is higher in the OO implementation as compared to the AOP counterpart.

*4.4. Threats to Validity.* The result of the case study is encouraging in that it indicates the viability of the aspect-oriented approach in improving maintainability. This is in line with other similar studies that have been conducted in the past. However, we need to be cautious before we try to generalize the results of our case study.

(i) The sample size is relatively small for our case study and would be difficult to predict if the same result holds for a very large system. In addition, in our case study, only selected crosscutting concerns were refactored from the OO versions of OpenBravo and Jasperreports using the AOP language—AspectJ. It would be good to have a complete AOP version of the OpenBravoPOS system to compare the maintainability of the two systems. Moreover, our maintainability assessment is based on a single system (OpenBravo-POS) which makes generalization of results difficult. One needs to carry out more experiments on various systems from various domains to have a more credible generalization.

(ii) Another issue related to our case study is that the people who did the refactoring of the aspects from the components were the same people who did the measurement of the maintainability of the system. This may create a potential bias. However, we tried by all means to restrict the refactoring such that the goal was to refactor the aspects and not to improve the maintainability of the system.

(iii) The assessment of changeability is not comprehensive enough. Even though we used similar procedures to other studies, the types of changes still need improvement. For example, Grover et al. [37] provided code-level changes that can be made at system level and component level. In addition, it provides criteria for minimum number of random changes. We will use this approach in our future work.

(iv) The structural complexity metrics selected considered each line of code to be uniform even though the effort required to make a call to a local module is less expensive as compared to a call to an external component [38]. This is an interesting phenomenon for COTS-based systems as the maintenance developer will have to learn how to call a COTS component. This

TABLE 9: Structural complexity metrics for the Jasperreports component.

| Type name | Type kind | LOCC | WOM | DIT | NOC | CBM | CDA | CAE | RFM | LCO | |
|---|---|---|---|---|---|---|---|---|---|---|---|
| JRFillObjectFactory | class | 1058 | 81 | 1 | 2 | 68 | 0 | 0 | 92 | 0 | OO |
| JRFillObjectFactory | class | 878 | 81 | 1 | 2 | 68 | 0 | 1 | 93 | 0 | AOP |
| RetrieveObjectAspect | aspect | 12 | 1 | 0 | 0 | 0 | 1 | 0 | 0 | 0 | AOP |

TABLE 10: Changeability results after maintenance task 1.

| | MA | MR | MM | OA | OR | OM | LA | LR | LM |
|---|---|---|---|---|---|---|---|---|---|
| OpenBravoPOS-SQLProfiling | | | | | | | | | |
| OpenBravoPOS | 1 | 0 | 1 | 2 | 0 | 3 | 20 | 0 | 0 |
| OpenBravoPOS-AOP | 1 | 0 | 0 | 2 | 0 | 0 | 12 | 0 | 0 |
| Jasperreports-SQLProfiling | | | | | | | | | |
| Jasperreports | 1 | 0 | 1 | 2 | 0 | 8 | 20 | 0 | 0 |
| Jasperreports-AOP | 1 | 0 | 0 | 1 | 0 | 0 | 10 | 0 | 0 |

TABLE 11: Changeability results after carrying out maintenance task 2.

| | MA | MR | MM | OA | OR | OM | LA | LR | LM |
|---|---|---|---|---|---|---|---|---|---|
| OpenbravoPOS-Logging | | | | | | | | | |
| OpenbravoPOS | 0 | 0 | 7 | 0 | 0 | 7 | 7 | 0 | 0 |
| OpenbravoPOS-AOP | 0 | 0 | 1 | 0 | 0 | 0 | 0 | 0 | 1 |

effect of the calls to a COTS component will also be investigated in future studies.

## 5. Conclusion and Future Work

In this paper, we have presented a case study for the assessment of the maintainability of an AOP-based COTS system by comparing it with its OO version of implementation. The COTS-based system used in our case study is OpenBravoPOS which is an open-source software used in retail business. For the assessment of maintainability, we used concern level metrics and structural complexity metrics. For both metrics, the results show that AOP-based implementation is more maintainable. In other words, most metrics show better maintainability values for the AOP version of implementation as compared to the OO version of implementation. In our case study, we refactored only 9.94% of the code for OpenBravoPOS and 6.78% for the Jasperreports. This might have an impact on the degree of maintainability improvement observed. Moreover, there are no threshold values specified for the values of each of the metrics in the literature. Had there been such threshold values, it would have been easier to see the acceptability of the improvement. This is one area for further investigation so that a maintainability index similar to the maintainability index of the traditional systems can be established for the AOP software.

In our case study, the concern level metrics are found to be good indicators of changeability of the system. For example, if 40 operations implement a given concern, when the concern is subjected to a maintenance task, we found that almost all these operations are to be affected. On the other hand, the structural complexity metrics are found to be poor indicators

of changeability as they do not capture some of the issues related to changeability such as changing a line of code. For example, if a line of code calling component A was replaced with a call to component B, then the structural complexity metrics would not change.

## References

[1] P. Jalote, An Integrated Approach to Software Engineering, Springer, Berlin, Germany, 3rd edition, 2005.

[2] I. Jacobson and P. -W. Ng, Aspect-Oriented Software Development with Use Cases, Addison-Wesley Object Technology Series, Addison-Wesley Professional, Reading, Mass, USA, 2004.

[3] X. Corporation, "The AspectJ Programming Guide," 2002-2003, http://www.eclipse.org/aspectj/doc/released/progguide/index.html.

[4] IEEE, "IEEE Standard Glossary of Software Engineering Terminology," IEEE Std 610.12-1990, 1990.

[5] H. Al-Kilidar, K. Cox, and B. Kitchenham, "The use and usefulness of the ISO/IEC 9126 quality standard," in Proceedings of International Symposium on Empirical Software Engineering (ISESE '05), pp. 126–132, November 2005.

[6] P. Oman and J. Hagemeister, "Construction and testing of polynomials predicting software maintainability," The Journal of Systems and Software, vol. 24, no. 3, pp. 251–266, 1994.

[7] I. Heitlager, T. Kuipers, and J. Visser, "A practical model for measuring maintainability—a preliminary report," in Proceedings of the 6th International Conference on the Quality of Information and Communications Technology (QUATIC '07), pp. 30–39, IEEE Computer Society, September 2007.

[8] M. Ceccato and P. Tonella, "Measuring the effects of software aspectization," in *Proceedings of the 1st Workshop on Aspect Reverse Engineering (WARE '04)*, Delft, The Netherlands, 2004.

[9] R. Burrows, F. C. Ferrari, A. Garcia, and F. Taïani, "An empirical evaluation of coupling metrics on aspect-oriented programs," in *Proceedings of the ICSE Workshop on Emerging Trends in Software Metrics (ICSE '10)*, pp. 53–58, ACM, Cape Town, South Africa, May 2010.

[10] M. Eaddy, T. Zimmermann, K. D. Sherwood et al., "Do cross-cutting concerns cause defects?" *IEEE Transactions on Software Engineering*, vol. 34, no. 4, pp. 497–515, 2008.

[11] A. Kumar, R. Kumar, and P. S. Grover, "An evaluation of maintainability of aspect-oriented systems: a practical approach," *International Journal of Computer Science and Security*, vol. 1, no. 2, pp. 1–9, 2007.

[12] U. Kulesza, C. Sant'Anna, A. Garcia, R. Coelho, A. Von Staa, and C. Lucena, "Quantifying the effects of aspect-oriented programming: a maintenance study," in *Proceedings of the 22nd IEEE International Conference on Software Maintenance (ICSM '06)*, pp. 223–232, IEEE Computer Society, September 2006.

[13] H. Shen, S. Zhang, and J. Zhao, "An empirical study of maintainability in aspect-oriented system evolution using coupling metrics," in *Proceedings of the 2nd IFIP/IEEE International Symposium on Theoretical Aspects of Software Engineering (TASE '08)*, pp. 233–236, IEEE Computer Society, June 2008.

[14] A. Przybyek, "Where the truth lies: AOP and its impact on software modularity," in *Proceedings of the 14th International Conference on Fundamental Approaches to Software Engineering*, Springer, Saarbrcken, Germany, 2011.

[15] A. A. Kvale, J. Li, and R. Conradi, "A case study on building cots-based system using aspect-oriented programming," in *Proceedings of the 20th Annual ACM Symposium on Applied Computing*, pp. 1491–1498, ACM, Santa Fe, NM, USA, March 2005.

[16] L. P. Tizzei, M. Dias, C. M. F. Rubira, A. Garcia, and J. Lee, "Components meet aspects: assessing design stability of a software product line," *Information and Software Technology*, vol. 53, no. 2, pp. 121–136, 2011.

[17] M. Lippert and C. V. Lopes, "Study on exception detection and handling using aspect-oriented programming," in *Proceedings of the 22nd International Conference on Software Engineering*, pp. 418–427, ACM, Limerick, Ireland, June 2000.

[18] OpenBravo, "Point of Sale Retail," 2010, http://www.openbravo.com/product/pos/.

[19] A. S. Foundation, "Apache POI—The Java API for Microsoft Documents," 2012, http://poi.apache.org/.

[20] BVBA, T.X., 2012, http://itextpdf.com/.

[21] A. S. Foundation, 2012, http://commons.apache.org/logging/.

[22] Jaspersoft, 2012, http://jasperforge.org/.

[23] K. Mguni and Y. Ayalew, "Improving maintainability in COTS based system using aspect oriented programming: an empirical evaluation," in *Proceedings of African Conference of Software Engineering and Applied Computing*, pp. 21–28, IEEE Computer Society, Gaborone, Botswana, 2012.

[24] M. Storzer, U. Eibauer, and S. Schoeffmann, "Aspect mining for aspect refactoring: an experience report," in *Proceedings of the 1st International Workshop Towards Evaluation of Aspect Mining (TEAM '06)*, Nantes, France, 2006.

[25] M. Robillard, "FEAT: An Eclipse Plug-in for Locating, Describing, and Analyzing Concerns in Source Code," 2005, http://www.cs.mcgill.ca/~swevo/feat/.

[26] M. Eaddy, "ConcernTagger," 2007, http://www1.cs.columbia.edu/~eaddy/concerntagger/.

[27] Metrics, 2012, http://aopmetrics.tigris.org/.

[28] N. Fenton and A. Melton, "Deriving structurally based software measures," *The Journal of Systems and Software*, vol. 12, no. 3, pp. 177–187, 1990.

[29] A. Garcia, C. Sant'Anna, E. Figueiredo, U. Kulesza, C. Lucena, and A. von Staa, "Modularizing design patterns with aspects: a quantitative study," in *Transactions on Aspect-Oriented Software Development I*, pp. 36–74, Springer, Berlin, Germany, 2006.

[30] M. Tritu, *Tool-Supported Identification of Functional Concerns in Object-Oriented Code*, KIT Scientific Publishing, Karlsruhe, Germany, 2010.

[31] C. Sant'Anna, A. Garcia, C. Chavez, C. Lucena, and A. V. von Staa, "On the reuse and maintenance of aspect-oriented software: an assessment framework," in *Proceedings of the 17th Brazilian Symposium on Software Engineering*, pp. 19–34, 2003.

[32] J. C. Taveira, J. Saraiva, F. Castor, and S. Soares, "A concern-specific metrics collection tzool," in *Proceedings of the Assessment of Contemporary Modularization Techniques at Object-Oriented Programming Systems and Applications (OOPSLA '09)*, Orlando, Fla, USA, October 2009.

[33] S. R. Chidamber and C. F. Kemerer, "Metrics suite for object oriented design," *IEEE Transactions on Software Engineering*, vol. 20, no. 6, pp. 476–493, 1994.

[34] S. K. Dubey and A. Rana, "Assessment of maintainability metrics for object-oriented software system," *SIGSOFT Software Engineering Notes*, vol. 36, no. 5, pp. 1–7, 2011.

[35] U. L. Kulkarni, Y. R. Kalshetty, and V. G. Arde, "Validation of CK metrics for object oriented design measurement," in *Proceedings of the 3rd International Conference on Emerging Trends in Engineering and Technology (ICETET '10)*, pp. 646–651, Karjat, India, November 2010.

[36] C. Babu and R. Vijayalakshmi, "Metrics-based design selection tool for aspect oriented software development," *SIGSOFT Software Engineering Notes*, vol. 33, no. 5, pp. 1–10, 2008.

[37] P. S. Grover, R. Kumar, and A. Kumar, "Measuring changeability for generic aspect-oriented systems," *SIGSOFT Software Engineering Notes*, vol. 33, no. 6, pp. 1–5, 2008.

[38] A. Endres and H. Rombach, *A Handbook of Software and Systems Engineering: Empirical Observations, Laws, and Theories*, Fraunhofer IESE, Kaiserslautern, Germany; Pearson Addison-Wesley, Harlow, England, 2003.

# Permissions

The contributors of this book come from diverse backgrounds, making this book a truly international effort. This book will bring forth new frontiers with its revolutionizing research information and detailed analysis of the nascent developments around the world.

We would like to thank all the contributing authors for lending their expertise to make the book truly unique. They have played a crucial role in the development of this book. Without their invaluable contributions this book wouldn't have been possible. They have made vital efforts to compile up to date information on the varied aspects of this subject to make this book a valuable addition to the collection of many professionals and students.

This book was conceptualized with the vision of imparting up-to-date information and advanced data in this field. To ensure the same, a matchless editorial board was set up. Every individual on the board went through rigorous rounds of assessment to prove their worth. After which they invested a large part of their time researching and compiling the most relevant data for our readers. Conferences and sessions were held from time to time between the editorial board and the contributing authors to present the data in the most comprehensible form. The editorial team has worked tirelessly to provide valuable and valid information to help people across the globe.

Every chapter published in this book has been scrutinized by our experts. Their significance has been extensively debated. The topics covered herein carry significant findings which will fuel the growth of the discipline. They may even be implemented as practical applications or may be referred to as a beginning point for another development. Chapters in this book were first published by Hindawi Publishing Corporation; hereby published with permission under the Creative Commons Attribution License or equivalent.

The editorial board has been involved in producing this book since its inception. They have spent rigorous hours researching and exploring the diverse topics which have resulted in the successful publishing of this book. They have passed on their knowledge of decades through this book. To expedite this challenging task, the publisher supported the team at every step. A small team of assistant editors was also appointed to further simplify the editing procedure and attain best results for the readers.

Our editorial team has been hand-picked from every corner of the world. Their multi-ethnicity adds dynamic inputs to the discussions which result in innovative outcomes. These outcomes are then further discussed with the researchers and contributors who give their valuable feedback and opinion regarding the same. The feedback is then collaborated with the researches and they are edited in a comprehensive manner to aid the understanding of the subject.

Apart from the editorial board, the designing team has also invested a significant amount of their time in understanding the subject and creating the most relevant covers. They scrutinized every image to scout for the most suitable representation of the subject and create an appropriate cover for the book.

The publishing team has been involved in this book since its early stages. They were actively engaged in every process, be it collecting the data, connecting with the contributors or procuring relevant information. The team has been an ardent support to the editorial, designing and production team. Their endless efforts to recruit the best for this project, has resulted in the accomplishment of this book. They are a veteran in the field of academics and their pool of knowledge is as vast as their experience in printing. Their expertise and guidance has proved useful at every step. Their uncompromising quality standards have made this book an exceptional effort. Their encouragement from time to time has been an inspiration for everyone.

The publisher and the editorial board hope that this book will prove to be a valuable piece of knowledge for researchers, students, practitioners and scholars across the globe.

# List of Contributors

**Yeresime Suresh, Lov Kumar and Santanu Ku. Rath**
Department of Computer Science and Engineering, National Institute of Technology, Rourkela, Odisha 769008, India

**Aftab Iqbal**
INSIGHT, NUI, Galway, Ireland

**Brian Henderson-Sellers**
University of Technology, Sydney, Broadway, NSW2007, Australia

**Wil M. P. van der Aalst**
Department of Mathematics and Computer Science, Technische Universiteit Eindhoven, 5612 AZ Eindhoven, The Netherlands

**Islam Elgedawy**
Computer Engineering Department, Middle East Technical University, Northern Cyprus Campus, Guzelyurt, Mersin 10, Turkey

**Nattakarn Phaphoom, Xiaofeng Wang and Pekka Abrahamsson**
Faculty of Computer Science, Free University of Bolzano-Bozen, Piazza Domenicani 3, 39100 Bolzano, Italy

**John Michura, Miriam A. M. Capretz and Shuying Wang**
Department of Electrical and Computer Engineering, Faculty of Engineering, The University ofWestern Ontario, London, ON, Canada N6A 5B9

**Kagiso Mguni and Yirsaw Ayalew**
Department of Computer Science, University of Botswana, Private Bag 0704, Gaborone, Botswana

Printed in the USA
CPSIA information can be obtained
at www.ICGtesting.com
JSHW051442221024
72173JS00006B/1557

9 781632 384218